MARIA, LADY NUGENT

LADY NUGENT'S JOURNAL

JAMAICA ONE HUNDRED YEARS AGO

REPRINTED FROM A JOURNAL KEPT BY
MARIA, LADY NUGENT, FROM
1801 TO 1815, ISSUED FOR
PRIVATE CIRCULATION
IN 1839

EDITED BY

FRANK CUNDALL, F.S.A.

SECRETARY AND LIBRARIAN OF THE INSTITUTE OF JAMAICA

WITH ILLUSTRATIONS AND MAPS

PUBLISHED FOR
THE INSTITUTE OF JAMAICA
BY
ADAM & CHARLES BLACK
SOHO SQUARE, LONDON
1907

PLYMOUTH
WILLIAM BRENDON AND SON, LTD
PRINTERS

BOOK-PLATE OF SIR GEORGE NUGENT

CONTENTS

160591

LIST OF ILLUSTRATIONS

PREFACE

OF the numerous books which have been published about Jamaica during the two and a half centuries of British occupation Lady Nugent's " Journal " is undoubtedly one of the most interesting. If every lady who has resided at King's House, since the days when Katherine, the ill-fated wife of Sir Charles Lyttelton, dispensed hospitality there for a few short months, had kept a diary like Lady Nugent's, we should be in the possession of a most valuable series of notes for a history of the development of the social life of the colony.

Lady Nugent's diary, we learn from internal evidence, was written for her pleasure and that of her children, and was not intended for publication, making, as it does, the frankest of references to private matters. But the two simple volumes (which were printed in London in 1839 for private circulation only, and are accordingly rarely met with) give a fuller insight into domestic matters in Jamaica, especially those surrounding the Governor and his circle, than we obtain in other writings.

In publishing a reprint of these journals it has been thought advisable to omit some parts which are trivial, some which it is needless to repeat (e.g. " The morning as usual," " N. rode out and I wrote," " Only our own family at dinner," " To bed at eight,") and much concerning the daily health of her children, which can be spared from a book intended for public perusal.

Lady Nugent (or Mrs. Nugent, as she then was) evidently made up her mind to eschew politics, the references to political affairs being very brief and occasionally very tantalizing. This is to be regretted, for she might have given us valuable information upon political affairs during the period in which her husband controlled the destiny of Jamaica (1801–1806). Her views on slavery and the condition of the slaves are of considerable interest.

Brief extracts from the portion of her journal dealing with her stay in England have been added, and a few notes have been included from the two volumes of journals kept in India, which were printed at the same time as the Jamaica volumes.

With respect to the illustrations, the portraits of Lady Nugent and Nurse Flora and the view of Government Pen are copied from the plates which, together with an elevation of King's House, formed the illustrations of the original volumes. One wonders whether Nurse Flora and Government Pen are her own productions or those of her instructor in drawing, Mr. Morelle, who had been " only a cook." To these have been added the portrait of Sir George Nugent, copied from an engraving by Woodman after a painting by Downman, to which Lady Nugent makes reference in the latter part of her Journal; a portrait of Admiral Duckworth, who was then naval Commander-in-Chief at Jamaica, and is frequently mentioned in the Journal; portraits of Lady Nugent's father and mother; views of King's House (Spanish Town), Admiral's Pen, and Bryan Castle, in Jamaica, and of the office of Lady Nugent's father in Perth Amboy; an illustration of a negro John Canoe, and Sir George Nugent's book-plate. A map of the island of the period of the Journal has also been included, as well as a plan prepared in order to show the places which she and her husband visited, on his tours of inspection.

In order to interfere as little as possible with Lady Nugent's story the notes in the text have been confined to those of a biographical and topographical character. The other notes have been inserted in the form of an introduction, with a view to supplementing the information given by Lady Nugent on Jamaica a hundred years ago. A few obvious misprints in the original Journal have been corrected.

The index contains the name of every person of importance in the colony at the period—naval, military or civilian.

The Editor's thanks are due to Mr. G. F. Judah of Spanish Town for much assistance in the identification of persons and properties in Jamaica, to Professor Hull of Cornell University and Mr. William Nelson, of Paterson, for information with regard to Lady Nugent's parentage, and to the Honourable Cortlandt Parker, of Newark, New Jersey, for portraits of General Skinner and his wife.

It is hoped that the Journal may prove of interest to Jamaicans and others to whom Jamaica history appeals, especially to Lady Nugent's countrymen in America.

F. C.

INSTITUTE OF JAMAICA,
    KINGSTON, JAMAICA.
    September, 1906.

CHRONOLOGY OF THE PRINCIPAL EVENTS IN THE LIVES OF SIR GEORGE AND LADY NUGENT, WITH SPECIAL REFERENCE TO JAMAICA

1757.	June	10.	George Nugent born.
1771.			Maria Skinner (Lady Nugent) born.
1773.	July	5.	N. appointed ensign in 39th Foot.
1777.	Sept.		N. joined 7th Royal Fusiliers at New York.
1778.	April		N. promoted captain in 57th Foot.
1782.	May	3.	N. obtained majority in 57th Foot.
1783.			N. promoted colonel in 97th Foot.
	End.		N. returned to England.
1787.			N. aide-de-camp to Lord Lieutenant of Ireland (Marquis of Buckingham).
1789.			*Revolution in France and in San Domingo.*
1790.			N. became captain and lieutenant-colonel of Coldstream Guards.
1793.			N. elected M.P. for Buckingham.
	Feb.	1.	*France declared war against England.*
			N. accompanied the Guards to Holland
			N. raised " Bucks Volunteers " (afterwards 85th Light Infantry) and appointed colonel Nov. 18.
1794.			N. went to Walcheren.
	Oct.		*Williamson made Governor of San Domingo.*
1795.			*Spanish portion of San Domingo ceded to France.*
1796.	Oct.	5.	*Spain declared war against England.*
1797.	March.		*Toussaint l'Ouverture appointed to command troops in San Domingo.*
	Nov.	15.	N. married at Belfast Maria, daughter of Courtlandt Skinner, late of New Jersey.
1798.	Aug.		*San Domingo evacuated by British.*
1799.	July to		N. Adjutant-General in Ireland, and represented Charleville, co. Cork, in last Irish
1801.	March		Parliament.
	April	1.	N. appointed Lieutenant-Governor and Commander-in-Chief of Jamaica.
	May	25.	Embarked at Portsmouth on *Ambuscade.*
	June	29.	Passed the tropic.
	July	20.	Anchored at Port Royal, Martinique.
		28.	Sighted Jamaica.

1801. July 29.		Landed at Port Henderson, and went to Spanish Town.
Sept. 12.		Admiral Lord Hugh Seymour died.
28.		Visited Clifton, in Liguanea.
Oct. 1.	,,	Papine and Hope.
3.	,,	Admiral's Pen.
9.		Arrival of Admiral Montagu.
20.		Assembly met.
Dec. 12.		prorogued.
28.		*Le Clerc reached San Domingo.*
1802. Jan. 26.		Admiral Sir J. T. Duckworth arrived.
Feb. 4.		Visited Bushy Park and Spring Gardens.
10.	,,	Mr. Israell, in Clarendon.
11.	,,	Mr. Osborn's, in Vere.
12.	,,	Pusey Hall and Moneymusk.
13.	,,	Old Harbour.
24.	,,	Bog Walk and New Hall.
March 5.		Started on tour round island; visited Simon Taylor's.
6.		Visited Albion.
7.	,,	Cow Bay and Montpelier.
8.	,,	Lyssons.
9.	,,	Bath.
10.	,,	Golden Grove.
11.	,,	Holland : the Moro.
12.	,,	Amity Hall and Merton.
13.	,,	Castle Comfort : the Bog.
14.		N. visited maroons at Moor Town.
16.		Visited Spring Gardens.
18.	,,	Kildare and Charlestown.
21.	,,	Fort Brunswick, Fort George (Port Antonio), Annotto Bay, Agualta Vale, Hopewell.
23.	,,	Nonsuch.
24.	,,	the Ramble.
26.	,,	St. Ann's Bay : Seville.
27.		*Treaty of Amiens.*
31.		Visited Arcadia.
April 2.	,,	Bryan Hall.

1802. April 4. Visited Falmouth.
            9.   ,,   Ironshore : Montego Bay.
           14.   ,,   Knockalva.
           15.   ,,   Paradise.
           16.   ,,   Savanna-la-Mar.
           17.   ,,   Black River.
           19.   ,,   Lacovia.
           20. N. visited Accompong.
           21. Visited Derry.
           22.   ,,   Porus.
           23.   ,,   Woods : Parnassus.
           24.   ,,   Old Harbour : home.
           26. Arrival of French officers from San Domingo.
     May 6. Went to Stony Hill.
          24. Review of 2nd West India Regiment.
     July 12-22. Visited the Decoy, in St. Mary.
     Aug. 24-27.   ,,   New Hall.
     Sept. 15. Aide-de-camp of Le Clerc arrived from San Domingo.
     Oct. 12. Birth of a son (George Edmund Nugent).
     Nov.   1. *Le Clerc died in San Domingo.*
     Dec.   Downes Skinner died.
1803. Jan. 12. Incorporation of the town of Kingston.
     March 14. Visited Berkshire Hall : the Decoy.
           22.   ,,   the Ramble.
     April 22. Returned home.
     May   12. French officers arrived from San Domingo.
     June 22. News of war with France and Holland.
     Aug.   1. French Deputies from San Domingo arrived.
     Sept. 8. Birth of a daughter (Louisa Elizabeth).
           25. N. made lieutenant-general.
1804. April 4. Arrival of Admiral Dacres in command of the station.
     June   9. Visited Stony Hill.
     July   7. Went to Mount Salus.
     Aug. 13. King of Mosquito Indians arrived.
     Sept. 9. Returned to Spanish Town.
     Oct.   8. *Dessalines declared Emperor of Haiti.*

1804. Dec. 18. Assembly prorogued.
1805. Feb. 19. Duckworth left and Dacres succeeded him.
March 10. Went to Port Henderson.
April 1. Martial law declared.
      19. Martial law ceased.
May 24. Martial law declared.
June 22. Martial law ceased.
      28. Lady N. and children embarked at Old Harbour on board *Augustus Cæsar*.
July 6. Passed Grand Cayman.
Sept. 4. Landed at Weymouth.
      7. Reached London.
      29. Visited Stowe.
Oct. 17. Returned to London.
Nov. 2. Visited Stowe.
      18. Visited Oxford.
      19. Visited Bath.
Dec. 18. Returned to Stowe.
1806. Jan. 15. Returned to Town.
Feb. 20. N. left Jamaica.
May 3. N. reached England.
      26. N. transferred to colonelcy of 6th Royal Regiment of Foot.
Oct. 9. Went to Exeter.
Nov. 28. N. made a baronet.
1807. Jan. 29. Returned to London.
April 27. Went to Stowe.
May 9. N. elected M.P. for Aylesbury.
Dec. 5. Birth of a son (Edmund).
      26. Infant son died.
1808. Jan. 21. Returned to London.
April 18. Went to Tunbridge Wells.
July 11. ,, Stowe.
      ,, Dublin.
      ,, Glasgow.
      ,, Edinburgh.
Oct. Lady N. purchased Westhorpe House.
Nov. 14. Went to Westhorpe.
1809. June. N. assumed command of Kent district.
July. Went to Ramsgate.
      Superintended transmission and return of Walcheren Expedition.

1809. Oct. 18. Returned to Westhorpe.
     Nov. 16. Birth of a daughter (Emily).
1810. Jan. 2. Visited Stowe.
        4. Lady N.'s mother died.
1811. March. N. appointed Commander-in-Chief in India.
     June 15. Birth of a son (Charles Edmund).
     July 27. Embarked on *Baring*—East Indiaman.
     Aug. 14–16. Madeira.
     Sept. 16. Crossed the line.
     Oct. 22. Sighted Table Mountain.
        23–28. South Africa. Stop with Governor, Sir J. Cradock.
1812. Jan. 14. Landed at Calcutta.
     March 22. Miniature by Chinnery.
     April 4. Lady N.'s brother (General Skinner) arrived.
     June 1. Sir G. sat for picture.
     July 1. Commenced tour up Ganges.
1813. June 4. N. made a full general.
     Aug. 9. Back at Calcutta.
        19. News of Lord Buckingham's death.
     Oct. 4. Lord Moira, the new Governor-General of Bengal and Commander-in-Chief of the forces in India, arrived.
        6. Sir G. resigned.
        12. Sir G. invested with the Order of the Bath.
     Dec. 28. Left Calcutta.
1815. Jan. 15–19. Ceylon.
     March 27 to April 4. Cape.
     April 30. St. Helena.
     May 6. Ascension.
     N. made a G.C.B.
1819. N. made an honorary D.C.L. of Oxford.
1819–32. N. represented Buckingham in Parliament.
1834. Oct. 24. Lady N. died.
1839. " Journals " privately printed.
1846. Nov. 9. N. made a field-marshal.
1849. March 11. N. died at Waddesdon House, Little Marlow.

A 2

INTRODUCTION

THE WEST INDIES, 1801–1805

MAJOR-GENERAL GEORGE NUGENT was Lieutenant-Governor of Jamaica from the 27th of July, 1801 to the 20th of February, 1806.

War with France had been continuous since 1793; but long before 1801 British naval supremacy had been established. British merchant ships carried on nearly all the trade, and their rivals had been swept from the sea. Martinique and St. Lucia had been captured from France, Trinidad and Tobago from Spain, against whom Great Britain had made good her title to British Honduras; Guiana and Curaçoa were taken from Holland, besides other minor conquests; and in 1799 Sir Hyde Parker had in eight months taken no less than 47 armed vessels and 225 merchant-men.

In July, 1801, there can have been little fear in Jamaica of foreign aggression other than the privateering raids that were then ever present. On October the 1st of that year the preliminary articles of peace were signed in London, and on the 27th of March, 1802, they were ratified by the Peace of Amiens. England gave up many of her West Indian conquests, but her naval supremacy remained.

The brief interval of peace was utilized by Napoleon in the disastrous attempt to reconquer Haiti, many allusions to which occur in Lady Nugent's Journal. A short summary of the confused history of that unfortunate island at that period is given below.

In 1803 war with France began again, and at the end of 1804 Spain joined her. The British recaptured most of the conquests given up by the Peace of Amiens.

Sir John Duckworth (whose name is frequently mentioned in the Journal) reported in November, 1803, that his squadron had taken forty-two vessels and destroyed two privateers in the last two months, and he was frequently the recipient of votes of thanks from various bodies in the island.

In 1805 French and Spanish privateers gave some trouble. In April Villeneuve captured an English convoy of fifteen ships, valued at five million sterling.

In that year Jamaica was on tenter-hooks of apprehension of French invasion, while Nelson chased Villeneuve out to the West Indies and back again ; or, as a local poet wrote—

> The combined fleet, with near 12,000 men,
> Which sail'd from Europe—has—sail'd *back* again,

and Dacres, the commander-in-chief on the station, detained for its protection four of the six ships of Cochrane's squadron which had come out in chase of Missiessy, and Nelson had hoped would reach him at Barbados.

Lady Nugent, however, seems to have understood better the principles of the " Blue-water School," for she writes in her Journal : " In fact, the security of this island depends mainly on our superiority at sea and the vigilance of our squadrons."

Lady Nugent left Jamaica in June, 1805, but General Nugent was still governor at the time of Trafalgar. The news reached the island on the 28th of December. January 10th was appointed a day of general thanksgiving, and great rejoicings took place ; but it is surprising that the island which paid worthy tribute to Rodney, and commemorated his victory by a dinner on the 12th of April for upwards of a quarter of a century, has allowed Nelson's memory to go unrecorded save for a tablet in Fort Charles, at Port Royal, telling of his sojourn there in early days, and, quite recently, the naming of a battery after him.

While commenting on naval affairs it may be mentioned that William James, the author of the well-known " Naval

History," lived in Jamaica, and practised as a proctor in
the Vice-Admiralty Court. He returned to England in
1812, and did not commence his history till 1819.

The poem given below is a specimen of Jamaica verse-
making of the time. It appeared in the *Royal Gazette* in
June, 1805.

LINES ON THE EXPECTED INVASION OF JAMAICA

Sons of Britannia! wield the lance,
  Defend Jamaica's isle,
Repel the rebel hordes of France,
  Nor let them touch its soil.

Fan in your breasts the gen'rous flames
  That feed the patriot's fire;
Your country calls—your country claims—
  The noblest deeds inspire.

What! shall this Isle defenceless fall
  A vile usurper's prey?
O! rather may we perish all
  Than crouch beneath his sway.

Sons of Jamaica! Britain's sons!
  The fiends of discord brave:
Grasp firm your swords, point sure your guns,
  And meet them on the wave.

O teach, O teach, the daring foe,
  Who threaten'd Britain's shore,
That British hearts, where'er they go,
  Are lions to the core.

Instruct them that the men they dread
  On England's flow'ry plain,
Do not in valour aught exceed
  Those on the Western main.

I see, I see, the haughty foe
  Presume to stride our shore,
I see him sink beneath our blow—
  Then seen, then heard, no more.

THE AFFAIRS OF HAITI, 1791–1806

As a Committee of the Jamaica Assembly reported in 1805, "the troubles of St. Domingo . . . originated in the bosom of the legislature of the Mother Country."

Before the outbreak of the French Revolution, in 1789, Haiti * had advanced further in the art of cultivation than any other West India island ; but the majority of the French planters, "flushed with opulence and dissipation, had arrived at a state of sentiment the most vitiated and manners equally depraved. The creole slaves looked upon the newly imported Africans with scorn, and sustained in their turn that of the mulattoes, while all were kept at a distance from the whites." †

On the 15th of May, 1791, the National Assembly decreed equal rights between whites and mulattoes. The blacks (instigated probably by the mulattoes) rebelled; but the rebellion was suppressed with the assistance from Jamaica of Admiral Affleck and H.M.S. *Blonde* and *Daphne*. The commissioners sent out from France to place matters on permanent footing did nothing, and returned.

On the 24th of September, 1791, the National Assembly annulled the decree of May, and the mulattoes and blacks joined in a fresh rebellion.

On the 4th of April, 1792, the National Assembly annulled the decree of the 24th of September, 1791, reaffirmed the principle of the decree of May, 1791, and sent out three fresh commissioners (Santhonax Polverel, and Ailhaud), with 8000 National Guards, to enforce the regulations.

---

* Haiti is the native name for the island which was called Hispaniola by the Spaniards. The French sometimes called their colony in the western part San Domingo. Haiti was the name adopted by the founder of the black republic, and is now applied to the western end as distinct from the eastern portion of San Domingo. The whole island is called at times either Haiti or San Domingo.

† *The Black Empire of Haiti*, Rainford. London. 1805.

The whites objected.   Two governors in succession were
sent home to France and guillotined.   The third resisted.
The commissioners enlisted the blacks and mulattoes,
offering them freedom and plunder against the whites, and
bloody results ensued.   Many planters emigrated to the
United States, England and Jamaica.   One in particular,
De Charmilly, influenced the English Government to send
instructions to the governor of Jamaica, major-general
Williamson, not only to protect the French *émigrés*, but
to send an expedition to take possession of such parts of
Haiti as were willing to come under the British flag.

For five years, 1793–1798, England occupied stations in
Haiti.   The commissioners withdrew to France, but the
intrigues of the French planters, the ravages of fever,
and, finally, the power of Toussaint l'Ouverture, compelled
evacuation.

Toussaint l'Ouverture (his cognomen, being due, it is
said, to his valour in causing a gap in the ranks of the
enemy) was an extraordinary man.   A pure negro, born a
slave, he made his way by character and ability.   He ruled
Haiti for four years with such success that, in spite of the
previous wars and devastations, he obtained an agricultural
crop equal to one-third of the best year of the French
planters.*   He took steps to establish freedom of worship,
formed an efficient police with the assistance of white men,
framed laws and maintained peace not only in Haiti, but
also nearly throughout San Domingo.

It is significant, however, to note that he, the first negro
in command of a number of Africans in anything like a
state of civilization, felt the need of enforcing labour in the
fields by military supervision.

On the 1st of October, 1801, preliminary articles of
peace between England and France were signed, and
Napoleon selected Haiti as a place of employment for
his soldiers.

On the 25th of January, 1802, General Le Clerc (Napoleon's

* In 1788 San Domingo exported 83 million lbs. of coffee.

brother-in-law) reached Haiti with 25,000 French soldiers. The Haitians resisted, and the savage war lasted nearly two years. Toussaint was treacherously taken prisoner—torn from his family by Le Clerc's order and shipped to France. He, "the most unhappy man of men," died in April, 1803, in the prison of Joux, near Besançon.

On the 1st of November, 1802, Le Clerc died, "leaving in the memory of his opponents a name blackened by the worst of crimes unatoned for by one single virtue," and the command devolved on Rochambeau (a planter), a worthy successor.

The leadership of the Haitians passed to Dessalines, who was both cruel and treacherous.

In July, 1803, war between France and England began again. A British squadron blockaded Haiti, and cut off French supplies.

On the 19th of November, 1803, Rochambeau capitulated to Dessalines. The British squadron captured three French frigates, twenty smaller vessels, and 8000 prisoners, and took them to Jamaica, where the cost of their maintenance was a source of much discussion between the Governor and the Assembly. Of the prisoners, about 1000 were on parole, and a source of much anxiety; the remainder were in "prison ships." This war cost France no less than twenty general officers and 40,000 men. The losses by fever were enormous.

On the 1st of January, 1804, Haiti declared her Independence, and on the 8th of October Dessalines was crowned as Emperor. The population was estimated at about 350,000, of whom 270,000 were agriculturists, 35,000 soldiers, the rest domestics, artisans, and the like.

Dessalines wished to restore to Haiti the prosperity it had enjoyed under Toussaint, but his rule was too bloody. He is said to have murdered 2400 people, white and coloured alike. Fear of disturbance spreading to Jamaica was very real. Haitian emigrants to Jamaica were considered dangerous; proclamations were issued against them by both Governor and Mayor and Corporation of Kingston, and many were shipped to New Orleans. So little did Dessalines realize his true mission as a negro leader that he tried to arrange with the British Government for the purchase of slaves, offering to open Haitian ports to British slave-ships.

He was murdered by a mulatto on the 17th of October, 1806.

CIVIL ADMINISTRATION OF JAMAICA, 1801–1805

The House of Assembly consisted during Nugent's governorship of forty-three members. The names of the members in 1801, and the constituencies they represented, are given in the table below.

The franchise, established by the law of 1681, for appointing the members of the Assembly, was still in force in 1802— " Freeholders in the same parish where the election is to be made." At a by-election in 1804, in St. Andrew, seventy-nine freeholders voted, forty-six for the successful candidate. The House met in Spanish Town, usually from October to Christmas, the time of year when the planters could be absent from their estates with least inconvenience.

The House voted about £15,000* a year for the maintenance of such roads as might be necessary to encourage settlers to cultivate lands at a distance from the sea. The money was paid in sums varying from £50 to £400 to groups of landowners for specific roads, the almost invariable result being that they reported in the following session that they had done the best they could with the money voted to them, but that they wanted more to complete the job. In those days a carriage road was made from Bull Bay, through Dallas Castle and Hall's Delight, to Hope. The road between Spanish Town and Kingston was under the direction of special commissioners. It is worthy of note that one reason that a squadron attended Nugent on his tours was that the state of the roads might render passage by sea desirable.

A survey of the island was made between 1800 and 1805 by James Robertson, and maps engraved on a scale of one inch to the mile, at a cost of £7500.† No regular cadastral

* The sums mentioned in this chapter are all Jamaica currency, of which £1 was then only worth 12s. sterling.

† The three maps of the counties with a key map, on a scale of ¼ inch to a mile, were published at a cost of twenty-one guineas the set.

survey has ever been made of Jamaica, though the question has been considered, and estimates prepared varying from £66,000 to £100,000.

The town of Kingston was incorporated on the 12th of January, 1803, under the name of " The Mayor, Aldermen, and Commonalty of the city and parish of Kingston." It forthwith passed ordinances relating to the Sabbath, distilling and sale of spirits, markets, slaughter-houses, fishing in the harbour, streets, lanes, penguin fences, riding, driving, drays, wherries, churchwardens, treasurers, blacksmiths, seamen, crimps, hiring of slaves, hawkers, pedlars, higglers, and dogs. Bread cost 7½d. for a 16 oz. loaf. A chaise and horses from the eleventh milestone on the Windward Road to Kingston cost £2, to Morant Bay £6 10s. Internal posts went (i) to leeward [i.e. westward]: (ii) to the north side : (iii) to windward [i.e. eastward] and (iv) to St. Mary, St. George and Portland. The mail packet to England sailed once a month.

The Church of England was established by law : jurisdiction having been given to the Bishop of London in 1748, and in 1800 Ecclesiastical Commissioners were appointed in Jamaica. The island was divided into twenty parishes. Each parish had a rector, with stipend of £420 a year and rectory. The rectors were in sympathy with the planters, and in many cases, if not actually opposed to, were lukewarm in carrying out any attempt to educate or even Christianize the slaves. A most intolerant Act* was rushed through the House on the 17th of December, 1802, forbidding any unqualified person from preaching to the negroes. Nugent approved it on the following day. Three Methodists applying to be qualified were refused by the magistrates who said they ought to be committed for daring to address the court. Another was sentenced to hard labour for a month for singing, which was declared to mean preaching. Another was sent to the workhouse. The Act was disallowed by the King in Privy

* An Act to prevent preaching by persons not duly qualified by law.

Council on the 23rd of April, 1804. The Assembly protested vigorously. Nugent was a religious man, and well aware, as the Journal records, of the lethargic condition of the clergy, but was probably unable to oppose the intolerance of the Assembly.

The principal newspapers were *The Royal Gazette* and the *St. Jago Gazette*, published in Spanish Town, and the *Cornwall Chronicle*, in Montego Bay. They consisted largely of extracts from English papers and advertisements. There was also a *Daily Advertiser*, published in Kingston; and the *Kingston Chronicle* was started in 1805.

The lavish hospitality of the period is well described in the Journal.

THE HOUSE OF ASSEMBLY, 1801

CONSTITUENCY	NAMES OF MEMBERS	
St. Catherine . . .	Philip Redwood	E. P. Lyon
	Wm. Mitchell	
Port Royal . . .	Fairlie Christie	James Stewart
	George Cuthbert	
Kingston	Eliphalet Fitch	John Jaques
	Alexander Shaw	
St. Andrew . . .	John Dawson	Thomas Kaylett
St. Thomas-in-the-Vale	Lewis Cuthbert	Robert Ross
St. Dorothy . . .	Wm. Jackson	Robert Ogilvie
St. John	William Thompson	John Quier
Clarendon	John Henckell	Joseph Israell
Vere	J. P. Edwards	Alexander Schaw
St. Elizabeth . . .	J. J. Swaby	H. Spooner
Westmoreland . .	W. R. Johnson	C. Mitchell
Hanover	Richard H. Reid	T. P. Tharpe
St. James	John Mowat	John Perry
Trelawny	James Stewart	P. Smith
St. Ann	Alexander Fullerton	James Henry
St. Mary	Charles Grant	T. Murphy
St. George	Henry Shirley	David Sherriff
Portland	Charles Bryan	J. S. Minot
St. Thomas-in-the-East	} Simon Taylor	{ Kean Osborne (the Speaker)
St. David	Robert Telfer	William Ker

The following is the Estimate of ways and means of the Colony's finances for 1803 :—

	£	s.	d.
Poll-tax at 8s.	115,000	0	0
Transient traders tax	2,000	0	0
Arrears of poll-tax, 1801	15,000	0	0
Deficiency and arrears	30,000	0	0
Land-tax and arrears	45,000	0	0
Negro duties (doubtful)	30,000	0	0
Rum duties	9,000	0	0
Additional duties	6,000	0	0
Arrears of taxes of former years . . .	30,000	0	0
Surplus of the revenue	20,000	0	0
Stamp duties	34,000	0	0
Debts to be recovered	2,000	0	0
Fees of private bill	240	0	0
Militia and other fines	1,000	0	0
	339,240	0	0
Balance of cash and surplus of revenue .	202,000	0	0
	541,240	0	0

MILITARY ADMINISTRATION OF JAMAICA, 1801–1805

Nugent was Commander-in-Chief as well as Lieut.-Governor, and was in constant controversy with the Assembly as regards military expenditure. The cost of the troops had much increased, the figures being as follows :—

In the year 1777 .	.	.	.	£18,750
,, 1783 .	.	.	.	£44,446
,, 1802 .	.	.	.	£189,599

The Assembly grumbled, asserting, as it always did, " that the colony was on the verge of ruin." It constantly protested, as it had done in Balcarres's time, against the cost of the subsistence of the white troops, but it objected specially to the presence of the 2nd West India Regiment of negro troops, raised in 1797, whom it considered "incompatible with our safety and pregnant with the most fatal calamities." Nugent offered to arrange for their withdrawal if the Assembly would consent to support 5000 British troops instead of 3000. But the Assembly, by a vote of twenty-four to six, decided that 3000 were sufficient, and the black troops remained.

Nugent reported on his arrival that the forts and barracks were insufficient and neglected, and he was very desirous of getting under his own control the expenditure on their maintenance.

Tables are given below showing the regiments in the island at the time, the names of the staff officers, and the localities of the forts and barracks. A list is also given of His Majesty's ships on the station.

The island militia totalled on paper to over 10,000 men, and consisted of whites and free people of colour; but its efficiency for military purposes cannot have been great, if we take as a sample the St. John's and St. Dorothy's regiment, of which Lady Nugent gives an amusing description in the Journal. The Duke of Clarence, who knew the West Indies, suggested in the House of Lords that corps of sepoys should be used there.

Below is given a copy of a Proclamation with regard to the inspection of the militia. In Nugent's time the militia were wont to muster once a week, and during martial law daily; in Kingston, where ball cartridge was served out, twice a day.

There was a law * at the time by which the planters were compelled to keep at least one white man for the first hundred slaves, and one for every additional seventy slaves. Failing this, they were put on the " mulct list " and fined. These men (i.e. those needed in addition to the white men which the working of the estate required) lived an idle life, and were probably not much use for work. They were all members of the militia.

Martial law was proclaimed for two short periods during 1805.

Lodgings were not all that the House was expected to provide for the troops. On one occasion the colonel commanding the 6th battalion of the 60th Regiment stated that the battalion in marching from Up-Park Camp to Cornwall Barracks had worn out nearly two pairs of shoes each, and asked for the same allowance for shoes as had been granted to other battalions of the same regiment. On another occasion the Deputy-Adjutant-General petitioned the House for lodging money, island pay, and " the usual allowance for his family," i.e. sixteen shillings per week for his wife, and eight shillings for his child.

H.M. SHIPS ON THE JAMAICA STATION, 1801

1 eighty (*Sans Pareil*).
2 seventy-fours (*Thunderer* and *Carnatic*).
3 sixty-fours (*Admiral de Vries, York*, and *America*).
1 fifty-four (*Abergavenny*).
1 forty-four (*La Vengeance*).
1 forty-two (*La Seine*).
1 forty (*Acasta*).
4 thirty-sixes (*Crescent, Nereide, Decade, Apollo*).

* An Act to oblige the several inhabitants of this island to provide themselves with a sufficient number of white persons, or pay certain sums of money in case they shall be deficient, and applying the same to several uses.

7 thirty-twos (*Amphion, Meleager, Lowestoffe,* *Juno,
Quebec, Retribution, Surprise*).
1 twenty-eight (*Circe*).
1 twenty-four (*La Legère*).
1 twenty-two (*Volage*).
2 twenties (*La Prompte* and *Tisiphone*).
2 eighteens (*Swallow* and *Bonetta*).
6 sixteens (*Albicore, Echo, Merlin, Calypso, Dark, Rattler*).
1 twelve (*Mosquito*).
And the hospital ship (*Winchester*).

The military forces then in Jamaica, taken from the
Jamaica Almanac for 1802, consisted of the staff, a hospital
staff, detachments of the Royal Artillery, the Royal Dutch
Artillery, the XX. (or Jamaica) Light Dragoons, the 1st,
4th, and 6th battalions of the LX. Foot,† the LXIX. Foot,
the LXXXIII. Foot, and the II. West India Regiment,
in addition to the island militia and artillery.

The Kingston regiment of foot militia had two battalions
of artillery and grenadiers, besides six companies to each
battalion of light infantry—the 2nd company was composed
of Jews, the 3rd of mulattoes, the 4th of quadroons, and
the 5th and 6th of blacks—all officered by white men.

The staff was as follows :—

His Excellency Major-General George Nugent, 85th Regiment.
Aide-de-camp and Military Secretary, Captain Walter Johnson,
60th Regiment.
Deputy-Adjutant-General, Major Charles Irvine, 62nd Regiment.
Deputy-Quartermaster-General, Lieut.-Colonel Charles McMurdo,
31st Regiment.
Acting Deputy-Master-General, Major Ed. Drummond, 60th
Regiment.
Assistant ditto, Cornet J. Nixon, 20th Dragoons.
Major of Brigade, Captain Augustus Gould, 20th Dragoons.
Island Engineer, Captain William Fraser, 60th Regiment.
Assistant Engineer, Captain James Lomax, 60th Regiment.

* It was in this frigate that Nelson came out to Jamaica, as
second lieutenant, in 1777.
† The 1st and 4th battalions were German protestants,
commanded by British officers. It was intended that they
should be disbanded and settled in the island.

Commissary-General, Matthew Atkinson, Esq.
Deputy ditto, Wellwood Hyslop, Esq.
Island Barracks-Master-General, Augustus Gould, Esq.
Second in Command, Major-General George Churchill.
Aide-de-camp, Lieut. Coatquelvin.
Major of Brigade, Captain Hampden Pye, 6th West India
    Regiment.

The following were the forts in Jamaica :—

Fort Charles, at Port Royal ; Fort Augusta, Apostles'
Battery, Rock Fort, all in Kingston Harbour ; Fort George,
at Port Antonio ; Fort Charlotte, at Lucea ; Fort Balcarres,
in Trelawny ; Montego Bay Fort ; Fort Haldane, in St
Mary ; Fort Lindsay ; Fort Ramsay, in St. Thomas-in-the
East ; Fort Dundas, at Rio Bueno ; and Fort Clarence, in
St. Catherine.

BARRACKS—1803

Names.	Numbers they will contain.	Numbers they are proposed to contain.
Spanish Town	500	100
Fort Augusta	500	500
Fort Charles	300	300
Kingston	200	70
Stony Hill	700	700
Port Antonio	200	100
Port Maria	80	50
Falmouth	60	50
Maroon Town (Trelawny)	200	300
Montego Bay	100	50
Lucea	80	50
Savanna-la-mar	100	50
Quashie River	80	80
Cornwall	—	300
Fort George Pen . . .	—	300

A 3

KING'S HOUSE, SPANISH TOWN.
May 24, 1804.

MILITIA GENERAL ORDERS

The Commander-in-Chief proposes to inspect the Regiments of Foot and the Troops of Horse-Militia of the several parishes of this Island, in the following order. The Colonels and Commanding Officers of the respective corps will therefore prepare them for his inspection without delay, and practice only such movements, etc., as have been directed by the Commander-in-Chief to be performed by the Foot and Horse Militia generally, in order to introduce an uniform system into that Service.

The Troop or Troops of Horse will be separately inspected immediately after the inspection of the Regiment of Foot of the same parish. The Arms and Appointments of the several corps must be very particularly attended to for the good state of which Colonels and Commanding Officers will be held responsible.

Forms of the Inspection-Returns, which will be required, will be circulated to the different Corps.

By order of the Commander-in-Chief,

J. TYRRELL, Sec.

INSPECTIONS OF MILITIA, 1804

CORPS	DATES OF INSPECTION
1. St. Catherine's Regiment and Troop.	Monday, June 11, on the Race Course, near Spanish Town, at half-past 5 a.m.
2. St. John's and St. Dorothy's Regiment and Troops	Thursday, June 14, at Spring Garden, at 10 a.m.
3. St. Andrew's Regiment and Troop.	Monday, June 18, at Half-Way-Tree, at 10 a.m.
4. Kingston Regiment and Troop.	Thursday, June 21, on the Race Course, near Kingston, at half-past 5 a.m.
5. Port Royal Regiment.	Monday, July 9, at Castile Fort, at 10 a.m.
6. St. Thomas-in-the-East and St. David's Regiment and Troops.	Tuesday, July 10, at Belvidere-Pasture at 11 a.m.
7. Portland Regiment and Troop.	Friday, July 13, at the Folly-Point, near Port Antonio, at 10 a.m.

CORPS	DATES OF INSPECTION
8. St. George's Regiment and Troop.	Monday, July 16, near Buff-Bay Tavern, at 11 a.m.
9. St. Mary's Regiment and Troop.	Thursday, July 19, at their Review Grounds, at 11 a.m.
10. St. Thomas-in-the-Vale Regiment and Troop.	Friday, July 20, at Shenton-Pasture, at 10 a.m.
11. Clarendon Regiment and Troop.	Monday, August 6, at their Review Ground, at 11 a.m.
12. Vere Regiment and Troop.	Tuesday, August 7, at the Alley, at 11 a.m.
13. St. Elizabeth Regiment and Troop.	Friday, August 10, at their Review Ground, near Black River, at 11 a.m.
14. Westmoreland Regiment and Troop.	Saturday, August 11, at Savanna-la-Mar, at 11 a.m.
15. St. James' Regiment and Troop.	Monday, August 13, at the Race Course, Montego Bay, at 11 a.m.
16. Hanover Regiment and Troop.	Tuesday, August 14, at Lucea, at 11 a.m.
17. Trelawny Regiment and Troop.	Thursday, August 16, at Falmouth, at 10 a.m.
18. St. Ann's Regiment and Troop.	Wednesday, August 22, at Seville-Pasture, at 11 a.m.

THE EXTERNAL TRADE OF JAMAICA, 1801–1805

Bryan Edwards, when he dedicated, in 1793, his history of the British West Indies to George III, called them " the principal source of the national opulence and maritime power " of England, and at that time the term " as rich as a West Indian " was proverbial.

In the year ending 5th of January, 1803, the direct trade between Great Britain and the West Indies employed 1060 ships, measuring 292,183 tons, and navigated by 16,793 seamen ; and the West Indies were then accountable for one-third of the imports and exports of Great Britain.

In 1802 the average price of sugar, published in the *London Gazette*, was thirty-six shillings and sixpence per hundredweight. That was " a period of the greatest de· pression " in Jamaica. In December the Assembly decided, at the suggestion of Simon Taylor, the richest man in the colony and one of the richest men in the empire, to instruct the island agent * to represent to the King " the necessity of adopting some measure of relief to prevent the ruin of the most important colony to the Crown."

For 1803 the price of sugar was fifty-two shillings and six-pence. A committee of the House of Assembly reported at this time that with a sale price of fifty-six shillings per hundredweight (or thirty-six shillings to the planter), " with peace prices and a fair price for rum, it is admitted that this return would just enable the sugar planter to continue his cultivation without loss." In spite, however, of these complainings, of war and of the doubt raised in the minds of planters by the Abolition movement, from 1788 to 1804, the export from Jamaica of sugar and of coffee (to the cultivation of which the disasters of San Domingo gave a great impetus) increased. In those days the planters, merchants,

---

* The office of Agent for Jamaica in London during Nugent's term of office was held first by Robert Sewell, then by George Hibbert, and lastly by Edmund Pusey Lyon. Sewell and Hibbert were members of parliament. Sewell's salary was £2,100 per annum.

and others interested were wont to meet and settle the rates of freight to be paid by the fleet of merchantmen which went home, four times a year, under the convoy of a man-of-war. In war time it was nearly three times as high as in peace. In October, 1803, for example, they decided—under the chairmanship of John Jaques, Mayor and Custos of Kingston—that the rates should be as follows : sugar, 7d. per cwt. ; rum, 9d. per gallon ; coffee, 10d. per cwt.; cotton, 2d. per ℔. in bags, or 1½d. per ℔. in seroons; logwood and other dye woods, £4. 4s. per ton.

The question of the commerce of Jamaica and of the West Indies generally was much complicated by the independence of the North American colonies. The inhabitants of the United States would not understand why they should not as a foreign state enjoy the privileges of trade with the British West Indies which had been their right before they revolted; and in this feeling they had the sympathy of many in Jamaica and elsewhere, who needed cheap supplies of lumber and provisions, and a handy market for their sugar; added to which in times of drought the need for prompt food supplies became acute. It is stated that 15,000 slaves died in Jamaica on account of shortness of provisions between 1780 and 1787 ; and Balcarres only averted famine by opening the ports of the colony to vessels of the United States.

Jay, in the treaty of amity, commerce, and navigation, which is named after him, sought to put matters on a better footing, and in the original treaty, signed in London in November, 1794, it was agreed that American single-decked vessels of seventy tons burden and under might trade with any merchandise which it was lawful to carry in British vessels to and from the British West Indies ; but the American senate in ratifying the treaty threw out this clause, and the matter was for some years left to royal proclamations, which varied from time to time, and gave rise to much difference of opinion between the home Government and local trade interests in the West Indies.

In 1802–3 the imports to Jamaica from the United States consisted of corn-meal, flour, bread, rice, fish, beef, pork, butter, peas, beans, corn, lumber, staves, and shingles ; and the exports were sugar, rum, ginger, pimento, and coffee. The trade then employed (as a result of sanction) as many bottoms (to use the official term for vessels) of American origin as of English.

A British Order in Council of the 21st of November, 1804, announced the termination of the trade with the United States in six months from that date, which had been based on an Order in Council of the 17th of July, 1800. This announcement caused much apprehension in Jamaica, especially amongst the leading merchants of Kingston. On the other hand, certain merchants, whose trade lay with the British Isles and Canada, stated in a petition to the King that all necessary salted provisions could be supplied from the British Isles in British bottoms and from British America.

" In 1799," the Assembly complained in 1803, " the impolitic attempt was made to make the foreign consumer of West India produce pay British duties." This presumably was in conformity with the revival of the Rule of 1756, that neutrals could not trade in time of war with colonies with which they could not trade in time of peace. And it was a recurrence of this state of affairs that the Jamaica merchants feared as a result of the Order in Council of the 21st of November, 1804. In 1806 the scarcity of provisions in the British West Indies was very great, and bounties were offered by the home Government on the salted provisions imported in British vessels from the North American colonies, the colonies to ultimately refund the bounties advanced.

In 1802, Pelham was Home Secretary ; Hawkesbury, Secretary for Foreign Affairs ; Hobart, Secretary for War ; St. Vincent, First Lord of the Admiralty ; Addington, Chancellor of the Exchequer ; and Liverpool, President of the Committee of Council for Trade and Foreign Plantations.

SLAVERY

The Journal gives a very vivid picture of slavery as it existed in Jamaica at the beginning of the nineteenth century. There were then about 300,000 slaves in the island. The statistics of those days are naturally unreliable, and the House of Assembly flatly refused to facilitate the collection of information about births and deaths. The average value of a slave was about £80, or perhaps £100. A negro man-cook was advertised for sale at £140, and Lord Penrhyn's agent claimed as much as £300 for a slave accidentally killed during the existence of martial law.

Lady Nugent's views on the subject evidently arose from her strong religious feeling, but they were at the same time very far-sighted. She saw that the evil of slavery was mainly in its effects on the white population.

During Nugent's time there was no rebellion of slaves. His predecessor, Balcarres, had suppressed a rising in 1798, and the next serious one was not till 1831, shortly before emancipation.

The only legislation which took place in Nugent's time in regard to slaves had reference to the trying of titles to slaves, to the prevention of intercourse between the slaves of the island and foreign slaves, and to the ascertainment of the value of slaves condemned to death, transportation, or imprisonment for life; a consolidated slave law having been passed in March of 1801, a few months previous to his arrival.

Although there were at the time many humane men in the island who treated their slaves well, these same slaves were by one and all regarded with very little difference from their four-legged stock.

Advertisements for runaway slaves and strayed stock were put in the newspapers side by side.

For example, the following advertisements, which appeared thus in the *Royal Gazette* for June, 1803, are only two of many such :—

SPANISH TOWN, *April* 18, 1803.

Strayed into the Two-Mile-Wood Savanna, near this town, a Spanish mule, lately from the ship; is marked A, within a circle on the buttock. Whoever will deliver the said mule at Ebony-Park pen, or at the Printing-Office, in this town, shall receive twenty shillings reward.

ST. ANN'S, *Jan.* 24, 1803.

Escaped from St. Ann's Workhouse, Plato, an Ebo, of a dark complection, 5 feet 6 inches high, belonging to the estate of Mr. Jones, of St. Ann's. Whoever will lodge the said Negro with the subscriber shall receive a Pistole reward.

WM. JONES TAYLOR (sub.).

Slaves and stock for sale were also advertised, as, for example, in the *Royal Gazette* for June 11th, 1803 :—

KINGSTON, *May* 24, 1803.

For Sale

302 Choice Young Eboe

NEGROES

Imported from Bonny in the ship Otway.

LUKE MANN, Master.

BOGLE, JOPP, & Co.

May 21, 1803.

For Sale, at Haddon Pen, near the Moneague,

50 CREOLE STEERS

Most of them fit for the Tongue. Apply on the premises.

A sugar estate was in those days as self-contained as a small village, with its hospital and resident, or at least visiting, medical man. Although the slave laws left much to be desired by philanthropists, the condition of slaves on the whole was not as bad as some writers, taking exceptional cases for the rule, have made out In the early days of slavery revolt was incited by each arrival of fresh negroes from the African bush; in later days, by the hope of obtaining emancipation and civil rights. Slaves were best looked after on those estates where the proprietor was resident.

Proprietors and overseers were required by law to give in at the vestry of their several parishes an account of provisions made for, and clothing delivered to, their slaves; to state that they had regularly inspected the negro grounds; and also give an account of the increase and decrease of slaves, with causes of decrease sworn to by the several doctors attending the plantations.

That the fear of rebellions, or at least outbreaks, on the part of the blacks was ever present is evidenced by the strong objection which the Assembly evinced to the maintenance of the recently formed West India regiment in the colony.

So far as their spiritual welfare was concerned, it is to be feared that the Church of England clergy scarcely fulfilled their mission. In 1798 an address was presented to the king praying for a new ecclesiastical institution. "Clergymen," Lady Nugent tells us, "make no secret of making a traffic of their livings," and she instances one faithful overseer who was rewarded by being made an island rector! The Moravians had been working quietly, as was their wont, for nigh on a century. The Wesleyan Mission had been founded in 1789; and Presbyterian and Baptist ministers were working in the island; but the Baptists, who afterwards played a large part in the emancipation of the slaves, did not actually found their mission in Jamaica till 1814.

George Nugent, the natural son of Lieutenant-Colonel the Honourable Edmund Nugent, 1st Foot Guards, was connected by birth with the earls of Fingal, barons Delvin, viscounts Clare, earl Nugent, and the earls of Westmeath. His father was the only son of Robert Nugent, Viscount Clare, afterwards Earl Nugent ; and had Sir George been of legitimate birth he would have inherited the earldom, for he was older than his only brother, Admiral Sir Charles Edmund Nugent. Their father died unmarried in 1771. Sir George's grandfather, the first Earl Nugent, acquired through marriage with rich widows a large fortune, and at the time of his death was regarded as a millionaire. This talent of his caused Horace Walpole to invent the term Nugentize to describe the actions of would-be imitators. By his first wife, a daughter of the 4th earl of Fingal, he had the son above mentioned, who pre-deceased him. His second wife, Anne Craggs, " a fat ugly dame," on her third marriage brought him great wealth, including Gosfield, in Essex, and £100,000, but no children. His third wife, Elizabeth Drax, widow of the fourth earl of Berkeley, also brought him a large fortune. The elder of the two daughters which she bore to him, Mary Elizabeth, married in 1775 George Grenville, afterwards Earl Temple, and later Marquis of Buckingham, the " dear Lady B.," of Lady Nugent's Journal. Middleton, near Newcastle, in Jamaica, is owned by Lady Kinloss, the daughter of the last duke of Buckingham. On the death of earl Nugent, in 1788, the title and real estate of about £14,000 per annum passed to the Marquis of Buckingham, who by royal permission assumed the surnames of Nugent and Temple, and obtained the privilege of signing Nugent before all titles whatsoever.

Earl Nugent's success in political life was fostered in great measure by his wealth, for political convictions he had none. His first seat in Parliament, that of St. Mawes in

Cornwall, he obtained with his second wife ; his money helped him to be made comptroller of the household of the Prince of Wales. He was a lord of the treasury under Pelham and Pitt, a vice-treasurer for Ireland, and for some years President of the Board of Trade ; and his money gained for him the viscounty of Clare, and the barony and earldom of Nugent.

He dabbled at times in poetry, and his ode to William Pulteny obtained great fame and high praise from Horace Walpole, albeit Gray suspected him of paying David Mallet, a protégé of his second wife, at times a collaborateur of Thomson, but a dramatist and a poet of short-lived fame, to write it, " his later and obviously unaided efforts being contemptible." At Gosfield, where he formed an extensive park, he entertained Goldsmith, who has passed his name on to posterity in his " Haunch of Venison," which winds up—

> To be plain, my good lord, it's but labour misplac'd,
> To send such good verses to one of your taste ;
> You've got an odd something—a kind of discerning,
> A relish, a taste—sicken'd over by learning ;
> At least it's your temper as very well known,
> That you think very slightly of all that's your own.
> So perhaps in your habits of thinking amiss,
> You may make a mistake and think slightly of this.

George Nugent was born on the 10th of June, 1757. He was educated at Charterhouse School, London, and the Royal Military Academy, Woolwich ; and was appointed ensign in the 39th Foot on the 5th of July, 1773. After serving at Gibraltar and on recruiting duty in England he joined, in September, 1777, the Royal Fusiliers at New York as lieutenant. He served in the expedition up the Hudson, at the storming of the forts of Montgomery and Clinton, and in Philadelphia. In April, 1778, he was promoted captain in the 57th Foot, and served in the Jerseys and Connecticut, and he must have there met the family of his future wife, when she was but a child. He was made a major in the 57th Foot in

May 1782, and the lieutenant-colonel of the 97th in the following year. He returned home and served in the 13th Foot. In 1789 he was transferred to the 4th Dragoon Guards, and in 1790 as captain and lieutenant to the Coldstream Guards. From 1787 to 1789 he was aide-de-camp to the Lord-Lieutenant of Ireland, his kinsman, the first Marquis of Buckingham. In 1793 Nugent accompanied the Guards to Holland, and was present at the siege of Valenciennes; but when the army went into winter quarters he returned home, and, aided by the Buckingham family interest, raised a corps of six hundred rank and file at Buckingham and Aylesbury, of which he was appointed colonel on the 18th November, 1793. These Bucks Volunteers afterwards became the 85th Light Infantry, and were, as we read in the Journal, stationed in Jamaica during his governorship. He was next in command of this regiment in Ireland and in Walcheren. He then joined the Duke of York's army on the Weal, and was appointed to command a brigade; but on Lord Cathcart's appointment to command that part of the army, he returned home, and was appointed to the Irish staff. He was also made captain and keeper of St. Mawes Castle, a post which his grandfather had tried in vain to obtain for his father in 1764.

From 1790 to 1800 he represented the borough of Buckingham in Parliament. He became major-general in May, 1796, and he commanded the Belfast district during the whole period of the rebellion. On the 15th of November, 1797, he married, at Belfast, Maria, seventh daughter of Courtlandt Skinner, formerly of New Jersey, then of Bristol, England, the authoress of the Journal.

From July, 1799, to March, 1801, Nugent was Adjutant-General in Ireland, and represented Charleville in the last Irish Parliament.

On April 1st, 1801, he was appointed Lieutenant-Governor and Commander-in-Chief of Jamaica, which he reached on the 29th of July, and where he remained until the 20th of February, 1806, a perilous period for the colony.

While in Jamaica Nugent acquired the rank of lieutenant-general in September, 1803. In those days the life of the Governor of Jamaica was a succession of reviews, audiences, balls, holding of Courts of Chancery, tours of inspection, and disputes with the House of Assembly, chiefly in connection with the question of restriction of trade with the United States, and the support of the military forces in the island. He was wont to attend at King's House for the purpose of seeing those who wished to interview him, on Tuesdays and Fridays between 9 a.m. and 2 p.m. On other days he could be seen at the pen.

Reminiscences of his governorship occur in Nugent Street, Spanish Town, and in Fort Nugent, near Rock Fort, not far from Kingston, which had been known as Fort Castile, it having been purchased in 1702 by the Assembly from Sir James de Castillo, a wealthy Spaniard, agent in Jamaica for the Royal African Company, who had built it at his own expense.

On the 28th of November, 1806, a few months after his return to England, Nugent was created a baronet of the United Kingdom, in recognition of his services.

He represented Aylesbury in the Parliament of 1806–7, and he commanded successively the Western and the Kent military districts. He was commander-in-chief in India from 1811 to 1813, and during that time Lady Nugent kept a journal, similar in style to that which relates her Jamaica experiences ; but his career there was not particularly distinguished, and ended prematurely by his resignation after the arrival as Governor-General of Lord Moira, who, if the Journal is to be believed, treated him with anything but consideration or courtesy.

But Lady Nugent's bitterness was evidently due to the fact that Moira was put over her husband's head. In the preface to the *Private Journal of the Marquis of Hastings*, edited by his daughter, the Marchioness of Bute in 1858, we read: "He was constituted both Governor and Commander-in-Chief by his own solicitation, not from an overweening love of power, but because he felt that under the then anxious state of Indian affairs it would be impossible for him to carry out his views of duty to his country with a divided authority ; and he therefore stipulated before he accepted the appointment for the labour and responsibility of both offices." But there is nowhere expressed in his journal any ill-will towards Sir George Nugent personally. On the contrary, under date 24 June, 1814, he writes: "This day I quitted Calcutta in form, having installed Sir G. Nugent as Vice-President. In strictness I cannot legally give him that title, but I wished to do it out of compliment."

Nugent became a full general in 1813, and was made G.C.B. in 1815, with the order of which he had been invested by Moira in India. In 1819 he was made an honorary D.C.L. of the University of Oxford, and was in that year returned once more for Buckingham, which he continued to represent until the passing of the Reform Bill in 1832. He lost his wife in 1834, after thirty-seven years of happy married life. He was made a field-marshal in 1846, and he died at his seat, Waddesdon House, Little Marlow, in Berkshire, on the 11th of March, 1849.* He was then the oldest general officer in the English army.

Of the five children—three sons and two daughters—

* The following is the inscription on his tombstone in Little Marlow Church :—

Sacred to the memory of Field Marshall Sir George Nugent Bart. G.C.B. who died March 11th 1849 aged 91 years and 9 months. He served 76 yrs with the British army in America and Holland, in Ireland during the rebellion, and had the command of the Western and Kent districts. He was also Governor of Jamaica and commander in chief in India all of which situations he held with credit to himself and benefit to his country. After 35 yrs of retirement in which he did much for the welfare of his parish he died in humble faith surrounded by his children who together with his friends and all connected with him will long revere his memory and lament his loss.

Hoc monumentum filius maereus posuit.

which Lady Nugent bore him, two, George Edmund, the second baronet, and Louisa Elizabeth, were born in Jamaica.

In the light of many details of little George's ailments set down in the Journal, but not reprinted, it is interesting to note that he inherited his father's longevity, and died at the ripe age of ninety.

Lady Nugent was the first native of the United States to preside over King's House, Jamaica, and probably the first American wife of a governor in any British Colony, albeit she was born while New Jersey still gave allegiance to the British Crown.

Her father, Courtlandt Skinner, was born in Perth Amboy, New Jersey, in 1728. This town,* which had lost much of its residential charm at that time, is now become quite cosmopolitan and is given over to coal and oil. Named after the Earl of Perth, who settled it in the late years of the sixteenth century or early years of the seventeenth — the title meaning Perth point — the town had amongst its early citizens the Reverend William Skinner, who was the first Rector of St. Peter's Protestant Episcopal Church, which was supported for some thirty years by the Society for the Propagation of the Gospel in Foreign Parts. He claimed amongst his friends to be a chieftain of rank of the MacGregor clan, who had been " out " in the rebellion of 1715, and Lady Nugent made allusion to this descent when she was at Edinburgh.

After the battle of Preston Pans, where he was wounded, he, dropping the name of his clan and adopting that of a friend named Skinner, escaped with Balmerino to Holland and subsequently found his way to Philadelphia. He there studied for the ministry, and, returning to England, was ordained, and received the appointment of St. Peter's, Perth Amboy, in 1724, where he laboured till his death in 1758. He had two wives: the first was a daughter of Christopher Billop, of Staten Island; the second was Elizabeth van Cortlandt, youngest daughter of Stephan van Cortlandt, of Cortlandt Manor (now Westchester), near New York city, sometime Mayor and Member of

* It has interest for Jamaica by reason of the fact that it is the port of registry of the vessels of the United Fruit Company.

BRIGADIER-GENERAL COURTLANDT SKINNER

Council of New York and Chief Justice—a son of the original settler from Holland.

William Skinner left four sons—Courtlandt, William, Stephen, and John. Courtlandt (he spelt the name Courtlandt, though other members of the family spelt it Cortlandt) became a lawyer, and practised first at Newark and afterwards at Perth Amboy. He rose to be King's Attorney-General of the province.

Though not of studious habits he, in this capacity, evinced great ability and integrity, and oratorical powers above the average. In 1761 he was elected to the Provincial Assembly from his native city, and four years later he was chosen speaker of that body.

At the commencement of the Revolution he, having sworn allegiance to the British Crown, remained true to his oath, though a leader of the Whigs, and strongly opposed to the encroachments of the British Ministry upon the liberties of the colonies. We read in Whitehead's *Contributions to the Early History of Perth Amboy and Adjoining Country* (New York, 1856) that "all his influence, which was very considerable, was exerted to bring about a restoration of the harmonious relations which had previously existed between the mother country and her American dependencies." But soon after the first blood was shed at Lexington, he openly avowed himself a loyalist, and, with the approval of General Howe, raised a brigade of loyalists—the New Jersey Volunteers, or "Skinner's Greens," or the "Tory Brigade of New Jersey," as they were called ; but the British Military were not popular in New Jersey, even with those who sympathized with their cause, and he only succeeded in raising 517 privates instead of the 2500 contemplated. His headquarters were at Staten Island, and he commanded, as brigadier-general over his brigade, at the battle of Springfield and several other engagements.

In Lee's *New Jersey as a Colony and a State* (New York, 1902) we read : "From the arrival of Lord Howe at Staten

▲ 4

Island early in July, 1776, the Tory element of New Jersey confined its efforts to argument, and supporting the three great figures of their cause—William Franklin, the statesman ; Jonathan Odell, the poet ; and Cortlandt Skinner, the lawyer-soldier.''

In 1752 Skinner had married Elizabeth,* a daughter of Philip Kearny of Amboy, also a lawyer, a son of Michael Kearny, a settler from Ireland, and Secretary of the Province, Surrogate and Clerk of the Assembly. Michael Kearny's second wife, and mother of Elizabeth, was Susannah Burley, widow of the Hon. William Burley (son, it is supposed, of Lady Barney Dexter), whose maiden name was Ravaud.

In February, 1776, Courtlandt Skinner's family was broken up, but after some time he was able to gather them together at Jamaica in Long Island.

When peace was declared the whole family, with the exception of one son, went to England, and were received with open arms. Skinner received compensation for the loss of the property he had forfeited as a loyalist, and also half-pay as a brigadier-general during his life. He died at Bristol in 1799. The following is the inscription on his tombstone in St. Augustine's Church, Bristol :—

" Near this place are deposited the remains of Brigadier-general Cortlandt Skinner. Born in New Jersey, North America, where he was many years his Majesty's Attorney-general. Died at Bristol, 15th March, 1799, aged 71. Descended from an honourable family in Scotland, of distinguished loyalty, he proved the inheritor of their virtues, in the steady performance of all the duties of life, which will make his death ever regretted by his family, most of all his afflicted widow, Elizabeth Skinner, who erects this monument to his memory.''

It is said, in letters written at the time, that he was there universally known and beloved, and the attention paid to

* The well-known Philip Kearny, general U.S. Army, known as " Fighting Phil," was one of her collateral descendants.

him during his illness truly remarkable, hundreds of
people that his family had never known, or scarcely heard
of, sending daily to inquire about his health. His widow
continued to reside amongst her children in England and
Ireland till her death in 1810.

They had five sons and seven daughters—William,
Philip Kearney, John, Cortlandt, Downs ; Susan, Eliza
beth, Euphemia, Catherine, Maria, Isabel, Gertrude.

The following particulars of them are gathered in the
main from Whitehead's book above quoted :—

William was placed in the English navy and died young.

Philip Kearny entered the army, and was taken prisoner
on one occasion by the French, and detained for some time
at Lisle. On his release and return to England, in 1799,
he found he had been promoted to an adjutant-generalship,
and before his death was lieutenant-general, commanding
at Bombay, while his brother-in-law was commander-in-
chief. He died in 1826, unmarried. He is referred to in
his sister's journal.

John was a lieutenant, was sent on board the *Phoenix*,
frigate, at Sandy Hook, and entered as a midshipman.
Soon after this, the *Phoenix*, on passing up the North River,
came within range of the guns at Fort Washington, and
young Skinner had the misfortune to have his right hand
shot off by a ball, which did no other injury on board.
He had previously, while playing in the market square
at Perth Amboy, lost the sight of one eye from a cork
dart ; and thus mutiliated he passed through life, a bachelor
ever active and cheerful, benevolent to a fault, an affectionate son and valued citizen.

As a post-captain he for many years commanded the
Holyhead packet, and while in the discharge of his duty
was accidentally drowned in 1830, being swept overboard
in a sudden squall. A monument, erected by public subscription, attests the estimation in which he was held.

Cortlandt was left by his father for several years in
America with his brother-in-law, William Terrill, but

afterwards went to England, and eventually established himself in Ireland, and died in Belfast.

He held different offices, and for several years was Comptroller of the Customs, being highly respected and esteemed.

Downs was named probably by the wife of William Franklin, Governor of New Jersey (son of Benjamin Franklin), as that was her maiden name. He went from England as Collector of Customs to the island of Jamaica, whither his brother-in-law, Sir George Nugent, was sent soon after as Lieutenant-Governor, and married there, his wife's name being Williams. He returned to England for his health in 1801, but finally died at Savanna-la-mar, Jamaica, in December, 1802. He left but one daughter, named after his mother,* Elizabeth Kearny, who married a Reverend Mr. Simpson of England.

Susan married Major Jasper Farmar, of the British Army, and after his death his brother, Thomas Farmar; and descendants bearing the name of Murphy were living in Nova Scotia when Whitehead wrote in 1856.

Elizabeth married William Terrill, of New York, and had four daughters, who never married, and one son, John.

Euphemia became the wife of Oliver Barberie, who studied law with her father.

Catherine married William Henry Robinson, son of Colonel Beverly Robinson, of New York. He was Commissary-General in the British Army, and went to Jamaica in 1806, and to Quebec in 1810. He was afterwards knighted. She died at Marlow, England, in 1843, aged seventy-five, and left several children.

Maria, the authoress of the Journal.

Isabel married a physician named Fraser while the family were on Long Island. He subsequently went to England, and she followed with her father at the close of the war. He apparently lived at Blackheath and practised in London. They had several children.

Gertrude married (in June, 1780, at Jamaica, Long Island) Captain Meredith, of the 70th Regiment of Foot, who died

---

* Lady Nugent calls her Bonella in the journal.

ELIZABETH, WIFE OF BRIGADIER-GENERAL
COURTLANDT SKINNER

previous to 1800, leaving her with four children, one of whom (Richard) became a captain in the British Navy. The eldest son, Cortlandt, was a captain in the Army in 1804.

Of Lady Nugent's early life little is known. She does not even tell us when or where she was born, nor is this information given on her tombstone. There is, however, a tradition in the family that she was born in 1771, and this is corroborated by the inscription on a memorial ring, sent at the time of her death to a member of the family, which reads: "Died Oct. 24th, 1834, aged 63 years." This being so, her birth most probably took place at Perth Amboy in the Skinner family house, which is thus referred to by Whitehead, writing in 1856:—

"Mr. Skinner's residence in Amboy stood on the bank, on the south-west corner of South and Water Streets, opposite the house of late years occupied by the Hon. James Parker.* It was of stone and brick, and not many years since a portion of the foundation remained to identify the spot. His office was the one now occupied by Mr. Parker on the opposite corner."

The Skinner house was burnt down in 1776; but the office is still standing.

We know that Maria was the fifth of seven daughters, but where exactly she came in the family of twelve is not recorded. She died at Little Marlow in 1834.†

* James Parker married Skinner's only sister, Gertrude.

† The following is the inscription on her tomb in the church:—

Sacred to the memory of Maria the much lamented wife of Gen. Sir George Nugent Bart. of Westhorpe House Bucks and daughter of Brigadier Gen. Cortland Skinner who died Oct. 24 1834 leaving her husband and children in the deepest affliction for the loss of one whose strictly religious principles, angelic temper and endearing qualities rendered her sincerely and universally beloved. She will long be mourned by the poor of the parish of whom she was for many years the devoted benefactress and friend.

Job 1. 21.
Rev. 14. 13.

She tells us that she was small in stature, and her portrait proclaims her of pleasing features.

She possessed deep religious feeling, domestic habits, and a sincere love of her children, and took a very genuine interest in the negro population, coupled with a keen appreciation of balls and dances and all kinds of social functions.

In this connection it is somewhat remarkable that she does not mention the name of Thomas Denniss, Surrogate of the Vice-admiralty Court, who was also Master of the Revels, a post which had been occupied half a century earlier by the notorious Constantia Phillips. As illustrative of the balls of that period there was published in London, in 1802, an engraving entitled: "A Grand Jamaica Ball, or, The Creolean Hop à la Mustee ; as exhibited in Spanish Town. Graciously dedicated to the Hon. Mrs. R——n,* Custodi Morum, etc.," with the following verses :—

> Farewell, ye girls! and still alas!
> As mama bids sad Red Coats shun ;
> But soon will each forsaken lass
> Most keenly rue the Dance she's run.
>
> Charmless you'll grow in person, face, and eye,
> Joyless in youth, old maids you'll useless die.

She was pre-eminently of a kind-hearted disposition, but was not easily imposed upon. The childlike manner in which she records her attempt to bribe a legislator in favour of her candidate for the agency of the island in England is interesting. She evidently had a good sense of humour, such as when she alludes to the terpsichorean qualities of candidates for the chief-justiceship, and the sweet smiles hastily assumed at her approach by virago-like hostesses.

She at times showed herself to be very emotional in character—the Irish blood which she inherited from her mother outweighing, in this respect, the more stolid mixed Scottish and Dutch characteristics which she inherited from her father.

* Mrs. Roden, mentioned frequently in the Journal.

LADY NUGENT'S PEDIGREE

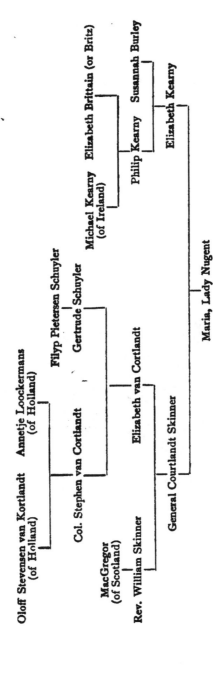

It is somewhat remarkable that in a land like Jamaica, where the beauties of nature appeal to one on every side—transforming even the most town-like of persons into lovers of the country—she makes but few references to the plants or scenery of the island.

COURTLANDT SKINNER'S LAW OFFICE AT PERTH AMBOY, NEW JERSEY

SIR GEORGE NUGENT

LADY NUGENT'S JOURNAL

CHAPTER I

I MUST preface my intended Journal by saying, that it commences immediately after we had terminated a residence of some years in Ireland, of which we were both heartily sick, tired, and disgusted; having witnessed during the Rebellion, which broke out in 1798, all the horrors of a civil war, during which my dear husband had the command in the north; so that he was not only obliged to meet the poor, infatuated, misguided people in the open field, but, after defeating them there, had also the distressing task of holding courts martial, and signing the death warrants of very many, which was indeed heart-breaking to us both.

After the suppression of the Rebellion, we wished to refresh ourselves and recruit our spirits, by returning to England; but Lord Cornwallis so earnestly desired that General Nugent would remain, and act as his Adjutant-General, that we took up our residence in Dublin, where we were aiding and abetting in all the odious *tracasseries* of the union between the two countries, till that point was carried. A change of Ministry then enabled General N. to resign his situation, and, to our great joy, on the 5th of April, 1801, we arrived once more in dear England.

A few days after our return, General Nugent was surprised by his appointment as Lt.-Governor and Commander-in-Chief of the Island of Jamaica. We were neither of us over well pleased ; but, like good soldiers, we made up our minds to obey.

As I had a cough, and was otherwise unwell from the anxieties of our Irish campaign, the doctors advised that I should not sleep in town.   General N. accordingly took a little place at Hampstead, where we spent a most agreeable time, till the first week in May, when we took up our abode at Reddish's Hotel in St. James's Street.   Our little home at Hampstead was so nice, that we regretted it very much. We had there dear Miss Acheson, and many visitors that I loved ; and, in short, I enjoyed my little abode so much, I should greatly have preferred remaining, instead of play-ing the Governor's lady to the *blackies :* but *we* are soldiers, and must have no will of our own.

May 22nd.—All things being ready for our departure, came the painful task of taking leave of our dear friends.—Could not sleep all night, and were glad when the bustle of the day began.—Had, soon after breakfast, a curious scene, with a despairing confession, about my friend Miss A., from Sir James Blackwood.   Could do or say nothing to lessen his *misery*, but left him, poor man ! to her *mercy*.—Then, dear Lady Buckingham,* Lady Temple, little Lady Mary, and Lord G. Grenville, came to our Hotel, and we took a most affectionate leave of each other.   I promised to send ac-counts of the Western World to my young friends, and dear little Lord George mounted the Hotel steps at parting, and just as I was about to get into the carriage, seized me round the neck, and gave me a *great* hug, and a most *sounding* kiss, before all the *beau monde* assembled in St. James's Street.   This did me a great deal of good, as, in spite of all our grief, we could not help laughing heartily. We then drove to Grosvenor Street, to take leave of my poor dear mother, and many dear friends and relations ; and, at 4 o'clock, started for Winchester, where we were most comfortably seated at supper by 11.—A servant was off some time before us, and had all the horses ready, so

* The cousin of General Nugent's father.

we made famous good speed, and, after we had dried our tears, we amused ourselves with reading the placards and advertisements, pasted on the walls, as we passed, and General Nugent was so ludicrous, with the discoveries he made on his side of the carriage, that he made me quite merry, in spite of myself.

23rd.—Breakfasted in the Cloisters with the Comtesse Du Paet.—Mrs. Wm. Mackinnon, Fred. Mash, and Tiny, were of the party.—Bade adieu to all, and arrived at Portsmouth about 3 o'clock.—Crowded immediately with visitors ; among them were the Naval Commander, &c. &c. ; and General Whitelocke* and his lady (he is Commandant), and we are to dine with them to-morrow. Then came Sir Charles and Lady Saxton, and she was my most amusing visitor ; she called me " your Excellency " five hundred times, I believe. At first I was rather frightened, and thought she was mad, but found her visit afterwards the most entertaining possible.—Had a little quiet dinner, and went to bed at eleven.

24th.—Captain and Mrs. Colville, with many officers and their wives, of both army and navy, came to pay their compliments after church.—Captain Colville commands *our ship*, the *Ambuscade*. He is the eldest son of Lord Colville, an old acquaintance of mine, and appears to be one of the most polite and agreeable of men.—Dined with General and Mrs. Whitelocke, and returned home at 9 o'clock to our inn.—I gave the gentlemen of our party *a fright*, which ended in discovering Billy Fitzroy and Mr. Dyke, who were in the next room. They joined our supper party, and were

---

* General John Whitelock, who, after a successful career, was cashiered in 1808 for his failure in Monte Video, had seen service in Jamaica in 1788 to 1795, in which year he became Colonel of the 6th West India Regiment. He married a daughter of William Lewis of Cornwall, Jamaica, sister of Matthew Lewis, Deputy Secretary of War, father of the celebrated Monk Lewis.

He served with distinction in 1793-4, in the expedition sent from Jamaica to San Domingo.

very merry, poor fellows. To-morrow they start for Egypt, and we expect to sail for the island of Jamaica. God grant us all a safe return to our native land.

25th.—Embarked on board the *Ambuscade* frigate, of 36 guns. The yards were manned, and we were received on the quarter-deck by Captain Colville, all his officers, and many other gentlemen. Mrs. Colville accompanied us on board, and I felt for her in parting with her husband; but they seemed to me to take leave with more good breeding and politeness than affection; so my commiseration was quite thrown away.—A salute, &c. and off we sailed from Spithead, towards the afternoon.—What little wind there is they say is against us, but the weather is so fine, and the ship so quiet, I don't much care about it. My maid Johnson, and our valuable Margaret Clifford, and the General's man Forbes, with William Hallam, were our only attendants.*—All seem happy and comfortable; only the poor maids don't like their bedroom, it is so open to the inspection of the ship's company, &c. who are constantly peeping at them.

26th and 27th.—Calm, and what little wind we have is contrary.—Sit on deck all the day, and amuse myself very well, talking to General N. about the future, and really enjoying the beautiful scene around us, as we move slowly on.

28th.—The wind was boisterous all night, and we were obliged to put into Torbay in the course of the morning.— Saw a poor little wherry, loaded with stones, founder; there were only two men on board, and they, I am afraid, perished.—I went down to my cabin, and could not help feeling very melancholy, though the gentlemen comforted me with the idea that the boatmen perhaps had saved themselves by swimming.

29th.—Fired a salute for the Restoration; told little Brooke the story of Charles the First, &c. after all the noise

* When the Duke of Albemarle came out more than a century earlier, in 1687, he had allowance of passage for one hundred servants and five hundred tons of goods.

was over.—The ship shook dreadfully, and so did I, for it was a frightful sensation altogether, though Captain Dunn told me, that Lady Horatio Seymour could fire off a gun herself. I can only say, that she has more courage, or better nerves, than I have.—Captain Talbot, R.N. and other naval visitors. Captain T.'s ship had lost a mast, which obliged him to put into Torbay.—Wind still very high, and the sea extremely rough. I don't feel in the smallest degree deranged by the motion of the ship; on the contrary, I continue to walk about, with General N.'s arm, though, as night comes on, I can't help being a little anxious.—We eat ginger-bread all the morning, and yet I am always ready for my dinner at 3 o'clock. I now begin to eat meat, and have a large glass of Hock every day, so I shall soon be a Hercules.

30th.—The wind fair.—Left Torbay soon after 8, and passed Plymouth before dinner.—In the evening fired at a vessel, and brought her to. She turned out to be only an English merchantman, from America. The sailors seemed disappointed; they had hoped for a battle, and a prize, I suppose. I was satisfied.

31st.—General N. and I read our prayers soon after breakfast; then, as usual, sat on the deck, where I am allowed a chair and small work-table, but the gentlemen could only sit on the guns.—Saw several merchantmen; one from Jamaica, in little more than a month.

June 1st.—Passed the Wolf Rock.—In the evening it rained; and blew rather hard. Not at all sick, but a little afraid when we went to bed.

2nd.—Came in sight of some Irish mountains; but there is so little wind, that we can scarcely get on at all.

3rd.—Got into Cove Harbour. Lord Gardner sent to us immediately. He is ill, but he lent us his yacht, and we went up the beautiful river to Cork. There General Myers received us, and we were paid the greatest attention to, being such great people as we are.

4th.—Poor dear old King George's birth-day! Parades,

feux-de-joie, &c. &c.—Invited to dinner by General Myers,* but declined, as we gave a *grand* dinner, at one of the principal inns, to Captain Colville, his officers, &c. In the evening I had all the ladies, headed by Mrs. Myers, to tea and coffee. It is wonderful how much a *high station* embellishes! —I heard it whispered on the parade this morning, that General Nugent was one of *the finest men* that ever was seen, and Mrs. Nugent, although small, *a perfect beauty!*

Speaking of my size, reminds me of some anonymous verses, left in Grosvenor Street for me, by a smart footman, who would give no name. I will insert them here.

ANONYMOUS VERSES

How many charms are there combin'd
  Within that little frame!
You seem by Nature's self design'd
  All Nature's love to claim.

How can so small a space contain
  So wondrous large a heart?
I fear this riddle to explain
  Would baffle every art.

'Twas thus I reason'd, till, at last,
  Made by experience wise,
'Twas only at my folly past
  I felt the least surprise.

Kind Nature's wisdom I confest,
  Who, with delightful art,
Whate'er she borrowed from the rest,
  Has added to the heart.

      Your sincere Friend and Admirer,
          ALDIBORONTIPHOSCOPHORNIO.

5th.—Did not leave Cork till this evening.—Received visits all day, and went to shops. General N. laid in a stock of wines for the voyage, those on board being very so so. I bought forty-five Bibles, and as many Prayer Books, for the poor sailors. They were all I could collect in Cork.

* Colonel of the 2nd West India Regiment and Commander-in-Chief of troops in the Windward Islands.

6th.—Sailed this morning; a nice breeze. I felt a little melancholy, at losing sight of land again; but I was soon cheered, for have I not my own little world with me, in my devoted husband and best of friends.

7th.—The Captain very cross; he cannot collect the Convoy as he likes, there are so many slow sailers. Colonel Noble, too, out of humour with his dinner, and his only consolation is the good wines that General N. brought from Cork. I cannot help laughing at their wry faces, and Captain Dunn tells me all their distresses for my amusement. General N. and I read in our cabin this evening, and then sat on deck till 10 o'clock.

8th.—Still very wry faces, and some salt tripe for dinner, that increased Colonel Noble's misery beyond anything. He wishes me to complain; my answer is, we are at sea, we cannot remedy it now, and besides, the biscuit and gingerbread are still very plentiful and good. How lucky it is that General N. laid in such a stock of gingerbread at Portsmouth.

9th.—The Bay of Biscay! The weather fine, and we are getting on prosperously.

10th.—The ships so close together all night, that drums were beaten, &c. to enable them to keep clear of each other; there being such a fog, that they could not well see.

11th.—The fog still continues, but the sailors say it will rain soon.

12th.—The wind blew hard, with rain, all night, but no fog. Taken aback during the night, which they say was a great risk for us all, but, thank God, we are safe. We are now going six knots an hour, but must soon slacken sail for the dull sailing ships.

13th.—High wind all night. I quaked a little, but put as good a face on the matter as I could.—The day as usual —some cross, some merry.—General N. and I read and talk, and amuse ourselves very well.

16th.—Keep our course, though the wind is not quite what Captain Colville likes, as I can see by his visage.

17th.—The wind fair towards evening, though not a great deal of it, and this I cannot say I regret.

19th.—Saw the Island of Madeira, about 3 o'clock, but not near enough to see what it was like; only it appears very high.—A turtle feast in prospect, and Colonel Noble happy.

20th.—Beautiful weather.—To-morrow we are to have our turtle feast.

22nd.—I have not been able to write since the 20th. We have had a dreadful shock. Poor Colonel Noble is no more! —On Saturday, he sate the greatest part of the day, as usual, talking to me on the deck. Captain Twysden, of the *Revolutionnaire*, part of our convoy, sent us a turtle on Friday, and said, as our cook was better than his, he would dine with us on Sunday, and partake of the feast. Poor Colonel Noble said repeatedly, on Saturday, that he was sure some contretemps would occur, and that we should be disappointed of our turtle. I made a joke of this. In the evening he was as well as ever; we played at whist, and all went on as usual till 10 o'clock, when he went on deck, while General N. and I were preparing for bed. Just before 11 o'clock, he came down to the cabin, and was whistling in a low tone all the time he was undressing. As there was only a curtain between his cot and ours, I could hear him distinctly. The instant he put the extinguisher on his candle, he called out that he was a dead man, and should die without assistance.—General N. was so sound asleep, that I could not wake him, and therefore ran myself to poor Colonel Noble's cot. The scene was frightful! All was done for his relief that possibly could be done, but by 2 o'clock he breathed his last. I have felt completely miserable ever since; the shock was dreadful, and, alas! I fear so unexpected and so unprepared! But God rest his soul in peace! On Sunday the 21st he was buried in the sea, and a most awful ceremony it is. The Captain read the Funeral Service. Young Noble knelt by my side the whole time. He is a fine young man, and General N. appointed him one of his Aides-de-Camp. I am sorry to say, that he shewed very little feeling ; however, he is very young, and had not, perhaps, been much with his father.

23rd.—The day calm, and the weather altogether delightful ; but I cannot shake off the recollection of poor Colonel Noble, and had a dreadful dream about him last night.

24th.—The weather still fine.—I am anxious about poor M. Clifford, who is very unwell. However, she is better this evening.

25th.—Came into the trade wind.—Beautiful weather.— Flying fish, &c.—Every thing is so new and so gay around me, that I find my spirits much better ; but I hate the cabin now, and live entirely upon deck.—My nightcaps are so smart, that I have tied up all my hair under them, and so sit on deck in the most comfortable manner ; for I found it impossible to keep my hair at all tidy and in good order. To tell the truth, I really think I look better in my nightcap than in my bonnet, or quite as well, and, as I am surrounded by men who do not know a nightcap from a day-cap, it is no matter what I do, so I please myself.

26th.—A sailor sent me a flying-fish for my breakfast. We all tasted it, but I cannot say I admire this food, pretty as it looks in the water. Feel less nervous the two last nights.

27th.—All well.—A nice breeze, and Captain C. less cross to his officers than usual.

28th.—Read Prayers in the cabin of Captain C. ; all the Service but the Litany, which I read. One little brig has lost a mast, and several vessels have left our Convoy. These are the only events of to-day, excepting that I was rather disgusted with an unfeeling trait of young Noble, but I do not like to think about it.

29th.—Pass the Tropic. Neptune and Amphitrite came on board, and there was a masquerade throughout the fleet, which lasted almost the whole day. General N. and I were unmolested, and allowed to see all the sport without any annoyance. Some poor men were sadly pulled about, and

shaved in the roughest manner, though all was done in
perfect good humour.

July 1st, 2nd, 3rd, 4th, 5th, 6th, and so on to Wednesday
the 15th.—No variety; but sometimes squalls and occasional
showers.—I have learnt to box the compass, and General N.
marks our daily progress on the map. One thing I must
mention, I have gone on, very regularly, with the education of my little pupil Brooke, who is a sad Pickle. I
have turned the greatest part of the History of England
into verse for him, to assist his memory, as to principal
events, &c.

16th.—Came in sight of Barbadoes. The first appearance of the island quite beautiful. It put me in mind of
the scenes in Cook's Voyages.

17th.—Early in the morning anchored in Carlisle Bay.
We were immediately surrounded by boats, with naked men
and women covered with beads, and bringing us all sorts
of tropical fruits.—The pretty Bridgetown, the hills behind
it, the palms of all sorts—in short, the whole—was most
picturesque, and altogether enchanting. Landed with the
usual fuss and bustle attending *Great People.*—Lord Seaforth's Aide-de-camp, to tell us that he was too ill to receive
us, owing to the explosion of an air-gun.*—Found excellent
accommodation at the inn ; much amused with the natives ;
in short, we were all delighted to be on shore again, and
were as merry as possible.—Gave a grand dinner to Captain
Colville and all the officers of the frigate, our own suite, &c.
&c. A turtle at the head of the table, and all sorts of odd
dishes covering it.—Had my own two maids, to prepare my
room for the night, intending to have a nice quiet sleep,
without rocking ; but, alas ! my repose was not a little dis-

* It had been the custom "from time" (as the saying is in
Jamaica) for the Governor of Jamaica to be entertained on the
way out by the Governor of Barbados. Lord Seaforth, the
Governor, had only arrived at Barbados early in 1801. During
his tenure of office, which lasted till 1806, he did much for the
amelioration of the slaves.

SIR JOHN THOMAS DUCKWORTH

turbed, by the large beetles and centipedes, that were discovered about the bed—General N. killed a huge centipede,
by dropping wax upon him, just as we were going to put
out the candles.

18th.—General N. and I up early, to the great astonishment of the natives, parading the town, exploring the
market, &c.; a carriage followed us, but we only made use of
it to go a mile out of the town, to procure money from the
Agent, from whose windows we saw a cart load of pigs and
poultry, all dead from the heat of the sun, and no doubt to
the great disappointment of the poor sailors, for whose
refreshment they were intended.—I ought to remark that
they were covered with large plantain leaves, so only imagine how great the heat of the sun must be.—Some officers
came to visit us, with running footmen, holding by their
horses' tails, and the whole scene was new and amusing in
the extreme.—I was sorry to embark again, which we did
in the evening, and sailed for Jamaica.—I must not omit
to say, that General N. was surprised at his bill, which was
sixty odd pounds, but our landlady remarked, that it was
nothing for the great Governor of Jamaica.

19th.—Little wind, and scarcely making any way, but
enjoy looking at the beautiful Barbadoes.

20th.—See St. Vincent's, St. Lucia, and other islands, and
in the evening we anchored in Port Royal Bay, Martinique.
Captain Dunn, young Duckworth, English, &c. all landed,
and I lost my little friend Brooke, who is gone on board
Admiral Duckworth's Flag-ship, as a Mid.*—The Diamond

---

* Admiral John Thomas Duckworth, who was born in 1747-8,
was Commander-in-Chief at Jamaica in 1803-5. He is remem-
bered in the Leeward Islands for his capture in 1801 of St.
Bartholomew, St. Thomas, and the other Danish and Swedish
islands; in Jamaica for his direction, in 1803, of the operations
which led to the surrender of General Rochambeau and the
French army in San Domingo, and for his brilliant victory, in
February, 1806, over the French under Leissègues off San
Domingo, when he brought three of the enemy's ships into Port
Royal, the other two being driven ashore and burnt. For this

Rock is very curious, it stands out so far into the sea, and is so high.*—Captain Colville very cross, not having been well received by the Admiral, on account of his incivility to Captain Dunn, his Flag Captain, whom he wished to leave at Portsmouth, and, after all, left a great deal of baggage for the Admiral there.

21st.—We received all sorts of civilities from the shore, but soon weighed anchor again, and took our leave, passing the beautiful town of St. Pierre. I must say that Martinique has altogether the appearance of a little Paradise.—The porpoises all to-day were innumerable.

22nd.—A poor seaman died last night, and was buried to-day in the sea. It was very melancholy, and reminded me of poor Colonel Noble; but I cannot say that his son seemed to feel it at all.

23rd.—Heavy squalls of rain and wind all night, and about 12, almost a tempest for a short time.

24th.—One of the ships in distress, having suffered from the heavy squalls, the *Midsummer Blossom* was ordered to take her in tow. We were obliged to lie to a long time, and the *Ambuscade* rolled dreadfully, as the wind was still very boisterous.

25th.—Getting on fast to our destination; the wind more moderate.

he received a pension of £1000 a year, the freedom of the City of London and a sword of honour, and £3000 from the Assembly of Jamaica for a service of plate. He subsequently damaged his reputation by his poor conduct of affairs in the Dardanelles in 1807.

* An islet which rises perpendicularly out of the sea to a height of six hundred feet, near Fort de France, in Martinique; is memorable in the annals of the British navy as having been commanded as a sloop. It was fortified and held by Commander James Wilkes Maurice from January, 1804, till June, 1805, when Maurice, having little powder and ball cartridges left, had to surrender to the French, who lost upwards of fifty, while Maurice had only two killed and some wounded. His garrison of one hundred and seven officers and men left with the honours of war.

26th.—In sight of St. Domingo ; the land high, but too distant to make any further observation.—The lightning in the evening was very vivid, but there was no thunder.

27th.—In chase of a Spanish vessel early this morning, but found she had a pass from the Governor of Jamaica, so could not detain her. The sailors again very much disappointed.

28th.—Come in sight of Jamaica. We were all up, and on the look-out by 6 o'clock. It appears beautiful.—Such hills, such mountains, such verdure ; every thing so bright and gay, it is delightful !—Not much wind ; it is now 7 o'clock in the evening, and we have only just anchored in Port Royal Harbour.—Thank God for all his mercies.—An express is just sent off to the Governor, in Spanish Town.— Colonel Ramsay of the Artillery, and Captain Coates of the 69th regiment, with a navy officer from Lord Hugh Seymour,* came on board immediately.—I am disappointed— I hoped to have landed instantly, but there is so much etiquette about it, that it is settled we are not to stir till to-morrow morning.

29th.—General N. landed at 6 o'clock, under salutes from the forts and all the ships of war in the harbour. The *Ambuscade* fired on his leaving the deck, and I lay down in my cot, with a pillow over my ears, the noise was so stunning. Major of Brigade, Gould, with numerous carriages, was waiting at Port Henderson, to escort us to Spanish Town. General N. accordingly proceeded with the Major of Brigade, and one of his own Aides-de-camp, leaving all the rest of the cavalcade to accompany me. This escort was a party of the 20th Light Dragoons, and he was received by Lord Balcarres, with all the garrison under arms, &c. &c.† To avoid this bustle, and the noise of

* Lord Hugh Seymour was naval Commander-in-Chief at Jamaica from 1800 to 1801. In August, 1800, Surinam had been captured from the Dutch.

† The period during which Alexander Lindsay, sixth Earl of Balcarres, controlled the destinies of the island as lieutenant-

salutes, I remained on board till near 10 o'clock. I then
landed, and found a chariot and four waiting for me, with
kittareens, &c. for my maids and the other domestics. I was
received, at the entrance of the King's House, by Lord
Balcarres, some of the Members of the Council and Assembly,
and the gentlemen of his own family, all with yellow
wrinkled faces.—Dined with this party at 5, had tea and
coffee at 7, and was glad to retreat to my own apartment
at nine.

30th.—Up at 6 o'clock, and much amused till 8 (when
we breakfasted) at seeing the black population, and the odd
appearance of every thing from my windows.—The King's
House,* which is now our residence, is a large brick build-

governor, 1795 to 1801, is memorable for the suppression of
the maroon rebellion in Trelawny. The immediate cause of
the outbreak was the flogging, at the workhouse at Montego
Bay, by a runaway negro (whom the maroons had captured),
of two maroons who had been convicted of stealing pigs. Leo-
nard Parkinson was one of their principal leaders. The House
of Assembly voted Balcarres seven hundred guineas for a sword
for his prompt actions which led to the suppression of the rebellion ; but General Walpole, who commanded the troops,
considered (and rightly considered so far as one can judge) that
Balcarres and the House had broken faith with the maroons
over the execution of the terms of peace by sending them off
the island, and he, on that account, refused a sword of honour
offered to him by the House.

It was during this governorship that Jamaica voluntarily contributed about £10,000 to help the mother country in her war
against revolutionary France in 1798.

* Previous to the building of King's House, the governors
lived at whatever house they chose ; e.g. the Earl of Inchiquin
is said to have lived in Eagle House, or, as the negroes call it,
" John Crow House." The plan of the existing building, now
leased to a citizen, was designed by Craskell, the island engineer,
during the administration of Lieutenant-Governor Henry Moore
in 1759-62, but the building was not completed till the arrival
of William Henry Lyttelton in 1762. The expense of building
and furnishing amounted to nearly £30,000 currency (or £21,428
sterling), and in Long's time (circa 1774) it was " thought to be

THE KING'S HOUSE, SPANISH TOWN

ing, of two stories high, forming one side of a square;
opposite is the House of Assembly; the two other sides
are formed by a Guard House and Public Buildings.* Our
apartments are very spacious, but very dirty. Immediately after breakfast, Margaret Clifford set the black ladies
to work, that our rooms may be a little less filthy before
we go to bed again.†

Lord Balcarres, and a large party of gentlemen, at breakfast.—I then retired to make my little arrangements, and
Lord B. and General N. began their discussions, which lasted
the greatest part of the morning.—At 5 o'clock we found a
numerous party assembled in the drawing-room. There
were only two ladies, Mrs. Roden ‡ and Mrs. Drewe, the
first old and plain, the other the reverse. Lord Hugh Seymour came for about half an hour, but could not remain

the noblest and best edifice of the kind, either in North America
or any of the British Colonies in the West Indies." Monk Lewis
not unjustly called it "a large clumsy-looking brick building."

* It is curious that she makes no mention of the Rodney
memorial, or of any of Bacon's monuments in the cathedral.
Nor does she later mention the iron railing which was imported
in 1802 at considerable expense to surround the garden between
King's House and the Assembly buildings.

† In 1803 there were thirty-three servants in the King's
House, the property of the Government.

Of men, eight house servants: Thomas, Prince, Jemmy,
Cupid, Harry, Bristol, Ford, Affleck; two in the kitchen,
(Primus and Quaw), five in the stables (Quaco, John, Jack,
Quamina, Hercules), and an infant, Philip.

Of women there were Nelly and Flora (superannuated), and
Phœbe, an old woman; three housemaids (Peggy, Margaret,
Rose), six laundry maids (Polly, Hannah, Grace, Emma, Sally,
Jenny), two kitchen-maids (Nancy and Eve), two children
(Betsy and Becky), and an infant, Mary.

‡ John Rodon was a member of the Council and Custos of
St. Catherine. The Council was as follows :—

President, Thomas Wallen ; Nathaniel Beckford, John Scott,
George Crawford Ricketts, John Rodon, John Lewis, James
Jones, William Dawes Quarrell, George Mackenzie, Francis
Rigby Broadbelt, Andrew Johnstone, Temple Luttrell.

c

for dinner.—All the gentlemen, civil and military, were introduced to me before we sat down ; I scarcely recollect the
name or visage of any of them, only they all looked very
bilious and very warm.   One gentleman seemed to suffer
exceedingly : for, in spite of his constant mopping, the perspiration stood like drops of crystal on his face the whole
time we were at dinner.   All took their leave soon after
nine.   No suppers are given in this country, and I am glad
of it, for I have neither strength nor inclination for late
hours.

31st.—I could not help laughing at a reply of Lord Balcarres, when I went down to breakfast.   I remarked to him
that it was a very fine day ; to which he answered, " Yes,
it is, but I assure you, Mrs. Nugent, you will be tired of
saying this before many weeks are over."   Captain Halkett
and Captain Loring, of the navy, at breakfast, in addition
to the staff.—I wish Lord B. would wash his hands, and use
a nail-brush, for the black edges of his nails really make me
sick.   He has, besides, an extraordinary propensity to dip
his fingers into every dish.   Yesterday he absolutely helped
himself to some fricassée with his dirty finger and thumb.—
Lord B. and General N. were discussing affairs all the morning.—Another large dinner party at 6.   Mrs. Roden again,
and Mrs. W. Bullock.*   The ladies told me strange stories
of the influence of the black and yellow women, and Mrs.
Bullock called them serpents.—The table to-day was loaded
with large joints of meat, turtle, turkies, hams, &c.—I must
not omit to mention here an extraordinary pet of Lord B.'s,
which makes its appearance every day in the dining-room.
It is a little black pig, that goes grunting about to every
one for a tit-bit.   The first day his staff appeared very much

* William Bullock was then assistant clerk to the Council.
When he died, in 1832, he was in possession of no less than five
public offices, of which the chief were Island Secretary and Governor's Secretary, with a recorded income of £4000 per annum
from only three of them, in addition to fees which were considerable.

shocked ; but, seeing me rather amused with the novelty
of it, they seemed reconciled.

August 1st.—It rains quite a torrent, and I have had a
great triumph over Lord B., in varying my remark ; and
I exclaimed, "What a sad rainy morning, my lord."—Only
a staff dinner to-day. I sat between Lord B. and Colonel
MacMurdo,* the latter actually dripping with perspiration.
He saw me looking at the drops as they fell from his forehead, poor man ! and this increased them almost to a
cascade.

2nd.—Read in our own room, for we cannot go to church
to-day.—Another tropical shower, and we had no close
carriage landed yet, and that which Lord B. sent for me,
to Port Henderson, was borrowed.† Lord B. and General
N. had a very long conversation, which lasted almost the
whole day.—Many new gentlemen at dinner, myself the only
lady.—Leave them early, and go to bed at 10.—To-morrow
Lord B. leaves the Government House, and then we mean
to have a thorough cleaning of this Augean stable.

3rd.—Up at 6.—A grand breakfast at 8, and a council at
10.—Lord B. set off immediately for his country-house,
called the Penn. A salute was fired, and all due honours
paid to him, as he drove off. General Nugent then walked
in procession to the House of Assembly, and was sworn in
as Lieut.-Governor and Commander-in-Chief. Then another
salute was fired, and he came back and held a levee. I remained above stairs until 4 o'clock, seeing all the proceedings from my windows, or the gallery round the Egyptian
Hall. I then went to the drawing-room, and received all
the ladies of Spanish Town, &c. the principal officers of the
navy and army, the members of council, and a number of
the gentlemen of the House of Assembly, who had come

* Deputy Quartermaster-General.

† Port Henderson was named after the owner of the land,
Colonel John Henderson, who was presented at Court in 1784.
It was founded in consequence of Passage Fort no longer
affording the necessary accommodation for ships.

to compliment the new Governor and his Lady; bowing, curtseying, and making speeches, till 6 o'clock. The ladies then dined with me in the Ball-room, and the gentlemen with General N. in the Egyptian Hall. My guests were forty in number, with ten gentlemen to carve for us. General N. had three or four times that number with him; but we should not call them *our* guests, as these dinners were given to us by the public.—I must remark the loads of turtle, turkies, hams, and whole kids, that crowded my table, and increased the heat of the climate. The room, too, was filled with black servants; and all the population, I believe, both white and black, were admitted to walk round the table, and stare at me after dinner. They did General N. the same favour, being, I suppose, very curious to see what sort of looking people we were; but their curiosity added most exceedingly to the heat, and, indeed, I never felt anything like it in all my life. At 12 o'clock all the ladies took their leave, and some of the gentlemen; but General N. left those that remained to enjoy their bottle, and he and I retired to our own apartment, but not to rest, for the garrison gave us a grand serenade, and the house was a scene of dancing, singing, and merriment almost the whole night.

4*th*.—This day we have kept to ourselves, and the house is put into as good order as we could prevail upon the poor blackies to do it. They are all so good-humoured, and seem so merry, that it is quite comfortable to look at them. I wish, however, they would be a little more alert in clearing away the filth of this otherwise nice and fine house.—Only our own staff at dinner, and as we were up at 6, and very busy all day, we took the liberty of going to bed at 9.

5*th*.—Up at 6.—Saunter from room to room, trying to persuade the blackies to follow Margaret Clifford's advice; and make the house clean as soon as possible.—General N. poring over papers all day.—Dine in the Council Chamber, but decide never to make that our dining-room again, the heat was so dreadful.

6th.—Reflect all night upon slavery, and make up my mind, that the want of exertion in the blackies must proceed from that cause. Assemble them together after breakfast, and talk to them a great deal, promising every kindness and indulgence. We parted excellent friends, and I think they have been rather more active in cleaning the house ever since.—Mean to give my first Assembly to-morrow, and am therefore in a great hurry to get all things into proper order. Doctor Lind and Captain Fraser, in addition to our staff party, at dinner.

7th.—General N. attended by some of his staff, went over to Kingston early this morning. A mulatto man, named Rogers, engaged as his valet de chambre. I rejoice that my dear N. will be much more comfortable with this man, I hope, as he is highly recommended. He has not been at all so with Mr. Forbes, who now leaves him.—Only the gentlemen of the family at dinner. Soon after 7, the ladies began to arrive, also many gentlemen.—Find a sad want of local matter, or, indeed, any subject for conversation with them ; so, after answering many questions about how I liked the country, &c. and being thoroughly examined by the eyes of them all, I sent for fiddlers, and we had a very merry dance till 11 o'clock, and before 12 they all took their leave. I mean in future not to attempt anything like a conversazione, but to have Friday dances.

8th.—Begin letters to England at 6 o'clock, but find that, at the request of the merchants, General N. had ordered the packet to be delayed, till the 17th.* I rejoice at this, as we shall now be less hurried.—Various strange fruits and curiosities sent me to look at to-day.—Mr. Matthews at dinner.

9th.—Could not go to church, as it is under repair, and putting in order.—Read prayers in our own room, and then

* The last occasion for which the packet was delayed was in 1891, when Sir Henry Blake detained it in order to send home an account of the opening of the exhibition by Prince George of Wales, on 27th January.

I marked places in several good books, for my own maids.—
Some new gentlemen at dinner. Mrs. Roden called, and
I took a short airing with her.—Mrs. Pye, &c. in the
evening.

10*th.*—General N. and I went out before breakfast, for
the first time.—We drove to Lord B.'s Penn.* Never was
there such a scene of dirt and discomfort. Lord B. was in
a sad fright, thinking that we should expect a breakfast.
However, upon his Secretary's whispering me, that there
was but one whole tea-cup and saucer and a half, we declared our intention of returning to the King's House, where
a party was waiting for us to breakfast.—The road to the
Penn is most exceedingly pretty. Penguin hedges, which
are like gigantic pine-apples, with beautiful red, blue, and
white convolvuluses running all over them. There was also
a variety of curious trees.—Only Captain Wright, in addition to our staff party, at dinner to-day.

11*th.*—The house appears now quite a Paradise, so clean
and nice after Lord B.'s dirty Penn. Some gentlemen, from
Kingston, to breakfast, and remain all day. Mr. Hanbury,
who was a sugar merchant, talked technically; and, in
speaking of some one, who was fond of good living, said, he
always liked to have his keg well filled! Lord H. Seymour
came in the morning, but could not stay to dinner.

12*th.*—General N. attended by Lieut.-Colonel Irvine, &c.
drove over to Kingston, and returned in the heat of the day.
Feel quite unhappy for fear my dear Nugent should suffer
by his imprudence; but he has promised to be more careful
in future.—General Churchill, and his Aide-de-camp, &c. at
dinner.

13*th.*—After breakfast, General N. walked out, to my
great annoyance and alarm, and to the surprise of every
one.—He says he forgot all about the climate, and does not

* For some reason the word "pen," which, derived from
the days when the wild cattle of the Spaniards were caught
and penned, is used for a farm in Jamaica, is often spelled
"penn."

feel the worse for it. However, Dr. Lind * has made him promise not to go out again in the heat of the day; at least not on foot.

14th.—The morning as usual.—Major and Mrs. Pye at dinner: she flattered me so much, that I was quite sick, and glad to dance off my ill humour in the evening.

15th.—Poor young Noble taken very ill. General N. sent off for the doctor, who pronounces it to be the yellow fever. I trust, however, it will be but slight, as he has not a tinge of bile in his complexion. But, alas! he has been very imprudent in drinking punch and sangaree, &c. The doctor said, in the evening, he could give no decided opinion, and we passed the night in much anxiety.

16th.—Poor Noble much worse. Feel sincerely for him.— Spend the day in our own apartment, as we have no church yet to go to.—Mr. and Mrs. Woodham, the Spanish Town clergyman and his wife, dined with us.†—Poor M. Clifford taken ill in the evening. Dr. Lind says, however, it is merely a bilious attack. Quite low, and feel really ill, with seeing and hearing of others being so.

17th.—General N. rose before 5, to review some troops. While he was dressing, a severe shock of an earthquake occurred. The doors flew open and shut again with a violent noise, and there was, at the same time, a great rumbling in the air. I leaped out of bed, for it shook dreadfully. —General N. had called out to the servants not to disturb me by opening the door so violently; but he soon found what was the case, and staid with me till I got a little composed, for indeed the visitation was most awful.—Poor Noble much worse, and General N. sent for another doctor. —The Attorney-General, &c. at dinner. Very uncomfortable, and thinking of poor Noble the whole time; but here no one appears to think of or feel for those who are suffering

* Charles Lind, surgeon of the forces, and inspector of military hospitals. He left the island on 30th of March, 1803.

† Rev. Robert Stanton Woodham was rector of St. Catherine and Chaplain to the Council.

from these frightful attacks.—A party in the evening.—Heartily glad when they were all gone.—Noble stationary, which they say is a good omen.

18*th*.—Noble better.—A large party at dinner; Lord Hugh Seymour and his Flag Captain (Penrose), the Rev. E. Ward, Mr. Mitchell, Colonels Gillespie and Wale, &c. &c.* Mrs. Pye the only lady.—Poor Noble's fate, they say, will be decided to-morrow. My anxiety is inexpressible.

19*th*.—Noble so much better that there are great hopes of his ultimate recovery.—Quite in spirits to receive my morning visitors, as well as my dinner company.—Lord Hugh Seymour, the Marquis de la Jaille, &c. &c. and a large party at dinner.

20*th*.—Noble out of danger, and taking bark.—Some new military people at dinner.—My mind quite relieved, and I went to bed comfortable.

22*nd*.—Drove out at 5.—All our baggage from England arrived safe this morning.

23*rd*.—Go to church in state for the first time. All the world staring, and the church crowded to excess.—A prayer against earthquakes, in which I joined most heartily. Received the Sacrament at our own desire, as it is only administered here three times a year. Several gentlemen visitors before dinner.—At dinner the Rev. Mr. Woodham and his wife, Mr. and Mrs. Roden, Colonel Wale, Captain O'Brien, &c. &c. and the Misses Rennalls.—Young Noble out of his room for the first time.

24*th*.—Lord Balcarres and a large party at breakfast. I behaved very ill, having placed an Aide-de-camp between me and his lordship; for really his hands, &c. were so dirty, I could not have eaten any thing had he been nearer.

25*th*. Drove out at 5, towards Port Henderson, our usual

* George Crawford Ricketts was Attorney-General. Rev. Edward Ward was Rector of St. Dorothy (Old Harbour). William Mitchell was Receiver-General, member of the Assembly for St. Catherine. Captain Hampden Pye, 6th West India Regiment, was later Major of Brigade on the staff.

road.—Major Cookson, Mr. Matthews, Major and Mrs. Pye, Mrs. Rossington, &c. dined with us.

26th.—Drove out a new road. All the country is flat, but very pretty. The farms are of various descriptions, and the orange trees, &c. lovely. I am told that the scenery of the interior is quite beautiful, and this I can well imagine, from the lilac-coloured mountains, and the variety of ground and tints, that I see from my window. General N. had a council at 9.—A large dinner party to-day, and very pleasant.—When I went to bed at 9, I found my maid Johnson ill, which lowered my spirits.

28th.—More of our English baggage arrived, and the morning was spent in seeing it unpacked.—A Mr. Rothey in addition to our staff dinner party.—A large party in the evening ; danced only two dances, as I can't help being a little afraid of the yellow fever.

29th.—General N. galloped to Port Henderson, and back again, to the great dismay of Colonel Irvine, &c. &c. who attended him. They complained sadly of fatigue.—After breakfast, had a great deal of conversation with Mr. Wood-ham, on the subject of the black domestics, whom I am in-structing, previously to their being christened.—Captain Manby, &c. &c. at dinner.—Drive out in the evening.— Desire the maids to take the carriage in the morning, as I don't mean to make the exertion myself. I cannot tell what it is, but this climate has a most extraordinary effect upon me ; I am not ill, but every object is, at times, not only uninteresting, but even disgusting. I feel a sort of inward discontent and restlessness, that are perfectly un-natural to me.—At moments, when I exert myself, I go even beyond my usual spirits ; but the instant I give way, a sort of despondency takes possession of my mind. I argue with myself against it, but all in vain. I acknowledge that I am ungrateful to that Providence, that has bestowed so many and such great blessings upon me, in the best and most indulgent of husbands, with the power and the in-clination to serve my fellow creatures ; but till the malady of the spirits has taken its departure, all these considerations, and even religion, are of no avail. As for poor General N. he feels it in a different manner. He is so over-worked in the writing way, and the different interests he has to attend to, that he suffers in mind, though, thank God, not yet in body.

30th.—Rise at 6, and was told, at breakfast, that the usual occurrence of a death had taken place. Poor Mr. Sandford had died at 4 o'clock this morning. My dear N. and I feel it very much, but all around us appeared to be quite callous. —Go to church at 10; uncomfortable, and absorbed in melancholy the whole service.—After church, studied an Exposition of the Catechism, that I might be able to explain more fully to the black servants, what they undertake in becoming Christians.—At 3 o'clock a large dinner party.— Captain and Mrs. Lomax the only new faces.—Poor Mr. Sandford was buried this evening; some of our staff attended.

The people here are so uncongenial to us, that I am often reminded of the complaint of the poor French emigré, that I met with in some late publication—" Toutes les pages du " livre de ma vie semblent effacées; il faut recommencer à " me faire connaitre, à me faire estimer.—Je me dis souvent, " je n'interesse aucun de ceux que je vois.—Je puisse vivre, " souffrir, mourir, sans exciter un sentiment.—Mon cœur " est surchargé de son propre poids; il voudrait se repandre, " mais non, il ne peut pas ici."—But, as long as we have each other, we are much happier than the poor emigrant, and have no right to complain.

31st.—We drove to Port Henderson at 5, and walked on the sea shore, which did our spirits good.—General N. un-usually busy all the morning.—Lord Balcarres, Major Alston, Mr. Douglas, and in short a large dinner party.— Feel much better in spirits from a determination to do my duty.

September 1st.—General N. much engaged with letters and papers all day.—Read, and try to regulate my feelings, till dinner time.—At dinner every thing in the best order. Our English china, &c. &c. all very nice.

2nd.—Take a delightful drive on the Kingston road.—I am determined not to lament, as I am too apt to do, for the illness and deaths I hear of daily, among various parts of our society.   Our own immediate family all well, excepting little bilious attacks from their own imprudence.   Thank God, the climate appears to agree perfectly with my dear husband.—A very large dinner party.—Colonels Gillespie,* Ainslie, &c. &c. with a few of the usual ladies.—Poor M. Clifford very ill indeed this evening ; ordered to take calomel, &c.

3rd.—Drove to Port Henderson.   Saw crabs innumerable crossing the road.—Lord Hugh Seymour and a large party at breakfast.   He staid and talked to me till 2 o'clock, General N. being engaged.   I then stole away to rest a

* Major-General Robert Rollo Gillespie, on whom the posthumous honour of a Knight Commandership of the Bath was inadvertently bestowed, entered the army in 1783, and was, in 1792, promoted to a lieutenancy in the newly raised 20th Jamaica Light Dragoons.   When in the following year the French planters in San Domingo applied to Jamaica for aid, he volunteered for service with the infantry, and in the campaign there distinguished himself by his bravery, returning home at the fall of Port-au-Prince.   On being appointed, in 1795, Major of Brigade to General Wilford he accompanied him to San Domingo, and soon afterwards, though small in stature, killed six men single-handed.   Returning to Jamaica, he assumed command of his regiment, and in 1799 was recommended by the Lieutenant-Governor and House of Assembly for the rank of lieutenant-colonel, and was so gazetted.   He was offered, by Lord Hugh Seymour, the military command at Curaçoa, but Balcarres said he could not spare him.   At the peace of Amiens, in 1802, when the 20th Light Dragoons were transferred to the English Establishment, Gillespie returned home in command, and the Assembly, glad to be rid of the regiment, voted one hundred guineas for a sword of honour for him.   He subsequently had a brilliant career in the East, and in 1812 he received the thanks of the Commander-in-Chief in India, Sir George Nugent, for services in connection with the Palimbang Expedition.

little, before dressing for our 3 o'clock dinner.—Talk again incessantly with Lord Hugh till half-past 6, when he took his leave, as we could not prevail upon him to take a bed, that he might avoid the dangerous atmosphere of the Lagoon, between Spanish Town and Kingston.—This has, indeed, been a fatiguing day, and not a moment have I had to myself, for reading, writing, or any occupation, but have gossiped from five in the morning till nine at night.

5th.—Dine at 3; our new guests were Mr. Batley, Mr. Bissett, and Mr. Carey. Leave the gentlemen, and drive out at 6. See Mr. March's Penn, called Belle Vue.*—Disappointed at not finding Mr. Johnstone at home, as we are told there is a great variety of shrubs and plants in his garden, worth seeing, and of course novel to us.

6th.—Colonel Wale and a military party at breakfast.— A large dinner party at 5.—The Custos and Mrs. Roden, Mr. and Mrs. W. Bullock, Mr. and Mrs. E. Bullock, Mr. Smith, King Mitchell, Mr. Cuthbert, Dr. Broadbelt, the Attorney-General, the President of the Council, Mr. Douglas, and several new military people.†—Colonel Irvine unwell.

7th.—Drive to Port Henderson at 5.—See a curious cold bath there.—It is under the rocks, quite separate from the sea, and yet the water is salt. It is said to be very dangerous, from the extreme cold, and several midshipmen have

* Belle Vue is three miles north-west of Spanish Town. It is the property of Mrs. R. Levy.

† Edward Bullock, an attorney, was Clerk to the Crown, Clerk to the Commissioners of Forts, and Captain of Fort Clarence. King Mitchell was William Mitchell, member for St. Catherine. Probably George Cuthbert, Judge of Vice-Admiralty Court. He was afterwards Usher of the Black Rod, 1806, and Member of Council from 1808 to 1821, when he became President. As President he administered the government in 1832 and again in 1834. Lewis Cuthbert was member for St. Thomas-in-the-Vale. He died in December, 1802. Francis Rigby Broadbelt, the son of a physician of the same name, whose monument by Bacon is in the cathedral at Spanish Town. John Smith was Postmaster-General.

lost their lives by bathing in it. Return home at 7. Find
Colonel Irvine still ill ; but the doctors say not in danger.—
Had a nice morning with my dear N. talking over many
interesting subjects.—At dinner, Major Mosheim, Mr. Carge,
67th regiment, in addition to our usual party.—In the evening Colonel Irvine worse, and I am indeed very uneasy
about him. The complaints in this country are, in fact, so
rapid and so mysterious, that one cannot feel a moment's
security.

8th.—General N. drove to Kingston this morning, in spite
of my persuasion. The heat is so dreadful, that I cannot
help feeling sadly afraid, but God will, I trust, be merciful
to me, and protect him.—Lord H. Seymour is ill from the
same imprudence.—The Speaker,* &c. called during General
N.'s absence, and I made the agreeable to him.—General N.
returned a little after 4.—Lord Hugh so unwell, that he has
gone on board ship, to try what sea air will do for him.

9th.—Colonel Irvine a great deal better.—Some new
guests at breakfast.—About 2 o'clock a dreadful thunderstorm. It was indeed frightful, but it has cleared the air,
and we breathe more freely in consequence. As the rainy
season is approaching, we shall soon have plenty of these
dreadfully refreshing showers, they say.

10th.—A bright and very hot morning.—Some gentlemen
at breakfast.—By one o'clock, black clouds over the mountains, and rumbling thunder till 3 ; but, alas ! no rain.—
Major and Mrs. Pye, Major Alston, &c. at dinner.—Leave
our guests, and intend to drive to Mr. Lewis's Coffee Mountain. After much wandering and fatigue, find our servants,
by mistake, had taken us to a Mr. Reid's. My dear N. not
well and much heated. Feel very uneasy about him, and
pray for him in secret the whole time.—Return to the King's
House, and our guests, with red eyes.

11th.—General N. went out early on horseback. I read
and amused myself in my own room, till breakfast time.—
At one, dreadful thunder and lightning, and a little rain.—

* Kean Osborne.

A few gentlemen at dinner, and a very large evening party.
—Major and Mrs. Heslop were of the party ; the lady talked
to me a great deal about my family—The gentleman, it
seems, was formerly in my father's regiment, and the lady's
sister nursed one of my brothers.—*N.B.* When I write to
my mother, ask her all about them.

    12th.—Drive at 5 to Mr. Lewis's Penn.—Enjoyed the
morning air in the mountains very much, and did not return till after 8.—The weather most exceedingly oppressive,
till a dreadful thunder-storm, with torrents of rain, cleared
the atmosphere.—At 4 o'clock the sun shone again, and we
sat down to dinner.—Soon after, an express from Port
Royal announced the awful and melancholy tidings of poor
Lord Hugh Seymour's death.*—We were indeed greatly
shocked. I could not help thinking of the risk my dear
Nugent ran, harassed as he is both in body and mind, in
this horrid country.—The sudden departure, too, of a
person I had seen so short a time ago, in the fullest health,
and looking forward to a long career of worldly enjoyment,
was too much for my spirits, and I was obliged to leave the
table.—Oh, my God, while scenes of this sort shew us more
than ever the uncertainty of this life, let them also teach
us to make the best use of our time ; that we may be found,
in some degree, perpared for that moment, in which we may
so suddenly be called upon.—Keep this sad news from poor
Colonel Irvine, who is still in such a weak state, that any
shock may be fatal to him.—General N. sent off an express
to Port Royal, with orders for all the proper arrangements
to be made, and has announced his intention of going himself to Kingston to-morrow, with all his household, &c. &c.
to attend the melancholy ceremony. I wish it was possible
to prevail upon him to remain at home, and not expose
himself to such risks at this unhealthy season ; but I know
persuasion is of no use, and I am therefore silent on the
subject.

    13th.—Had a dreadful night ; was restless, and had fright-

* He died at sea.

ful dreams.—General N. was up at 3, and was just stepping into the carriage, when another express arrived from Captain Bayntun, R.N. at Port Royal, saying, that as a ship must be sent immediately to England, to announce the death of poor Lord Hugh, it was thought advisable to send the body home in a leaden coffin. This is, indeed, a relief to my mind, as my dear N. will not be exposed to the risk, which I had apprehended he would have to encounter to-day.

Poor Lord Hugh sailed in the *Tisiphone* only on Thursday morning, and died before 8 on Friday. It seems that, just as the ship got under way on Thursday, he received a great shock, on hearing of the arrival of the *Topaze*, with the loss of Captain Church, and twenty or thirty of his crew, by the yellow fever. It is sad, too, to think, that poor Lord Hugh had not the smallest idea of his approaching end, but was almost in the act of arranging business when he expired. The last day he dined with us, he and I had much conversation ; he spoke of the chance of Lady Horatia Seymour's recovery, with almost sanguine expectation ; but, alas ! I fear by this time, she, too, must be no more, and his poor children orphans indeed. Of his own strength he boasted much, and shewed me his giant hand ; but in this deceitful dreadful climate what does strength avail ?—Major and Mrs. Pye and our usual staff dinner.—Found in the evening, that Colonel Irvine had been told of poor Lord Hugh's death, and bore it better than, in his weak state, could have been expected.

14*th*.—Drove to Bellevue very early. Return to breakfast, and employ the morning in my own room.—Write to Lord W. &c. &c. an account of poor Lord Hugh's illness and death.—My dear N. is now, in his character of Chancellor, sitting in the Egyptian Hall all day, surrounded by lawyers.* I have been to peep at him from the gallery several

* Until 1842, when a new Judicature Law, which transferred to a Vice-Chancellor the authority of Chancellor, came into force, the governor, for the time being, was ex-officio Chancellor of the Island, and sat in the Chancellor's Court.

times.—The heat is intolerable. Not a breath of air, and
the thermometer from 90 to 95. I wish it would rain,
but, alas! there is only distant thunder and lightning, and
all the rain falls provokingly on the mountains,—Received
several visitors in my dressing-room—Some officers of the
67th regiment, &c. &c.—Dine at 6 in the library.—A party
of lawyers, in addition to the staff. Poor Colonel Irvine
crawled to see me for the first time. He is sadly low, and
looks wretchedly.

15th.—Don't drive out, but order chocolate in my dressing-room, that I may have leisure to make my arrangements
to go into the country, which I hope to do to-day. All our
attendants were sent off at 12. Received Mr. Douglas, &c.
in my own apartment. He took leave on going to Curaçoa.
—The Chancery Court over to-day at 4 o'clock. Set out for
Bellevue,soon after.—A snug, comfortable, and cooler dinner
than we have enjoyed for a long time.—Explored the
rocks round us, admired the immense bamboos, and spent
a delightful evening till 9, when we went to bed to avoid
the innumerable insects, that put out our candles, in spite
of the large glass shades.—Here I must mention, among the
agrémens of this climate, the innumerable musquitoes, that
have almost eaten us up, and certainly spoilt our beauty.
My face, neck, hands and arms, have been martyrs.

16th.—Our landlord, Mr. March, and Captain Taylor,
were of the party.—General N. off on horseback, before
8 o'clock, for the King's House, to perform the duties of
Chancellor.—Wrote to dearest Lady Buckingham, &c. &c.
to go by the *Sting* tender, that conveys poor Hugh's body
to England.—General N. returned at 4 o'clock—Skerrett,
and another officer of the 83rd regiment, and two of the
staff, attended him. They left us soon after 8, and we went
to bed.—This day General N. decided Mr. Irvine's cause in
his favour, to the great satisfaction of the public, and was
particularly happy himself in seeing others so.

17th.—The musquitoes tormented us all night, and the
morning was more than usually sultry.—Soon after 7,

General N. rode to Spanish Town. I begged to remain in
the country to avoid the great dinner to be given to the
lawyers to-day.—At 12 o'clock, a sudden and frightful
high wind, and the house shook dreadfully. This was succeeded by tremendous thunder and lightning, and torrents
of rain.—Towards 5, a dead calm, very sultry, exactly like
a vapour-bath, and not a breath of air.—Poor Colonel Irvine
drove out to avoid the crowded dinner, and dined *tête-à-tête*
with me. Drank tea at 7, and before 10 my dear N. returned, having had an immense and broiling party. We
have only now to rejoice that it is over.

18*th*.—Major Alston, Captain Johnson, &c. at breakfast.
Soon after, all rode into town, with General N.—Pass the
morning quietly ; read and compose for the blackies.—
Dress for dinner at 3. Then walk with Cupid and my umbrella towards Spanish Town, in hopes of meeting General
N. Dreadfully sultry ; only distant thunder and no rain
to-day—Obliged to return.—Wait till 5, when General N.
&c. &c. arrived to dinner.—All left us at 8, and we were in
bed at 9.—Received a letter from Captain Penrose, R.N.
requesting that I would keep the French books, lent me by
Lord Hugh Seymour.

19*th*.—A long discussion on Burns' Poems.—Prevail
on General N. not to go into town to-day. Spend a
most comfortable and social morning.—At dinner Mr.
March, Major Maxwell of the Dragoons, Captain Taylor,
&c. &c. · In the evening made melancholy, by hearing
of the death of Captain Macnamara, R.N. and several
other officers.

21*st*.—Dinner at 4, Major Gould, &c. came with General
N. The weather too hot to move.

22*nd*.—Very frightful thunder and heavy rain during the
night.—General N. and Colonel I. drove to town, in the
curricle, before 8.—The air is cooler—The thermometer is
at 83.—Spend a comfortable morning ; read and think a
great deal. Religion is now my greatest source of happiness.—I thank God for the blessings I enjoy, and I pray

D

ever to be resigned to his will.—General Churchill and ten guests at dinner to-day.

23rd.—General N. off early, as usual, for Spanish Town. —My prayer has been to-day, that we may have grace to do our duty in this foreign land, and be allowed to return to our native country, there to shew our gratitude, by devoting ourselves to the welfare of our fellow creatures.— General N. and only two of his staff came out to dinner, and we felt very comfortable in being so quiet.

24th.—Mr. Douglas and several gentlemen at breakfast ; I thought he was at Curaçoa long since.—General N.'s second great dinner to the lawyers to-day.—Margaret Clifford and the blackies with me till 4, when I was glad to see Colonel Irvine, as the thunder and lightning have been very dreadful the greater part of the day. The house shook, and there is scarcely a dry place in it, for the torrents of rain have burst in, in every direction.—A beautiful calm moonlight night at 9, when my dear N. came home, having run away from his lawyers as soon as possible after dinner.

25th.—Leave my little quiet abode, and breakfast at the King's House, with a crowd, at 8 this morning.—Saw Mr. March, and invited him for the evening, and have a handsome present ready to send him to-day.—All the morning, my poor dear N. harassed with business.—In the midst of his Chancery, he is called upon for some military and then some commercial affairs, and then must turn his attention to the French and St. Domingo ; and all this hurry and occupation increases the heat of the climate most exceedingly. Poor fellow ! I am sure I feel it all equally with him.—Mr. and Mrs. Batley, General Churchill, and in short a very large party, at dinner.—My visitors this evening very numerous. Open the ball with General Churchill, and finish it with Mr. Affleck.—To the great astonishment of some of the company, General N. and I sat together, and conversed the greatest part of the evening.—In fact, he has many and great vexations, and we have but little time to talk them over. I only pray his health may not seriously suffer.

26th.—Breakfast in my own room for a wonder.—My spirits are worn out with my poor dear N.'s worries and vexations.—Put on great spirits, however, and pretend to be gayer than usual.—After the Court of Chancery had broken up, we set off to Bellevue, with only two of the staff, and enjoyed a quiet dinner, rejoicing to be so snug after the bustle of the week.

27th.—We spent the morning all alone, which was delightful.—After our duties, General N. wrote some despatches of moment. I read, wrote, and sketched by his side.—We agreed that we had scarcely ever read our prayers with more fervour, than we did this day—I am sure it was from our very hearts.—Drove in the curricle to Spanish Town, at 5.—Found the dinner party assembling.—Dressed immediately, and dined at 6.—Mr. and Mrs. Woodham, Major and Mrs. Pye, Captain Taylor, 67th, Mr. George Cuthbert, Messrs. Nixon, Parkinson, and Vidal, 20th Dragoons, dined with us, in addition to our staff.

28th.—Set off before 5 for Mr. Cuthbert's in Liguanea. —General N.'s man Rogers, and my maid Johnson, with various blackies, in attendance upon us. Some of the staff were of the party, and one of Mr. Cuthbert's servants as a guide. The road beautiful and romantic, overhung with bamboos, and different picturesque trees and shrubs. Then, again, opening to a great width, and the soil like the bed of a river, owing to the torrents that occasionally pour down from the mountains. The palms and cotton trees on each side of it were quite majestic. It was all singularly beautiful, and my delight was increased upon arriving at Clifton (Mr. Cuthbert's seat), which is indeed indescribably lovely.* The views from it are quite enchanting. We found some of our staff there before us, and Mr. Cuthbert and his son waiting breakfast for us.

As soon as I could get away from the party, I went to my own room, the better to enjoy the landscape, as from my windows it is enchanting indeed. Imagine an immense

* In Gordon-Town, now the property of Mr. W. G. Clark.

amphitheatre of mountains, irregular in their shape and various in their verdure ; some steep and rugged, others sloping gently, and presenting the thickest foliage, and the most varied tints of green, interspersed with the gardens of little settlements, some of which are tottering on the very brinks of precipices, others just peep out from the midst of cocoa-nut trees and bamboos, the latter looking really like large plumes of green feathers. The buildings are like little Chinese pavilions, and have a most picturesque effect. In front is a view of the sea, and the harbours of Kingston, Port Royal, Port Henderson, &c. full of ships of war and vessels great and small ; the whole affording an exceedingly busy and interesting scene. The plain, from the Liguanea mountains, covered with sugar estates, *penns*, negro settlements, &c. and then the city of Kingston, the town of Port Royal, all so mixed with trees of different sorts, and all so new to an European eye, that it seemed like a Paradise ; and Clifton, where I stood, the centre of the blissful garden. Clifton stands upon a small mountain, and the plain in front, to the sea side, is about four miles in extent. The way to the house winds up the mountain by a rugged road ; the house itself is in the midst of a garden. Its form is the usual one, of one story with a piazza, &c. The garden contains a great variety of flowering shrubs and fruit trees, and the hedge round it is of lime trees, kept constantly cut, which makes it thick and bushy. The limes were ripe, and the yellow tint mixed with the bright green had a beautiful effect. Here and there the logwood was seen, which is something like our hawthorn. In other places are seen rows of orange trees, the fruit just turning yellow ; mangoes, red and purple ; forbidden and grape fruit, in clusters ; the acqui, a tree that bears a large scarlet fruit, the inside of which, they say, when dressed is like a sweetbread ; and the avocado pear, or real vegetable marrow, which poor Lord Hugh told me he ate for his breakfast on his toast, instead of butter.* There were also pomegranates, shad-

* In the West Indies avocado pear was called midshipman's butter.

docks, &c. in abundance, and a tree, that looks like the cherry at a distance, but is redder and much larger. Coffee, too, is a very pretty shrub, bearing a bright red berry. Besides these, there are several trees from which perfumes are made, but I forget their names. One had a narrow long very green leaf, and a very bright pink flower, which looks at a distance like a large full blown rose. Another tree has small dark green leaves, and tufts of scarlet flowers, something like the geranium. But it is quite impossible to describe the great variety of beautiful plants, trees and shrubs, that at this moment delight my eyes, and regale my nose. General N. and I spent the whole morning, looking about and admiring every thing, as far as the scorching sun would permit.—Only a Mr. Stimpson added to our dinner party, when the table groaned, as usual, with piles of food, and not an inch of the table-cloth was to be seen.

29*th*.—At 4 o'clock, General N. &c. set off to review the troops at Stony Hill.*—I took a walk in the garden till the heat drove me in. *Tête-à-tête* with mine host at breakfast. Had a learned conversation on the cultivation of sugar-canes, the population of the negroes, &c. Mr. C. told me he gave two dollars to every woman who produced a healthy child ; but no marriages were thought of ! ! After I had got all the information I wished from Mr. C. I went to my own room and amused myself very well till dear N. returned ; when we met with as much joy as if we had parted for months. He took some tamarind drink, and slept till dressing time.—An immense party, from Kingston and Up-Park Camp, at dinner, but no ladies, to my great joy ; so I did as I pleased, ordered tea in my own room, and went to bed at ten.

30*th*.—General N. started at 4 this morning to review the troops at Up-Park Camp.†—I had a nice early walk in the sweet garden, and conversed a great deal with Mr. Cuthbert,

* The old barracks are now used as a Reformatory.

† Purchased by the Crown in 1780: it had for a time been occupied by Rodney.

at our tete-à-tete breakfast, on the state of slaves in this country, &c. &c. He is a sensible man ; but we are creatures of habit, his mind is prejudiced, and I fear his heart is hard.—My dear N. returned at 3, and, while he refreshed himself with a nap, I read and kept off the Musquitoes from him. Several gentlemen at dinner, in addition to our party, whose names I don't recollect. No ladies ; so I have had my tea, and now am enjoying the cool breeze from the mountains, until my dear N. comes from the dinner party. In the mean time I shall take a review of the week, as far as it has hitherto passed. It has been quiet and comfortable. I have heard much of slaves, plantations, and counting-houses, but these subjects are new, and I have curiosity. For the principal part of my comfort, I have seen my dear N. composed and cool. He has had what for him is moderate exercise, and he has had relaxation of mind ; his countenance is quite changed, it is now placid, cheerful and serene ; he has no more that hurried heated manner, that has too often made me miserable. Oh, my God ! grant to him health of mind as well as of body, and enable me, as far as may depend upon my conduct and ability, to contribute to his welfare and happiness. Grant that I may conquer every propensity that may occasion him the smallest uneasiness, or make me less worthy of the blessings thou hast bestowed upon me. Teach me to suppress all sinful repinings, and to become entirely resigned to thy Divine will. With this prayer I shall go happy to bed, though it has thundered and lightened dreadfully, and the rain is now pouring in torrents.

⊙ *October* 1st.—Up at 4, and dress by candle-light. The fire-flies looked beautifully in the hall, as we passed through to our carriages. The walls were quite illuminated.

Drove to Mr. Hutchinson's place, called the Papine estate. A large party of gentlemen, and a grand cavalcade of all descriptions. All sorts of meats and fruits at breakfast. See a fine bamboo walk afterwards, reaching from one end of the garden to the other. Every ten or twelve feet there is a cocoa-nut tree, as a pillar to support the feathering bamboo. Nothing could well be more beautiful. The bread-fruit tree is here in great perfection. The Jack-fruit tree is like an enormous pumpkin, growing on the trunk, as it is too heavy for the boughs. There is also an infinite variety of beautiful flowers ; in short, the garden is the best and most curious I have yet seen.—The situation of the house is bad ; it lies low, and it is shut out from the sea breeze, by what is called the Long mountain, and from the land breeze, by a range of mountains, under which the house is placed. Mr. Hutchinson is a quiet, awkward Scotchman, and so overcome by the honour we have done him, that it is quite distressing to see the poor man.

About 10 we drove to the Hope estate.* We took a cross road, through a sugar plantation, or rather cane-piece, as it is called ; a negro man running before the carriage, to open the gates. The Hope estate is very interesting for me, as belonging to dearest Lady Temple,† and I examined every thing very particularly. It is situated at the bottom of a mountain, and as the Hope river runs through it, the produce is more certain than on estates in general, which often suffer from the great droughts in this part of the world. A severe hurricane alone can affect it. It is said to be an old estate, and not further improveable than yielding, as it does now, 320 hogsheads of sugar.—They say that, though it is incapable of yielding more, it is better, as being a sure produce, than most estates in the island, which are liable to great vicissitudes.—As you enter the gates, there is a long range of negro houses, like thatched cottages, and a row of cocoa-nut trees and clumps of cotton trees. The sugar-house, and all the buildings, are thought to be more than usually good, and well taken care of. The overseer, a civil, vulgar, Scotch officer, on half-pay, did the honours to us ; but, when we got to the door of the distillery, the smell of

* The present botanical gardens. The great house stood where the superintendent's house now is.

† Afterwards Marchioness of Buckingham.

the rum was so intolerable, that, after a little peep at the process, I left the gentlemen, and went to the overseer's house, about a hundred yards off. I talked to the black women, who told me all their histories. The overseer's chere amie, and no man here is without one, is a tall black woman, well made, with a very flat nose, thick lips, and a skin of ebony, highly polished and shining. She shewed me her three yellow children, and said, with some ostentation, she should soon have another. The marked attention of the other women, plainly proved her to be the favourite Sultana of this vulgar, ugly, Scotch Sultan, who is about fifty, clumsy, ill made, and dirty. He had a dingy, sallow-brown complexion, and only two yellow discoloured tusks, by way of teeth. However, they say he is a good overseer; so at least his brother Scotchman told me, and there is no one here to contradict him, as almost all the agents, attornies, merchants and shop-keepers, are of that country, and really do deserve to thrive in this, they are so industrious. I should mention that there is an excellent hospital on this estate, which is called a hot-house, where the blackies appear particularly comfortable, and well taken care of.

Return to Clifton to dinner; some dreadful peals of thunder this evening; for we are so near the mountains, it is quite terrific, and the house seems shaken to its very foundation; but, after our fright, we shall have a nice clear and cooler air to comfort us.

2nd.—Dress by candle-light, and off at 4 o'clock.—The morning darker than usual, and the fire-flies more brilliant; all the walls seem covered with gold spangles. We drove first to Kingston, and I was left at Mr. Atkinson's,* while General N. reviewed the 69th regiment, quartered in the town. Mr. A. made grand efforts to amuse me during his absence. The mountain wind, the sea breeze, slaves, plantations, and the prices of different articles, were the edifying topics, till a little after 7, when breakfast made its appearance, and Mr. A.'s spirits were relieved by the appearance

* Matthew Atkinson was Island Secretary.

of Mrs. Pye, who came to offer her services, hearing that
I was in Kingston.   Poor man, he seemed very happy, so
was I.   Some officers came soon after, and we sat down to
the usually profuse breakfast.   Afterwards, Mrs. Pye took
her leave, Mr. A. and Mr. Bogle (his partner) went to their
counting-house, and the officers to their camp.   General N.
brought General Churchill and some other officers with him.
Admiral Smith * and several officers of the Navy called.—
At one, General N. and I drove about town, and then to
General Churchill's Penn, to see his monkey and other
curiosities.—Back to Mr. Atkinson's ; dress and dine with
a large party, at 6.   General C., Mr. Simon Taylor,† Mr.
Cuthbert, &c. &c. &c. officers of the Army and Navy, and,
in short, half Kingston and Port Royal, but no lady ; so
I did not meet the gentlemen after dinner, but went to bed
at half-past nine, to be off early next morning for home.

   3rd.—Up at 4, and drive to the Admiral's Penn.‡   Ad-

   * Not to be confounded with Sir Sidney Smith (1764–1840),
the defender of Acre.
   † Simon Taylor sat in the House of Assembly from 1763 to
1810. He is said to have exercised greater influence in Jamaica,
and for a longer period, than any other individual, not even
excepting the Prices or Beckfords.   Immensely wealthy, he had
all the planter's prejudices, especially against dissenters.   He
left behind him the greatest fortune which perhaps any West
Indian had acquired.   As showing the value of sugar estates
in Jamaica about the middle of the eighteenth century, it may
be mentioned that Taylor gave £100,000 (sterling) for Holland
in St. Thomas-in-the-East.   He was a friend of Nelson for
nearly thirty years.   He was much disliked by the dissenters.
It was at his instigation that the Assembly, on 17 December,
1802, passed the "Act to prevent preaching by persons not
qualified by law," which was disallowed by the King ; and he
took a leading part in the Assembly's opposition to the abolition
of the slave trade.   He was buried at his pen in Liguanea, but
when this was sold his body was removed to Lyssons.
   ‡ The Jamaica station was at that time one of the most important in the British Empire. In 1773 the House of Assembly
resolved, probably at the instance of Rodney, then admiral on
the station, to purchase the house formerly occupied by Sir

miral Smith and a party met us. See the house, grounds, and stables, and select what furniture we wished to have, as all was to be sold. Feel truly melancholy, in thinking of the sad fate of its late possessor, and was glad to return to the carriage. Arrived at the King's House, and breakfasted at 8, with the sun broiling over our heads, and the heat tremendous. Hear a great deal of gossip from some of our staff about favouritism ; for I am such a great lady, that all I say and do is remarked upon. Mrs. Pye, &c. are spoken of as in my confidence, and likely to guide me in my conduct towards others. What ninnies ! But to avoid cabals, I determine not to go to Port Royal on Monday, and so I shall not have that lady in my train, and shall prevent at least some remarks. I mean, as much as possible, to live alone at my private hours, and so put an end to all these silly jealousies.—After breakfast, General N. held a Court of Ordinary in the Egyptian Hall, which lasted till 4 ó'clock. We had only our usual staff dinner, and slept at dear little quiet Bellevue.

4th.—Breakfast at 7, read our prayers, then walk about the gallery, and have a snug conversation, which we enjoyed very much.—General N. made memorandums for the business of to-morrow, and I wrote French verses, and translated them for his amusement. They were very bad, but very affectionate, and he wishes me to keep them ; but some future day they may make me blush for their want of merit ; so I shall give them to the winds.—Drove to the King's House before 5 ; some clouds obscure the sun, and make the heat more supportable.—Dined at 6 ; the clergyman and his wife, Major and Mrs. Pye, Captain Taylor, &c. &c. with our usual staff dinner.

William Burnaby, Admiral Keppel, and Admiral Parry, for the use of the Commander-in-Chief. Gayton was probably the first admiral to inhabit it. He was followed, amongst others, by Sir Peter Parker, Joshua Rowley, Gambier, Gardner, Sir Hyde Parker, Seymour, Montagu, Duckworth, Dacres, Cochrane, Popham, and Sir Charles Rowley. The house is now used as a Union Poor House for Kingston and St. Andrew.

ADMIRAL'S PEN

5th.—General N. &c. off to review the troops at Port Henderson.—As soon as I had breakfasted, made arrangements for his comfort, and mean to surprise him with a cool writing room, when he returns. Saw Monsieur Grandjean d'Aubancourt in my dressing room, and settle for his breakfasting here every morning, and reading French to me for an hour. He thinks my verses very good, but, query, does he speak the truth ?—Read Mrs. Haverdon's papers with real interest and attention ; write and tell her, that all that can be done in her case shall be done.—General N. returned at 3, and was delighted with his new apartment, to my great joy.—Set off after dinner for Bellevue, much against the advice of Dr. Lind, as it was quite dark.

6th.—Have not suffered at all for our great imprudence, and, though the musquitoes were in myriads about our beds, we had a tolerable night, and went, at gun-fire, to see Mrs. Pennington's Mountain.—Don't like it half as well as Bellevue, which I mean to try and persuade Mr. March to let to us.—After our breakfast, Captain Fraser, &c. about barracks. A good deal of jobbing going on, but General N. is determined not to countenance it.—Much rain, with thunder and lightning, the greatest part of to-day.

7th.—General N. gave audience to Monsieur Brunel, &c. from St. Domingo.—Wrote to Mr. March, and sent him a present, of porter, hams, &c. all just arrived from England, and a great treat here.—General Bell, &c. dined with us.— Hear of the arrival of our carriages from England.—Drive with General N. in the curricle, as usual, to Bellevue, and enjoy sleeping once more in the fresher and purer air of that place.

8th.—A sad head-ache all this evening.—Some of the staff at breakfast, and some Kingston gentlemen on business with General N.—Rain, thunder and lightning, at intervals, all day.—Dine at the King's House, at 5 ; Colonel Maclean, Monsieur Grandjean, &c. at dinner. Carriages ordered for the navy officers to-morrow evening at Port Henderson.

9th.—The carriages went at 4, but returned empty, as

Admiral Montagu's arrival at Port Royal has kept all our navy friends there. Am not very sorry, for I still have a head-ache, and am not very equal to any great gaiety.—Read and converse with Monsieur Grandjean, for an hour after breakfast, and have begun to write an Abridgement of French History.—At dinner, General Bell, Mr. Rose, Mr. Minot, Colonel Gillespie, Captain Macdonald (just from England), Mr. H., Colonel MacMurdo, Mr. Matthews, Admiral Smith, and the eternal Major and Mrs. Pye, in addition to our staff.—In the evening an immense party, but not so many ladies as usual, on account of the torrents of rain.

'10th.—Was present at the review of the troops in this garrison, at 5 o'clock.—Colonel Gillespie, &c. breakfasted with us afterwards.

13th.—Drive to the Government Penn * at 6; the works there going on slowly, and Jones, the head workman, says, that, although Lord Balcarres said he would lay out £700 in repairs, he had limited him to £55 !

14th.—General N. surprised us by walking off at 6, to see a Penn, or rather a mountain, belonging to Mr. March, two miles off. He did not seem to be the worse for it, and I trust will not suffer; but such walks are very imprudent.—The Secretary, &c. with papers to sign, and, after breakfast, we were left to ourselves; when General N. wrote his speech. We actually now feel the cold quite uncomfortable. The heavy rains have so saturated the walls with damp, and the squalls of wind are so powerful, that they pervade everything, and we live in almost a bath; so I fear we must soon leave this dear pretty quiet retreat.

15th.—A pain in my head and shoulders from the damp air last night; but drive into town to breakfast. Find Lord Balcarres and a large party.—After breakfast, read and go through my usual avocations with Monsieur Grand-

* Government Pen, or Government Park as it is now called, is three miles south-east of Spanish Town. It is now under lease to the United Fruit Company.

jean.   Dr. and Mrs. Ludford arrived at 10—Conversed with
them till 2.—Very unwell ; and I mean, as symptoms arise
of any illness, always to mention it ; because, if I should
die in this country, it will be a satisfaction to those who are
interested about me, to know the rise and progress of my
illness, &c.

16th.—Still unwell, but carriages are gone for the Navy,
and I must do my best to be gay.   At half-past seven,
Captains Bayntun, Cathcart, and Loring, Dr. and Mrs.
Ludford, &c. &c.—Then Lord Balcarres, Captain Woolley,
Mr. Carthew, Mons. Le Vaillant, Major and Mrs. Pye at
dinner.—A large evening party of ladies, and crowds of
gentlemen, both civil and military.   All in high spirits, and,
in spite of my illness, I danced, and was as gay apparently
as any of them ; though the enquiries of my people shewed,
that I did not disguise quite so well as I thought.

17th.—Get our English letters.—All well, thank God !
General N. all the morning reading his despatches.   Dr. and
Mrs. Ludford at Kingston all day, so we were left to ourselves.—Only our usual dinner party, with Monsieur Grandjean, our eternal guest now, poor man !

18th.—Drive out with General N. at 6 o'clock, and go to
church at 10.—Our English carriage and four horses for the
first time.—A large party at dinner.—Still unwell, and glad
to go to bed at nine.

19th.—Drive out at 6.—The Marquis de la Jaille in addition to our breakfast party.   Then the Attorney-General,
to consult with General N. about his speech, and some few
alterations were made.—Read as usual with Monsieur
Grandjean.—Mr. Warren, our chaplain, made his appearance for the first time.—All the morning interrupted by
visitors, that I am obliged to receive.—General N. held a
privy council at 5, to whom his speech was read.—At 6
a dinner in the Great Hall ; about forty or fifty guests.
I dined in my dressing-room, with Mrs. Pye and Mrs. Ludford.

20th.—At 4, the House of Assembly met, and came over

to the King's House, in grand procession. General N. read his speech, and they departed to discuss it.

21st.—Send out cards for my balls, and distributed to the black women, gowns, petticoats, &c. and various presents for my wedding day. Dr. and Mrs. Ludford took their leave at 3.—Messrs. Bogle, Atkinson, Forbes, B——, Donaldson, &c. at dinner, with Mr. Corbet, the St. Domingo agent. After dinner had a great deal of conversation with Mr. Corbet, about General Toussaint l'Ouverture, which was particularly interesting.* He must be a wonderful man, and I really do believe intended for very good purposes.

22nd.—The actual rainy season, they say, set in last night ; and I believe it, for we were so uncommonly chilly, that we kept the counterpane on all night, and this morning it rains torrents.—We could not drive out, and I amused myself till 8, in translating General N.'s speech into French, for Monsieur Grandjean's edification.—At breakfast, Mr. Corbet, &c.—Drove, with some of the staff, to Lord Balcarres's auction.—Every article had its price put upon it, by Lord B. himself, who was present the whole time, and had his emissaries to bid for him, till all was sold at his own price, which was always more than their worth ; consequently most of the things remain on his hands.—Returned and read French with Monsieur Grandjean, for a couple of hours ; then gave audience to the old superannuated President of the Council,†who wanted me to patronize a decayed milliner of bad character. Altogether it was an unpleasant business, and I got rid of it civilly, but decidedly.—A very flattering answer to General N.'s speech came over from the House of Assembly.—The Members of the Council sent one

---

* Toussaint L'Ouverture, the negro patriot, one of the liberators of Haiti, gained and maintained unsullied, during a very chequered career, passed in most troublesome and uncertain times, a reputation for ability, courage, resourcefulness, and justice. If charges of harshness were at times true, who shall wonder ?

† Thomas Wallen.

equally so, and General N. replied to all at half-past four.
—We went to dinner at 6.—Mr. Corbet, Colonel Skerrett,
Mr. MacCluny of the 87th, &c. dined with us, and all
departed at nine.

23*rd.*—General N. rode out at 6 ; I had not had a good
night, and did not accompany him.—Read and converse,
after breakfast, with Monsieur [Grandjean] D'Aubancourt,
in my dressing-room, till 12.—Afterwards received a few
visitors in my own room.—General N. and I then had a
tête-à-tête, and conversed a good deal upon the subject of his
situation, &c. and he sent several messages to the House of
Assembly. He has strange people to deal with. The trade of
this island has been for a long time much injured, and several
merchants almost ruined, by the constant depredations of
small privateers and feluccas, which infest the coast ; while
the navy are engaged in distant pursuits. Admiral Montagu,* who succeeds to the naval command, *pro tempore*, has
offered, at the representation of General N. of the necessity
of keeping cruisers to guard the coast, that he will station
his ships, so as to intercept these mischievous privateers ;
this offer was very handsomely made in a letter to General
N., who shewed it to the gentlemen in Council, when it was
drily received, as a matter of perfect indifference ; although
not many weeks since, the remissness of the navy, in this
respect, was not only complained of by them, but was a
cause of general complaint. Many very severe philippics
appeared in the newspapers against poor Lord Hugh Seymour, on account of the cruisers not doing their duty in
guarding the trade. But such are these people, and such is
their littleness, that because they suppose that General N.
has the order of ministers to employ black corps in the
island, they seem determined to do every thing to make his
situation uncomfortable, and to discourage every arrangement, though for their own good and advantage. He must,
however, do his duty, and it is to be hoped that time will
bring all things right.—Dined at 5—The two Mr. Cuthberts,

* Rear-Admiral Robert Montagu.

E

Colonel de Charmilly,* Mr. Warren, Captain Taylor, Mr. Matthews, Monsieur Grandjean, &c. in addition to the staff. —In the evening a very large party, and much dancing.— We had three hours to-day of the heaviest rain I ever saw : it came down like a torrent.

24th.—Drive out.—Admiral Montagu, and some of the Navy, at breakfast, at 8.—At 10 received several visitors.— I forgot to say, that although Dr. and Mrs. Ludford did take their leave, they returned, and were still our guests.—Found time before dinner to translate one of Sappho's Odes from the French. It is addressed to the Rose, and is very pretty.

25th.—Drove to the Penn at 6.—Went with Lord Balcarres to see the garden, or rather where the garden has been, for not a plant of any kind is there existing at present. —A party at breakfast, and go to church at 10.—After church, visit Mrs. Bailey and Mrs. Romsey.—Find at the King's House all Lord B.'s poor negroes, to solicit favours. Make them all as happy as I can, by promising kindness.— At dinner, Monsieur and Madame Grandjean and Mademoiselle Robert, Mr., Mrs. and the Misses Warren, Mr. and Mrs. Woodham, Major and Mrs. Pye, and some officers of the Navy and Army. A strange mixture of people altogether, and a most laughable party.

26th.—After breakfast, drive to the Penn. The sun extremely oppressive. Lord B. very civil, but, I am sure, very much annoyed. Dr. Ludford, who was of the party,

---

* Colonel Venault de Charmilly, a planter in St. Domingo, of fourteen years residence, and Member of the General Assembly of that colony, was charged with the duty of negotiating with Lieut.-General Adam Williamson the capitulation of the French part of the island. He was strongly in favour of St. Domingo going under the suzerainty of England. In 1797 he wrote a letter which was published in London in both French and English, criticising unfavourably that portion of Bryan Edwards's " Historical Survey of St. Domingo," where it reflected on the conduct of the French in the colony, in which he gave many evidences that Edwards had written his account of that island on insufficient information.

taken ill of *the* fever, in consequence of the heat ; and, indeed, it is very unsafe to go out so late in the day.   We
all felt the heat very much.—Poor Mrs. Ludford was very
uneasy, but the fever is not thought serious.—Mr. Corbet,
&c. at dinner.

27th.—Dr. L. better this morning.—General N. and I
drove towards Kingston at 6.—Read, &c. with Monsieur G. after breakfast ;   then received a visit from
the Attorney-General, with his niece, in my dressing-
room.—Only Grandjean and our staff at dinner.—Dr. L.
getting well.

28th.—At 5, drive on a new road, by the river side, and
enjoy it much.—After breakfast read with Grandjean, as
usual.—The Attorney-General many hours in conference
with General N. on the subject of black corps, &c.   Employ
myself and the maids in decorating the ball-room.—Send off
Baptiste (our French cook) to Kingston, with orders for
ornamental cakes, &c.—A grand dinner given to-day to
General N. by *King* Mitchell.—Mrs. Pye and Mrs. Ludford
with me.—To bed early.

29th.—Drive out at half-past five.—The Attorney-General
again at breakfast this morning.—A long conference, and
all about General N.'s message, respecting black corps, &c.
—I feel very anxious myself for the issue, as it is all such a
source of vexation to my dear N.—Read with Grandjean,
write English letters, dine at 5, and the eternal Major and
Mrs. Pye of our party.

30th.—Up at gun-fire.*—Did not drive out, but General N.
rode.   I was glad of the excuse to be quiet till breakfast
time, as I was kept awake by the band of the 20th dragoons,
that regiment having given a parting dinner to the 67th.—
Dr. and Mrs. L. took leave, on account of their child's illness.   Do all I can to comfort them before they left us, as
we feel a particular interest for them, on account of Colonel

* 5 a.m.   The port of Kingston was then open to shipping.
At 6 p.m. a second gun warned ships to anchor off Port Royal,
and at 8 p.m. a third gun warned them to lie outside Port Royal.

and Mrs. M. Murray, and Sir J. and Lady M. Murray.—
Dress for dinner at 6.—My evening party full of ladies, but
not so many gentlemen as usual ; owing, I imagine, to the
dinner and serenading last night.   General N. did not make
his appearance, but left me to do the honours, as he had so
many letters to write, and so much business of various kinds
on his hands.   Poor fellow, he works hard, and I do indeed
pity him !

November 1st.—Hear of the death of George the Second,
who was assassinated, and King Stephen proclaimed as
Regent.   The Commander-in-Chief sent the intelligence
from the Musquito Shore, with his mark by way of
signature.*—An immense dinner party of gentlemen at 6.—
Dined in my dressing-room.   Wrote and read, and waited
for General N. till near 12, whose party found it so agreeable, he could not get rid of them before that hour.

2nd.—General N. inspected the 20th dragoons at 6.—
The morning as usual.—I gave each of the white servants
a present for our wedding day.—Captain Taylor came to
take leave for England.—Gave him some medicines, &c. foi
his voyage.—Hear of the arrival of a packet from England.

3rd.—Give Colonel MacMurdo a present of comforts for
his voyage to dear England.—Pass part of the morning in
inspecting the decorations of the ball-room.—Dress soon
after 7, and at 8 all the company were assembled.—General
N. and I then went down to the Great Hall, at the door of
which all the staff were paraded, and we marched up to the
sophas, at the upper end, to the tune of " God save the
King."   General N. then went round the room, attended
by most of the staff, and spoke to all.   The ladies were then
handed up to me, one after the other, and made their
curtsies.   After all this ceremony was over, I opened the
ball, with a Member of Council, then danced with a Member
of the Assembly, then with a military man ; and, having performed all these agreeable duties, seated myself in state till

* A document signed with the mark of Peter, King of the
Mosquito Indians, is in the Institute of Jamaica.

supper time.—Handed to supper at 12 o'clock by Mr. Scott the Member of Council, with whom I opened the ball ; but after supper, I forgot all my dignity, and with all my heart joined in a Scotch reel.—Many followed my example, and the ball concluded most merrily.

4th.—So tired I could not get up till 7. A large breakfast party.—After reading with Grandjean, lounged away the morning in my dressing-room.

5th.—General N., &c. went with old Grandjean to the Penn, early this morning, to arrange about the garden.— After the usual breakfast, gave my last lecture to the blackies, and finished my Christian story. I consider them now so well acquainted with their expected duties, that I have appointed the Rev. Mr. Warren* to be here to-morrow, at 12, for the purpose of baptizing them. Saw the Rev. Mr. Woodham, also, upon the same subject, and he approved, as well as Mr. Warren, of the little Catechism I have arranged for their use, and the progress of their instruction. —Major Drummond, just arrived from Turkey, and Mr. Davis, our only new guests at dinner to-day.

6th.—Drive to the Penn at gun-fire.—Settled all about the apartments we are to inhabit, their being painted, &c. —Return to a large party at breakfast.—Captain Parker came ; he is newly arrived.—At 12, Messrs. Warren and Woodham, with their families, came ; all the servants were assembled in the chapel, and the gentlemen of the staff as witnesses.—Twenty-five of our black domestics were made Christians, and I trust will be so indeed. After the ceremony, cake and wine, in large pieces and glasses, for the newly made Christians.—Captain Parker, Major Drummond, &c. &c. at dinner ; and a large party in the evening, and we danced till the usual hour, eleven o'clock.

7th.—General N. went to Kingston, with part of the staff, at 6. The rest breakfasted with me at 8. Captain Parker went to Port Royal, immediately after.—Left alone part of the morning, with Major Gould, who entertained me with

* Domestic Chaplain to the Governor.

an account of Lord B.'s *domestic* conduct, and his ménage here altogether.   Never was there a more profligate and disgusting scene, and I really think he must have been more than half mad.   I was glad to get to my own room, and employ my time more profitably than in listening to such horrid details.—Found Major and Mrs. Pye in the drawing room, with the family assembled, at 6.   General N. came soon afterwards, and we went to dinner.   He brought me a very nice wedding present from Kingston, as our anniversary is to-morrow week.

8th.—Don't drive out, but read till breakfast.   After church, shut myself up for some hours, composing instructions for the new made Christians.—At dinner, Mr. Warren and family, Mr. and Mrs. Woodham, Major Cookson, Colonels Ainslie and Skerrett, Mr. Nixon, &c.

9th.—General N. rode to Mr. Hanson's Penn at 6, and has ordered sheep, &c. for our Penn, in a most farmer-like manner.—Major Cookson, &c. at breakfast.

10th.—Drove, at half-past five, to Major Cookson's Penn. The morning delightfully cool.—The Attorney-General, &c. at breakfast.—General N. full of business, and really nearly hurried and worried to death, the whole day.—I employed my morning, translating all the family, but especially kitchen, regulations into French, for the benefit of Baptiste, who is a St. Domingo *gentleman*, and scarcely understands a word of English ; so now I hope the cuisine will go on more prosperously.

11th.—Had a pleasant drive.—The horses were much quieter than they have hitherto been, and the black postilions understand them better.—Saw the Penn, and settled many important affairs with Jones.—Had a long conversation with Mr. Warren, about the blacks.   I don't think he is much interested about their spiritual welfare, but he is a well-meaning man.

15th.—This is our fourth Wedding Day.   God bless and preserve my dear husband, and continue to us our present happiness.—General N. much better, but staid at home,

while I went to Church with the staff.   Delighted to see the
black servants look so well, so orderly, and behave so properly during the Service.—Assembled them all afterwards,
and gave them each a dollar for a Wedding present.—Their
wish was, that General N. and I might live happy together,
till our hair was as white as their gowns.   They don't know
what snow is, or I suppose they would have said snow,
rather than gowns ; but their muslin was very clean and
white.—Dined at 5, with a very large party.—Poor General
N.'s looks shew how ill he has been the last two days ; it is
really astonishing, to see so robust and florid a man so soon
changed ; but he has much fatigue both of body and mind,
and this, added to the climate, keeps me in constant alarm.
—God preserve him !

16th.—Thank God !   N. is much better, but we did
not drive out.—A note in the evening from General
Churchill, telling us of the death of his mother, Lady
Mary Churchill.

17th.—Drive to the Penn at 6.   After breakfast very
busy, with Johnson, M. Clifford, &c. &c. decorating the ball
room.—Dine at 3 with General N. in my dressing room.—
Try to get rid of my head-ache by a little sleep.—Dress at
7, and enter the ball room with General N. &c. in great
state.   A very large party was assembled, and all the
benches were full.   Open the ball with the Attorney-General.
Then dance with a Member of the Assembly.   Begin the
ball after supper again, with the Commanding Officer of the
Military, and then, having done my duty, steal away to bed,
and leave General N. to do the honours.

19th.—General N. drove me to the Penn at 6.—I don't
think any year of my life I ever read half as much as I
have done since I came to this country ; in spite of the musquitoes, that constantly annoy every one who is sitting at
any quiet occupation.—Don't dine till half-past 7, on account of the House of Assembly sitting so late.   The
Speaker, the Attorney-General, and eleven Members, at
dinner, besides our own party ; only two ladies.

20th.—Drive to Port Henderson, and bring Captain Colville and several of his officers. Mr. Criek, Mr. Becker, and Mr. Henry, also came to breakfast, and staid all day.—A larger assembly than usual in the evening. Dance down twenty-three couples, to begin the ball, and half kill poor Captain C. who, being an honourable, was obliged to be my partner.—Heard the delightful news of peace,* and the evening ended very merrily.

Till the Session is over I can only speak of events, and make no remarks, for I have not time. I ought to have mentioned, that, after the two first dinners were given to General N. and me, there was a demur about what the third entertainment should be. I was referred to, and named a ball. This pleased all parties, and it is soon to take place.

21st.—Don't drive out, but, after breakfast, send off Captain C. and his party, in the sociable, to Port Henderson.— The rest of the day much as usual, every one talking of and delighted with the idea of peace ; though there are some who don't seem as well pleased with it as we are ourselves.

22nd.—General N. and I passed a comfortable morning together afterwards, anticipating the delights of home, and talking over our prospects of returning to dear England soon. Fourteen people in addition to our staff party, at dinner.—Very much shocked in the evening, by a sad account of the massacre of three hundred and seventy white persons in St. Domingo. How dreadful, and what an example to this island.

23rd.—Drive to the Penn.—All the gentlemen of our family, excepting Major Drummond, gone to dine with Captain Colville, on board the *Ambuscade.*—The Marquis de la Jaille, Monsieur Brunel, and Monsieur Grandjean, our only party at breakfast.—General N. held a Court of Appeal at 10, which lasted till 3. He then gave audience till 5 to Monsieur Brunel, on the subject of St. Domingo ; and, as dinner was ordered at that hour, it was so late that he did

* The peace which resulted in the Treaty of Amiens, 27 March, 1802.

not change his Chancery dress, but sat down in black.—
After dinner, as there were only Major and Mrs. Pye in
addition, Major Drummond and I had a long conversation
on the subject of religion.   He appeared to be particularly
well informed, and had read much upon serious subjects.   I
have lately devoted much of my time to Mr. Wilberforce's
works ;   therefore his conversation was very interesting to
me.   He is a young man, and has been running a great deal
about the world, which makes his thinking so seriously the
more extraordinary.

   25th.—The carriages were sent to Port Henderson for
some Navy men.   We had twenty at breakfast and at
dinner, in addition to our party.—Much talk about peace ;
some pleased, some the reverse.   I am of the contented
party ;   and went to dress in great spirits for the grand ball,
given me to-night by the Council, &c. :   put on my smartest
dress, with a gold tiara, and white feathers, and made myself look as magnificent as I could.   At 8, was received at
the entrance of the House of Records by the Members of
Council, some of the Assembly, and some military.   Was
conducted to a sort of throne, covered with pink silk and
draperies festooned with flowers.   The decorations of the
room were beautiful, and the supper was superb :   one dish
I shall never forget ;   it was a roasted peacock, placed before
me, with all the feathers of the tail stuck in, and spread
so naturally, that I expected every minute to see him strut
out of the dish.   Danced myself almost to death, to please
both civil and military, army and navy, and staid till
1 o'clock.

   26th.—A party of Navy officers to breakfast, and Monsieur Pechon.   The breakfast was crowded with visitors,
before I could make my escape.   Very much fatigued, and
lie down afterwards till 3.—My dear N. had prepared a little
luncheon for me, of a couple of snipes, which we enjoyed
very much, talking over England, &c. and the peace.—
Twenty-four guests added to our dinner party ;   only six
ladies of the number.   Retire at ten.

27th.—General N. rode out at 6.—I was so tired I rested a little longer than usual.—Send the carriages for Navy officers.—Eighteen new people at dinner.—The Speaker and Mr. Scott were the only civilians ; the rest were of the Navy and Army.—A very large party in the evening, and the Navy men skipped away famously.

28th.—Don't drive out, but send the carriages for more Navy friends, Captain Freemantle, &c. &c. &c. and we had an immense party all day.   General Churchill, and Captain Coatquelvin,* came to dinner also.   After the party broke up, kept my eyes open half an hour later than usual, to talk to Captain F. of England, and of English friends.   He hates this country, and is most dreadfully alarmed at the climate.

29th.—Send Captain F. in the sociable to Port Henderson, with several other officers.—Mr. Colin Donaldson, the new clergyman, at dinner, with Mrs. Warren and Mrs. Woodham, General Churchill, Captain Coatquelvin, Mr. W. Bullock, &c.—Heard of the arrival of an English packet, just as we were going to bed, and longed for the news of the morning.

30th.—Before 6, large despatches, but very few letters, though those were comfortable.—General N.'s regiment (the 85th,) is at Madeira.

December 1st.—A more than usually warm morning.   See the bills of fare for dinner and supper, and pity poor Baptiste, &c. &c. who, they say, have sat up all night preparing them.—Send carriages for Captains Penrose, Essington, Foley, Freemantle, &c.—General N. had to hold a Court of Appeal, and then a Privy Council, after breakfast, so that I was obliged to entertain the gentlemen all the morning.   However, the task was easy, as the novelty of all things was quite enough for them, and they took particular interest in the decorations of the supper room, &c.—In the evening, I danced with all my Navy friends, and I thought they would have twisted my arms off, and broken my neck,

* Captain S. Coatquelvin, of the Royal Dutch Artillery, aide-de-camp to General Churchill.

in their wild spirits; and this was shockingly indecorous, after our stately and solemn entry into the ball-room, which astonished them very much, as they told me afterwards.—One of the black women produced two boys, this morning. Went to see them, and they were exactly like two little monkies.

2nd.—Give orders to have all the remains of the supper distributed. Send the old Custos some rich cake, as he is as fond of such things as a child. To the shopkeepers, &c. in Spanish Town, cake, &c. also. The rest was given to the blackies, which made them all very happy.—General N. was engaged in Court, till 3. We then drove with the Navy captains to the Penn.

3rd.—General N. accompanied our Navy guests to Port Henderson. He and the staff on horseback, and they in the sociable, drawn by four fine new horses. Each of them, one of the Aides-de-camp told me, cost General N. £200, and the horse the servant rode was of the same price. Good animals of the sort are of course very dear in this country. —A small dinner party to-day, and a nice little conversation, in the evening, on the subject of religion, which here is quite a treat to me ; Major Drummond and Dr. Lind are both very good men.

4th.—Mrs. Pye called to say, that she and Major Pye were going on a cruise with Captain Penrose. Invite them and some Navy men to dinner.—The poor Chief Justice is just dead, and the house is beset with applicants for the situation.* However, General N. has made up his mind on the subject, and it is to be made known to the happy man to-morrow. The Chief Justice's illness lasted only two days ; but he was a worn out looking skeleton, poor man, and had not stamina, I am sure, to withstand any illness.—At 7, a very large party in the evening, and the candidates for the Chief Justice's situation particularly smiling and attentive. Some of them danced merrily on the occasion, and particularly when they were my partners.

* The Chief Justice was William Jackson.

5th.—Drove to Port Henderson, at 6.—Only the Speaker at breakfast, who attended General N. and the staff to the funeral of poor Mr. Henckell.—On returning to the King's House, Mr. Kirby, (one of the barristers,) was immediately declared the new Chief Justice.—The Judges of the Court, (none of whom are lawyers,) were expecting this appointment, so I suppose it will be rather an unpopular act. However, they all expressed their approbation, on account of Mr. Kirby's character, and many because he was a lawyer, which the late Chief Justice was not. Besides, the deceased had the superintendence of so many estates, that it was impossible for him to attend properly to the duties of his office. He had charge of Lord Balcarres' property, who, the scandalous " Chronicle " * said, received a douceur of a thousand guineas for giving him the appointment. General N. has made it a point with Mr. Kirby, that he should hold no second situation, but devote himself solely to his duties as Chief Justice ; it is therefore to be hoped, that all will go well.—Although we dined late to-day, on account of finishing despatches for the *Ambuscade*, General N. went to his room immediately after dinner, and I joined him, to take copies, or make duplicates, of many papers going to England, that he does not wish others to see.

6th.—Drive to Port Henderson, soon after 5 ; all the staff with us. Baptiste and his myrmidons had gone on some hours before. At breakfast, omelettes, fricassees, &c. all prepared. Captains Colville, Foley, Essington, Penrose, Freemantle, &c. landed from Port Royal, just as we came to the inn door.—Breakfast at 7.—Talk over dear home, and our English friends. Gave Captain Freemantle a hundred messages and commissions. Then took leave of all at 9 o'clock, half laughing and half crying, but putting the best face upon it that I could ; and we arrived at the church door, just in time not to keep the Service waiting. Mr. Supple read the prayers, and Mr. Donaldson preached be-

* The " Cornwall Chronicle," founded in 1773. The " Kingston Chronicle " was not founded till 1805.

fore us for the first time.   They are both young men, candidates for livings ; and General N. is determined not to
give one away, without being well acquainted with the
character and talents of the gentleman whom he appoints.
Mr. Supple read very well, only he has rather a discordant
voice and Irish accent.   Mr. Donaldson does not appear to
have a sufficiently powerful voice ; but he was so nervous
to-day, that it was impossible to judge fairly.   His discourse
shewed more knowledge of the narrative part of Scripture,
than talent to draw sound inferences from his text ; *mais
nous verrons.*—In addition to the clergymen who read and
preached, the Rector and his wife, Mr. and Mrs. Clements,
Doctors Walker and Gallagher, Mr. Blake, 20th dragoons,
and Mr. Handfield of the Navy, formed our dinner party.

7th.—Read a shorter time than usual with Grandjean this
morning ; he talks so much, and stays so long, that he teases
my poor dear N.   Admitted Mr. Ward, poor Lord H. Seymour's Chaplain, and had a long conversation with him, in
my dressing-room.   He is a most sincere Christian, and a
most excellent man, and truly interested in the cause of
religion, particularly in the instruction of the poor negroes.
Our dinner would have been very comfortable, if Grandjean
had not made his appearance, and bored General N. sadly.

8th.—It is not 6 o'clock, and the thermometer is at
summer heat.   I am writing *en chemise,* and don't find it at
all too cool.   The rains have ceased for ten days, and they
say we shall have no more showers till May.   During the rainy
season, there were not above two or three days on which
we could not take an early drive in the morning, or have a
nice one in the evening.—However, when it does rain, it
comes down like a torrent, and converts the streets into
rivers ; but the sun and the heat of the earth absorb all
moisture almost immediately, so that, if we have no rain
before May, we shall indeed be burnt up.→Poor N. still so
unwell, that Dr. Lind ordered quiet, and some medicine.
Remain with him all the morning, but he was obliged to
see several persons on business.—One of the little twins,

born last week, died to-day.—Send for Mr. Woodham, and had the other christened Philip King. Margaret, one of the black maids, and two of the footmen, lately christened, stood sponsors. They appeared much flattered at being selected for the office, and promised to do the duties of it, poor things !

9th.—I would give any thing for a little rest and quiet, but must exert myself at dinner, to make the agreeable to the big wigs.—Went to the drawing room at 6, though the House of Assembly did not break up till much later.—At dinner, Mr. Speaker (Osborne), Mr. Scott, and the other Members of Council, Messrs. Edwards, Lewis, Murphy, Thorpe, &c. &c. all Members of Assembly ; Colonel Gillespie, and several military men. No ladies, so I got to bed early.

10th.—General N. full of business all the morning; but he is so much better he does not mind it.—Feel quite subdued, but don't complain, and anticipate a quiet evening, as General N. and his whole staff dine with *King* Mitchell.— Took my dinner in my dressing room, and read till a little after 9, when General N. came home, and gave me an account of his party.—A loaded dinner, as usual in this country, but better served, and more *recherché*, than is generally met with. Mr. Mitchell is a coarse looking man, but humane, and treats his negroes most kindly. He disgusted me very much the other day, by making a joke of poor Lord Hugh's death ; but it is a common custom here.

11th.—General N. wrote his take-leave speech, and the House, thank God ! is to be prorogued to-morrow. Bathe at 3 o'clock ; then dress for dinner. Eight or ten people, in addition to our staff.—While we were at table, the Speaker came to say, that the House did not wish to break up till 9 to-morrow morning. Agreed to by General N., and the Session will conclude ; and they say it has been the quietest and most peaceable ever known here. A large party, and much merry dancing, in the evening.

12th.—Colonel de Charmilly, &c. &c. at breakfast.—At 9,

the House met. At 11, General N. made his speech, and prorogued the meeting, according to the usual forms. As soon as possible after, the greatest part of the Members set off for their homes, as happy, I dare say, to depart as we were to see them go away.—Monsieur Grandjean, Madlle. Robert, Major and Mrs. Pye, &c. at dinner. Some singing afterwards.—At 8, all took their leave, and we went to bed. General N. delighted to have a respite from such continual tiresome business, and I equally so, from a constant round of company.

13th.—General N. rode out early. After church, a despatch from St. Domingo. Toussaint is determined to keep his command. This reminds me of a conversation General N. had with Colonel de Charmilly, who said that General Toussaint, he was sure, would negotiate with France, and for a compensation resign his command. General N. thought differently, and that he would retain his power as long as he possibly could ; that he would probably call upon the whites to join him, and, in case of their refusal, a general massacre of those unfortunate people would be the consequence, that is, if he found himself at all pressed by the French force sent to St. Domingo. General N. thought, also, that he would be likely to burn the towns, and retire to the mountains. The sequel of the disastrous history of that wretched country, will prove which is the right opinion. At present, General Toussaint having declared exactly what General N. thought he would do with respect to his government, had sent secret advice to all the white inhabitants, to come over to this island as soon as possible, with what property they could collect.

14th.—General N., after writing a few despatches, began to read a novel, called The Infernal Quixote.* I rejoice to see him so much disengaged and at his ease already, as to

* No copy of this book is in the British Museum Library. It may have been inspired by *The Spiritual Quixote* of Richard Graves, published in 1772 and frequently reprinted down to 1808.

mix amusement and light reading with his worrying and serious occupations.—Major and Mrs. Pye set off to the country to-morrow, with Mr. Herring; all took their leave, and I can't say that I am sorry.

15th.—Drive to the Penn. Lord Balcarres' cattle have ruined our garden; but I cannot help laughing at the rueful faces of our blackies.—Write English letters all the morning after breakfast.

16th.—Drive again to the Penn, with Clifford in our *suite*, driven by old Grandjean; she set the black women to work, and I hope now that the house will be clean.—Write English letters all the morning.—Poor Johnson was more than usually cross.—Mr. Hall, Grandjean, and two friends of Captain Johnson's, that were at the Charterhouse School with him, all left us at eight.

17th.—The gentlemen of the family, except Colonel Irvine, set off for Kingston, where General Churchill and Colonel Gillespie give a ball to some French ladies. We sent excuses. General N. had a great deal of St. Domingo business, and sat writing the whole day in my dressing room.—Very comfortable indeed.

18th.—At 6, Colonel Irvine went in the sociable to bring a cargo of Navy officers, who all arrived for breakfast.—Hear of the arrival of a packet.—General N.'s despatches all he could wish (thank God!). All his applications attended to. Poor Irvine confirmed Deputy Adjutant-General, with the rank of Major in the Army, and, in short, nothing could be more comfortable in every respect. My letters were from my brother, Lady Temple, Lady Mary, and Lord George Grenville, all of whom write in the greatest spirits, and give the most delightful accounts possible.—At 5, Captains Lobb, Stephens, Meades, &c. exceedingly lively and pleasant; as indeed every thing has appeared to me since the good tidings from England. My English letters always put me in a state of happy fuss for a day or two after their arrival.—A nice dance this evening.—The Navy men very happy, and all was gaiety.

19th.—Have a more than usually fine *déjeuner à la four-chette* for our Navy friends, who started immediately after for their ships.

20th.—General N. rode out early.—To church at 10.—The rest of the morning, my dear N. and I passed in reading and writing, and interesting talk. Confess my misery, that the dear name of mother will never greet my ear probably.—My mind relieved, and promise never to be so ungrateful to Providence any more ; but to be resigned to His will, who knows what is best for us, and above all to be grateful for the many blessings I enjoy.—Mr. and Mrs. Woodham, Captain Cross, Messrs. Hiatt, Hylton and Lewis, Mr. Nixon of the 20th dragoons, at dinner.—Grandjean and Baptiste bring in their *projets* for family arrangements, to our great amusement.—General N. gave Mr. Nixon,* to-day, the appointment of Assistant Deputy Quarter-Master General, and he dined with us the first time, as a member of the family.

21st.—All the morning my dear N. writing in my dressing room, while I drew, read and wrote by his side.

23rd.—Drive to the Penn at 6. All getting in beautiful order. Busy making my arrangements.

24th.—Some vulgar Messrs. Gallagher, from Ireland, of our party.—General N.'s business and worries decrease rapidly, and we shall now, I trust, be very comfortable.—Dine at 5.—Only the Irish gentlemen at dinner.

25th.—Christmas Day ! All night heard the music of Tom-Toms, &c. Rise early, and the whole town and house bore the appearance of a masquerade. After Church, amuse myself very much with the strange processions, and figures called Johnny Canoes.† All dance, leap and play a thousand anticks. Then there are groups of dancing men

* Cornet J. Nixon, 20th Dragoons.
† An interesting account of John Canoe is given in Belisario's "Sketches of Character," (Kingston, 1837). This form of entertainment, which interested Monk Lewis in 1816, is now almost entirely fallen into disuse.

F

and women. They had a sort of leader or superior at their head, who sang a sort of recitative, and seemed to regulate all their proceedings ; the rest joining at intervals in the air and the chorus. The instrument to accompany the song was a rude sort of drum, made of bark leaves, on this they beat time with two sticks, while the singers do the same with their feet. Then there was a party of actors.—Then a little child was introduced, supposed to be a king, who stabbed all the rest. They told me that some of the children who appeared were to represent Tippoo Saib's children, and the man was Henry the 4th of France.—What a *mélange !* All were dressed very finely, and many of the blacks had really gold and silver fringe on their robes. After the tragedy, they all began dancing with the greatest glee.—We dined in the Council Chamber, but went to bed early, but not to rest, for the noise of singing and dancing was incessant during the night.—I must not omit to say, that Mr. Ward called. I gave him one of my catechisms for the blackies, and one to send to Mr. Wilberforce.

26*th*.—The same wild scenes acting over and over again.

27*th*.—The town very quiet.—To church at 10.—A particularly full congregation, and the heat excessive.—Colonel Gillespie, &c. and young Lake arrived ; the latter so like all his family ! Not more than twenty-one, and yet he looks thirty-one, so thin, pale, and wrinkled.—Dined at 5. Warwick Lake, the clergyman and his wife, &c. of our party.

28*th*.—The Christmas sports recommenced, and we don't like to drive out, or employ our servants in any way, for fear of interfering with their amusements. Poor things, we would not deprive them of one atom of their short-lived and baby-like pleasure.—The whole day, nothing but singing, dancing, and noise.—Dined in the ball-room, every thing in confusion. A bad dinner ; no servants to attend ; and I am sorry to say, more than half our family tipsy. Major Mosheim and young Lake did not seem quite so lenient

JOHN CANOE

about it as we were ; the former seemed to think that German discipline would be useful, and the latter that of the quarter-deck.

29th.—Sent young Lake back to Port Royal.

30th.—Drive to the Penn. Very busy all the morning after we returned.—Read Wilberforce, and have Cowper's Poems sent me by the Rev. Mr. Ward.

31st.—I packed up papers and books for the Penn, where we hope to dine to-day. This is the last day of the year, and I rejoice, as time passes, to think, that every day, now, will bring us, please God we live, nearer to dear England, and our domestic comfort there. I will begin the new year, at the Penn, by instructing the poor negroes, and if I do but succeed in making them the better understand their duties as Christians, I shall be happy indeed ; and I pray for a blessing on my efforts for that purpose.—Drive to the Penn, all the staff attending, at 2 o'clock.

CHAPTER II

JANUARY 1, 1802—DECEMBER 31, 1802

January 1st.—At 6 a party of singing men and women at our door, and all our servants, &c. dancing mad, I think. Give them a holiday.—Some of the staff come to breakfast, and another party to dinner, but left us early, and we went to bed at 8.—We have had no rain since the last week in November, but the heat is very supportable. The north wind blows furiously from 12 till 4 o'clock, and then dies away into a perfect calm, before the sun sets. The mornings and evenings are delightfully cool, and the nights so much so that we can bear a counterpane as well as a sheet upon our bed; but in the middle of the day it is very warm indeed, and if it were not for the sea breeze, would be almost intolerable. The sun is never under a cloud, but shines unremittingly, from half-past six in the morning till the same hour at night; but almost the instant the sun sets, the night comes on. No twilight, either in the morning or evening.—Received many compliments to-day, upon the new year, particularly from French people. Answer all in the best manner I can.

2nd.—A head-ache. General N. rode out, and then went to town, with the staff gentlemen that came to breakfast.—Spent the morning alone.—Some pan sugar also, from Mrs. Lewis. The new sugar is excellent, drank in cold water; and I like the pan sugar of all things.—Sent, in return, a purse to Mrs. Jones, and some wreaths of flowers to Mrs. Lewis's daughters. In short, all sorts of civilities have passed between us.—Our staff came to dine, and two of them remained to sleep at the Penn.

3rd.—Send the servants and all the family to church.—
General N. detained by business, and I staid with him.—
Write to Lord George Grenville, and send him some sketches
of Christmas gambols, and a view of our Penn.   Read with
dearest N. till dinner time.

4th.—Only two of the staff at breakfast, and they went
to town soon after.—Enjoyed looking over our little farm.
Two lambs born.   They were the sixth since we took the
Penn.   How prolific !—Many negroes came to make complaints of their masters.   It will be all investigated fairly,
so I shall make no remarks at present ; but it is a difficult
situation for a Governor.—Are invited by the Custos and
his lady for Twelfth Night.—Only a family party to-day.
Major Drummond, for the first time since his illness, and
means to remain.—Play cassino in the evening till 8.   The
gentlemen then go to town.—This day has been quite comfortable and rural, and I have enjoyed it beyond measure.
General N. and I walked out, and looked at our ducks,
chickens, &c. in the evening.

5th.—Our stud not arrived from Spanish Town, so we
walked in the veranda only till breakfast time.—Teach
Cupid (now George) part of his catechism.—Only Major
Codd in addition to our staff party.

7th.—Mr. Sandford Peacocke introduced at breakfast by
Mr. Cuthbert.

9th.—Find all the gentlemen in the breakfast-room, when
I make my appearance.—Afterwards hear Cupid and Bristol
their catechism.—Three of the staff staid to sleep.

10th.—To church at half-past nine.   A good sermon, but
the bats made such a loud chirping noise all the time, that
I could hardly hear any thing.—The heat was excessive.—
In the morning a carpenter, from Spanish Town, applied to
General N. to respite a slave, sentenced to be hanged to-
morrow.   The law of the land is, it seems, that three magistrates may condemn a slave to death.   This case was, that
two slaves, one, an old offender, the other, a boy of sixteen,
robbed a man of his watch, &c.   The old man shewed the

boy how to get in at the window, and gave him all his instructions, while he remained on the outside, and received
the things stolen.   The old man has been condemned to
hard labour, and the boy to be hanged.   General N. made
every exertion, but in vain, to save the life of the boy, and
send him out of the country ; but it appears that it could
not be done, without exercising his prerogative very far,
and giving great offence and alarm to the white population.
—This law of the three magistrates appears to me abomin-
able, but I am too little versed in such matters to do more
than feel for the poor sufferer.—Found to-day that we had
fourteen people at dinner, when the cook only expected a
very small party: poor man !—Mr. and Mrs. Woodham,
Mr. Corbet, Mr. Wakefield, Mr. Smith, Mr. Williams, Mr.
Parkinson, &c. were of the party.—Walked on the lawn
with Mrs. Woodham after dinner.

   11*th.*—Cupid and Bristol are almost perfect in their catechism.   Finish Addison on the Christian Religion, and have
been much gratified with the perusal.—Dine at 3 ; Colonel
Ainslie, Captain Maclean, and the staff, at dinner.—Settled
that Boisdabert's poor little negroes shall be sent to the
black corps, at Fort Augusta.   I rejoice at this, for they
would be starved if they returned to their impoverished
master.

   13*th.*—Study Wilberforce till breakfast time.—Colonel
Cookson, Captain Perkins, R.N. at breakfast, and remain
all day.

   14*th.*—A present from Mr. Hanson, of a peacock and two
hens.

   15*th.*—My dear N. went at 4 to review the militia at
Kingston.   All the staff, excepting Major Drummond, with
him.—Write, &c. till breakfast ; then Major and Mrs. Cookson, their two daughters, and a little boy, a black maid, and
two men, came on a West India visit, to spend the day.

Mrs. C. is a perfect Creole, says little, and drawls out that
little, and has not an idea beyond her own Penn.   Had
fruit for the children at 10 ; then second breakfast a little

after 11.—Dined at 3, and the hopeful family took their leave at 6.—General N., &c. returned at 12, and had evidently taken too much wine, but appeared perfectly well.

16th.—General N. complains a little of head-ache, but is not ill.—Plant some balsams.—Dine with our family party, at 3.

17th.—Send off a carriage to Port Henderson, for Captain Parker, R.N.—Go to church at 10. A good sermon, and the church less warm than usual. Spend an hour at the King's House ; then return, and meet a party at the Penn, at 3 ; Mr. and Mrs. Woodham, Messrs. Blake and Vidal of the 20th dragoons, Captain Parker, &c.

19th.—Despatches sent off to England, conveyed by Capt. Milne.—Drive out after dinner in the sociable ; Captain Parker with us. Visited Messrs. March and Hanson at their Penns.—Then tea, coffee and cards, and to bed at nine.

Just as we were taking leave for the night, came despatches from Lord Hobart, brought by the *Racoon* sloop of war. They were delightful ; and General N. has the satisfaction of finding that he has in every respect anticipated the wishes and orders of Government, on the subject of St. Domingo, even to the expressions to be made use of to General Toussaint, respecting the neutrality of England, &c. A large naval force is ordered out here, and General N.'s regiment (the 85th), is coming from Madeira, as well as some artillery, to reinforce us. So now we go to bed contented and happy in our minds. Mine, however, is merely a reflected happiness, in seeing my dear husband pleased ; otherwise, these warlike preparations make me tremble.

20th.—General N. drove Captain Parker, in the curricle, to Port Henderson, at 5.—The Speaker, Mr. Edwards,* &c. in the piazza, when I came out to breakfast.—Expect Sir J. T. Duckworth in a few days.

21st.—A cloudy morning, and an appearance of rain on

* J. P. Edwards, of Pusey Hall, member for Vere.

the mountains.—Receive a present of an immense quantity of peacock's feathers.—At dinner, a larger party than usual ; Messrs. Cross, Hanson, March, O'Farrell, &c.—Have coffee, cards, &c. till 8.   Only Captain Cross, of the 20th dragoons, remained.

22nd.—Begin Sketches in my Green Book.—A letter from Admiral Montagu, announcing the certainty of Sir J. Duckworth's coming to succeed him in the command.

23rd.—General N. off at 5, to fix upon the site for a new barrack at Stony Hill, and to arrange the quarters for the 85th regiment.   I did not get up, but found a note on my dressing table, from my dear N. with his good wishes, &c. as he expects to be absent the whole day.—Set all the blackies to scrape and clean all round the house, the lawn, &c.   Treated them with beef and punch, and never was there a happier set of people than they appear to be.   All day they have been singing odd songs, only interrupted by peals of laughter ; and indeed I must say, they have reason to be content, for they have many comforts and enjoyments. I only wish the poor Irish were half as well off.   Had a visit and a good long conversation with Mr. Ward to-day.

24th.—My dear N. being obliged to go to Fort Augusta to-day, we did not go to church.   Had prayers in the dining room for all the servants.   They behaved very devoutly.— Mr. Jennings and Mr. Bailey, from Fort Augusta, and old Grandjean, at dinner.

25th.—An English packet, and letters by Major Cameron at breakfast.—The Court of Chancery begins to-day.— Read, write, draw, and teach the blackies their catechism, from the time General N. went, till he sent a dragoon with my letters, at 2 o'clock—At 4 my poor N. came home, much exhausted, by attending to the long causes and the fatigues of Chancery.

26th.—General N. walked out with his gun at 6.   I sat in the piazza, and saw the sun rise most beautifully from behind the mountains.   Nothing, certainly, can exceed the beauty and enchanting scenery of this country.   Immense

GOVERNMENT PEN

mountains, covered with the thickest wood, of the most
lively green ; others, rocky, and looking quite blue. Then,
here and there, tufts of green upon their craggy and tremendous looking sides. Then, the fertile plains and plantations and penns, all mixed. When the sun first rises, all
this is particularly beautiful, for the mist is cleared away
gently, like a large transparent curtain, through which we
see the *silver* hills, and bright green woods, &c. The dew
is very heavy, and all the animals about the house seem to
enjoy the coolness of the ground in consequence, in the early
morning, though they are panting and appear miserable
with the heat, during the middle of the day, their mouths
open, and the poultry with their wings distended, all seek-
ing the shade.—General N. in Chancery again.—On returning to dinner, he presented Mr. Supple with the living of
St. Dorothy's, and means to name Mr. Ward for St. Ann's,
a much better living, vacant by the death of poor Mr.
Holmes, a young man, only a few months in the island.—
Heard of the arrival of Sir J. T. Duckworth. A salute
fired, &c.

27th.—A modest request from Mr. Peacocke, that General
N. would endorse a bill to the amount of more than £3000 !
His plea is, that, his brother having been General N.'s Aide-
de-camp in Ireland, he takes the liberty of a friend. *Decline
his proof of friendship.*

28th.—Have a correspondence to-day with the Rev. Mr.
Ward, on the subject of St. Ann's living, by General N.'s
desire. He is an excellent man, and, if possible, too con-
scientious.—Mr. Hinchcliffe, Mr. Affleck, &c. at dinner.

29th.—The Court of Chancery as usual, and every day for
a fortnight.—My day as usual, driving out, reading, writing,
and teaching the blackies.

30th.—I now bathe in cold water, and then write, &c.
some times *en chemise*, and this makes me cool and comfortable for the rest of the day.—It is quite wonderful how time
flies in this monotonous life, and I have scarcely hours
enough for my occupations.

February 1st.—Dress by candle-light, and set off for the race-course. General N., &c. on horseback; myself in the sociable. Took up three Spanish Town ladies on my way, Mrs. Hughes, and the Misses Rennalls; and asked others to breakfast.—General N. reviewed the Spanish Town militia, who performed exceedingly well, though it was ridiculous to hear the negroes, who were spectators, laugh at the Jew company when it fired, which it did very badly—" Now Massa Jew! Dat right! dat well, Massa Jew!" &c. All the officers of the militia breakfasted with General N. at the King's House, and a party of ladies with me at the Penn, and never was there any thing so completely stupid. All I could get out of them was, " Yes, ma'am—no, ma'am," with now and then a simper or a giggle. At last, I set them to work stringing beads, which is now one of my occupations; and was heartily glad when their carriages came at 2 o'clock. I also drove to the King's House, and sat listening to a cause in the Court of Chancery, between two slave merchants, and was not a little disgusted with some details that came out in evidence.—At half-past five all concluded, and we got home to dinner soon after 6.—Mr. Wickey, recommended by General Grenville to General N., dined with us. He is exactly like a man who has been buried and dug up again; so pale, lean, and miserable looking. Went to bed very tired.

2nd.—Captains Penrose and Walker, R.N. at breakfast. They staid almost the whole morning. Then came Mr. Spires, and Mr. Hardy with letters from Lord Longueville.

3rd.—General N. &c. went to Port Henderson, and brought Sir J. T. Duckworth, Captain Dunn, &c. to the Penn, to breakfast, a little after 7 o'clock.—General N. had much business about barracks, &c. with Captain Fraser, the island engineer, so that I am left to amuse the Navy men. Admiral Duckworth is as fond of early hours as we are, so we went to bed at 9 o'clock.

4th.—Dress by candle-light, at half-past five.—The

Admiral, &c. set off for Port Henderson, and we for Bushy
Park estate, Mr. Mitchell's, where we breakfasted in the
Creole style.—Cassada * cakes, chocolate, coffee, tea, fruits
of all sorts, pigeon pies, hams, tongues, rounds of beef, &c.
I only wonder there was no turtle.   Mr. M.'s delight is to
stuff his guests, and I should think it would be quite a triumph to him, to hear of a fever or apoplexy, in consequence
of his good cheer.   He is immensely rich, and told me he
paid £30,000 per annum for duties to Government.   His
house is truly Creole.   The wood-work mahogany—galleries, piazzas, porticoes, &c.   In front a cane-piece, and sugar
works, with plenty of cocoa-nut trees and tamarind trees,
&c.   He seems particularly indulgent to his negroes, and is,
I believe, although a very vulgar, yet a very humane man.
     After breakfast, set off to Spring Gardens, to review the
militia of St. John's parish and St. Dorothy's.   Spring
Gardens was formerly a fine place, but its owner now lives
in England, and the house and every thing are neglected.
The situation is beautiful.   I saw an immense fig-tree, with
a palm growing out of the top ; it had a most singular
appearance, but how the palm was engrafted, no one could
tell me.   The house has carved mahogany doors, &c. and
many remains of its former magnificence.
     On the lawn we found the regiments assembled, and spec-
tators of all colours crowding the place.   Kittareens,†
horses, and mules, in abundance, attending.—The whole review, in fact, was most funny.   Not one of the officers, nor
their men, knew at all what they were about, and each had

     * Or Cassava.
     † Kittereen—a kind of covered vehicle.   In the west of
England formerly applied to a kind of omnibus, and in the West
Indies to a one-horse chaise or buggy.   Gardner, in his " History
of Jamaica," states in error that it took its name from its being
made in Kettering.   The derivation from the car ran by Christopher (Kit) Treen between Penzance and Truro is also doubtful.
In Jamaica Lady Brassey, when she visited the island in 1883,
applied it to a vehicle something like the modern buggy, but
simpler in construction.

displayed his own taste, in the ornamental part of his dress. They were indeed a motley crew, and the Colonel whispered me—" Ah, ma'am, if the General did but know half the trouble I have had to draw up the men as you see them, he would not ask me to change their position ; for what they will do next I don't know. You see I have drawn a line with my cane for them to stand by, and it is a pity to remove them from it." Poor man ! I did pity him, for at the first word of command they stared, and then moved in every direction, and such a scene of confusion at any review I believe was never beheld.—A magnificent second breakfast, which succeeded this display, proved that, at Spring Gardens, the business of ménage, or eating and drinking, was better understood than military tactics.

After their repast, Colonel Ogilvy wished me to receive the thanks of the corps, for attending the review ; but I begged leave to decline the display, and as soon as possible we all returned to Bushy Park, where we arrived to rest ourselves about 4. Had a profuse dinner at 5.—Sick of so much eating and fatigue, and get rid of the remembrance of it all by going soundly to sleep at 9 o'clock.

I don't wonder now at the fever the people suffer from here—such eating and drinking I never saw ! Such loads of all sorts of high, rich, and seasoned things, and really gallons of wine and mixed liquors as they drink ! I observed some of the party, to-day, eat of late breakfasts, as if they had never eaten before—a dish of tea, another of coffee, a bumper of claret, another large one of hock-negus ; then Madeira, sangaree, hot and cold meat, stews and fries, hot and cold fish pickled and plain, peppers, ginger sweetmeats, acid fruit, sweet jellies—in short, it was all as astonishing as it was disgusting.

5*th*.—Do not feel the least fatigued to-day. Write my journal, &c. before breakfast. Soon after, some gentlemen of the *Sanspareil*, Mr. Lutwidge, and Mr. Ward arrive.— Write, and endeavour to console Mrs. Heslop, for her husband's dismissal from the army, and promise General N.'s assistance to herself, &c.

6th.—Not quite well early this morning, but meet Mr. Ward, &c. at breakfast, and at one we all set off to visit Sir John Duckworth on board the *Leviathan*. Find the boats waiting for us, and we were received with due honours. Before dinner, were shewn every part of the ship, and were delighted with the neatness and wonderful economy of the whole. A large party of Navy officers, &c. at dinner. Bring young Brooke home with us in the evening. The poor child was rejoiced to see me.

7th.—Made some visits in Spanish Town, and, when we returned to the Penn, found Capt. Campbell and Mr. Brown, just arrived from England. The latter brought letters from dear Lady Buckingham and Lady Temple, with some beautiful millinery as presents from Lord Buckingham, and from dear, kind Lady Temple. Our two new visitors, and the clergyman and his wife, the Rev. Mr. Harrison, &c. at dinner.

8th.—General N. off to review the militia of St. Thomas's Parish, at a very early hour.—Had no visitor this morning, but Mr. Sinclair, of the *Santa Margaretta*. Tried to make young Brooke read, and employ himself usefully. He is a sad Pickle, and keeps me in a constant fright, he is so mischievous and daring. Scold and laugh at him by turns. He seems affectionate, and I hope to lead him right at last.

10th.—Set off to-day for the parish of Clarendon. A large company was assembled at Mr. Israell's, to meet us.* The house is a long low building, with outside and inside very like a barn. A loaded table, and Mrs. Israel continually walking about the room, pressing every one to eat. There was a new fish, the Mountain Mullet, very small, but excellent, and having expressed my approbation, it was with great difficulty I escaped Mrs. Israell's intention to make me sick, by devouring the whole dish, or rather dishes, of marrow-like little fish. The conversation of the hostess was

* Joseph Israell was member for Clarendon. He owned Orange River.

not very interesting, but rather curious. The extent of Mrs. Israell's travels has been to Kingston, and she is always saying, "When I was in town;" she says too, that frost and snow must be prodigious odd things. The daughter has been brought up at the *Queen Square Boarding School*, and is much looked up to by her mamma; and she, in return, is in constant anxiety, for fear they should be guilty of some mistake, &c. This difference of education is, I think, a real and mutual misfortune.—About 8 began dancing. Broke the fiddle-strings. Poor Blackie was in despair, and so were some of the ladies. I rejoiced secretly, and we got to bed soon after nine.

11*th.*—Set off very early, to review the militia, at Walker's Inn. Mrs. Israell, her daughter, &c. with me, in the sociable. Mr. Israell, in his full uniform, with General N.; and Mrs. Israell talking of her husband as a great hero.—A large party of ladies, &c. at the Inn to receive me. Get to Mr. Osborne's (the Speaker), in Vere Parish, at 3 o'clock.—Mr. Ashley and Mr. Shaw the only strangers; but a large party in the house. Woods is the name of the place. Like all West India houses, it is neglected, and the grounds are wild. An excellent, but profuse dinner, as usual.—Heard such frightful stories of scorpions, that I lay awake half the night in terror of them.

12*th.*—Set off early for Pusey Hall, the estate of Mr. Edwards, and to review the Vere militia. The house is neat and comfortable, but the sugar works are so near, that, as this is crop time, we were much annoyed by the noise. After the review, had a profuse breakfast, and at 4, sat down to an immense dinner, with all the gentlemen of the militia, &c.—We then proceeded to Mrs. Sympson's estate, called Money Musk. Mrs. Sympson is a widow for the second time, and has an estate of ten or twelve thousand a year, which she manages entirely herself. They say she is an excellent planter, and understands the making of sugar, &c. to perfection. She has had many proposals, but finding all her admirers *interested*, she has wisely declined taking a

third husband. The widows Henckell and Bailey were staying with Mrs. Sympson. Alas! how often in this country
do we see these unfortunate beings! Women rarely lose
their health, but men as rarely keep theirs. May God protect my dear, dear husband! Returned with our cavalcade
to Woods, in the evening.—Annoyed sadly by musquitoes,
and my little protégé Brooke's face is terribly disfigured by
them. Captain Parker says his tough skin is proof against
their attacks, and, if so, it must be tough indeed.

13th.—Dress almost in the dark, intending to set off for
home, without disturbing the family; but find them all up,
and a fine breakfast prepared. Set off, as soon as possible
after, for Spanish Town. Arrived at 11 at Old Harbour Inn,
and have a second breakfast. We left our horses to be led
on, and proceeded with those provided for us, and arrived
at home a little after 4. Began dressing immediately, for
Mr. Cuthbert's dinner to Admiral Duckworth. Fortunately, the Admiral sent to say, that the sailing of the
packet on Monday would prevent his coming, so we sent
our excuses, and dined with only the staff, and got to bed
at 9. Heard this evening of the arrival of the 85th regiment
from Madeira.

14th.—Captain Parker took leave, for Port Royal, after
church.—Some officers of the 85th.—All the day, hurry and
bustle.—Poor General N. overwhelmed with business of all
sorts, and he must make a report on all subjects by the
packet that sails to-morrow. Feel for him, and make myself useful when I can; but alas! it is but little I can do to
assist him. Sent off the despatches by a dragoon at 6, and
then to dinner with some of the 85th, in addition to our
usual and Sunday dinner party.

15th.—General N. rode into Spanish Town before breakfast.—Sent a carriage to Port Henderson, for Colonel Gordon, Colonel Roberts, and some gentlemen of the Assembly,
and I had to talk all day, as General N. was much engaged
with business.—After dinner all went away, and we to bed
at eight.

G

16th.—Began to teach French to young Brooke. At dinner Colonel Gordon, Colonel Brisbane, Mr. Oliver Herring, Mr. Dobbin, and Captain Maclean. They all went at 8 ; and about 10 our repose was disturbed by a dragoon, with General N.'s letter-bag, as a packet had arrived.

17th.—Send carriages for the Admiral, &c. to Port Henderson. We had a very pleasant party at breakfast, both civil and military.—Mr. Ward called to take leave for England.—Major Aston, &c.—After dinner, General N. and I drove out with little Brooke, leaving the rest of the party to take their coffee : called upon Dr. Lind, to consult him about my health, which has of late been a little deranged, and I have lost my appetite ; we were afraid that the climate had seized upon me, but Dr. Lind says, that I shall probably be quite well in time, and that I had better take no medicines, but leave myself to nature. The moon shone delightfully as we returned. Nothing could be more beautiful than the evening.

18th.—General N. off before day, to review the troops in Kingston and St. Andrews.—Not well all day.—Only a small dinner party.—Despatches from St. Domingo, at 7.— General N. returned at 9, and opened them. The French have landed 20,000 men, and the consequence is just what General N. predicted. The whites have all been taken into the mountains. Many of them were dragged there, bound hand and foot.—Cape François, &c. have been burnt ; in short, it seems Toussaint's plan to distress the French as much as possible, by burning the towns, and harassing them from the woods and mountains, where the blacks have already taken refuge. How dreadful a business it is altogether ; and, indeed, it makes one shudder, to think of the horrible bloodshed and misery that must take place, before any thing can be at all settled in that wretched island. Poor dear N. was sadly hurt at all this news, and was also greatly fatigued, having, in addition to reviewing the Kingston and St. Andrew's regiments, seen his own corps, the 85th, at Stony Hill. The staff are not only astonished at the fatigue he undergoes, but those who attend him are not a little alarmed for themselves ; though many of them go in kittareens, &c. when he rides.

19th.—Mr. Carthew, once Secretary to Mr. Pitt, and Mr. Bogle, came to breakfast. General N. went with them to the King's House, and swore in Mr. Carthew as Collector of the Customs at Kingston. Major Drummond and I copied the French despatches, and General N. made his Report to-day, upon the subject of St. Domingo ; all of which is to go by the *Raven* sloop-of-war to England to-morrow.—Mr. Sherriff, Mr. V., Mr. Bogle, and Mr. Carthew, all at dinner.—A large party.

20th.—For a wonder only ourselves at breakfast.—General N. then settled barrack business with Captain Fraser.—He had next the disagreeable task of announcing to Colonel Ainslie and Major Forsyth, the Duke of York's commands, that they should leave the service. He feels this disagreeable and painful business very much. However, by every account it appears that they have merited the severity shewn them, and so he must endeavour not to think of it. At dinner Mr. and Mrs. Herring, Doctor, Mrs. and the three Misses Rennalls, Miss Hanson, Mr. and Mrs. Roden, Mrs. and the three Misses Lewis, Colonel Brisbane, and Colonel Roberts, which, with our own family, amounted to nearly thirty.

21st.—Not well. Have the Psalms and Prayers read at home.—General N. not at all comfortable, and very anxious about St. Domingo, &c.—Mr. Corbet, &c. on business the greatest part of the day.—At 3, Mr. and Mrs. Woodham, Mr. Corbet, &c. at dinner, and we were glad to get rid of all, and to bed at eight.

22nd.—Alone with little Brooke.—General N. off at 4, to review the Port Royal militia, to consult with the Admiral, &c.—Poorly all day.—Gave French and English lessons to Brooke.—General N. came home, thank God, quite well, notwithstanding all the fatigues of the morning ; for he went to Fort Augusta and saw a detachment of the

85th there.—At dinner we were shocked to hear of a mutiny on board the *Seine* frigate, and ten mutineers to be tried immediately. What a dreadful thing to think that these poor creatures may so soon be sent out of this world, with all their sins upon their heads ! I thank God that I am not a man, to run either the risk of such offences against society, or the being obliged to pass sentence upon them.

23rd.—The carriages sent to bring the Admiral, young Baker, Colonel Brisbane, and Major Otway, 85th, to dinner.

24th.—Dress by candle-light, and set off, with an immense party and cavalcade, for the Walks,* and New Hall (Mr. Mitchell's) four miles beyond Spanish Town. We entered the Walks, which is really the most romantic, beautiful, and picturesque road I ever saw or could imagine. The road winds along the side of a mountain, very narrow, and, excepting in a few places, excavated in the rock ; only room for a carriage. There is a precipice on one side, and the rocky mountain hanging over your head as you pass on. At the bottom of the precipice is a clear, beautiful, and rapid river, and, on the other side, another high mountain rises almost perpendicular, covered with trees and shrubs. In some places the road was really awfully beautiful ; the height of the mountains, on each side, throwing a very dark shade, and entirely excluding the sun, and almost the light. Then the roar of the river beneath, which was quite sublime. In some places, large fragments of rock, which had rolled down the precipice with the trees and shrubs upon them, looked like islands. We were all in curricles, gigs, or kittareens, or I don't know how we should have got on, the road was so narrow in many places.

About half way through the walk, which is six miles long, there is a most beautiful but tremendous bridge to pass, composed of logs and earth, and without railings or defence of any sort. Just after you cross the bridge, the mountains take a different form. They are exactly perpendicular, with the trees growing as it were out of the rock, for

* Now called Bog Walk.

you scarcely see a vestige of earth. The road then runs
down close to the roaring river, winding most beautifully,
and the rocks, &c. projecting at different intervals, that I
almost fancied the horses' heads would come against a rock,
and we should find ourselves quite shut in.

We arrived at Mr. Mitchell's Penn before 9, and, after
eating an abundant *creole* breakfast, set off for the sugar
works. Sir J. Duckworth, Mr. Mitchell and myself, were
in a carriage. General N. and suite on horseback.—We
then examined the whole process of sugar making, which is
indeed very curious and entertaining. The mill is turned
by water, and the cane, being put in on one side, comes out
in a moment on the other, quite like a dry pith, so rapidly
is all the sweet juice expressed, passing between two cylin-
ders, turning round contrary ways. You then see the juice
running through a great gutter, which conveys it to the
boiling-house. There are always four negroes stuffing in
the canes, while others are employed continually in bringing
great bundles of them.—Then after the juice is expressed,
the pithy stuff, which is called trash, is conveyed to a place
below the boiling-house, to keep the fire going constantly.
In the boiling-house there are nine cauldrons ; three of
them merely simmer the sugar. This throws up all scum
and useless particles to the top of the cauldron. The pure
liquor then runs into the first boiling cauldron, and so is
conveyed to another, till it granulates. After that, it is
carried by a large gutter into a large trough, called a cooler,
from whence the negroes take it in pails-full, and put it into
the hogsheads, and so ends the process. Those casks, however, have holes bored at the bottom, and, being on stands,
the coarsest part, called molasses, runs through, and is used
in the distilling of the rum. Four negroes attend the mill ;
two put in the cane, one receives the dry cane, and throws
it into the trash house, and there is always one attending
to see that all is right and done well. At each cauldron in
the boiling-house was a man, with a large skimmer upon a
long pole, constantly stirring the sugar, and throwing it

from one cauldron to another. The man at the last cauldron called continually to those below, attending the fire,
to throw on more trash, &c. ; for if the heat relaxes in the
least, all the sugar in the cauldron is spoiled. Then there
were several negroes employed in putting the sugar into the
hogsheads. I asked the overseer how often his people were
relieved. He said every twelve hours ; but how dreadful
to think of their standing twelve hours over a boiling cauldron, and doing the same thing ; and he owned to me that
sometimes they did fall asleep, and get their poor fingers
into the mill ; and he shewed me a hatchet, that was always
ready to sever the whole limb, as the only means of saving
the poor sufferer's life ! I would not have a sugar estate
for the world !

After this, we went to the distillery, but this I cannot so
ь. 'll describe ; but it seems that the molasses and dirty part
of the sugar ferments, and, after passing through fire and
under water, in a long tube, it becomes a strong spirit.
They have a sort of glass bead, by which they try the
strength of the spirit, but I could not comprehend that part
of it ; and the smell of the dunder, as it is called, made me
so sick, I could not stay to make a minute enquiry.

Returned to New Hall about 2 o'clock, drank the juice
of a common orange and a Seville orange mixed, which is
very refreshing, and then laid down to rest till dressing time.
Find after all, that I have only half-an-hour, and therefore
merely make a little change, and join the gentlemen at
dinner. It is wonderful the attention that is paid me, and
the care that is taken of me ; all I say and do is perfection,
for I am the only woman ! Not well at dinner, and the
loads of hot meats, &c. were disgusting. Every man was
on the alert to serve me ; laugh it all off, and get into the
carriage with great glee that is to carry us home to-night,
upon a perilous journey back, through the beautiful Six
Miles Walk.—Invited to a Jew's wedding, but, after a little
debate, agree that it is better to drive through Spanish
Town to the Penn, and promise ourselves to attend the next.

25th.—Admiral Duckworth, young Baker, &c. off at 6. On parting, the Admiral made very fine speeches, and said this was a Paradise, and General N. and I were the Adam and Eve of it, we were so happy and so much in love with each other ! ! At dinner, Colonel Ramsay, R.A., Major Stehelin, Major Cookson, Captain Hardy, Mr. Supple, and Mr. Bruce, who has come on a visit of a few days.—Walk after dinner, with the *boys* of the party, and play cassino with them after the visitors go away.

26th.—General N. in town, immediately after breakfast. Sick, and lie on the sopha, pretending to the boys to read all the morning—Meredith, Brown, and Brooke.

27th.—General N. and I on horseback soon after 5. In the hedges we saw clusters of the red (Liquorice) beads, sold in the jewellers' shops in England. They grow on a sort of vine, and are in pods like peas, and spread over the trees in great clusters, looking beautiful. General N., to please me, plucked them as we passed through the lanes, and filled his pockets with them ; but when we came home, he was covered with black ants, and really tortured with them, and obliged to change every thing before breakfast.

March 1st.—Captain Garth of the *Tartar*, with despatches, from the Governor of Cuba, for General N.—To-day I made the boys string beads, instead of teaching them any thing, I was so very poorly.

2nd.—General N. in town early, to swear in Custom House officers, &c.—Send away all our young friends, preparatory to our tour.—Send the carriage for Sir J. Duckworth, Captains Dunn, Walker, and Garth. Have also Captain and Mrs. Elrington, and Captain and Mrs. Davis, 69th regiment, the Attorney-General, Mr. Bullock, Mr. Campbell, &c. at dinner.—Walked in the garden with the two ladies, and all took their leave at 8 o'clock. Then came Mr. Douglas ; have refreshments for him, and hear all his St. Domingo news, &c.

3rd.—Mr. Douglas left us after breakfast.—Employed all the morning in giving orders for our tour round the island.

—Captains Maitland and Munro* of the 85th regiment, with Major and Mrs. Pye, at dinner.

4th.—Don't feel well, but see Baptiste, Hallam the butler, &c. and make all proper arrangements, previous to leaving home.—Mr. Drummond, of the second West India regiment, at dinner. Retire early, for to-morrow we begin our grand tour. Only sorry I am so very complaining, and feel so unequal to all exertion ; but I will do my best, and be as merry as I can.

5th.—After an immense fuss, hurry, and bustle, we started from the Penn at half-past two o'clock, with an enormous cavalcade ; carriages, horses, sumpter mules, &c. &c. Detained by business at the King's House, for an hour. Then, delayed by various difficulties, on the road ; but we arrived all safe, and in high preservation, at Mr. Simon Taylor's in Liguanea.† As there were merely gentlemen of the party, I only brushed the dust off, and went down to dinner at 7 o'clock, they no doubt thinking me very smart. A most profuse and overloaded table, and a shoulder of wild boar stewed, with forced meat, &c. as an ornament to the centre of the table. Sick as it all made me, I laughed like a ninny, and all the party thought me the most gay and agreeable lady they had ever met with, and Mr. Simon Taylor and I became the greatest friends. When I left the gentlemen, I took tea in my own room, surrounded by the black, brown and yellow ladies of the house, and heard a great deal of its private history. Mr. Taylor is the richest man in the island, and piques himself upon making his nephew, Sir Simon Taylor, who is now in Germany, the richest Commoner in England, which he says he shall be, at *his* death.—Did not return to the gentlemen, but went to bed as soon as my coloured friends left me.

6th.—Breakfast at 6, and start for Albion,‡ another place

* Lady Nugent misspells it Monro.

† Now called Vale Royal, the property of the Rev. H. Scotland, not far from King's House.

‡ A well-known sugar estate, whence Albion sugar takes its name, as white vacuum pan sugar was first made at this estate somewhere about 1870.

MARCH   ALBION   89

of Mr. S. Taylor's. Leave my dear N. at Rock Fort, to
review the Yallahs and Bull Bay Companies of Militia, as
well as to view the Fort. At Albion I found a large party
of gentlemen assembled.—General N. came about 3. We
dined at 5. I tried to taste the brawn, but it made me
sicker than ever.—The road this day was beautiful, but tremendous. Steep rocky roads, rivers to ford, high rocky
hills to pass over, thick woods for the carriage to be dragged
through, aloes and a variety of beautiful plants and shrubs
in full bloom, and innumerable parties of negroes, laughing,
dancing, and singing, and dressing their food on the road-
side, and all hurrying to get to Kingston ; for, alas ! Sunday
is the great market day. It is a sad custom, but I fear
difficult to reform or alter in any way. After giving audience to the coloured ladies, went to bed at nine.

7th.—Reading our books, and dearest N. with me.—Then
set off at 7 for the Speaker's. First go to Cow Harbour, and
see a small fort there ; then, after a most delightful drive,
something the same as yesterday, only more majestic and
awful, fording large rivers, &c. we arrived at Montpellier,*
where there was a large party assembled.—Mr. Robinson
and Mr. Milner were the only two gentlemen new to me.

The house is most delightfully situated, on a little mountain, and in front is the sea. Behind are mountains rising
above mountains, and the famous Blue Mountains in the
distance. Beautiful trees and shrubs round the house. In
short, it is altogether indescribably beautiful.

I went to my own room, and lay down to read, as usual.
My favourite book just now is Dodd's Reflections upon
Death.† On asking Johnson (who is deaf), for it, she said,
" Pink or blue to-day, ma'am," thinking of my shoes, as
always being the colour of my dress.—Dinner, Creole-
French, and very good ; but I was very sick, and wished

* Originally settled and named by Peter Vallette, a French
Huguenot, about 1736-7.

† First published in 1763, frequently reprinted till 1822. The
author was hanged for forgery in 1777.

myself in bed, where I soon was, after giving audience, as usual, to the coloured ladies, while I took my tea, and leaving the gentlemen to their cigars, &c. for which, I am sure, they were much obliged to me.

8th.—Write my Journal before we breakfasted ; set out to review the St. Thomas in the East, Yallahs and Morant Companies of Militia, at Belvidere. The Speaker drove me in his curricle—The rest of the party were on horseback. After the review, we all went to a place called Licence,* another estate of Mr. Taylor's.—The situation is high, and the view magnificent.—The musquitoes tormenting !—An immense party at dinner.—My usual levee of coloured ladies. One told me she was twenty-four years old, and shewed me her grand-child. I found afterwards that she was fifty-four ; but they have no idea of time or distance. They reckon the one by the number of Christmas masquerades they can recollect, and for the other they have no scale. If you ask how far to such a place, they will say, " two or tree mile," if it should be twelve or fourteen. If it exceeds that, they say, " far enough, massa," or " too far, massa."

9th.—Devoured by musquitoes all night.—Set off for Bath immediately after breakfast, with an immense cavalcade of gentlemen on horseback, or in kittareens, sulkies, &c. &c. in addition to our own party. Stopped at Mr Baillie's Penn,† just above Morant Bay. General N. &c. crossed over to see a fort and block-house, and I proceeded, with the rest of the party, to Bath. A most beautiful and romantic drive over mountains, on the ledges of precipices, through fertile vallies, &c.—Bath is truly a lovely village,

* Or Lyssons. Simon Taylor and Sir John Taylor, Bart., his brother, are buried there. The great house was destroyed by fire shortly before the Morant Bay Outbreak of 1865.

† The site of the present Court-house. The original Court-house was burnt down in the rebellion of 1865. Morant Bay was first named Freeman's Bay, by the owner, Thomas Freeman. Peter Vallette, who first laid it out as a town, called it Peterborough.

at the bottom of an immense mountain. The houses are surrounded with gardens and cocoa-nut trees, and there is an immense row of cotton trees in front, most magnificent, and like our finest oaks. General N. came at 4.—Dined at 6.—Mr. Cuthbert and Mr. Chief Justice are here, for drinking the waters. They joined our party, and drank punch made of the Bath stream. I tasted it, and it is sickly, nauseous stuff.—To bed before ten.

10th.—Up at 5.—Set off on horseback, in my night-cap, dressing gown, and pokey bonnet, with General N. and a party of gentlemen. The road is the most beautiful thing I ever saw, narrow, and winding for two or three miles up a mountain. A dreadful precipice is on one side, at the bottom of which runs a river ; but bamboos, &c. growing thickly up the sides of the mountain, lessened one's fears for the narrowness and height of the road.

The bathing-house is a low West India building, containing four small rooms, in each of which there is a marble bath. Then there is another house for infirm negroes, &c. In fact, a kind of public hospital with baths, and they tell you of wonderful cures performed by the waters. I drank a glass of it first, which was really so warm, that it almost scalded my throat. I then went in for twenty minutes, and had the heat increased till I got familiarized to the bath, which I really found most delightful and refreshing. I must, however, mention an adventure of the Governor's Lady. The old woman attending the bath was very anxious to see her, but her pokey bonnet covered her face, and her dressing-gown concealed her person ; but as the lady was stepping out of the bath, in a perfectly undisguised state, she heard a voice near her, and perceived, under the door, a pair of black eyes, and indeed a whole black face, looking earnestly at her ; for the door was half a yard too short, and the old woman's petticoat had been applied to the breach ; this she had slyly removed, and laid herself down on her stomach to peep. The Governor's Lady gave a great squall, and away ran the old woman.

After I came out of the bath, I drank another glass, and

then proceeded down the mountain, at the bottom of which
is a botanical garden.   We rode, and were really much gratified, in seeing the variety of plants, shrubs, and trees, all
so new to an European eye.   The bread-fruit, cabbage tree,
jack-fruit, cinnamon, &c. were in great perfection ; as like-
wise were the sago, and in short a number of beautiful
shrubs I can't describe, and some of them as curious and
extraordinary as they are beautiful.—The leaf of the Star
Apple-tree is like gold on one side, and bright green on the
other.   Another tree, the name of which I can't recollect,
was purple on one side, and also green on the other.   The
Otaheite apple is a beautiful tree, bearing a bright pink
blossom, like a tassel ; but it is impossible for me to describe all the beautiful plants I saw.   Besides, we were
obliged to hurry home, a shower of rain coming on, which
prevented our beginning our journey till 10 o'clock, when
we proceeded to Golden Grove, another estate of Mr. Simon
Taylor's.   I cannot here avoid mentioning, that Mr. Taylor
is an old bachelor, and detests the society of women, but I
have worked a reform, for he never leaves me an instant,
and attends to all my wants and wishes.   He recollects
what I have once commended, and is sure to have it for me
again.   Every one of the party is astonished at this change ;
but I believe he takes me for a boy, as I constantly wear
a habit, and have a short cropped head.

   The road to-day was bad and intricate, so that we were
obliged to have a guide to Golden Grove.   After fording
Sulphur and the Devil's River, we arrived safe there.   It is
an excellent house, surrounded by sugar works, cocoa-nut
trees, &c.   We drove up just at the dinner hour of the
negroes.   Never in my life did I see such a number of black
faces together.   We went into the sugar works, ate sugar,
talked to the negroes, &c. ; but another shower of rain
coming on, obliged us to go to our own apartments.   I put
on my dressing-gown, and attempted to rest, but was every
instant interrupted by mulatto ladies, with one curiosity or
another in the eating way.   A conch was first brought to
me.   It was a delicate white on the outside, and a beautiful

pink in the inside.   It was just caught, and the women told me that they put a little fire to the shell, and it instantly left its dwelling, poor little fish.   A turtle, and several curious fish, were also introduced for my inspection.   So, as I found I could get no rest, and was uncommonly well after bathing this morning, I dressed, and walked about the house till dinner time.   A little mulatto girl was sent into the drawing-room to amuse me.   She was a sickly delicate child, with straight light-brown hair, and very black eyes. Mr. T. appeared very anxious for me to dismiss her, and in the evening, the housekeeper told me she was his own daughter, and that he had a numerous family, some almost on every one of his estates.   The housekeeper's name was Nelly Nugent.   She told me that her father was a Mr. Nugent, from Ireland, who had been some years ago upon that estate.   She of course considers herself a connection of ours, and we were consequently well acquainted in a short time.—Our dinner, at 5, was even more profuse than usual. A great variety of fish, barbacued hog, fried conchs, &c. ; in short, I can't recollect half the strange dishes—but I tasted of a great many, and particularly of the black crab pepper-pod [pepper-pot], which was very good indeed.*

According to usual custom, when I went to my bed-room, I was surrounded by all the mulatto ladies the neighbour-hood afforded.   One little black girl came to beg that I would take her with me.   She was a remarkably thick-lipped and ugly, but intelligent child.   She could say the Lord's Prayer perfectly, but could not tell how she had learnt it ; both her father and mother are field negroes, and neither of them can say their prayers.—This led me to talk of the field negroes, with my friend Nelly Nugent, who told me that Saturday and Sunday were allowed them to work in their own gardens, and to raise provisions for themselves. The smallest children are employed in the field, weeding and picking the canes ; for which purpose they are taken from their mothers at a very early age.   Women with child work

* Black crab is one of the delicacies of Jamaica, others being ring-tailed pigeon, calipever and mountain mullet.

in the fields till the last six weeks, and are at work there again in a fortnight after their confinement. Three weeks in very particular cases are allowed, but this is the very longest time. Nelly Nugent remarked, however, that it was astonishing how fast these black women bred, what healthy children they had, and how soon they recovered after lying-in. She said it was totally different with mulatto women, who were constantly liable to miscarry, and subject to a thousand little complaints, colds, coughs, &c. Indeed, I have heard medical men make the same observation.—Soon after 9, the gentlemen began to smoke. General N. left them, and we went to bed.

11th.—General N. &c. &c. set off at 5, for Rocky Point. I wrote and amused myself till 9, when they all returned to breakfast.—The Speaker is quite ill to-day. I don't wonder at it, for he eats so enormously, that it is impossible he should escape indigestion.—Soon after breakfast we went to another estate of Mr. Taylor's, a few miles from Golden Grove, called Holland,* where we found a profuse second breakfast prepared for us. Visited the sugar works, &c. The house is a good one, but the situation is low and damp, and I should think not healthy. The negro-houses are extremely pretty. All neatly built on the borders of Plantain Garden River, and innumerable cocoa-nut trees are mixed with the gardens and houses.

Return to Golden Grove at 3, and half-an-hour after set out for the Moro, Mr. Scott's, of the Privy Council. I went in Mr. Taylor's carriage to the bottom of the hill. We then all mounted our horses, and for two or three miles clambered up a steep road, with a precipice on one side, really frightful, which almost terrified me out of my little wits ; but I made up my mind there was no danger, being mounted on an old quiet horse of Mr. Scott's, that travelled up and down the hill every day, and was perfectly acquainted with all the difficulties of the road. The Moro † is a good house, situated on the pinnacle of a mountain. You can't go ten

* Taylor had given £100,000 sterling for this estate.
† Moro formed part of Hordley Estate.

MARCH   GOLDEN GROVE   95

yards from the door, without descending ; but the view is
really charming.   In front you see a rich vale, full of sugar
estates, the works of which look like so many little villages,
and the soft bright green of the canes, from this height,
seems like velvet. The Guinea-corn fields make a variety
in the green, and the canes that are cut are of a brownish
hue ; which, with the cocoa-nut and other trees, make a
delightfully varied carpet.   Plantain-Garden River runs
through the whole, and loses itself in the sea, at the bottom
of the vale.   On the other side of the vale, hills rise over
hills, some clothed in wood, some in canes, and all have
small settlements here and there.   Then, the rest of the
view, as far as the eye can reach, is all sea ; and as there
are many shoals and rocks, on this part of the coast, you
see it constantly foaming over them.   There is, however, a
good harbour, at Rocky Point, for vessels to come up and
take the sugars from the several estates, which are carried
down Plantain-Garden River in boats.

Our dinner, at 6, was really so profuse, that it is worth
describing.   The first course was entirely of fish, excepting
jerked hog, in the centre, which is the way of dressing it by
the Maroons.   There was also a black crab pepper-pot, for
which I asked the receipt.—It is as follows ; a capon stewed
down, a large piece of beef and another of ham, also stewed
to a jelly ; then six dozen of land crabs, picked fine, with
their eggs and fat, onions, peppers, ochra, sweet herbs, and
other vegetables of the country, cut small ; and this, well
stewed, makes black crab pepper-pot.—The second course
was of turtle, mutton, beef, turkey, goose, ducks, chickens,
capons, ham, tongue, crab patties, &c. &c. &c.—The third
course was composed of sweets and fruits of all kinds.—I
was really sicker than usual, at seeing such a profusion of
eatables, and rejoiced to get to my own room, and, after my
usual levee of black and brown ladies, to go to bed.—I pitied
poor Mr. Osborne, he was in the situation of Tantalus, and
obliged, among all the good and savoury things, to dine
merely on the wing of a boiled turkey.

12th.—Up at 6—Wrote my journal, and soon after break-

fast the whole party set off on horseback for Amity Hall,
our carriages were sent round to meet us, by a different
road. After ascending a very high hill, the view was lovely ;
but, as it was only a more clear and full one than that from
the Moro, I shall not describe it. Staid half-an-hour at
Amity Hall, then joined our carriages at the bottom of
Featherbed Hill, where we took leave of our good friend,
Mr. S. Taylor, and of Mr. Scott ; the rest of the party proceeding with us to Merton, the estate of Mr. Bryan.   When
I expressed my regret at parting with Mr. Simon Taylor, he
said, " I am very sorry, too, Ma'am, but good Almighty
God, I must go home and cool coppers."   I thought really
he was going home, to have all the large brass pans emptied
to cool, that I had seen the sugar boiling in, and that it was
part of the process of sugar making ; but I found he meant
that he must go home, and be abstemious, after so much
feasting.

The road to-day was beautifully romantic, but tremendous.   Merton is an excellent house, and delightfully situated, having a fine view of the sea, and Manchineal Harbour.
It does not stand above ten yards from the edge of a precipice. Mr. Bryan is in England, but his agent, Mr. Milner,
received us.   Salutes were fired from the block-house, and
the ships in the harbour.—I walked about the lawn, and
talked to the negro children, who were weeding, superin-
tended by an old woman.   I gave them a little money, and
this brought almost all the negroes of the estate about us ;
for I found that the works were stopped, and the negroes
had been given a holiday in consequence of our arrival.
Poor creatures, they seemed much pleased, and talked a
great deal, but I could scarcely understand a word they said.
General N. returned, and we sat down to dinner, profuse as
usual, at half-past six.   I was glad to get to bed as soon as
possible after.

13th.—Breakfast before 8, and then set off for Castle
Comfort, the estate of Mr. Jones. Mr. Orr received us,
with a large party of gentlemen of the country, and the
Members for the Parish, as usual. The road frightfully

beautiful !—Had a sumptuous second breakfast, and walked about after, till the carriages were ready. Saw a most beautiful tree, called the Scarlet Bean. It is like a large coquilecot-geranium ; for the leaves fall off as soon as the flowers make their appearance. The floor of one of the rooms in the house particularly struck me. It was of zebra wood, the ground like satin wood, the stripes mahogany colour, and all so polished that it was quite dangerous to walk upon.

At 3 set off for the senior Mr. Bryan's estate, called the Bog, a mile beyond Port Antonio. The road was very hilly and rocky, but, as usual, extremely picturesque. I counted thirteen gentlemen on horseback, who had joined our party. These, with our former friends, servants, sumpter mules, &c. formed an immense cavalcade. At Port Antonio, the whole neighbourhood was assembled to stare at us. A salute was fired from the ships in the harbour, and the Fort saluted also as soon as we entered the town ; where we were met by several officers of the 60th regiment, quartered there. The guns happened to be particularly near, which put our horses in a fright. Off they set, the rest of the party, sump- ter mules, &c. joined in the scamper, and we went through the place as if we were mad ; turning over the old women's baskets, and knocking down every thing in our way. I felt in a sad fuss, but, fortunately, our horses were stopped a short distance from the town, and all arrived safe at Mr. Bryan's at half-past six. We were received by him, and a Mr. and Mrs. Cosens. Mrs. Cosens is the first white woman, except my maid, that I have seen since we began our jour- ney.—At 8 we had a dinner, in the usual style of plenty, and we went to bed as early as we could, heartily fatigued with the day's journey.

14th.—General N. set off at 4, to see a settlement of the Maroons, called Moortown.*—I breakfasted at 8, with the family here, and a small party. After breakfast, converse

* In 1805 there were maroons as under—Charles Town, 256 ; Moore Town, 318 ; Scot's Hall, 50 ; Accompong, 198. Total, 822.

H

a good deal with Mrs. Cosens, who appears a very pleasing young woman.

The situation of this house is beautiful, but it is very odd and looks dark and gloomy. All the others we have been at were painted and newly done up, for our reception, while this is dirty and comfortless ; but, as they have taken great pains to mend our roads, and seem particularly anxious for our accommodation, we ought not to complain of slight inconvenience. Every one appeared here in a bustle, nothing but running in and out ; the old gentleman himself, I believe, intended to dress the dinner, for I have seen him constantly going into the kitchen, or cook-room, as it is called in this country. The idea of making so much fuss, and giving so much trouble, disturbs my repose.

Feel uncomfortable about poor little Cupid, who was sadly hurt yesterday by a vicious mule ; he is, however, better to-day.—General N. did not return till near 8 o'clock. —A feast had been given him by the Maroons, of jerked and barbecued hog, plantains, yams, &c. After that there was one dance, and then their war exercise concluded the fete. We sat down an immense party, between 8 and 9. To bed at twelve.

15th.—At 5, General N. went to review the battalion of the 60th regiment, at Port Antonio, to inspect their barracks, &c. A second edition of salutes and firing.—I breakfasted with the party here, and, immediately after, we all set off on horseback, to see the review of the Portland Militia, a little beyond Port Antonio, where we were joined by General N. and his cavalcade. A tent was prepared for us, with fruit, wine, &c. I had my saddle changed, and put on a beautiful grey horse, belonging to an officer of the 60th regiment ; and, after the review, I rode it back to Mr. Bryan's, to which we were attended by an immense number of gentlemen on horseback, and sat down, a large party, to a second breakfast at 2 o'clock. I liked my little horse so well, that General N. paid a hundred pounds for him, and sent him to the stable immediately.

Notwithstanding the fatigues of the morning, my dear N.

was obliged to go, at 4 o'clock, to dine at Port Antonio,
with the officers of the militia.   I dined with a small party
of about twenty-two people.—After dinner, had a conversation upon religion.   Some of the opinions of the gentlemen were shocking.   Not one professed to have the least
religion, and some said it was all a farce.   I took courage,
and expressed my disapprobation.   This brought some
awkward apologies, and so ended the conversation.

   16th.—Breakfast at 8 ; a very large party.—Mr. Sherriff,
Member for St. George's, and some gentlemen of that
parish, came to advise us to proceed immediately on our
journey, as much rain had fallen in the mountains, and
there was a prospect of more ; which, in all probability,
would render the rivers impassable before the next morning.   We therefore sent our excuses to the 60th regiment,
with whom we were to have dined, and set off, at about 11,
for the parish of St. George.   The speaker and Mr. Edwards,
&c. took their leave, and we proceeded, with almost an
entire new party, to an estate of Mr. Shirley's, called Spring
Gardens.—My little attendant, Cupid, much better, and
able to attend us.

   I rode the first four or five miles, the roads being very
bad, and remarkably narrow, and winding on the edge of a
frightful precipice ; but, to the astonishment of all, General
N. drove the curricle the whole way.   At the River Grande*
I was obliged to get into the carriage, and we forded it extremely well ; but it was very deep, and I trembled the
whole time.   Then we had hills to mount, and the sea shore
to encounter, with the waves dashing against our horses'
feet, till we arrived at Swift River, which was so deep, that
boats were in waiting for us ; but General N. preferred
fording it, so we sent a black man on, to wade through before us, and we got over safe ; though, as everything was
wet through, my gingerbread nuts were spoiled.   They
were a *delicate* attention of Mr. Simon Taylor's, and the only
thing that relieved my sickness.—Again we had sea-shore,
mountains, precipices, and sloughs, till we came to Spanish

   * Generally called Rio Grande.

River. After that the road improved, till we got to Spring Gardens, though it was still very hilly and rocky. It seems the roads being so very bad was owing to our being a few days sooner than we were expected ; though there were hundreds of negroes at work, they could not clear away or mend half the bad places. Got to Spring Gardens about 6 ; my maid did not arrive till near 7, which alarmed me very much. Went to dinner about 8, very, very sick, and more so than usual, from the fright and fatigue of the day.—Had a light all night, and was so unwell that I could not sleep at all.

17th.—Did not get up till 7.—Mr. Fitzgerald, and Mr. Murphy and Mr. C. Grant, the two members for St. Mary's, came to join our party.—General N. full of business till 2. He and I then took a walk in the garden, which is an excellent one, and kept in very good order. Saw a great number of curious trees and plants, amongst which were the chocolate-tree, &c. &c. I found five or six strawberries, some roses, and a variety of beautiful flowers.—Dined at 6, with a very large party.

This house is a very good one, placed at the top of a hill, at the bottom of which, on one side, are the negro houses, neatly laid out into a street, with a stream running through the vale, plenty of cocoa-nut trees and plantations. The vale, on the other side, contains the garden, which is also well watered by a river, that comes from the mountains ; and the gardener told us that alligators often appeared on its banks, which rendered it dangerous for bathing. In front is the sea, sugar works, cane pieces, &c. While we were in the garden this morning, two poor negroes, who had been in chains nearly a year, came to General N., to ask him to intercede for them, and they were accordingly released in the evening.

18th.—Up at 6.—A large party at breakfast, and set off immediately after for Kildare, the estate of Mrs. Fitzgerald. The road tremendous. First, under a frightful rock, the sea beating against our horses' feet ; and then over a still more frightful mountain ; but General N. drove

the carriage the whole way, a thing never attempted before.
We proceeded a few miles beyond Kildare, to review the
St. George's militia, after which we all rode on to Charles-
town, a Maroon town.—The Maroons are composed of the
descendants of those who made their escape during the
Spanish dominion, and were established on lands by the
British Government, after the conquest of the Island.
Many of them, however, were runaways from estates of
British planters, at a later period, and before their treat-
ment was so lenient as it is at present, and before the treaty
made with all the Maroon towns by Governor Trelawny.*

The Maroons received us as if they were much pleased
with our visit ; the women danced, and the men went
through their war exercise for us.   The dancing was exactly
like that of the negroes at Christmas, and their military
manœuvres seemed to consist entirely of ambuscade ;
taking aim at their enemy from behind trees, leaping up,
and rolling about, to avoid being wounded themselves.
Altogether it was so savage and frightful, that I could not
help feeling a little panic, by merely looking at them.

The women were all dressed with a variety of trinkets and
finery, and many not unbecomingly, though very fantasti-
cally.   Their band was composed of all sorts of rude instruments, neither very musical, nor with much variety of
cadence.   The Coromantee flute is a long black reed, has
a plaintive and melancholy sound, and is played with the
nose.—Charlestown is situated between two high hills, with

* In March, 1738, during the governorship of Edward Trelawny, there was concluded, as the result of years of guerilla
warfare, a treaty with the maroons of Trelawny, in Guthrie's
Defile, (when Dr. Russell, the representative of the Army, exchanged hats with Cudjoe, the maroon chief), by which the
maroons received full pardon with privilege to possess for ever
1500 acres of land between Trelawny Town and the Cockpits,
the maroons undertaking to take part in any action of the Government against rebels or invaders.   The memory of Cudjoe's
brother, Accompong, still lives in the settlement of that name
in St. Elizabeth.

cocoa-nut trees, &c. up to the very tops, with little huts up the sides of the hills, each having a piazza in front, and a little garden, looking really picturesque. — The Maroon clergyman preached for us, as he called it, which was merely repeating a part of our Morning Service, and murdering the sense of it most completely.

At 4, General N. went to dine with the militia gentlemen ; and at 6, I sat down with Mrs. F. and a party here.—This day I have suffered more than usual from sickness, and find in Mrs. F. a very pleasing, sensible, motherly woman, and like her much.

19th.—General N. off early, to see a situation in the mountains for a barrack.—I breakfasted with a large party here. —My dear N. came back at 12, quite wet through, and all splashed with mud ; for, though it is dry here, there has been much rain in the mountains. Poor fellow, he has indeed a great deal of fatigue, but he does not seem to mind it ! He changed his dress, had a second breakfast, and then we began our journey again, along the sea shore, through rivers, over rocks and stony roads, till we arrived at Mr. Sherriff's coffee estate. Passed Alligator Pond, which they say abounds with those monsters, but we did not see any of them.

We found Mrs. Sherriff, her mother Mrs. Strachan, and a Miss Cumming, dressed ready to receive us, all in their best. Mrs. S. is a fat, good-humoured Creole woman, saying dis, dat, and toder ; her mother a vulgar old Scotch dame ; and Miss C. a clumsy awkward girl. The house is a good one, quite new, and every thing neat about it. It is situated in the midst of mountains, out of which issue abundant streams of water ; all up the sides of the mountains are plantain and cocoa-nut trees, and coffee bushes. The coffee is a beautiful shrub, bearing a white flower on the stalk, and the leaf is a most brilliant green.

We dined at 6. A large party. In the evening the house was very damp and cold, owing to the numerous streams that run about it, and the great quantity of rain that gene-

rally falls in the mountains, at this season of the year. We
had a wood fire, which I found extremely comfortable, as
I am still very unwell, and susceptible of the smallest change
in the atmosphere. This house is perfectly in the Creole
style. A number of negroes, men, women, and children,
running and lying about, in all parts of it. Never in my life
did I smell so many.

20th.—Did not breakfast till 9.—Saw a flight of parrots
this morning, all chattering as they flew. They are said to
be very destructive to cocoa-nut and plantain trees. The
negroes eat them, and some people make soup of them.—
Went to the coffee works, and saw the process of preparing
coffee, &c.—Mrs. Sherriff had a cabbage tree dissected for
me. It is really very curious and beautiful. They grow
wild in the woods, are eighty years coming to perfection,
and for a dish of cabbage you cut down the whole tree, as
the top of it is the only part eaten, and the tree dies when
that is taken off.

At dinner a large party of men.—In the evening a fire
again, and we all agreed it was very comfortable.—When
the gentlemen joined our party, there was a vulgar Mr.
Murdoch so drunk, that I called for my maid, and went
to bed.—I think nothing so hideous and disgusting as a
drunken man, and how happy am I that my husband joins
with me in this opinion, and I never have seen him in the
least intoxicated.

21st.—We took our leave a little after 7, and proceeded
towards Annotta Bay. The firing from Fort Brunswick
frightened the horses, and terrified me not a little. General
N. examined the fort, &c. We then sent our servants forward to Agualta Vale, and proceeded ourselves six or seven
miles farther up the country, to look for a situation for a
barrack, on Mr. C. Ellis's estate, called Fort George.* The
situation is pretty, but the house is merely one fitted up for
the overseer. There was wine, biscuit, &c. prepared for us,
and I could not help observing, although the gentlemen of

* Still the property of the Ellis family.

our party had all eaten and drank at Fort Brunswick, they
did the same here, and I am sure so much eating injures the
health of many of them.   General N. and I touched nothing
at either place.

We now returned to Annotta Bay, where we were saluted
again, on our way to Agualta Vale.   At 6 we pursued our
journey again, to Mr. Grant's, in St. Mary's.   We were be-
nighted, and, after a tedious, doubtful, and frightful drive,
we arrived at his estate, called Hopewell, at about 10.   I
forgot to mention, that we had a profuse second breakfast
at Agualta Vale, which was in every respect an immense
dinner, though otherwise denominated.   A large dinner
was prepared for us at Mr. Grant's, but a little soup was the
only thing any of us could take, except one gentleman, who
declared it was only the fifth time he had eaten in the course
of the day, and he stuffed of every thing, even to mince
pies, the first I have seen in this country.

My maid did not arrive till after 11.   The mules had
taken it into their heads to lie down two or three times in
their way.   Poor creature, I pity her very much ; she has
no associates, and no equals ; she is left to the care of
a parcel of blacks, and every thing is new and strange
to her.   However, she bears it extremely well, and
makes no complaints.   We went to bed as soon as possible ; and did indeed sleep most profoundly, being all much
fatigued.

22nd.—All well, except the gentleman who ate so much
yesterday.—A dragoon with despatches.—No English mail
yet, but a packet expected every hour.—This house is a
very good one, every thing neat about it, and it commands
a view of a very beautiful country.   The estate is just now
worth clear £18,000 per annum.   It is wonderful the immense sums of money realized by sugar in this country, and
yet all the estates are in debt.—Read, &c. in my own room,
all the morning.   A large party of gentlemen at dinner, at 6.
—Get to my room at 9.—Dismiss my mulatto friends as
soon as possible, and go to bed.   Several of them gave me

their histories. They are all daughters of Members of the Assembly, Officers, &c. &c.

23rd.—Leave Hopewell at 12.—Arrive at the house of the late Mr. Bryan Edwards,* called Nonsuch, about 2. The road very rough, but the country pretty. Miss Murphy and Miss Spencer there to meet me, and several gentlemen. The place is pretty, surrounded by cocoa-nut trees, with a magnificent cotton tree in front of the house ; but every thing wears the appearance of age and neglect. All the doors, wainscoats, &c. are of mahogany. At 6 the usual profuse dinner.

In the evening, the conversation fell upon hurricanes, when many frightful stories were told. This reminds me of a strange circumstance, that was related to me by Mr. Shaw, Member for Kingston, when we were at Spring Gardens. Messrs. Grant and Murphy also attested the fact, therefore I will relate it.† About six or seven months ago, Mr. Shaw saw from his window dark clouds arise from opposite points, accompanied by sudden and violent wind. They seemed at first to have a conflict ; at last they united together, and came towards the house, in a great black column. The house was situated upon an eminence, in the parish of St. George, and fronting the sea ; but, as there were deep ravines on both sides, Mr. Shaw hoped the wind would be attracted by one of them. However, it made directly towards the house, and he and his servants had just time to escape with their lives, when the whole was carried away, scattered, and sunk in the sea, and now not a vestige remains. These columns of wind I have observed several times, but had no idea they were ever so serious in their effects. However, this is a most uncommon instance, and affords much matter for wonder and conversation.— Did not get to bed till eleven. These are sad hours in this climate, but it can't be helped.—Less sick to-day than usual.

* The Historian of the West Indies.

† Thomas Murphy was Custos of and member for St. Mary ; Alexander Shaw, member for Kingston ; Charles Grant, member for St. Mary.

24th.—Awoke at 6 by English letters. Every thing pleasant.—N.'s public letters delightful.—Breakfast, and set off at 9, for the review of the St. Mary's militia. The two young ladies and myself in a phaeton ; General N. and Mr. Murphy in another ; the rest of the party on horseback. Our servants, mules, &c. were sent on to the Ramble, Mr. Murphy's estate. After the review a sumptuous second breakfast, consisting of hot fish, all sorts of cold meats, pies, &c. abundance of cakes, confectionary, fruit, &c. and the greatest variety of wines.—Mrs. Edwards, Mrs. Cruikshanks, and Miss Bigsby, were introduced to me.—Set off a little before 4, for the Ramble, with an immense cavalcade of horsemen, &c.—Mrs. Murphy, Mrs. Mason, Mrs. Cox, Miss Hicks, three Misses Murphy, and Miss Spencer, composed the lady-party ; the men in crowds.—Dined a little before 7.—Began dancing at 10.—I steal away before 12. N. soon followed my example, for we were both heartily fatigued with our journey, society, &c.

25th.—Breakfast at 8.—General N. &c. set off immediately after, to see the fort at Port Maria, &c. &c.—I walked with the ladies in the garden, to the bath, and about the grounds, till our horses were ready, when we all mounted, attended by a few gentlemen, and went to a cottage, a mile or two off, which belongs to Mr. Murphy. From that went to Mrs. Mason's ; from both of which places we had fine views of the country, the sea, &c. Mrs. M. joined our party, and we all returned to the Ramble about 2, and sat down to a second breakfast.

I now found the reason that the ladies here eat so little dinner. I could not help remarking Mrs. Cox, who sat next to me at the second breakfast. She began with fish, of which she ate plentifully, all swimming in oil. Then cold veal, with the same sauce ! ! Then tarts, cakes, and fruit. All the other ladies did the same, changing their plates, drinking wine, &c. as if it were dinner. I got away to my own room as soon as possible, lay down and slept for an hour ; and then read till 6.—Soon after, General N. re-

turned, and we went to dinner at 7.—Began dancing a little
after 10.—We got away, and to bed before one.

26th.—Up at 6.—Breakfast before 8, and then walk
through the sugar works, &c. &c. At 10, began our journey. Very bad roads. Did not get to Mr. Shaw's till
near 2. An immense second breakfast was prepared. Mrs.
Shaw, Mrs. Lewis, Miss Shaw, and Miss Henry, were the
ladies.—At 5, we all mounted our horses, and proceeded to
St. Ann's Bay. The road was frightful ; so narrow and
rocky, and the precipices dreadful. Arrived at General
Rose's at about 7. The family were General and Mrs. Rose,
Miss Chambers, Miss Whitewood, Captain and Mrs. Carr.
A profuse dinner, and to bed at ten.

27th.—A large party at breakfast ; and, immediately
after, we all started for the review of the St. Ann's militia.
The ground was crowded, and I was introduced to a hundred people. The heat was excessive. After the review,
General N., escorted by the cavalry, and attended by all the
gentlemen of the country, and I by a number of women,
returned to Seville. A tedious introduction and conversation then took place ; the men drank all the sangaree, and
then the party dispersed. Immediately, sets of singing
women sent me word of their approach. They danced, and
sung several songs ; some made in honour of General N.
and some of me, till we were heartily tired of them. General
N. then dressed, and went to dine with the military, and I
sat down, at 6, with a party of ladies and a few gentlemen,
to dinner. More ladies in the evening, and the gentlemen
joined us at ten.

This is really a most uncomfortable house ; the servants
awkward and dirty, the children spoiled, and screaming the
whole day. As for the ladies, they appear to me perfect
viragos ; they never speak but in the most imperious manner to their servants, and are constantly finding fault. West
India houses are so thin, that one hears every word, and it
is laughable, in the midst of the clamour, to walk out of
my room, and see nothing but smiles and good humour,

restored to every countenance in an instant. The old
gentleman and lady are really diverting. They never agree
upon any point ; but she generally gets the better, from her
extreme volubility ; and always, when she stops to catch
breath, she exclaims, " But now, Mr. Rose, let me speak ; "
then off she sets again with as much vivacity as ever. The
daughter seems perfectly worthy of such a mother ; but I
am ungrateful to make these remarks, for they are very kind
and friendly to us, though I heartily wish it was over.

28th.—At breakfast General N. received an express, and
set off for Spanish Town, at 12 ; as it was necessary he
should call a council, and decide upon some measures respecting St. Domingo, as well as give notice, for the assembling of the Legislature, to take into consideration communications which he has received from Ministers. I am
really unhappy at this, for various reasons ; the fatigue he
must undergo, and the risk he must run, from mountainous
bad roads, in crossing the island, as well as from the great
heat of the climate. Another reason is, my being left alone
in such a house, so really unwell as I am. He said he would
be back on Tuesday night, but that is impossible, without
his suffering dreadful fatigue.

Passed the greatest part of the day in my own room, crying and reading, till 6 o'clock, when I joined a large party
at dinner. I ate little, and talked less. The chattering Mr.
Whitehorne was on one side of me, and really wore down
my spirits, and put me out of patience, by speaking with
his mouth full, and obliging me constantly to change my
plate. I am not astonished at the general ill health of the
men in this country ; for they really eat like cormorants
and drink like porpoises. But to-day I am out of humour,
and see every thing *en noir*.—Almost every man of the party
was drunk, even to a boy of fifteen or sixteen, who was
obliged to be carried home. His father was very angry, but
he had no right to be so, as he set the example to him.—
Went to my own room at 12, but not to sleep, as they kept
up their jollity much later. This, with the absence of my

dear N., and my anxiety on his account, kept me awake almost the whole night.

29th.—Thank God, in good health this morning. Ask for blessing for my dear husband.—If I were the Queen of Sheba, I could not be made more fuss with than I am here. It is really overpowering. A word from me decides every thing with the ladies, and a look sets all the gentlemen flying to anticipate my commands. The ball they are to give me occupies every one.—A hundred messages from the stewards in the course of the morning.—What hour shall the ball begin ? what door shall I enter ? &c. &c. Please the ladies, by making my maid arrange their dresses for the evening. —My little attendant, Cupid, is ill ; the complaint announced to be repletion.—Only gentlemen at dinner.— Start for the ball at 8, with a grand cavalcade. Received at the door with great ceremony ; led in by two stewards, and followed by a large party of gentlemen, the music playing God save the King. Immediately on my being seated on the state sopha, all the company came up, and paid their compliments. I then opened the ball with Mr. Henry, one of the members for the parish, and really a gentleman-like man. After dancing a little, the carriages were ordered; but first I walked about the room with my suite, and after curtesying and making fine speeches, took my leave, with the same ceremonies with which I entered ; and got home at 2 o'clock.—I slept soundly.—I could not help laughing, as we entered the hall at Seville, to see a dozen black heads popped up, for the negroes in the Creole houses sleep always on the floors, in the passages, galleries, &c. Got to bed about three.

30th.—Rise early, and was in the breakfast room before any of the party. Dr. Western in addition to our number. —This day, in spite of my fatigues, I felt particularly well and comfortable, as I expect my dear good N., and to-morrow we shall be able again to continue our journey.— A great many gentlemen called in the morning, to make enquiries after the ball. Steal away to my own room as

soon as possible, for, towards the middle of the day, I began
to feel a good deal tired, with talking, the bustle of people
coming and going, and the incessant noise of the children,
not to mention the continual scolding at the servants, which
is to me the most distressing thing in the world.—Am the
first in the drawing-room at 5 o'clock.—Wait dinner till 6.
All the company assembled, except General N., who had not
arrived. Endeavour to be reconciled to his absence till to-
morrow, when, to my great joy, just as we were going to
place ourselves at table, he made his appearance. He did
not leave Spanish Town till 12, being obliged to hold a
council this morning. This is really a great fatigue, and
more than he ought to risk.—Major Gould seems to feel it
infinitely more than General N., however ; the latter looking as perfectly well and in good spirits as usual, while the
poor Major appeared at least twenty years older. Unfortunately, soon after they came in, the horse, which drew
the gig the whole way, died of the complaint they call the
pant, which is very common with horses not bred in the
West Indies ; and this was an American horse, therefore
not accustomed to the climate. He was really a fine animal,
and cost General N., three or four months ago, two hundred
pounds. What a mercy that the horse was the only sufferer!
To bed by twelve.

31*st*.—Breakfast at 8, and take leave of the family, &c.
&c. at Seville, and set off at eleven for Arcadia. After a
pleasant, though rather a hilly and rocky drive, reach Rio-
bueno, where we met the members of Trelawny Parish, and
other gentlemen, Mr. McAnuff,* agent for Mr. Barnett, who
is the proprietor of Arcadia estate, came to invite us there,
accompanied by a Mr. Galloway and a Captain Sherry.
Mr. Barnett is married to a Miss Markham, daughter of the
Archbishop of York, and they have lately left this country.
Found a profuse second breakfast prepared for us, at the
inn, and, after General N. had inspected the forts, &c. we
proceeded to Arcadia, where we arrived at 6. Found a

* John Clinton McAnuff was adjutant-general of militia.

party ready to receive us, and sat down to dinner before 7. To bed early.—Every thing here is so quiet, clean and comfortable, that we feel ourselves in Arcadia indeed.

April 1st.—This day year we left Ireland. What would I not give, if we had now so short a voyage to make to England; but I won't think of it.—Much refreshed by our comfortable night's rest. My dear N. quite cool and well to-day. Yesterday he complained much of head-ache, which alarmed me a good deal, as it is always the forerunner of evil in this country.

This house is not large, but it is very neat and convenient. It stands on a high hill, overlooking the sea, and a great extent of beautiful country; it is surrounded with very fine orange trees, &c. The ladies, who spent the day with me, were Mrs. Galloway, Miss Howorth, and Mrs. Littlejohn; and at dinner we had a fresh relay, Mr. and Mrs. Easton, Dr. Littlejohn; and in short, a large party.—Get to my own room before ten, but obliged to give audience to all the black and brown ladies in the parish, while I was undressing.

2nd.—Up early.—General N. made arrangements for expediting our tour, on account of the situation of St. Domingo, and the private intelligence he had received from Lord Hobart,* about the treaty with France.—As soon as breakfast was over, a party of gentlemen, headed by General Bell and Mr. Cunningham,† arrived to attend us to Falmouth and Montego Bay. General N. then left us for Mahogany Hall, and to-morrow he is to proceed on, and view the Black Grounds, Quashie and Mouth rivers, to fix on situations for barracks.

At 4, General Bell and myself, in his phaeton, and the rest of the gentlemen in kittareens, and on horseback, went to Bryan Hall, to dine with Mr. and Mrs. Galloway.† The

* Robert, Lord Hobart, afterwards Fourth Earl of Buckinghamshire, was the Secretary of State for the Colonial and War Department. Hobart Town, Tasmania, is named after him.

† James Galloway and John Cunningham were of the magistracy of Trelawny.

Hall was the seat of the late Bryan Edwards, where he wrote the greatest part of his History of the West Indies.[*] It is really a beautiful place ; the house is a good one, and tolerably well furnished, and has a Turkey carpet in the drawing room—an extraordinary sight in this country. The house stands rather higher than Arcadia, and is surrounded by Pimento (Allspice) groves, so laid out, as to make the prospect of the sea and the country more picturesque, through vistas. The pimento is a large fine tree, with the brightest green foliage imaginable. The process of preparing the allspice is merely picking it and laying it in the sun to dry, and then thoroughly cleaning it by taking off the rough husks, &c. About eighteen or twenty years ago, this was a very valuable and productive article to the island ; but, latterly, there has been little or no demand for it, on account of the great supply of spices from the East Indies.—A large party of gentlemen, but only three ladies besides myself. Felt more than usually sick during dinner time, and was glad to get back to Arcadia. Took leave of all my gentlemen as soon as I arrived.—I then went to bed, but not to sleep, being very ill all night.

3rd.—Called my maid, and had some tea at 6. Then sent my excuses to the gentlemen, and remained in bed. Miss Howorth and Mr. Miller came to attend me to Mahogany Hall, to meet General N. on his return there.—Found myself too unwell to rise. Miss Howorth sat by my bed-side

---

[*] Bryan Hall, now called Bryan Castle, in Trelawny, was, together with the neighbouring estate of Brampton, now called Brampton Bryan, settled in or before 1792. It is within three miles of the Port of Rio Bueno, A view of the great house is given in Hakewill's " Picturesque Tour in the Island of Jamaica," London, 1825.

In 1792 Edwards had permanently left Jamaica. He sat in the House of Commons for Grampound, and supported the slave trade with certain restrictions. He was reported by Wilberforce to be a powerful opponent to abolition. His history of the West Indies was first published in 1793 ; it subsequently ran into a fifth edition in 1819.

BRYAN CASTLE

1

till one ; I dozed till four, but was so unwell, notwithstanding, that I could scarcely dress for dinner ; but looking
most impatiently for the return of my dear N. to comfort
me.—At half-past five, went to the drawing room, to receive the 'grand Monde.' Looking out for General N. till
near 7, when a message arrived to tell me that he could not
come back till later in the evening. Soon after 9, he
made his appearance with his party. They had had a most
fatiguing day ; thirty miles of shocking bad roads, or rather
no roads at all, through the woods ; the trees and bushes
so thick, that they were obliged to have negroes going on
before to clear the way, and they themselves leaping their
horses over stumps at almost every step. Thank God, my
dear N. does not appear to have suffered in the smallest
degree, nor does he complain of fatigue.

4th.—Full of business, and writing letters, to go by the
express to Spanish Town. Leave Arcadia about 12, and
arrive at Falmouth to dinner. The streets crowded with
people, and a negro market held in front of General Bell's
house. The negroes seemed very happy, selling their yams,
cocoa-nuts, plantains, &c. and salt fish. When we shewed
ourselves in the piazza, they laughed, danced, bowed, curtesied, and grinned, and used every possible grimace to
express their happiness in seeing us. I took a fancy to an
immense water-melon, which my maid secured for me, and
I devoured it all, while I was dressing for dinner.—A very
large party.—General and Mrs. Bell are very comfortable
people. Their house, and every thing about them, is in the
best order, and there is a white woman for a housekeeper.
They have no children, but have adopted a niece (a Miss
Virgo), who lives with them.—Several ladies at dinner, and
more in the evening ; but we were all in bed by eleven.

I must not forget to record a funny adventure of my poor
deaf maid Johnson. General N.'s Military Secretary has
the same name, and he had driven her out to-day in his
kittareen ; consequently the servants supposed they must
be man and wife, and therefore they only prepared one

apartment for them. As soon as I was undressed, she retired to her bed-room, where she was not a little surprised
to see a military coat, boots, &c. When the servants answered to her questions, " Only the Captain's, Ma'am," she,
not liking to acknowledge she was deaf, nodded her head
as usual, and said, " Very well, very well."—The musquito
net was comfortably tucked round her, and she was enjoying her first sleep, when the Captain was shewn in, who, in
his turn, was not a little surprised to find that he was only
to have half a bed, and that his questions were answered
with " Only Missis, Sir." The light awoke Johnson, who
began to vociferate most loudly, and it was some time before
good order was restored, by the Captain retiring to the
pallet prepared for the *Femme de Chambre*.

5*th.*—General N. off to review the detachment of the 60th
regiment, quartered here, and to breakfast with the officers.
—Nothing but guns firing, drums beating, and all sorts of
noise. I breakfasted with the ladies here, people crowding
in upon us continually, till 11, when we all set off for the
review, and were attended back by an immense party to
second breakfast ; after which we retired to our own room,
to rest a little. At 5, General N. went to dine with the
officers of the Trelawny militia, which he had also reviewed
in the morning.—I sat down to dinner with no less than ten
ladies.—About 8, a number of gentlemen came to attend us
to a ball, given at a Mr. Baillie's. Danced only three
dances, and got away at 12, rather sick, and much fatigued.

6*th.*—Very unwell, but a great crowd of people at breakfast. However, we contrived to pass part of this morning
in our own room.—Dined at half-past five. A large party ;
Navy officers, &c. I forgot to mention Admiral Duckworth's attention, in sending Captain Loring, with a small
squadron in command, to attend us round the coast. The
Navy men have been great acquisitions to our society on
our tour ; but, from the state of the roads, we have not
been obliged to accept of their services at sea. Indeed,
General N. is determined not to quit terra firma, if he can

possibly avoid it. At 9, we all went to a public ball, given
to us by the gentlemen of the parish. I opened the ball,
and danced a few dances. Supper at 12, and got home before 2.—The ladies all very fine, and the gentlemen particularly civil and attentive.

7th.—General N. &c. off for the Maroon Town at 5,
to view the place, and to inspect the 2nd battalion of
the 85th regiment, just arrived from England.—For a
wonder, a *tête-à-tête* breakfast with Miss Virgo. Mrs. Bell
was in her bed with a head-ache, and all the gentlemen were
gone with General N. A Mr. Heywood called, and kept me
an hour talking of Southampton, and my old friends there.
Get to my own room to rest. At 2 the *white* housekeeper
came and said, " Ma'am, shall I have the honour to offer you
your breakfast," luncheon being always called so.—Mine
consisted of chicken soup, ham, oysters swimming in oil, &c.
—The *sight* of the oysters and oil was sufficient for me ; but
I have observed that the ladies here eat a great deal of it.—
Went at 4, with the ladies, to dine with a Mrs. Mitchell,
three miles out of town. Tired to death, making the agreeable till after 6, when we went to dinner. The Navy officers,
and a large party as usual.—Got away before ten.

8th.—Only ladies at breakfast.—Immediately after, Cap-
tains Loring, Johnson, and Barry, of the Navy, Captain
Carr, 83rd regiment, Mr. Hiatt, a planter, &c. At 1,
General and Mrs. Rose, Mrs. Carr, Mr. and Mrs. S. Rose, &c.
Soon as the party dispersed, went to my own room, looking
out for my dear N. We had frequent showers this morning.

Amused myself with reading the Evidence before the
House of Commons, on the part of the petitioners for the
Abolition of the Slave Trade. As far as I at present see
and can hear of the ill treatment of the slaves, I think what
they say upon the subject is very greatly exaggerated. In-
dividuals, I make no doubt, occasionally abuse the power
they possess ; but, generally speaking, I believe the slaves
are extremely well used. Yet it appears to me, there would
be certainly no necessity for the Slave Trade, if religion,

decency, and good order, were established among the negroes ; if they could be prevailed upon to marry ; and if
our white men would but set them a little better example.
Mrs. Bell told me to-day, that a negro man and woman of
theirs, who are married, have fourteen grown up children,
all healthy field negroes. This is only one instance out of
many, which proves, that, the climate of this country being
more congenial to their constitutions, they would increase
and render the necessity of the Slave Trade out of the question, provided their masters were attentive to their morals,
and established matrimony among them ; but white men
of all descriptions, married or single, live in a state of licen-
tiousness with their female slaves ; and until a great reformation takes place on their part, neither religion, decency
nor morality, can be established among the negroes. An
answer that was made to Mr. Shirley, a Member of the
Assembly (and a profligate character, as far as I can understand), who advised one of his slaves to marry, is a strong
proof of this—" Hi, Massa, you telly me marry one wife,
which is no good ! You no tinky I see you buckra no content wid one, two, tree, or four wifes ; no more poor negro."
The overseers, &c. too, are in general needy adventurers,
without either principle, religion, or morality. Of course,
their example must be the worst possible to these poor
creatures.

    General N. came home a little after 5, extremely well,
and in excellent spirits, thank God ; but wet through, as a
great deal of rain had fallen in the mountains. Dressed,
and went to dine at Mr. Galloway's at 6.—Got home as soon
as we could, and to bed at twelve.

    9th.—During breakfast, a crowd to take leave of us.
About 12, we left Trelawny Parish, and started from Falmouth for Montego Bay. About six miles on our journey,
Mr. Cunningham's chaise and four met us. Proceed in it
to Iron Shore, the estate of Mr. Irving ; found an immense
party, and a great second breakfast ready. A large old
house, and the situation beautiful.—Proceed on our journey

to Montego Bay. Arrived at Mr. Cunningham's at 6 o'clock.
Found fifty people assembled to meet us, was introduced
to the crowd, and then hurried to our rooms to dress. Sat
down to dinner at 7.—An additional company ; altogether
sixty or seventy people. Every face perfectly new to us,
for the glare of the sun had so dazzled us, on our first arrival
and introduction, that it was quite impossible to distin-
guish a feature, or hardly black from white.—The dinner
was in the usual abundance, and consisted of every Jamaica
delicacy ; and we were pressed to taste of so many things
that it was scarcely possible to avoid being stuffed into a
fever.—Began dancing at 10 or 11. Danced with various
partners till 1, and then got to my own room at last,
where I found General N. who had stolen away half an hour
before.

This house is as comfortable as possible. The rooms are
good, and well furnished, and the situation is delightful.
The town of Montego Bay is situated in an amphitheatre of
very high hills. In front a most beautiful bay, full of vessels, and open to the sea. On the hills are all the gentlemen's houses, or those not immediately shop-keepers. These
are interspersed with gardens, palms of all sorts, &c. So
that, from the town, quite up to the tops of the hills, you
see nothing but villas peeping out from among the foliage.
Mr. C.'s house overlooks the whole town, bay, &c. &c. and
altogether the prospect is lovely. Nothing can exceed the
hospitality of our host and his wife. They have a numerous
family, and a crowd of relations, constantly with them.
Every thing wears the appearance of content and cheerfulness ; the children are well managed, and not young enough
to disturb one with their noise. The heat, however, is
great, and we suffer a good deal from occupying the state
apartments ; which here, as well as at Falmouth, are, from
12 o'clock in the day, entirely exposed to the sun.

10th.—General N. set off with his *suite* at 4 o'clock this
morning, on board the *Syren* frigate, Captain Loring, for
Lucea. Here we had an immense dinner party, as well as

breakfast and second breakfast, and crowds of visitors all day. Among the ladies that came to dinner was a Mrs. Russell, an English woman, and the wife of an officer in the artillery—a very pleasing person. As the Navy officers were of our party, we had a dance in the evening ; and, having rested so much during the day, I rather enjoyed the gaiety.—To bed at 12 o'clock.

11*th*.—An immense breakfast party at 8, and at 10 we all went to church. The congregation very respectable, and a number of the military. The prayers were read by a Mr. Barnet, and Mr. Ricard preached. Before the service began, I was surprised, and not a little shocked, at Mr. Ricard's proposing to me to dismiss all the congregation for an hour or two, as *his Excellency* would probably land by that time ! Of course I declined. After the service, when I remarked the number that had attended, Mr. Ricard very coolly told me, that was on account of our being here, for that he had in general scarcely any congregation, and the military had not been in church for nearly three years !— A splendid second breakfast was given me by Mrs. Grey, a sister of Mr. Cunningham, and at 3 o'clock we all returned home, to meet General N. who had just landed. Guns firing, and a great crowd, as usual ; the whole place being in the greatest bustle.—An immense dinner party—*all* the Navy officers, a number of the military, and gentlemen of the country ; four ladies, besides those of the family, Mrs. Evans, Mrs. Coward, Mrs. Landsdown, and Mrs. ——, I forget her name.—To bed at 12 o'clock.

12*th*.—A large breakfast party, and we all started for the review ground at 10 ; Mrs. and Miss Cunningham and myself in a chaise and four, and all the rest in kittareens and phaetons, and on horseback.—After the review went a-shopping with the ladies.—All the shop-keepers' wives shook hands with the ladies of my party, and appeared perfectly on a footing with them, talking of the review, the ball to be given to-morrow, &c. A more than usually large second breakfast at Mr. Cunningham's to-day, on account of the review.—Soon after 5, General N. went to the public dinner, and I sat down to mine at 6, with a number of ladies, and a few *civil* gentlemen, as all the military were with General N. In the evening, many more ladies and gentlemen, and about 10, several from the grand dinner, with General N., who took his leave of the company almost immediately.— I danced till a little after 12, and then, when supper was announced, pleaded fatigue, and got to bed as soon as I could, having scarcely an atom of strength left.

13*th.*—This is to be a grand day, and all the house was in a bustle very early.—Soon after breakfast, held a *council* with the ladies, to decide upon the dresses for the evening. Get my maid to work for the young people, to make them smart for the ball, and *advise* also with Mrs. Cunningham, upon the subject of her cap, &c.—My dearest N. full of business, settling disputes between the military and civilians, and harassed with their complaints and nonsense till after 6.—Then hurried to dress, and dine, about two miles out of the town, with the Custos and his lady, a Mr. and Mrs. Mowat.—Find sixty-two people assembled, and the clergyman ready to make Christians of three of their children, the eldest of whom was about four years old, and the youngest as many months, and for this last we were sponsors.—The heat was dreadful, and the crowd so great at dinner, that there was scarcely room for the servants to change the plates. The smell, added to the intense heat, altogether was very near overcoming me, but I tried to support it as well as I could, and rejoiced when an express arrived from the town, to say the ball-room was full, and all the world waiting for us. The few moments of fresh air between the dinner and the ball-rooms were a real treat ; but when we arrived at the latter, the crowd was so great, that the heat if possible surpassed the former. However, the smell of the blackies and of the hot meats was absent, and that was some comfort. But never shall I forget the combination of a crowd of Creoles, and a mob of blackies, with turtle-soup, pepper-pot, and callipash and callipee, at

Mr. Mowat's, as long as I live in this world !—General N.
and I both began the ball.   He at the head of one set, and
I at the head of another, and my partner was so anxious to
exhibit me, that I was obliged to jig to the very bottom of
the dance, which consisted of no less than thirty-one
couples !—Supper at 2 o'clock, and we felt ourselves bound
to remain for it, as such preparations had been made, that
it would have been a *sin* to disappoint the steward, &c.—
but conceive our fatigue !   Poor dear Nugent had a restless
night, and so had I, and he complained sadly of heat.

14*th.*—We can scarcely say that we have been in bed, for
we did not lie down till past 4, and were up again at 6,
hoping to get away from the kindness of the crowd here at
an early hour.   Both of us half dead with the heat, and
with aching heads from the fatigue and want of sleep.—A
large party to breakfast, at 8.—Constant visitors till 12,
when we set off for the parish of Hanover, a party of gentlemen, civil and military, accompanying us.—Met by Colonel
Malcolm and his friends, on the road.—General N. inspected
a barrack as we passed on to Knock-Alva,* the estate of
Mr. Malcolm the Colonel's elder brother.

The country beautiful, and the roads tolerably good.
Arrive about half-past four, and intend to keep my room,
and recruit my strength and spirits a little, as I am the only
lady, and this is a bachelor's house ; but my dear N. is so
unwell, that the doctor says he must go to his bed immediately, and, in consequence, I am doomed to go to dinner ;
for as our host has been at much trouble and expense, to
prepare for our reception, it would be the *acme* of cruelty
not to look at the dinner at least.—Cry and lament myself
all the time I am dressing, not only on account of my own
fatigue, but from alarm and apprehension about my dear,
dear husband !   Sit down soon after 6, with twenty gentlemen, to a loaded table, extending all the length of the
piazza.   Three courses were served with the greatest bustle
and confusion, the servants nearly knocking each other

* Knockalva is still in the possession of the Malcolm family.

down in their hurry and awkwardness ; for I suppose it is
an age since they have had such fine doings.   The dinner
was so tedious, and I felt so really unwell, that I begged
leave to retire before the cloth was removed, and then it
was near 11 o'clock.—Take a little tea with my dear Nugent,
who is, thank God, much better, and get to bed as soon as
I can.   He has had a refreshing sleep, and the doctor's pre-
scriptions appear to have done him a great deal of good.

   15th.—Up at half-past four, and hope to make our escape
before Colonel Malcolm is stirring, but find the house lit up,
and a profuse breakfast prepared.   Take some tea only, but
feel much better than yesterday.   God be praised, dearest
N. quite well again.   Set off for Paradise, the estate of Mr.
Wedderburn.   A large party, breakfast ready.   A good
house, and lovely situation altogether.   As soon as breakfast was over, we proceeded to the review ground, near
Savannah la Mar.   Meet a number of ladies, and Major and
Mrs. Dunbar gave us a grand second breakfast, after the
review of the 83rd, which succeeded the Militia review ; and
this was rather hard work for poor General N. who had also
to inspect the barracks, hospital, &c.

   Drove to the Custos, Mr. Murray's, in his carriage, which
I rejoiced to find waiting for us, on the review ground.   Mr.
and Mrs. M. are a comfortable old couple, and made us
welcome in a plain manner, and with less fuss than we have
been used to, and so we promise ourselves a little rest and
quiet here.   We were allowed to remain without interrup-
tion, in our own apartment, till near 6, when General N.
went to dine with the Militia, and I sat down to a profuse
dinner, with many ladies, but very few gentlemen.   The
dinner very dull indeed ; the ladies almost mute, and
staring at me, which obliged me to keep up the conversation
as well as I could, the whole time, with Mr. Stewart, clergyman of the parish.   He appeared rather an illiterate person,
though a well meaning man ; but much cannot be expected,
when it is known, that, only a few years since, he was an
overseer, on Mr. Wedderburn's estate of Paradise.   It seems

Mr. Wedderburn, to reward his services as an overseer, purchased the living of Savannah la Mar, and the Bishop of
Man ordained him !—In the evening, more ladies and gentlemen, in crowds, many of whom came with General N. from
the dinner.—A dance as usual. At 12, we got away to our
rooms, but I could not rest or be satisfied, till I got a little
piece of salt ham, that I saw on the supper table, as we
passed near where it was laid. This seemed to cure my
sickness, and I slept most comfortably after it.

Good Friday, 16th.—Make early reflections, and explain
the meaning of the day to the black servants that are
with us.—Breakfast at 7 o'clock ; a number of gentlemen,
who, with Mr. Murray, attended us, to look at the church.
It is better fitted up than usual, and altogether looks very
nice and respectable.   I only regretted we could not remain
for the service of the day, though it seemed doubtful whether
there was to be any ; but I dare say, if we had staid, Mr.
Stewart would have put on his canonicals.   We then visited
the court-house, which is a very good building ; and after
driving all over the town, went down to the Bay, where,
while General N. was inspecting a small work for the protection of the harbour, I heard a full account of the dreadful
hurricane in the year 1780, from a gentleman who was present at the time.   He shewed me where the sea had rushed
in, and carried all before it, and then retreated, bearing
away with it to the deep many houses with their hapless
inhabitants, almost in a moment.   Our landlord and landlady had only time to get out of their house, when it was
blown down, and their only place of shelter was in the body
of an old carriage, taken off its wheels, and placed on the
ground.

At 10, began our journey again ; the heat excessive. A
beautiful road along the coast.   Arrived at the farm, Mr.
Wickey's estate, soon after 2 o'clock.—Two Mr. Jones's,
and a Mr. McFarlane, with Mrs. Wickey, to receive us. Our
own party, however, was sufficiently large to fill his house,
which, although the situation is pretty, looks miserable, and

is very low, as well as most intolerably hot.   The master of
it is a wretched looking man, and all the household are
equally meagre, and indeed appearing as if they were half
starved ; but we had a coarse greasy feast, and were glad
to pursue our journey as soon as possible, which we enjoyed
particularly, for it was a lovely moonlight night, and the
roads were uncommonly good, having been prepared on
our account.—Arrived at the parsonage, Mr. Warren's, in
St. Elizabeth's, a little before 12 o'clock.   A large party
was assembled to receive us, but we begged only to take tea,
and go to our rooms, as soon as all the bows and curtesies
were over.

17th.—Up at 6.—Poor D.'s wife, with her pretty little
girl, came to spend the day with me.   I was rather pleased
with her appearance and manner, and delighted with the
child, it is such a dear little thing.—General N. went to
Black River, to review the St. Elizabeth's militia, while I
spent a most fatiguing morning, talking to a dozen women.
Mrs. and the Misses Shakespeare, Mr. and Mrs. Vassal, Mrs.
and Miss Hylton, and Miss Williams, in addition to the party
already in the house.—In the evening a large assembly,
chiefly of gentlemen, who accompanied General N. from
Black River.   A dance, and to bed soon after 12 o'clock.—
Mr. Warren's two sons sad objects—they have St. Vitus'
dance, and are both quite deformed, and poor General N.
was quite uneasy at their handing me about, and shewing
me so much civility ; but I tried to look at them as little as
possible.

18th.—Up at 6.   Explain the day to the servants, and
gave them the same present that I did on Good Friday.—
I am, at this moment, admiring from my window one of the
largest and most beautiful acacia trees I ever saw.   It is in
full bloom, and quite lovely.   My maid tells me that the
negroes say that they make a very good aperient medicine
from it.

At 10, go to Black River, about five miles off, to church.
The building is shabby and much neglected.   All the con-

gregation, excepting our party and nine other persons, were
either black or brown.   I cannot help here remarking, that
the clergyman's wife, Mrs. Warren, excused herself from
attending, on account of the service being so long to-day.
Her married daughter, too, who is the widow of the late
Chief Justice, did the same.   At the Communion, there
were only one old white man and woman and one *brown*
lady, besides ourselves, for the clergyman's two daughters,
who came with us, left the church with the rest of the congregation ; and yet they are certainly of an age to join in
the service, being nearer to thirty than twenty years old.
But, altogether, it was a most extraordinary scene ; for,
just before the service began, and when I thought the
church doors were to be closed, in walked a strange gentleman, and took his seat in our pew, and began making fine
speeches, about our going to his house to-morrow.   This
invitation General N. very civilly declined, while I kept my
eyes upon my book, and said nothing.   General N. opened
his, but the gentleman still talked on.   The clergyman went
to the altar, and every thing appeared quite ready to begin
the service.   General N. then said, " Pray, Sir, do you stay
for the Communion ? "   " Oh, no," was the answer, and
then, after a few bows, and a few more speeches, off he
walked.   It is scarcely necessary to say, how much we were
disgusted at this conduct ; but I am sure that the poor man
had not the smallest idea of the impropriety, to say the
least of it.   When we went up to the altar, the clergyman
began *his civilities*—first asking whether we would prefer
having the bread and wine brought to our pew ; then hoping
the heat was not too great ; and, in the midst of the service,
stopping to enquire whether I wou'd like a window opened
that was over the altar.   I said not a word, and General N.
shook his head, saying, " Please to go on, Sir, I beg ! "   All
this time, the young ladies were talking and laughing, loud
enough to be heard, as they sat in the carriage at the church
door ; and, in short, it was altogether shocking.—We drove
afterwards to Luana, where Mrs. Williams gave us a grand

second breakfast.—Little B. very pretty and very engaging.
She came with her mamma to the parsonage.—Miss Williams, Miss Hylton, &c. all remained till 9 o'clock, when
they took their leave, and we were glad to get to bed early.

19th.—Set off soon after breakfast for Lacovia, the estate
of our host, the Rev. Mr. Warren. The two Misses Warren
accompanied us, and the two sons would hand me to the
carriage, to General N.'s great annoyance.—Captain and
Miss Owen there, and another breakfast ready, though it
was only 10 o'clock. The house and the place altogether
very ugly. But there were some remarkably fine mango
trees, loaded half with fruit and half with blossoms, which
had a very extraordinary effect.—At one o'clock a third
breakfast of fish, hot stews of all sorts, &c. and at 3 we pursued our journey to Windsor.—The road lovely. Arrive
soon after 5. Received by a Mr. Armstrong (a Scotch overseer) and his friends. The proprietor of the estate is a
Kingston merchant, and rarely comes here.—The house is
old, and much out of repair, but the place is famous for an
excellent garden. While dinner was preparing, General N.
and the gentlemen walked to see it, but I begged to rest a
little, feeling much fatigued.—A very coarse dinner, but the
poor man had done his best, and no doubt thought it very
fine ; and so it was, if abundance of beef and pork could
make it so.—To bed before 10, and all glad to rest ourselves.

20th.—General N., &c. off at 4, for the town of the Accompong Maroons.—At 7, sat down in the piazza to a complete
overseer's breakfast of salt fish, salt beef, Irish butter, &c.
&c. As my poor maid was the only white person in the
house besides myself, I sent for her, intending she should
make the tea, and take her breakfast with me. But she
was so very mincing and miserable, that, as I had no appetite myself, I took one cup of tea, and then left her to enjoy
the delicate fare alone. I had a nice walk in the garden,
which amused me extremely, till the excessive heat drove
me in. The trees and plants very curious, and in great

variety ; not only natives of this country, but also from Otaheite, the Cape of Good Hope, &c. The gardener is an intelligent Scotchman, and seems perfectly well acquainted with his business. He made me remark the Otaheite plum particularly ; it bears a bright pink blossom, like a tassel, and although some of the branches were covered with them, others were loaded with fruit, some of the fruit quite green, others quite ripe ; and all round the tree the ground was covered with the blossoms that had fallen, to make way for the fruit, and was really like a bright pink carpet. The camphor, cinnamon, sago, &c. &c. in great perfection. There was the largest jack-fruit tree I ever saw, and the most abundant mango and bread-fruit trees. A very good bath and fish pond in the garden, but the late dry weather has destroyed all the fish. However, the gardener told me as soon as the rainy season began, he would fill the pond immediately, by sending negroes to the mountains in the night, with lanterns, and they could fetch abundance.— General N. returned about 3 o'clock ; he had been very much gratified by his visit to Accompong.—A Mr. Vernon and Mr. Griffiths were added to the party. Dinner at 6, and to bed at ten.

21st.—General N. off early to see Hector's. River, &c. Mr. Vernon, Major Drummond, and Captain Johnson break-fasted with me, and we then proceeded to Derry, Mr. White's estate. Nothing could well be more frightful than the road —hills and precipices continually, and one hill extended six miles, with a narrow road full of stumps and rocks. The views were beautiful between the openings of the moun-tains ; fine vales, covered with sugar estates, penns, &c. One place that we passed was called Paradise, and a Mr. Angel was the inhabitant. At 2, reached Derry. It is a lovely romantic situation ; and, as we passed through the woods to the house, we saw several flights of parrots, and various curious birds. A fine second breakfast prepared for me, by Mr. White, who, with his nephew, was waiting to receive us.—I have taken some soup, and am now going to rest myself a little, if the black and brown ladies will allow me.—At 6, General N., &c., and all wet through, the mountain showers were so heavy.—To bed at 11 o'clock.— I can't sleep all night, thinking of our host, who is certainly the ugliest man I ever saw—but so civil !

22nd.—The morning much cooler than usual, owing to the height of the situation.—Soon after breakfast set off for Porus, an estate of Mr. Conolly's, an Irish lawyer, who, I believe, never visits this country. The drive lay through woods ; the trees fine, and a variety of beautiful shrubs. The wild pine is particularly curious ; it shoots out from the branches of trees, and has the oddest effect.—Reach Grove Place at 1. A superb second breakfast ready ; but, as there was no cover for our horses, and the clouds seemed to threaten rain, we were persuaded by another Mr. Vernon, who had joined our party, to proceed on without delay to Porus, where we arrived at 3 o'clock. Mr. Grey and Mr. Lafnan, Mr. Conolly's agents, received us.

Porus is very pretty—surrounded by woody mountains. The house stands in the midst of a garden, and you enter it under a bower of granadillas, the blossom of which is exactly like large Passion-flowers. The trees in the garden are loaded with fruit, and the mango trees, in particular, are quite bowed down by the weight of theirs.—Try to lie down, and read a little, by way of resting myself ; but the heat is excessive, although my room is all doors and windows, and quite open to the garden.—Have a great deal of talk with some of the black women of the house. There is an old negro man here, who was coachman to Lord Portland, when he was Governor of this island in 1721.* He is still healthy and active, and this reminds me of an old woman, who died while we were in St. Mary's, who was so old that no one could tell her exact age ; but, from known circumstances,

* Henry, Duke of Portland, was Governor from 8 December, 1722, to 4 July, 1726, when he died. The parish of Portland bears his name. Titchfield, Port Antonio, is named after his second title.

K

she had certainly seen her 140th year* ! Does not this prove
how congenial the climate is to their colour ?

23rd.—Up at 6, and set off, as soon as we had taken our
breakfast, for Woods, the estate of Mr. Osborne, Speaker
of the House of Assembly. Stop a few moments at Par-
nassus. The road unusually good. Before we reached our
destination, General N. and I had a most extraordinary
vision. He was driving me in the curricle, and we were
some distance before our party, who drove slower that we
might avoid the dust. We came to the top of a hill, and
just as we were about to descend, General N. drew up with
astonishment at the prospect before us, and we both thought
we must have mistaken our road most strangely. We knew
that our journey was quite inland, and that, on the road to
Woods, it was quite impossible we should see the harbour
of Port-Royal, or any place on the coast ; and yet before us
appeared an expanse of water, a headland with ships lying
at anchor, some with their sails half exposed to the sun, as
if to dry, and others with their sails close furled ; in short,
it was a perfect view of a harbour with its accompaniments.
Soon, however, it began to change, and as we moved gently
forward, descending the hill, nothing but a plain with sugar
estates was before us, and no water or ships to be seen. I
have read of these things, but never before saw the effects
of vapour.

We found a large party and second breakfast at Mr.
Osborne's, about 2 o'clock. Mr. and Mrs. Ashley, Mrs.
Rossington, and Miss Faro, were the only new people, but
Mrs. Rossington I had seen before, and I must, at the con-
clusion of this day, tell an adventure, in consequence of her
advice.—After dinner, we had a dance, in which I joined,
though I was so unwell with a cold, that I had much rather
have gone to bed. Mrs. R. said she had a receipt that would
certainly cure me, and my maid was sent for it, as soon as
I was in bed. It tasted very sweet and nice, and I never
slept better in my life. When I awoke in the morning, however, I felt a little giddy, and when I thanked Mrs. Rossing-

* *sic.*

ton for her medicine I told her so. She asked how much
water I had put to it ? I said none at all. She exclaimed,
" Why, it was only the ingredients of very strong punch,
and you should have put at least half a pint of hot water to
it ? " So I was certainly very tipsy, but I slept so sound
that I knew nothing of it.

24th.—We could not begin our journey home till near 10.
Stop at the inn, at Old Harbour, for two or three hours, as
some of the mules were ill. Then sent all the baggage and
stuff on before us, and drove the backway to our Penn; avoid-
ing all the fuss and bustle of going with a great cavalcade
through Spanish Town. Several gentlemen, however, came
to greet us on our return home, and staid dinner.—To bed
before 10, however, and feel delighted to think that we have
no journey to make to-morrow, and I thank God sincerely
for all his goodness and mercy.

I will conclude my tour through the island with a few
remarks. In this country it appears as if every thing were
bought and sold. Clergymen make no secret of making a
traffic of their livings ; but General N. has set his face
against such proceedings, and has refused many applications for the purpose. He is determined to do all he can
towards the reformation of the church, and thus rendering
it respectable. It is indeed melancholy, to see the general
disregard of both religion and morality, throughout the
whole island. Every one seems solicitous to make money,
and no one appears to regard the mode of acquiring it. It
is extraordinary to witness the immediate effect that the
climate and habit of living in this country have upon the
minds and manners of Europeans, particularly of the lower
orders. In the upper ranks, they become indolent and in-
active, regardless of every thing but eating, drinking, and
indulging themselves, and are almost entirely under the
dominion of their mulatto favourites. In the lower orders,
they are the same, with the addition of conceit and tyranny ;
considering the negroes as creatures formed merely to ad-
minister to their ease, and to be subject to their caprice ;

and I have found much difficulty to persuade those great people and superior beings, our white domestics, that the blacks are human beings, or have souls. I allude more particularly to our German and our other upper men-servants. —It was curious to observe, when we were entering any town, the number of trunks, band-boxes, &c. that were hurrying to the different houses, and the same at our departure, all going back to the country again, and all on negroes' heads ; for, whenever the ladies go to town, or are to appear in society, their black maids and other attendants start off with their finery in cases, or tin boxes, on their heads. Trunks of any size are carried in the same manner. In short, every thing is put upon the head, from the largest to the smallest thing ; even a smelling-bottle, I believe, would be carried in the same way. I have often, on our tour, seen twelve or fourteen negroes in one line of march, each bearing some article for the toilette on his head.—The Creole language is not confined to the negroes. Many of the ladies, who have not been educated in England, speak a sort of broken English, with an indolent drawling out of their words, that is very tiresome if not disgusting. I stood next to a lady one night, near a window, and, by way of saying something, remarked that the air was much cooler than usual ; to which she answered, " Yes, ma-am, *him rail-ly too fra-ish.*"

25*th*.—My dearest N. very unwell, and kept his bed till 2 o'clock.—The staff and Mr. Scott of the Council breakfasted with me. Had a long conversation with the latter, on political subjects ; and, as his was a visit of business, General N. saw him in his bed-room afterwards. Mr. G. Cuthbert, also, about a place in the Custom House, for a friend of his, as one of the officers is dead.—Give the servants an entertainment in the evening, and a dollar each. Poor creatures, they seemed the happiest of the happy, dancing and singing almost the whole night.

26*th*.—Colonel Roberts and Major Mackenzie of the 85th, Dr. Lind, Major Pye, and Captain Fraser, &c. at breakfast.

—My dear N. better, but so harassed with business, that he has hardly a moment to himself, and we can scarcely speak to each other. Made a present to the white servants to-day. —Dine between 5 and 6. General Churchill and his Aide-de-camp, Mr. Scott, the gentlemen of the 85th, and Mr. Hanbury, in addition to our party.

27th.—Soon after 6, sent off carriages for General Le Clerc's Aide-de-camp, Colonel Bourke, and the other French officer, who have just arrived from St. Domingo. They came to breakfast about 8. General Churchill, &c. and about thirty people, at breakfast. Wore my new Neapolitan mantle, sent me by dear Lady Buckingham.—The gentlemen seemed to be bragging Republicans, and General Churchill and I had a great deal of fun, in questioning them about their adventures in St. Domingo, and were indiscreet enough to make our remarks to each other in English, thinking that they did not understand us ; but we found, afterwards, that they had only pretended to be ignorant of English, for when General N. sent an Aide-de-camp with them to do the honours of the King's House, &c. to them, as he could not speak French, they were quite fluent in English. So poor General C. and I are in a sad scrape.— Admiral Duckworth and his son added to our party at dinner.—The Frenchmen all went to Kingston, and the Admiral remained for the night.

28th.—Sir John Duckworth set off at 5.—The late Attorney-General of St. Domingo, for our Government, was at breakfast,—strongly recommended to General N. by the Duke of Portland. Also Mr. Cuthbert, Mr. Lindo, and Major Mosheim, with some of the staff. Soon after, Captain Hogg and his son came.—General N. full of St. Domingo and other business, and sadly bored by insignificant people. Got rid of them all in the evening, and go to bed at 9 o'clock.

29th.—Soon after 7, Dr. Lind, Mr. Corbet, Mr. Hanbury ; and Mr. Hyslop, to be sworn in for his appointment in the Custom House. Then Colonel Lethbridge, of the 60th regiment, just arrived from England. After a great deal of talk, get away to write our English letters. Only Mr. Corbet and Mr. Hanbury remain for dinner. General N. had a great deal of business to transact with Mr. Corbet, about St. Domingo.

May 1st.—Send carriages at 1, for Sir J. Duckworth and the Navy men, and at four for the French gentlemen.—General N. busy all the morning with his English despatches.— Twenty-eight people at dinner. Sir J. Duckworth was obliged by business to leave us early, and the rest all took their leave by ten.

2nd.—The horses were galled and tired by their frequent journies during the last week, so we said our prayers at home. Kemble* went to Kingston, to take possession of the appointment given to him by General N.—Only Duckworth remained at the Penn for the night.

3rd.—A dreadfully hot morning.—Mr. and Mrs. and Mr. W. M. Murphy, Mr. and Mrs. Woodham, Mrs. and the Misses Rennalls, Mrs. and the Misses Lewis, Captain Penrose, and Mr. Ward—the two latter gentlemen to take leave for England. All left us by 1, and we wrote English letters till dinner time, and then despatched them by a dragoon to Port Henderson.

4th.—Drive to Port Henderson at 5, and bring young Meredith, Brown, and Rogers, to the Penn.—Mr. and Mrs. Hibbert,† Mr. and Mrs. Hughes, the Rev. Mr. Scott,‡ and Mr. Cuthbert, at dinner.

---

* There were Kembles of New Jersey, connected with Lady Nugent by marriage.

† The Hibbert family was long connected with Jamaica. Two Thomas Hibberts, and a Robert Hibbert, who were members of the Assembly. Thomas Hibbert, the elder, who arrived in Jamaica in 1734, built Headquarter House in Kingston, long known as Hibbert House. George Hibbert, an alderman of the City of London, and Member of Parliament, was agent for Jamaica in England; he played a large part in the establishment of the West India Docks, and in the foundation of the London Institution, of which he was president for many years; he was also chairman of the West India Merchants in London.

‡ Rev. A. J. Scott was rector of St. John, now called Linstead.

5th.—General N. off at 4, to review the 69th regiment. Find Captains Ross and Hatley, R.N., in the breakfast-room.—My dear N. back at one, not the worse for the excessive heat, thank God. The Navy men, and Mr. Drummond of the 60th regiment, in addition to our staff party.

6th.—Set off at 5 for Stony Hill.—General N. drove me in the curricle. My maid was driven by Mr. Duckworth in a gig. General N.'s man Rogers, with various blackies on horseback, and our own horses, were sent on before. The staff joined us near Spanish Town. Arrive about 9, at the bottom of Stony Hill. Major Gould and our horses already there. Mount and ascend the hill. At the barracks we were received by Colonel Gordon and the officers of the 85th regiment, and a large party, assembled for breakfast. After which the regiment was reviewed, the barrack was inspected, and we saw the men at dinner.—The band played for me all the morning, stationed in front of my window. Highly gratified in every respect. General N. complimented the regiment, and we took our leave, all parties thoroughly well pleased.

At the bottom of the hill find our carriages ready ; but then it was near four o'clock, and the sun broiling over our heads furiously, and the dust intolerable.—A large party assembled at the Admiral's Penn. The dinner had been waiting some time, and Sir J. Duckworth was so impatient, that it was announced to us before we were ourselves half dressed. Poor dear N. was worse off than myself, as he had to shave, and had only just begun. Got ready as soon as possible, and beg the party to sit down, and that General N. would soon join them. He came in about the middle of the dinner, in as high a fever as myself. Two tables were laid, for an immensely crowded party. Only two ladies besides myself, Mrs. Peacocke and Mrs. Griffiths ; so there was no dancing, and we got to bed as soon as we could.

7th.—General N., thank God, quite prosperous this morning, and he set off at 5 to review the 6th battalion, 60th regiment, at Up Park Camp. A lage party of naval men

to attend the Admiral and me, to a breakfast given by Mr.
Griffiths.　General N. met us there.　A room as full as possible ; and, what with the heat of the sun and the crowd,
the atmosphere was almost insupportable.　The breakfast
table was loaded with ragouts, fricassées, &c. and beef-
steaks ! !　As General N. had business in Kingston, we got
away as soon as we could.—Return to the Admiral's about
4, dress and dine almost immediately.　A large party—Mrs.
Hibbert, Mrs. Symes, Mrs. and Miss Cochrane, were the
ladies to-day.

　　8th.—General N. off soon after 4, to review the 2nd battalion, 60th regiment.—A large party, of Navy officers in
particular, to breakfast with the Admiral ; I making the
agreeable to them as well as I can.—Mrs. Griffiths called
soon after, and we all drove to Kingston, to shop and visit.
The heat dreadful.　Got back at 3 ; my dear N. was just
returned.　Both of us half-fatigued and hurried to death ;
the first with the heat, and the second with the Admiral's
impatience to sit down to dinner, for fear it should be spoiled.
The party was a complete crowd.—Before 6 drove to Greenwich, where the Admiral's barge was in waiting for us, and
we rowed to Port Henderson ; there we took to our carriages, and got safe to the Penn soon after nine.

　　9th.—Up very early, but can't get to church ; there being
such a crowd of people, and my dear N. so full of business.
—Captains Ross and Hatley of the Navy, Colonel Gordon
and some officers of General N.'s regiment (the 85th),
Colonel Roberts, Captains Maitland, and D'Arcy, and (I beg
his pardon) Major Mackenzie.　Then to dinner came Colonel
Gillespie, 20th dragoons, Colonel Brisbane, 69th regiment,
Major and Mrs. Pye : in all twenty-six people.

　　10th.—Up early, and again an immense party ; twenty to
breakfast.　Soon after General N. went off to his Court of
Chancery, and was not at home again till near 6.　He was
much fatigued, and worn out with long causes.　Major
Mackenzie, 85th, Mr. White, Mr. Hely, 69th regiment, and
altogether twenty-five people at dinner.

11*th.*—The Speaker, Mr. Edwards, &c. at breakfast. General N. at the King's House soon after.—Captain Elrington, 2nd W. I. regiment from Fort Augusta, in the morning.

12*th.*—Drive to Port Henderson soon after 5. Received Mr. Scott at breakfast.—General N. at the King's House all the morning.—Dr. Lind says that no one can be going on better than I am, and I trust in God he is right.—King Mitchell, the Speaker, Mr. Edwards, Mr. Hinchliffe, Rev. Mr. Scott, and a large party, at dinner.

13*th.*—Mr. Campbell, and Mr. Jones, at breakfast. General N. as usual, at the King's House, as Chancellor, all the morning.—For a wonder, all our staff dine out.

14*th.*—Mr. Peacocke, with the staff, at breakfast. At 5, General N. with delightful letters, and several nice presents, from dear Lady Buckingham and dear Lady Temple. Twenty-six people at dinner, among them were the new Attorney-General,* Mr. Ross, Mr. Redwood, Messrs. Jackson, Affleck, and Lewis, privy counsellors, Captain Mends, R.N. Captain Brown, 20th dragoons, Major and Mrs. Pye, &c.

16*th.*—Honourable Major Macdonald, and several of the staff at breakfast. At dinner, Mr. and Mrs. Woodham, Mr. Edwards, Captain Dickson,† and Mr. Kelly (just from England) and Mr. Parkinson, 20th dragoons, &c. &c.

17*th.*—At dinner, Major and Mrs. Pye, Captain Bartlett, and Lieutenant Le Breton of the Engineers, from England, and another lieutenant of the same corps, whose name I could not learn. Mr. Bankes and Mr. Foster, of the Navy, with the staff.

18*th.*—Colonel Ramsay and Major Cookson at breakfast, with Mr. Halkett, and Mr. Grant, just arrived, who remained all day.—Talk a great deal about England to-day, but, alas ! our new comers don't know any of our friends.

19*th.*—Colonel Gordon, Captain Dobbin, Mr. March, and Mr. O'Farrell, at breakfast. Have a long conversation with Colonel G. afterwards. Send carriages for the Admiral, Captain Boyle, &c.

* William Ross.
† Sometimes written by Lady Nugent as Dixon.

20th.—Sir J. T. Duckworth off at 5, for Port Royal. Colonel Gordon went long before.—Captain Elrington at breakfast.

21st.—A very large party of lawyers at dinner. Three ladies, Mrs. Hughes, Mrs. Tonge, and Mrs. Cunningham, and Mr. Redwood,* a clergyman from Montserrat, to whom General N. has given a living at the request of the Speaker, were also of the party.

23rd.—General N. so much engaged that we can't go to church. Send the staff and the servants, and we staid at home together.—Mr. Corbet on St. Domingo affairs ; and Mr. and Mrs. Woodham, and Mr. Drummond, of the 60th, at dinner. Am so unwell that I am obliged to leave the table.

24th.—After a restless night, up before 4, and off for Fort Augusta. Arrive there just as the sun was rising, and General N. immediately reviewed the 55th regiment, which had just landed. A grand breakfast.—Then the 2nd West India regiment was reviewed. Walk down the line with General N. and speak to many of the new soldiers ; though they did not understand, they tried to look pleased.—Cake, wine, &c. set out at Mrs. Cruchley's, who, with Mrs. Elrington, did the honours of their apartments to me. Return to the Penn a good deal fatigued, but my dear N. was obliged to start for Spanish Town immediately, to hold a Bishop's Court. He returned to dinner at 6.

25th.—Drive to Port Henderson at 5, where General N. inspected some invalids of the 55th regiment. He bought a fine American horse. He did not go to the King's House, but staid at home, and wrote letters all the morning.—At dinner, Colonels Lethbridge and Roberts, and Dr. Veitch.

26th.—Kemble came to-day to thank General N., and seems very happy in his situation.

27th.—The blackies perfect in their prayers. Read to them myself this evening, and intend doing so in future.

28th.—Colonel de Charmilly and Mr. Lewis at breakfast. —Give a farewell dinner to the officers of the 2nd West

* Evidently a relative of the Hon. Philip Redwood, then Speaker.

India regiment and their wives. All depart at ten, excepting Mrs. Elrington, who sleeps here.—We had a few drops of rain to-day for a wonder, and how tantalizing that there were not a few showers.

29th.—Rise at 5, and write letters for General N. till breakfast time, and begin again immediately after, and write till 1, when he despatched forty circulars to the different Members of the Assembly, upon the subject of the ensuing meeting.—At dinner, only Mrs. Elrington and our staff.—Heard the servants their catechism, and to bed at nine.

30th.—The Admiral, &c. send to beg for the carriages. This prevents us from going to church. These Sunday parties are sad things; but in the present instance it can't be avoided. Read prayers at home.—Sir J. T. Duckworth, Admiral Campbell, and Captains Dunn, Gardner, Eyles, Grindal, and Mends; in all about twenty-four. All left us for Port Royal at 8, and we were in bed at nine.

31st.—Drive to Port Henderson at 5. Took leave of Mrs. Elrington, and sent her under the escort of Captain Duckworth to Fort Augusta.—All the morning preparing despatches to go by the *Juno* frigate to England.

June 1st.—Send off my letters by Hallam, who goes in the *Juno* to England.

2nd.—Try to drink the Spa water,* but it won't do.—At dinner only Mr. Colman, of the 60th, and our own party.—Drive to see poor little Dr. Lind, who is ill in bed, but not I trust seriously so. He thinks well of my case, and I am happy.

3rd.—Drive to Spanish Town at 5 o'clock. Give orders for the grand dinner to-morrow. Only Captain Macintosh, of the 85th, added to our party to-day. General N. has given him a fort, and he seems delighted.

4th.—General N. &c. started early for Spanish Town. The troops out. Salutes, &c.; and then a levee held.—Mrs.

* This probably refers to the spring near Silver Hill Gap, in the Blue Mountains, which was formerly known as the Jamaica Spa.

Pye and Mrs. Elrington came to dine with me, and General N. had all the civil and military at the King's House, to celebrate the King's birth-day. *A great let off.* Returned to the Penn at 10, and all in bed soon after. God bless our dear good old King!

5th.—Major Mosheim, Captain and Mrs. Elrington, and Mr. and Mrs. Davies, 2nd W.I. regiment, at dinner.—Almost all our servants ill with the fatigues of yesterday.

6th.—Whitsunday.—Up early, and to church at 10. The service well performed, and the Communion well attended. —Only Mr. and Mrs. Woodham, Monsieur and Madame Grandjean, and Madlle. Robert, at dinner.

7th.—General Churchill and his Aide-de-camp, &c. at breakfast. General C. &c. amused themselves as well as they could, for General N. was obliged to attend to business. Major and Mrs. Pye, Captain and Mrs. Elrington, and Major Stapleton, added to our party at dinner.

8th.—Major and Mrs. Pye came to enquire, and remained to breakfast. The whole morning strong symptoms of all going on right and well with me, and though very poorly, I rejoice and keep up my spirits.

9th.—Captain and Mrs. Elrington went back to Fort Augusta.—General N. and I most comfortably alone all the morning. He wrote a letter to the Speaker, and I worked by his side.—I am now teaching some of the ladies to make shoes, in the style of Vanderville, and am very busy at the pattern pair.

10th.—My dear husband's birth-day, and may God bless and preserve him in all things! Offer up this morning a more than usually fervent prayer for his welfare. He is, however, sadly harassed with business, and has scarcely ever the pen out of his hand. Colonel Gillespie and Mr. Edwards to breakfast. A great deal of conversation after, with the latter. When they were gone, my dear N. finished his speech, message, &c. and is now ready for the opening of the session. Colonel Roberts, Major and Mrs. Pye, &c. at dinner. To bed at 10, but poor General N. had to write to the Admiral, and so much to arrange in the way of business, that he was much later.

11th.—General N. off, at 4, to review the 20th dragoons. Not well enough to go with him.—An immense party at dinner, at 5, and a dance in the evening. Colonel Gillespie and I opened the ball, and, in spite of my illness, this morning, I got through all extremely well, and did not get to bed till half-past twelve.

12th.—General N. and part of his staff went to visit Admiral Campbell. Colonel Roberts, Mr. Lester, and Mr. Sutherland of the 85th, who slept here, breakfasted with me. About 1, General N. returned much heated, and more fatigued than usual. Persuaded him to lie down, and, in consequence, he was much refreshed by 5.—At 6, a large party, General Rose, &c.

13th.—Send the chariot for Miss Murphy and Major and Mrs. Pye.

14th.—General N. &c. early in Spanish Town, to meet the Council, &c. The Attorney-General and Mr. Campbell, 2nd West India regiment.

15th.—Rise very early, anxious for the result of the business to be brought before the Assembly, and particularly on account of all the vexations that may arise to my dear husband. Mrs. Pye, Mrs. Griffiths, and Mrs. Elrington, and Lord Aylmer,* &c. at breakfast.—General N. went to town at 2, and returned before 6.—Much business expected to-morrow.—Lord Aylmer and I had a great deal of talk about old times.

16th.—The Speaker, Mr. Scott, Mr. Murphy, &c. &c. and some military. Two young Messrs. Murphy, Mr. Grant, and Colonel Skerrett, were among our guests.—Most of them returned to dinner at 6, so we did not get to bed till half-past ten o'clock.

* Matthew, 5th Baron Aylmer, who was born in 1775. He was colonel of the 18th foot. He had married in 1801 Louisa Anne, daughter of Sir John Call. He apparently did not bring her to Jamaica. Aylmers, in St. Catherine, was settled by Colonel Whitgift Aylmer in the seventeenth century.

17th.—At breakfast, Mr. Simon Taylor.—General N. went to Spanish Town, and sent his first message to the House of Assembly, on the subject of his communications from Lord Hobart.—Dine at 6. The Speaker, General Rose, Captain Carr, &c. added to our party. Anxiety has made me so unwell, that I can scarcely sit out the dinner, and was glad to get away, and go to bed, without seeing any more of the gentlemen.

18th.—Only our own party at breakfast, and dine between 2 and 3 o'clock ; after which General N. went into Spanish Town, for the meeting of the Assembly.—At 6, Mrs. Elrington and Miss Murphy accompanied me, and we all dressed for the ball at the King's House. An immense crowd of gentlemen, but few ladies, as, at this season of the year, they are all in the country. I declined dancing, and no one seemed surprised ; but I promised old Sir John Duckworth * to open the first ball with him after October next. God grant it, and how happy I shall be then ! Even at this distance of time, the happiness is almost too great to think of. I played cassino, and did all I could to keep the *big wigs*, &c. in good humour.—We supped between 12 and 1, and got home at 4 o'clock, my knee aching with making curtesies, and my temper tried with amusing and making fine speeches ; but, thank God, my dearest N. is not at all the worse for the anxieties and his writing fatigues, &c. which have been severe of late.—I must mention, that I wore a pink and silver dress this evening, given me by Madame Le Clerc, and which was the admiration of the whole room.

19th.—Don't get up till 8, and breakfast at 9. Sir J. Duckworth, Admiral Campbell, and several Navy men, at breakfast. They staid all the morning, and we dined at 4 ; having an addition to our party of some officers of the 85th. My dear N. sat down, but, after taking a little soup, was obliged to be off to Spanish Town, where indispensable business awaited him. He returned at 8, and the party was kindly broken up. Only Captain Elrington and young Drury staid to sleep. To bed soon after 9, fatigued both

* He was only fifty-five.

in body and mind, and very anxious for my dear N., who has many embarrassing affairs on his hands at present, and every thing going wrong in the House of Assembly.

20th.—Our thoughts are so engaged with business that we have no comfort of our prayers to-day.—My dear N. is much harassed.—At dinner, Mr. and Mrs. Woodham, the Pyes, the Murphys, and the Elringtons—the latter left us in the evening, to go on board the *Druid* frigate. Heard of the arrival of a packet, just as we were going to bed.

21st.—At breakfast, the Speaker, Mr. Edwards, and the Reverend Mr. Scott. All went with General N. to Spanish Town after, and Miss Murphy also left the Penn. Glad to be alone, and read my English letters sent me by express from the King's House. All pleasant, but the fuss and agitation of reading them increased the heat so much, that I was quite ill when General N. returned home to dinner at 6. —Feel more annoyance than I own, when I think of the vexatious proceedings of the House of Assembly, and also my dear N.'s fatigues and anxieties.

22nd.—The Pyes, Mr. Herring, Mr. Griffiths, and some military, at breakfast.—General N. went to town at 11, and then all the rest departed, and I was happy to be left alone. —The Speaker and a few Members dined with us.

23rd.—The Reverend Mr. Donaldson only, in addition to our staff, at breakfast to-day. General N. went to the King's House, to prorogue the Assembly, and came back to dine at 5.

24th.—Drive to Port Henderson, and return before 7.— Messrs. Grant, Minot, Corbet, and Whitfield, with Lord Aylmer, at breakfast, and Mr. Murphy and Major Maitland added to the party for dinner.

25th.—Drive to the Salt-Ponds early.—Only our own party at breakfast.—The morning quiet. Captains Carthew and Mends of the Navy, Mr. Colman, the Pyes, Messrs. Griffiths and Kemble, at dinner. The latter is now Surveyor of Kingston, and my brother Downes Collector of Savanna la-Mar.

26th.—Captains Bartlett and Carr at breakfast.—Send for the Admirals, &c. at 2, to dinner. They, together with Lord Aylmer, Colonel Roberts, and Mr. Nixon of the 85th regiment, the Reverend Mr. Scott, Captain Walker, R.N. &c. formed our party. The Admirals slept here, and we played cards.

27th.—A cloudy morning.—The Admirals went away early.—A few showers in the course of the day.—After we returned from church General N. was full of business, and sat up late writing, after our dinner party broke up.

28th.—At 4, General N. off, to see the troops embark at Port Henderson. Mr. Scott returned with him. General N. engaged all day with English despatches. I also write my letters.

29th.—Writing all day. Only Lord Aylmer at dinner.

July 1st.—Drive to the King's House before 5.—Send carriages for Navy men.—A very large party at dinner, and all left us before 10, excepting Lord Aylmer and Mrs. Pye, who remain at night.

2nd.—Up very early, and finish my letters before breakfast.—Lord Aylmer came to gossip in my own room, while General N. finished his, and this was not till our dinner time. Feel low and unwell all dinner, thinking of England, &c. Lord A. left us at 6, to embark for England.

3rd.—Drove to Spanish Town early, but am particularly heavy, and feel the heat exceedingly all day.

4th.—To church at 10, and bring back with us Monsieur Grandjean and Madlle. Robert.—Not well, and retire to my own room, and leave them to amuse themselves. Have a consultation with Dr. Veitch, and dress for dinner in much better spirits. Several officers of the 85th, and altogether a very large dinner party.

5th.—Copy despatches for General N. from 5 till near 9, and am delighted to be useful. Colonel Rumsey and a party at breakfast; and feel so much better to-day, that, as soon as they were gone, wrote again, not only my own letters, but helped to copy my dear N.'s.—Mr. Cuthbert and

Mr. Lindo upon business.   The latter about lending money
to the French in St. Domingo.—Send off our despatches by
the *Crescent* frigate, Captain Carthew.

6th.—General N. reviewed the 2nd battalion of the 85th
regiment, on the race course,* near Spanish Town, before 6,
and returned before the sun was over-powerful.   At 4, my
dear N. off for Spanish Town again, to dine with the 85th.
—Mrs. Pye, Kemble, and Duckworth, to dine with me.

7th.—General N. up at half-past two.   I also got up, and
wrote Mems, for him, while he dressed.   At half-past three,
he was off for Kingston, Stony Hill, &c. about barracks, and
other military arrangements.   I laid down till 5, but could
not sleep, I was so uneasy about my dear N., who has so
much fatigue of body and mind, and in such broiling weather.   After breakfast Mrs. Pye was sent for express, Mrs.
Rossington being taken very ill in Spanish Town ; and she
was dead at 11 o'clock, only having complained a few hours
before.   Very much shocked, and feel quite unwell in consequence.

8th.—Have had a tolerable night's rest, and cheer myself
with looking forward to the return of my dear husband.
God protect him !   All the party went into Spanish Town,
after breakfast, and I remained at home till dinner time.

9th.—Colonel Gordon, and some of the 85th, at breakfast.
About 2 o'clock, the Admiral, his Secretary, Captains Mends
and Ross, of the Navy, with some civilians, made a large
party.   Had spasms in my side all dinner time, and went
to bed as soon as our guests left us, before ten.

11th.—Feel so well that I return thanks fervently to God,
and now look forward with more certainty and joy than
ever to the arrival of my expected darling baby.   Mr. Gore,
of the *Cerberus*, at breakfast.—Read prayers at home, Mr.
Woodham being so ill he could not leave his house.—Mrs.
Pye took leave in the evening, and we were in bed at ten.

12th.—Up at 4, and set off for the Decoy,† Mr. Murphy's

* Now no longer used for racing.
† Formerly the property of Sir Charles Price, for many years
Speaker of the Assembly.

L

estate, in St. Mary's parish.—Arrive at Berkshire Hall at half-past nine. Find a breakfast prepared, and Mr. and Miss Murphy waiting for us.—Proceed on our journey at 11. A dreadful hill to mount, and the heat beyond description. A tremendous thunderstorm met us, just as we were in a narrow road, with a great precipice on one side, and a hanging rock on the other. The flashes of lightning, and the rain, beating in our faces, almost blinded the poor horses as well as ourselves. We were wet through, for General N. was obliged to throw away the umbrella to save our lives, as we were very near being down the precipice. The kittareen, that was driven by Captain Johnson, close behind us, was thrown down the precipice, and dashed to pieces, but he was active and saved himself.

Arrived at the Decoy about 2, but so stiff and heavy with the weight of water about me, my shoes even being full, that I was obliged to be lifted out of the carriage. My clothes were immediately taken off by the ladies of the house, who thought I was all over bruises; but soon found that the green and yellow stripes on my skin proceeded only from the dye of the umbrella having run in streams down my back. I was washed all over with rum, and then took some warm soup, and in two hours I was as well as ever and as gay. My dearest N. would not take care of himself, and only thought of me, so I fear he will suffer. God grant he may escape, and all the party; for, like myself, every creature is wet through.—Only Mr. Hinchliffe, who came with us, in addition to the family party.—Very snug and comfortable, and all uncommonly cheerful and well, this evening.

13th.—All well, except being a little stiff this morning. My dear N. really enjoying himself very much; walking about, shooting, and fishing on the lake, till dinner time. Dine at 4.—A nice walk in the garden in the evening. Fine broad gravel walks, cabbage and cocoa-nut trees, and many ornamental shrubs. Have a syllabub on the lawn. The gentlemen play at bowls, and the young people swing. The comparative coolness of the climate is quite refreshing, and all things are so comfortable about us, that I felt almost as if I were in England; and, besides, I have so many secret sources of comfort and delight at present, that my mind is in a heavenly state, and I am as perfectly happy as any mortal can be.—Two Messrs. Grant joined our party, but we all separated, and went to bed at nine.

14*th*.—Up at 5, and walk in the garden with my maid. At 7, we all assembled at breakfast.—Visit the dairy, &c. and feel quite well, but my dear Nugent's hands are very much inflamed and swelled, and his face is redder than ever, from being so much exposed to the sun all day yesterday. Captain Cox from the East Indies, and Kemble and Duckworth came.—At 8, I went to bed from prudential motives. The rest of the party went at ten.

15*th*.—An early walk again.—A working party of ladies in the morning.—More gentlemen joined us at dinner to-day, and we had a large party.—In the evening in the garden, bowls and syllabub, &c. and then cards till ten.

16*th*.—Walk more than an hour in the garden with Miss Murphy, and my maid attending us.—A large breakfast party at 7. General N. rather heated and not quite well. Oblige him to rest and be quiet, till dinner time. Some people, however, upon business. Captain Vanderbrooke, &c. of the 60th. I was in hopes we should not have had anything of the sort, for a few days at least. In the evening General N. quite well, and I am happy.

17*th*.—An early walk as usual. After breakfast, General N., with a party of gentlemen, explored the country on horseback, and came back much pleased with the views, &c. Dine at 4 o'clock. Afterwards ; first, the usual lawn amusements, and then chess and cards till 9. I played at the former, beat and was beaten.

19*th*.—Before I returned from my morning walk, the Chief Justice, Mr. Kirby, and Mr. Cuthbert, arrived.—Some of our party returned to Spanish Town, and Majors Irvine and Drummond replaced them ; so they will all in turn enjoy a little cooler atmosphere.

20*th*.—Mr. K. and Mr. C. off early.—At 4, our packet letters ; all delightful. Go to dinner in high spirits, at 5. A little thunder and rain, for about a quarter of an hour, and then beautiful and fresh all the evening ; quite delightful.

21*st*.—A grand holiday given to the blackies, on our account. A most amusing dance on the lawn, and all very merry.

22*nd*.—Rise soon after 4, and breakfast at 6.—Begin our journey homewards. A sad fright soon after we started. The horses took it into their heads to back partly down the hill. Thank God, no accident, and I behaved quite heroically ! The reflection on the dear one I have in charge, gave me presence of mind, and a degree of fortitude I did not think that I possessed ; thank God ! Carried in a chair to Berkshire Hall, where we took leave of our kind host and his daughters, and paid my black ponies for my journey. Arrive at the Penn, without accident or fright, at 4.

23*rd*.—Colonel Roberts and Mr. Mackenzie, of the 85th, and Mr. Gore, R.N., at breakfast.

24*th*.—Our new butler, Short, arrived.—Drive to Dr. Lind's in the evening.

25*th*.—Colonels Gordon and Roberts, of the 85th, and Captain Bartlett, of the Engineers, at breakfast.—Only Captain Bartlett and Lieutenant Le Breton, R. E. in addition to our party of the staff. To-day I have written to some, and lectured others, of the young men of our staff. All very silly people, but I keep their folly from General N. as well as I can.

26*th*.—General Churchill, Mr. March, &c. at breakfast, and also some officers of the 2nd battalion of the 85th.— Send off our despatches by the *Sans Pareil*, and dine at 4. —Then a drive to Dr. Lind's. He pronounces me very flourishing. Alas ! poor man, he appears sadly declining, I am grieved to say.

27th.—Major Mackenzie, and Messrs. Nixon and Rogers, of the 85th, at dinner.—Drive out in the evening on the race-course.

28th.—Colonel Gordon and the Pyes at breakfast. Major Pye just returned from St. Domingo, whither General N. had sent him on a mission to General Le Clerc. He brought me a second cargo of Parisian fashions, from Madame Le Clerc (subsequently La Princesse Borghese), sister to the great Buonaparte.—In the evening, drive to Port Henderson, where Colonel Gordon embarked for England on board the *Nimrod* frigate, commanded by Captain Mends.

31st.—King Mitchell, the Attorney-General, and a large dinner party.

August 1st.—The Admiral, &c. attended our family prayers.—Capt. Honyman, R.N. came to ask our commands for England.

2nd.—Sir J. Duckworth, &c. left us.—Officers of the 2nd battalion of the 85th at breakfast. Dine at 3.—Visit Dr. Lind in the evening.

3rd.—Young Creek and Grace, of the *Ganges*, at breakfast.—General N. went to the King's House soon after, to hold a Board of Works. Expected all the officers of the 85th, second battalion, at dinner. A delightful tropical rain kept most of them from coming. Those that did come got away soon after 8, and we went to bed, much refreshed by the air being cooled.

4th.—Sent Grace and Criek to Port Henderson at 4.— Only Major Mackenzie at dinner.

5th.—Out, before gun-fire, in the carriage, by myself. Only the maids. General N. rode.—Captain Bartlett, &c. at breakfast.

7th.—Mr. and Mrs. Woodham, and their little girl, Captain Bartlett, and Mr. Le Breton, &c. at breakfast. They all took their leave at 10.

8th.—Mr. Woodham too weak to perform the service, so we read prayers at home.—Despatch our English letters before dinner.—The Grandjeans, Mademoiselle Robert, Mr.

Edwards, 5th West India Regiment, Mr. Colman, 60th, Mr. Thompson, 85th, &c. were our guests.

9th.—A dreadful and sudden tornado for half an hour this morning. The whole house in consternation, for fear of a hurricane. General N. in alarm for me, and thinking of a place of safety. However, all passed over, and we were truly thankful.—Only Major Gould and Mr. Brown at dinner. Set off immediately after for the Admiral's Penn.— Mr. Waterhouse, Mr. Ludlow, and some Navy men.

10th.—General N. off before 5, for Up Park Camp, on barrack business.—Some Kingston ladies after breakfast. Go into town with them to *shop*, &c. Return at 3, and try to rest a little.

11th.—All our party go to breakfast, at Mr. Griffiths', at 8. All the gentlemen attend my dear N. to his daily labours of inspection of barracks, seeing about *money matters*, &c. at Kingston. Soon after 2, he returned for me, and we went back to the Admiral's Penn.—A large party of Navy men, Army, &c. at 4. The ladies were Mrs. Griffiths, Miss Moss her sister, Mrs. Symes, and Miss Cockburn her sister, soon to be married, they say, to Captain Ross, R.N.

12th.—Return home before breakfast.—My dear N. full of business, and writing despatches for England, to go by the *Topaze* frigate, Capt. Honyman.—A magnificent present of peaches to-day from Sir J. Duckworth; a very great treat to me.

13th.—Drive to Spanish Town, and look at a house soon to be occupied by Mr. and Mrs. Murphy. See Dr. Lind. He says I do a great deal too much. Determined to rest; to bed at eight.

14th.—Take my walk till sun-rise in the Piazza.—Captain Bartlett at breakfast. Mr. Ramsay came to pay General N. an escheat.—Dine at half-past three, and drive out. Lose our way in a wood, and don't get home till past 8, much fatigued.—Make Captain Johnson read prayers, and hear the servants their catechism, and go to bed myself.

15th.—At dinner, Mr. and Mrs. Woodham, Major Maitland, 60th, Captain Jeffries, 60th, Mr. Thompson, 85th, and three officers whose names I did not hear.

16th.—My dear N. and I talk over many interesting arrangements, in the Piazza, before breakfast.—Only Mr. Edwards, 6th West India regiment, with our staff at dinner. —Drive to Port Henderson.

17th.—General N. out with his gun till 7.—Receive dear English letters. Every thing delightful. All our friends well, and General N.'s public despatches of the most flattering nature. His conduct in all respects highly approved of, thank God! His applications, too, all attended to, and all successful.—Drive to Dr. Lind's, and have the happiness of telling him of General N.'s success in his favour. Call also for General N. to make communications to Mr. Cuthbert and Mr. Mitchell.—Have prayers, and go happier to bed than usual, and feel uncommonly well. Ease of mind is the best medicine for all my little ills, I am sure.

18th.—I often think what a curious sight it would be in England, to see General N. and me, in only our *robes de chambre*, strolling about at daylight, eating fruit, &c. This morning was fresher than usual, and we really enjoyed ourselves. Captain Bartlett and Colonel Roberts at breakfast ; they staid all day.—Write letters to go by the *Syren* frigate. —Call upon Mr. March, &c. after dinner.

19th.—Send the carriage early to Fort Augusta, for Captain and Mrs. Elrington, and their little girl, only five weeks old. All day nursing the little baby. Feel deeply at the sight of an infant. A sort of happy agitation kept me awake all night. Oh, my God, hear my prayers, and grant me the blessing of a healthy child, endowed with such good and amiable qualities and disposition as may make it a blessing to its dear father and myself, and grant it may ever be worthy of thy care and protection, by doing good in its generation, and serving thee faithfully all its days, through our Lord and Saviour Jesus Christ.

20th.—Up at half-past five. Send for the baby, and walk

with it in the Piazza.—Finish our letters, to go by the *Syren*.
—At dinner, Captain Carr, Mr. D'Arcy Whittington (a complete quiz), &c. were of our party.

21st.—Send to Port Henderson for the Admiral, &c.
Mrs. E. confined to her bed, and the poor baby not at all
well.—Dined with the gentlemen at 4. Feel very uneasy,
from hearing the poor baby crying continually. Obliged to
play my part, and have cards, &c. to amuse my gentlemen.
—The baby better.

22nd.—Walk with General N. in the Piazza till sun-rise.—
Our house overflowing with guests.—Go to church at 10.
—Mrs. E. well enough to return to Fort Augusta at 2.—A
large party at dinner. Mr. Supple, the new clergyman, was
of the number.

23rd.—Sir J. Duckworth, and Captains Dunn and Ross,
amuse themselves exceedingly well, and give me no trouble,
while General N. goes on with his business uninterruptedly.
—Twenty-six people at dinner, the principal guests being
of the Council and Assembly, with General Churchill, his
Aide-de-camp, &c. All go to the King's House in the evening, where we had a ball and supper. Did not get to bed
till 1. This is not keeping strictly to poor little Dr. Lind's
quiet directions; but, though I was as merry as any of
the party, I did not even think of dancing.

24th.—Dine at half-past two. Then all set off, at 4, for
New Hall, King Mitchell's. Get there before 8, and feel so
fatigued that, as I was the only lady, I long to go to my own
room and to bed immediately, but the heat and the musquitoes would scarcely let me sleep the whole night.

25th.—After breakfast the gentlemen attend General N.
to explore the country. I kept quiet, but took too long a
walk in the evening, and was glad to get away from the
party, very early.

27th.—Up very early. The heat, the musquitoes, the
roars of laughter from the gentlemen till a late hour, and the
dancing and jollity of the servants all night, all combined
together to spoil our repose, so that we got very little sleep,

and I feel this now very much. My dear N. is, thank God, quite well, and that is a consolation.

27th.—Start at daylight for home.—The Admiral and Captain Dunn near having their necks broken, by the horse Captain Dunn was driving becoming unruly, and the carriage was indeed in a sad shattered state, in consequence. All get home safe, however, thank God! and soon after breakfast, all retire to sleep, and rest ourselves. I undressed completely, and had a most sound and refreshing nap; and, when we all met at dinner, were very merry, and there was no complaint.—Captain Dunn drove the Admiral to Port Henderson, but we gave them a quieter horse, and all was well. Only Mr. Hanson, in addition to our dinner party to-day.

28th.—General N. off before daylight, to look for a lady donkey for me, as I am desired to drink the milk every morning, to keep up my strength in this cruel hot weather. But it is my mind more than my body that is affected, by hearing of the constant deaths that occur at this very unhealthy season, which always throws a gloom over this time of the year; and, just now, the island is particularly sickly. Keep up my spirits as well as I can, and try to think of everything cheerful.

29th.—Go to church at 10. The rest of the day quiet, and only Mr. and Mrs. Woodham in addition to our staff, at dinner.

30th.—Up at 5.—The appearance of the morning most extraordinary. All over the mountains to the east, were thick clouds, apparently tinged with fire. From these issued rumbling thunder, and vivid flashes of lightning. This lasted for a quarter of an hour, and was most awful. Then, the sun broke through all with his brightest rays, and nothing could be more sublime. The black clouds became first a sheet of fire, and then dispersed entirely. After looking with wonder and admiration, and some little anxiety, at this scene, my dear N. and I had a most delightful conversation, on the subject of our happy prospect in becoming a father and mother. Our hearts are full of gratitude and joy, and we said our payers with more than usual fervour this morning.—After breakfast, he went to hold a Court of Chancery, at the King's House, and I remained quietly alone till 3, when he returned with the staff, and after our family dinner drove me to Dr. Lind's, whom we found better.

31*st.*—General N. again in the Court of Chancery all day. —Poor Henry Rogers taken ill. Send for Dr. Adolphus.*— A shower of rain, of ten minutes only, was so heavy, that it prevented us from driving out this evening.—Henry Rogers much better.

September 1*st.*—General N. in the Court of Chancery, and I pass my morning alone ; for, as there are only young Aides-de-camp here, I leave them to themselves.—Dr. Adolphus came to tell me that Henry Rogers was much better.—My dear N. much fatigued when he returned from Spanish Town.

2*nd.*—General N. out with his gun early. I walked in the Piazza.—The Pyes and Captain Bartlett to breakfast.— Thank fortune the odious Chancery Court is over to-day. My dear N. home at three. Take a delightful drive in the evening, and to bed early.

4*th.*—General N. rode out with Rogers, Duckworth, and Drury ; but I preferred being quiet till breakfast.—General N. read prayers for me, for I was too much fatigued.

5*th.*—General N. rode with the young Aides-de-camp, and I kept quiet, for the heat is most oppressive.

6*th.*—Only Captain Bartlett at breakfast.—General N. now rides, and I keep quiet in the Piazza before breakfast. Captain Bartlett, as usual, attended General N. to Spanish Town, to hold a Board of Works. I employed my morning most delightfully, in making arrangements for my nursery, and for the accommodation of our gentlemen in town, who must now soon leave the Penn.—My dear N. read to me for an hour, on his return home.

7*th.*—My little lady donkey arrived, and I took my dose. —General N. out with his gun, for an hour before breakfast.

* Afterwards Sir Joseph Adolphus.

—The morning quiet.—Mr. and Mrs. Hughes, Mr. and Miss
Affleck, Captain Saunders, Captain Bartlett, and his officers,
at dinner.   The heat intolerable, and all the party panting
and perspiring to excess.

9th.—Find the ass's milk agree extremely well with me,
but it can't revive my spirits quite, or make me forget the
many who are suffering from illness at this cruel season of
the year.—Send carriages for the Admiral, &c.—A large
party ; Messrs. Hylton and Goreham were the only civilians.
—Doctor Adolphus taken ill at dinner, and obliged to go
home.   The heat more than usual, and all complaining.
The present season, they say, is more than usually sick.
Numbers, both civil and military, are ill, and most of the
medical staff too, which is particularly distressing.

10th.—General N., the Admiral, &c. all rode out early.—
After breakfast, the usual routine ; writing, reading, and
creolizing.*—An immense party at dinner.—Mr. Mitchell,
Mr. Cuthbert, Mr. Shand, Mr. and Mrs. Roden, Mrs. and the
Misses Rennalls, Dr. Broadbelt, &c. were of the number.
Send to Port Royal, for young Brooke and Pakenham.   We
all gasped in the Piazza, after dinner, but really could not
play at cards.—The night a perfect calm, and the moon so
bright, that I got my small Bible, and read some verses in
it, as easy as I could by daylight.

11th.—All up at half-past four.—Drive with the Admiral
to Port Henderson.   He went on board the *Leviathan*, and
General N. went to Fort Augusta, to inspect the invalids
there, and to see what can be done for the comfort of the
poor sick soldiers.   I returned home a little melancholy ;
but, thank God, this dreadful season of the year is so far
advanced.   I now long for two months to be over.—General
N. did not get home till 1.—Am wretched on account of
the heat, but he has not suffered from it.   Only a morning
party.—Drove to Major Cookson's Penn in the evening.

12th.—The heat so great, that I can't go to church.

* cf. J. McLeod, " Voyage of Alceste " (1818): "Creolizing
is an easy and elegant mode of lounging in a warm climate."

Prayers at home.—The Woodhams, two Messrs. Hylton, &c. at dinner.   The heat overpowering, and I am now in a constant state of fatigue from it.

13th.—Major Otway, of the 85th, dined with us.   Drive to Dr. Lind's.

14th.—All our gentlemen, excepting Major Drummond, Rogers, and Drury, gone to dine on board the *Leviathan*. Feel ourselves very comfortable, in having such a snug party.—Send off carriages for Dr. and Mrs. Ludford to-day, and expect them to-morrow by dinner time.

15th.—My domestics are so zealous in giving me the ass's milk, that I am obliged to beg they will not get up in the middle of the night ; for now they bring it to me at three instead of an hour and a half later, which is rather hard upon me, as well as themselves.—Just as we had breakfasted to-day, an Aide-de-camp of General Le Clerc's (Capitaine le Brun) arrived with despatches.   He gives a sad account of the state of the French troops in St. Domingo.   In the course of the last few months they have buried 14,000 men of the yellow fever.   Fifteen general officers have also died, with a proportion of other officers.   Captain Le Brun says, that they have had 25,000 men well, and now not 5000 effective men remain ; and that their guards have been obliged to be made up latterly of black troops ; rather a dangerous experiment under their present circumstances. The island is full of brigands, who come in strong parties from the mountains, and harass the troops continually ; murdering, also, not only every white man they meet, but any black man they suppose to be attached to the French cause.   In short, nothing can be more dreadful than the account this poor young man gives, who appears really sinking into his grave from hardship and fatigue.   He and Colonel Bourke are the only two remaining Aides-de-camp out of ten that General Le Clerc brought with him from France !   He laid down almost all the morning.   We had a present, of English cut-glass and trinkets, made up for Madame Le Clerc, and have purchased a hobby-

horse, with silver appointments, for her son, Astyanax
Le Clerc.

Mr. Forbes, from St. Domingo, joined our dinner party,
with Monsieur Grandjean and Mr. Thompson, of the 85th;
and Dr. and Mrs. Ludford came just before we sat down.
Had a little conversation with him, in the evening. He
thinks me very large, I am sure, from what he said, but
thinks me wonderfully well. Our minds are now at rest,
for, having the doctor in the house, we need not fear a
surprise. I only think about it with joy and thankfulness.

16th.—The ass's milk at 4 this morning. Beg for another
half hour to-morrow; for it is not day-light now, till much
after that time.—General N. drove the doctor into Spanish
Town. On their way they met a Mrs. Hamilton, the wife
of one of the Irish soldiers of the 85th. It seems that she
has come to offer herself as my nurse. I like her appearance
very much. She is pretty and good humoured, which
makes Doctor L. anxious I should take her, and he has persuaded General N. it will be such a good thing to have her
in the house, in case I can't take charge of the dear baby
myself. I have consented, if her character answers, to
receive her, and to give up the delightful idea of nursing,
if it should be found best for the darling child.—Drive out
in the evening, but my mind so agitated all day, that I am
quite unwell, and good for nothing. Mr. Holmes, of the
85th, and Captain Bartlett, our only additional guests
to-day.

17th.—Don't sleep all night for thinking of nurse Hamilton and the future. After breakfast, Dr. and Mrs. Ludford
go to Spanish Town. My dear N. and I all alone during
the morning, and he consoles me very much; for he says
it would be impossible for me to do justice to my dear baby
in this horrid climate, and with the many anxieties of a
public situation, and that Mrs. Hamilton's fair and fat
little boy shews what a good nurse she really does make.
Try to be satisfied.—Am much shocked to hear of Captain
Bartlett's being seized with the yellow fever. He only left

us at 8 o'clock last night, in perfect health, and now they
say that his life is almost despaired of. As soon as we had
dined, General N. drove into Spanish Town, and we called
upon Doctor Rennalls, desiring that he would also take
charge of Captain Bartlett, and at General N.'s expense,
that nothing may be omitted to save the poor man. Major
Maitland rather better, and hopes are entertained of his
recovery. Call upon the Attorney-General.

18th.—The Attorney-General, his bride, and her mother,
Mrs. Tinker, at dinner.

19th.—Visit poor Captain Bartlett. Hear that his symptoms are more favourable.—Mr. Griffiths, Mrs. Rennalls,
Mrs. Israell, the Honourable Mr. and Mrs. Leslie, General Le
Clerc's Aide-de-camp, the Commissary-General, &c. &c. in
all twenty-eight people, at dinner. Much fatigued, though
much amused. The Leslies perfect strangers, and boring
poor General N. sadly about their affairs.—I was cruelly
fatigued too, and the thunder and lightning were so frightful, the greatest part of the night, none of us could sleep.
The rain fell in torrents, but for this we are most grateful.

20th.—Feel good for nothing, but my dear N. is much
cooler, thank God ; for he is so full of business, I don't know
how he will ever get through it all. What with St. Domingo,
the black corps question, and the Court of Chancery, (which
begins again to-day), it is enough really to distract him.
Both of us shocked, too, by hearing that poor Captain
Bartlett was given over.—Mr. Leslie and a large party at
breakfast. General N. went into Spanish Town soon after,
attended by all his plagues. Did not return till 4. The
heat dreadful ; but it threatens rain again to-night. God
grant we may have it.—Some cases of claret sent by the
French to General N., which he immediately ordered to be
returned

21st.—Dr. and Mrs. Ludford off, at daylight, for Kingston.—General N. and I comfortable and alone, till breakfast, when the Admiral and a large party came, for whom
we had sent carriages early. General N. and all the family

went into Spanish Town, and the latter attended poor Captain Bartlett's funeral. General N. in the Court of Chancery all the morning, and I had to amuse the Admiral, &c. Perhaps it was better for me, as I should otherwise only have thought of poor Captain B. who had so often been our guest, and to whom we had taken a great liking. —A remonstrance from the French officers, about the claret, sent as a present, *they said*, from General Le Clerc ; still coolly refused, and for particular reasons, but too long to state to-day—however, I hope to amuse myself shortly, with detailing this transaction, so worthy of the modern French character. In the evening, drive with the Admiral and his party to Port Henderson.

23rd.—Up at gun-fire. The heat dreadful.—General N. in Spanish Town, the whole morning. Drive to Dr. Lind's after dinner, but hurry home on account of a threatened thunderstorm. The air was quite on fire. I just got in before the rain began, which poured down like a torrent. Then came the most tremendous thunder, with flashes of lightning almost blinding. We sat round the table, and were taking some wine and water with Dr. Ludford and Henry Rogers,* who had both come in wet through, when, all at once, there was peal upon peal, and so rapid, that I asked General N. to see by his watch if there was the interval of a second between them, in order to judge of the distance ; but, just as I spoke, the house seemed to be on fire, and two dreadful claps of thunder came as it were at once. All I recollect was, finding myself under the table, on my knees, and quite *crumpled* up. The Doctor ordered the table to be removed, and no one to touch me, but to let me straighten myself gradually. Soon after, I was able to move, and, after a hearty fit of crying, and seeing that no one was hurt, and the thunder becoming every minute more distant, I recovered myself entirely. All the servants had run out of the house, in spite of the rain ; and they say that a ball of fire passed close to the offices, but fortunately

* Henry Rogers was later captain of the 2nd West India Regiment.

no one was hurt. Yet the whole thing was, for a moment, more tremendous and frightful that I can possibly describe. All was comparatively quiet by 10, when we went to bed, only the rain pouring, and the thunder distant.

24th.—No one the worse for the fright of last night, and I slept well, notwithstanding, to the Doctor's great astonishment, who did not know what might have been the consequence.—General N., the Doctor and his lady, in Spanish Town all the morning.—Alone with my own agreeable thoughts till dinner time.—Heavy rain in the evening.

25th.—Up before daylight.—General N. finished his Chancery business to-day, to my great joy.—A large party at dinner, at 5. The Admiral, Mr. Mitchell, the Attorney-General, and Mrs. Ross, Mr. Tinker, Mrs. and Miss Rennalls, Mr. and Mrs. Hughes, Mr. and Miss Affleck, &c. &c. twenty-six in number. The whole party dispersed at 9, excepting the Admiral. About 10, a shock of an earthquake, that alarmed me a good deal, and another at half-past one, shook our bed very much. Keep myself as composed as I can, but cannot help feeling the greatest alarm.

26th.—The Admiral off at 6, for Port Royal. I think he was as much frightened at the earthquake as I was, for he looked *blue* when he talked of it this morning. All the family went to church, except myself. The Doctor thought I had better rest.—Only the Woodhams at dinner. Thank God we have had neither thunder nor earthquake to-day.

27th.—Major Ottley just from England, came to breakfast, and Captain Drummond, 2nd W. I. regiment, they both stay all day.—Poor Captain Johnson ill.—After dinner, took leave of our party, and drove to enquire about him, and see Dr. Lind.

28th.—Mr. Le Breton on business as engineer, now that poor Captain Bartlett is no more.—Feel the heat sadly, and am very faint and poorly till dinner time, and indeed after. Then better, and go to bed comfortable, having had a most refreshing drive.

29th.—Colonel Roberts and Captain Munro of the 85th,

and Captain Elrington, at breakfast. They staid all day ; and the 85th men to sleep.

30th.—We were awoke, in the night, by another shock of earthquake ; it was not severe, yet most awful.—My dear N. and I comfortably alone till one, when General Churchill and Captain Coatquelvin came to spend the day. Left them, with Colonel Roberts, Captain Munro, &c. to creolize. General N. found General C. so sound asleep on the sofa, in the drawing room, that we were tempted to play him a trick, by making an old black woman steal a pair of gloves, which awoke him in horror. He bore it, however, with great good humour, and it served for a laugh the rest of the day.—Captain Monro went back to Stony Hill ; Colonel Roberts remained.

October 1st.—Nurse Hamilton came ; feel half angry at her superseding me in one of the most precious parts of my expected duty, but play with her fair little boy, till I was quite in good humour with the mother.—Colonel Roberts returned to the regiment. Still full of jealousy and worry about nurse Hamilton, for why should I not be a mother indeed.

2nd.—Colonel Ramsay and Major Cookson, R.A. at breakfast, and Mr. Douglas of the 85th. The latter taken ill, and obliged to lie down all the morning. Soon as it was cool enough, order the carriage, and send him to his quarters, at Fort Augusta, and we took our drive to the race course.

3rd.—General N. read prayers to me at home, and our morning would have been quite satisfactory, if it had not been for the English despatches, to be closed to go by the *Tisiphone.* At 5, a large dinner party. The Honourable Mr. and Mrs. Leslie, sad bores to General N. Mrs. Woodham, too, exhibited herself in an odd way, talking all sorts of nonsense, though this rather amused many of the company. My dear N. really worn out with letters and applications, &c.

4th.—General N. off, before 4, for Kingston, to settle a variety of affairs.—The heat most oppressive, and the mus-

M

quitoes in swarms. I am so tormented by them, that I can get no rest.—Have the staff with Dr. and Mrs. Ludford to dine with me at 5.

5th.—Dr. and Mrs. Ludford went into Spanish Town for the morning.—Admiral Duckworth returned with General N. to dinner, having joined him at the King's House.—Drive to Fort Augusta with him after dinner.—Before we retired to our nests we were almost devoured with musquitoes, and when there were dying with the heat; but there is an appearance of more rain, and so I trust the atmosphere will soon be cooled.

6th.—The morning cooler, but the musquitoes, if possible, more intolerable than ever. Their buzzing really makes me nervous.—Only Major and Mrs. Pye.—Advised by Dr. Ludford not to drive out any more, till after my confinement.

7th.—Poor Mr. Radford, of the Engineers, died this morning, and Mr. Le Breton is dangerously ill. Try not to dwell upon these horrors, but alas! how can I help it. Some nice showers to-day. Nothing new in society here, but all talking of the yellow fever, &c.

8th.—Feel very low. Poor Mr. Le Breton is also dead of the fever. Nothing can be more melancholy than the accounts from all parts of the country. Endeavour to support myself as well as possible, but my mind is sadly harassed with a thousand fears for my dearest N. and many friends.—Poor young Brown much affected by the death of his brother officers, and kindly reprimanded, and put in arrest, by General N. for a supposed fault, to prevent his attending the funeral this evening.

9th.—Rise early, as usual, and try to shake off my depression of spirits, by playing with nurse Hamilton's baby, and thinking of my own.—General N. went into town, and was full of business all the morning. Dr. L. also absent till dinner time.—Get Mrs. Ludford to help me to make camphor bags, for all our friends, to preserve them from infection.

*   *   *   *   *   *

NURSE FLORA

Here has been a great chasm in my Journal, and, oh my God! with what gratitude and joy do I once more renew my usual occupations! But I will try to detail the past as accurately as I can. About 3 o'clock on Sunday morning, the 10th of October, I began to feel very unwell, but I did not see the doctor till 5, when I was sitting on the sofa, and all things were prepared for the approaching event. At 8, the staff, and Mr. Perry, a Member of the Assembly, came to breakfast. I sat down with them, and endeavoured to appear at ease; but I suffered sadly, and was forced to go to my own room before they took their leave. From that time till half-past five o'clock on Tuesday evening, my misery was great indeed; but the moment my darling boy was born compensated for all past suffering, and never can I forget the delightful sensation of first beholding my precious child, and feeling that I was a mother. Oh my Heavenly Father, how shall I ever express my gratitude to thee, or the joy that now fills my heart, for the great blessing thou hast bestowed upon me! My future life, prolonged as it may be, will be too short, to shew the sense I have of thy bounties and mercies. Yes, even if it should be lengthened to the utmost extent of the age of man, at every moment that I breathe I will endeavour, as much as in me lies, to promote thy honour and glory; not only with my lips but in my life, by giving up myself to thy service, and doing all the good I can to my fellow-creatures. That child, too, thou hast given me, that precious child, shall be taught, as far as I am capable, to glorify thee by word and deed. Endow him, oh my God! with such good and holy dispositions, as may render him always acceptable in thy sight. Grant that he may be a faithful servant to thee; a comfort to his dear, dear father, and myself, and an useful as well as amiable member of society, kind and compassionate to the poor, and that he may, in every action of his life, prove himself a faithful follower of our Lord and Saviour Jesus Christ.— Here I must again leave off writing; for my heart is still too full, and my frame too weak, not to feel the exertion

and excitement of writing. I cannot yet be at all composed
or coherent. A few days will, I trust, give me more strength
of both body and mind.

Before I attempt to begin my Journal regularly, as usual,
I will try to describe some of the *agrémens* of a Creole confinement. First, the heat is so dreadful, that it is impossible
to go to bed. Then, to mitigate it a little, the blinds are
kept closed. Then, the dark shade of the room brings
swarms of musquitoes. With these teasing, tormenting insects I am half buzzed out of my senses, and nearly stung
to death. Then, the old black nurse brought a cargo of
herbs, and wished to try various charms, to expedite the
birth of the child, and told me so many stories of pinching
and tying women to the bed-post, to hasten matters, that
sometimes, in spite of my agony, I could not help laughing,
and, at others, I was really in a fright, for fear she would
try some of her experiments upon me. But the maids took
all her herbs from her, and made her remove all the smoking
apparatus she had prepared for my benefit.

The very night my dear baby was born, it was nearly devoured by the musquitoes, in spite of all my care, in ex-
posing my own arms and neck to their attacks ; and, for a
day or two, his dear little eyes were almost closed up.—
Poor nurse Hamilton suffered sadly from the heat, in keeping him under my curtain, and behaved so kindly that I am
quite *reconciled* to her.—My English maids too, were so
attentive, and took such care, that old nurse Flora should
not pinch, or suffocate me to death with her charms, that
I shall not forget it. As for Margaret Clifford, I am sure
if I had been her own child, she could not have appeared to
feel more.

The morning after my darling boy was born, I was
allowed the luxury of a warm bath, of all sorts of sweet
herbs and scented leaves ; such as orange blossoms, &c. It
was so contrived, that I could enjoy it without much fatigue
for a few minutes, and those few minutes were an indescribable refreshment. This I continued every day, while I

kept my room.   The third day I sat, or rather lay upon my
sofa, with my *cherub* on a pillow by my side ; and who can
describe or imagine my delightful sensation, in looking at
this dear baby !   My heart is always in prayer, and never
can I be sufficiently thankful.

Past the first three weeks quietly.—Did not admit all our
family, but had two or three only to visit me, and now and
then to dine.—On the 30th of October, however, they all
came once more, as usual, and our former way of life was
renewed.—My dear N. was engaged every morning, with
the House of Assembly, but the great happiness he feels,
when he returns from the labours of the day, in seeing our
little darling, makes him forget all, and join with me in my
joy and delight.   I am indeed thankful, and only wish all
the world felt the gratitude and happiness I do, or had cause
to feel it equally with myself.   In speaking of the kindness
of domestics, I ought not to forget Cupid, who was the picture of woe I am told, and would neither eat, drink, nor
sleep, while I was ill ; and then danced and sung, and
seemed half mad with joy, when my dear baby was born.
And I have rewarded him, by letting him be the first of all
the blackies about the house to see the baby, and he is also
to be his valet-de-chambre by-and-bye.

*   *   *   *   *   *

November 1st.—I will now resume my journal, and go on
regularly, as usual ; and what an additional subject I have
—the progress and improvement of our dear little boy !—
I rise now at gun-fire, and take my walk in the Piazza, for
it will be three weeks to-morrow since my confinement ;
but I find the comparatively cool air strengthens me, though
I don't go out, because I don't wish yet to leave my dear
baby, and go into the world, which I must do if I am seen
beyond the lodge gate.   We have our staff now, as usual,
at breakfast and at dinner, with Dr. and Mrs. Ludford ; but,
as we are not upon ceremony with them, all goes on well,
and as we like.

2nd.—The early morning happy in the society of my dear N. and baby. He makes an excellent nurse already, and I delight in seeing him so happy. At 10, he went to Spanish Town, as the House of Assembly meet again to-day ; but he has had a holiday since Friday, and this is the case every week, that the Members may attend to their private affairs. —A most comfortable evening, and to bed at 8.

3rd.—A day of distress. Soon after General N. went into Spanish Town, this morning, and Mrs. Ludford also had gone to visit and shop, poor nurse alarmed me with looking very unwell, and seeming really to have a fever. I prevented her nursing the dear child, till I could get the doctor's opinion. Doctor Adolphus luckily arrived, and prescribed for her, and desired that we would feed the little darling till she was better. Kept all my anxiety from my dear N., who is obliged to remain at the King's House, as it is Wednesday, and his dinner day to the Assembly. Forty or fifty dine with him on this day every week.—Passed a miserable day, and was quite overcome when General N. came home at 10.

7th.—The Admiral, &c. only, in the day, and all arrangements were made for the christening of the dear little man. —At 4, the company assembled. They consisted of some few ladies, Mrs. and the Misses Murphy, Mrs. Woodham, Mrs. Pye, Mrs. Ludford, and Mrs. Elrington, who were staying at the Penn. There were about twenty or thirty gentlemen ; Sir J. T. Duckworth, General Churchill, King Mitchell, Simon Taylor, Mr. Scott, Mr. Warren, &c. &c.

After dinner, the black servants, about forty men and women, with their children and sweethearts, &c. had a dance in the back Piazza ; the white ladies and gentlemen having had theirs before we sat down to dinner. At half past 8, the whole family were assembled in the Piazza, and the guests in the dining room. The dear baby was christened by the names of George Edmund.—The Rev. Mr. Woodham performed the service. Admiral Duckworth and King Mitchell stood proxies for the Marquess of Buckingham and

Admiral Nugent, and Mrs. Murphy and Mrs. Ludford for Lady Gage* and dear Lady Buckingham.

After the ceremony, cake and wine were handed round, and all the gentlemen stood up to drink the new Christian's health, with three times three. The white and black servants, too, had cake and wine, and vociferated heartily also. After which, the blackies sang and danced and made merry. My dear baby looked beautiful in his christening dress, and was wrapped, by way of mantle, in a beautiful muslin handkerchief, embroidered in gold, sent me by Madame Le Clerc. I am much flattered by the pleasure all the Members of the Assembly, &c. expressed, on the birth of our little boy. He is, it seems, the first child that has been born in this situation ; for none of the former Governors have had children, excepting Sir J. Dalling, and they were not born in Jamaica.† Old Mr. Simon Taylor and Mr. Mitchell could never say enough upon the subject, and they seemed to think that he should now be so attached to the island, and should become quite one of themselves. I own, although I am grateful for their kindness, I could not carry my gratitude so far. As to Mr. Simon Taylor, he really talked to me like an affectionate father, though in a sort of gruff way.

8th.—General N. took his little boy his usual walk at gunfire ; for he has done this every morning, since the dear child was a fortnight old. He makes, indeed, an excellent nurse, and spends every leisure moment in playing with his darling little son. Should this book be ever read by our dearest George, he will then know that, should there be any fault hereafter in our care of him, or any mistakes in his education, &c. the errors have been those of our judgment

* A cousin cf Lady Nugent, only child of her uncle, Colonel William Skinner.

† Henry, the infant son of Sir Charles Lyttelton, who lies buried in the cathedral, was born at sea on the way out ; he survived his landing less than six months. Elizabeth, daughter of Sir William Beeston, who represented Port Royal in the first House of Assembly, and was Lieut.-Governor and Governor from 1692-3 to 1701-2, lies buried in the cathedral ; she died on 18 August, 1693, in the eighteenth year of her age.

only, or an over-anxious tenderness ; for never did parents feel a more lively affection for a child, than we do for him, nor look forward to its future happiness and respectability with more anxiety than we do to his. His welfare is, indeed, far beyond our own. We would, either of us, willingly sacrifice our lives even, to promote his interest. Our prayers to God are more fervently offered for him than they ever have been for ourselves.

Although still agitated with the interesting event of yesterday, this has been a day of peace, joy, and comfort inexpressible.

9th.—Yesterday my cards of thanks were distributed, and I expect all the world to drink caudle. General N. took the baby his walk, but has promised me never again to lay his little charge down on a sofa, and run with his gun to shoot a hawk, which I found he had done to-day. General N. in Spanish Town early, and at 12 the ladies began to come. Cake, caudle, chocolate, &c. were devoured. The baby was shewn in his little cot, and much admired ; the gauze curtains and bows of ribbons being particularly becoming. I sat in state till near 4 o'clock, and then, finding no more guests arrive, went to rest.—Had a sad alarm, for poor Clifford, I found, had been taken ill with a sad pain and inflammation in her leg. Send a carriage immediately for Dr. Adolphus, who, thank God, does not think seriously of her case. Heard, before dinner, that Captain Munro, of the 85th, was dying,* and many others ill. I do my best, but how can one help such melancholy circumstances preying on the mind ! General N., too, has received a card, to attend the funeral of poor Miss Affleck. She was a fine young woman, and, when she dined here last, was anticipating the pleasures of my intended balls, for which she had just received her cards.

10th.—Poor dear Clifford better, and nurse and baby merry, and as well as possible. Find a large party in the breakfast room.—General N. away all the morning, to meet

* Captain George Ross Munro died on November 11th, 1802. A monument to his memory is at Fort Augusta.

the Assembly, and to give his weekly dinner, and did not
get home till 10. The two ladies and the staff absent all the
morning. I nursed the baby, and amused myself, and was
as happy as I could be under present circumstances.

11th.—Send carriages for the Admiral, &c. and had a
large breakfast party.—Clifford better.—Crowds of ladies,
from 12 till 3 o'clock. All chattering, gossiping, eating
cake, and drinking caudle, &c. I can't say I enjoyed the
party much, for I was kept in a fidget about my dear baby.
Some one took him out of his cot, contrary to my wishes,
or rather orders ; I did not see it done, however.—They
pulled him about and passed him from one to the other, till
I thought they would break his neck. At 3 I was heartily
fatigued, and glad to see them all depart. There were two
Mrs. Baillies, Mesdames Clements, McGlashan, Tonge, Cookson, Yeates, Maxwell, Crackley, Ecuyer, Fermor, Ramsay,
Milwood, two Mrs. Bullocks, Roden, Sheriff, two Misses
Armstead, two Rennalls, Misses Hanson, Fermor, Cargill,
Kelsall, Mrs. Ross, Mrs. Tinker, Dolmage, Kelsall, Simon,
&c. &c. ; but I don't recollect the names of half that came
to-day. Only Mr. Corbet at dinner.—Opened a little book
to-day, to keep an account of my dear baby's health, and
know, from hour to hour, how he goes on, that I may be
ready in case of any illness.

12th.—George took his walk in the Piazza, with his papa,
and they both enjoyed it very much. Soon after, General
N. went into Spanish Town. The Admiral, Captain Dunn,
Mr. Edwards, &c. came, but only staid till 2, for second
breakfast. Feel the time lost, as I could not be with little
George. A white satin hat for him to-day, and sent him,
dressed very smart, to meet his dear papa, at half-past five.

13th.—Little George and his father took their walk early,
as usual.—Find Mr. Murphy and Mr. Sherriff in the breakfast room. They are deputed, by the House of Assembly,
to congratulate me on my recovery, and the birth of my
dear little boy, and to say that that House wished to give
me an entertainment on the occasion, and requested I would

name the day.—In consequence, Tuesday the 30th, is fixed upon for that purpose ; and though I feel very grateful for this attention, yet I dread the fatigue of balls, &c. the present session, and, more particularly, because they will oblige me to be so much absent from my little darling. But it can't be helped, and I must only try to make up my mind to little crosses, and think of my great blessings.

At 12, the ladies began to come again. They were chiefly from Kingston to-day, mixed with the military and members' wives, from Spanish Town again. The crowd and heat were very great, but I got through all much better than the last time, as my wish not to have the baby taken out of his cot was complied with, and so my mind was at ease.

14th.—The early morning as usual. To church at 10. After the service, a certain number of ladies and gentlemen staid, and I returned thanks, and then the Communion was administered to us. Called at the King's House afterwards, and found a present of six ring-tailed pigeons, from my friend Mr. Simon Taylor.—At dinner, the Woodhams, Pyes, Major Maitland, Captain and Mrs. Lomax, Dr. Adolphus, &c. Prayers, and to bed at nine.

15th.—This day five years I was married, and I can say sincerely from my heart, that I have never one moment repented it, nor have I ever experienced the smallest degree of slight or unkindness from my dear husband ; and this year finds me a happier woman than ever I was in my life. I am so truly blest, that if I could but see my dearest N. a little less fatigued with business, and a little less anxious, I should pronounce myself that *rara avis*, a perfectly happy human being. I have all my heart can wish ; an excellent husband, a beautiful, fine and healthy boy. We have not only an independence for ourselves, but ample means to serve our fellow-creatures. In short, we have all that any reasonable beings can possibly want or wish for ; and oh, my God, give us grateful hearts, that we may be worthy of the continuance of thy great and manifold favours and mercies.

The Rev. Messrs. Warren and Scott * came to breakfast. It was the first time I had seen the latter since he was struck with lightning ; and, poor man, he is a sad object ; he is deaf, his ideas are confused, his speech is imperfect, half his teeth are gone, and his whole frame is shaking and shattered. From his former liveliness and intelligence what a change ! But may these misfortunes here be beneficial by turning his thoughts more to hereafter ! The sight of him, however, made me very low, and, unfortunately, he remained all the day.—In the course of the morning, the officers of the 60th came in a body, to congratulate me upon dear George's birth. Was glad when the visit was over, as all these demands upon my time are cruel interruptions to my morning engagements.

16th.—A new carpet for dear baby. A beautiful tiger skin, on which he lies in the veranda, and enjoys the fresh air, early in the morning.

17th.—Doctors Broadbelt and Adolphus, soon after, to see Mrs. Ludford, who, they say, has a strong tendency to consumption, but that she is in no immediate danger.—My dear boy is prospering, but, alas, we must soon think of giving him the small-pox.

19th.—This is to be a day of bustle and fatigue, and to-night I give my first ball this session.—Send for the Admiral, &c. early. At breakfast, in addition to the Navy, Colonel Roberts and Mr. Hogg, of the 85th. At second breakfast, Captains Walker and Dundas, of the Navy. Joined the party, but all went to dine at King Mitchell's. I dined alone here, with only Mrs. Ludford, and at 8 went to the King's House, to meet my company. Dear little George was with me while I dressed for the ball, and really seemed pleased with my gay appearance ; for I put on one of Madame Le Clerc's spangled dresses, on purpose, and the glitter I am sure attracted his notice. Opened the ball with the Admiral, according to promise. At supper my little darling's health was given with three times three. General

* Rector of St. John.

N. thanked them, and drank success to the Island of Jamaica. I only curtesied, but my heart was full. My fatigue was so great all day, that General N. kindly got the chariot as soon as supper was over, and we brought off Drury and Rogers with us, to sleep here, leaving Mrs. Ludford, &c. to follow at leisure. Found the dear boy sleeping nicely in his cot at half-past two o'clock, and went to bed satisfied and thankful; but the noise I had heard of cheering, &c. at supper, the speeches, and the fatigue, altogether, were almost too much for me.

20th.—Was told this morning two melancholy circumstances. My poor little Cupid's mother (Venus) died at the King's House, on Thursday. They had kept her illness from me out of kindness, but every thing had been done for her comfort, &c. I am assured. The other is the death of poor Mr. Blakeney, of the 85th. The chief cause of his death was the distress of his mind (poor fellow) for the loss of his brother officers. Poor Captain Munro's death, in particular, affected him. It is remarkable that poor Mr. Blakeney had scarcely any fever, and his death was almost sudden.

21st.—General N. crowded with unexpected business, and trying to get through all in time for church; and particularly as we have asked for the Sacrament to be administered to us to-day. Order our breakfast in our own room, and I help to copy as well as I can, but, in spite of all, found it impossible to be ready by 10. I therefore wrote to Mr. Woodham, begging that the service might proceed without us, and that we would be at church in time for the Communion, &c. Accordingly, we went at 12, but the sermon had begun, so we retired to the King's House, that we might not distract the congregation; but returned exactly in time for the Sacrament, at which Mr. Kirby, just from England, assisted Mr. Woodham. Returned to our business, at the Penn, with satisfied minds. My dear N. finished all his despatches before dinner; but really the fatigue was overpowering. He copied Simon Taylor's calculations, made out all the St. Domingo Reports, &c. &c. in all of which I could be of no use, to my great regret.—At dinner, the Woodhams, Messrs. Herring, Donaldson, &c.

22nd.—The Assembly have sent out their cards for the grand ball and entertainment, to be given to me.

23rd.—Received an express from Stony Hill, giving an account of the death of poor nurse's husband. Poor creature, I don't know how to tell her, and am much distressed on her account. Get Mrs. Ludford, towards evening, to break it to her, and do all I can to comfort her. She has promised to feel as little as possible, on account of the dear baby ; and I will do all I can for hers.

24th.—Out early in the sociable, with nurse and dear baby.—Poor nurse trying to look cheerful, not to distress me. Make her some presents, and talk of her boy, &c. and we returned home tolerably at ease.—Mrs. Murphy and her daughters at breakfast.—Quite grateful to poor nurse, for keeping up her spirits as she does.—Heard of a packet, and immediately after, my dear N. received his English despatches. Nothing can be more flattering than the expressions of all his official correspondents. Our private letters also delightful, and most cheering to the spirits.—At dinner Colonel Malcolm, member for Hanover, and Dr. Maxwell. General N. shocked Colonel M. when he introduced dear George, by saying, how much obliged our little man had been, for his hospitality in the spring.

25th.—General N. drove with me and the nursery party to Port Henderson, in the sociable, and we enjoyed ourselves very much.—Dr. Ludford went to Kingston, to see the child from whom our dear boy is to be inoculated, and brought such quantities of baby's things, sent by the packet, and just landed from England. Much admired, and a great amusement to us all day.

26th.—Dr. L. returned from Kingston, and at 12 o'clock my beloved child was inoculated. Much agitated, in consequence, the rest of the day, but obliged to dress, and go to the King's House, soon after 4. Find most of the company assembled. Sit down at 5, with about thirty or forty people at dinner. The dancing people began to come before the cloth was removed. Only open the ball with Sir J. Duckworth, and then walk about, and say civil things, till about 11 o'clock, when we returned to the Penn. General N. and I sat up afterwards to discuss the politics of the day. Much of an uncomfortable nature has been debated in the House of Assembly, and the Members are more than ever divided, and more than ever inclined to cavil at every measure of the British Government. I regret all deeply, on account of my dear N ; but he will do his duty, and trust to the rest.

27th.—Mr. Corbet at breakfast. One of the Aides-de-camp made me his confidant, about his pecuniary distresses : do what I can to relieve his mind ; but these sort of things make me exceedingly uncomfortable, and particularly on account of the friends of these very inconsiderate young men.

28th.—Mr. Stewart,* of Trelawny, at breakfast. I don't like him at all, he seems such a republican. Am very low, and unwell all the morning. My dear boy again inoculated, as the first attempt does not appear to have answered. This keeps me in great anxiety.—Mr. Stewart returned to dinner, with Dr. Adolphus.

29th.—Drove to Port Henderson, at day-light.—Thank God, our dear child appears to have taken the infection, but I hope what was done yesterday will not increase the eruption.—Rain at 4, and so heavy, that none of our expected company came to dinner.—Young Grace only.

30th.—Dress at 7, for the ball given to me to-night, by the Assembly. Dear little George at my toilet. For the benefit of posterity I will describe my dress on this grand occasion. A crape dress, embroidered in silver spangles, also sent me by Madame Le Clerc, but much richer than that which I wore at the last ball. Scarcely any sleeves to my dress, but a broad silver spangled border to the shoulder

* James Stewart, the Custos.

straps. The body made very like a child's frock, tying behind, and the skirt round, with not much train. A turban of spangled crape, like the dress, looped with pearls, and a paradise feather ; altogether looking like a *Sultana*. Diamond bandeau, cross, &c. ; and a pearl necklace and bracelets, with diamond clasps. This dress, the admiration of all the world over, will perhaps, fifty years hence, be laughed at and considered as ridiculous as our grandmother's hoops and tissures appear to us now.—But, to return to our proceedings ; all well here at 8, and we started in high spirits for the ball. We were met at the door by the four stewards, and marched up the room to the tune of " God save the King." I then stood by the state sofa, receiving the compliments of all the company, and making curtesies for near an hour. After which, I opened the ball with the Admiral, danced with a Member of Council and one of the Assembly, and then thought it *dignified* to play a rubber of cassino. This over, General N. and I walked about the room, toadying and being toadied till supper time. A splendid supper soon after 12. Transparencies and appropriate devices, &c. Soon after we had sat down, the company all stood up round the table, with filled glasses, and drank my health, with a fine complimentary speech, and three times three. Then General N.'s health followed, with the same sort of speech, and applause ; and last of all, our dear child's health, with blessings and good wishes, most grateful to our hearts. General N. thanked them, and I curtesied and looked my thanks, but I could not speak, and really felt so much overcome with the whole thing, that I was glad when the uproar ceased, and the attention of the company was drawn to some other toasts, proposed on the part of General N. about the concerns of the Island, Kingston,* &c. Got back to the Penn at three.

December 1*st.*—Up at 8. What an hour for us ! General N. in town all the morning. At 5, some gentlemen, and Mrs. Griffiths, Miss Moss and Miss Williams, at dinner.

* About this time Kingston was anxiously expecting to receive its charter of incorporation as a city.

2nd.—Dear babe and his arm as well as possible. Crowds of visitors all the morning, coming and going till 4 o'clock. Then drive with General N. to Spanish Town. We gave a dinner to a large party of the Assembly, at the King's House, and Mrs. Ludford and I dined quietly with the Murphy family.

3rd.—Dressed and went into town. A great crowd. Sit between Mr. Mitchell and Simon Taylor; both very kind, and telling me to please myself, and leave the company to take care of themselves; but hear at 8, that all is going on well at the Penn, and I begin the ball, which was at last adjourned to the Egyptian Hall, for the company became so numerous that the gallery, where we usually met on Fridays, could not contain half of them. One of the longest and most disagreeable evenings I ever spent, but get away at eleven.

4th.—My dear N. full of business, all the morning, with Mr. Corbet and Sir R. Basset *; the latter endeavouring to vindicate his conduct, when he was Superintendant of Honduras. Mr. Corbet was bringing forward his proof to the contrary; being employed some little time since by General N. to enquire into the charges, brought against Sir Richard Basset by the settlers of Honduras.—It appears altogether to have been a scene of the saddest fraud and peculation possible. Yet the wretched man looks so miserable, that I can't help pitying him, as he is dismissed the service; and it is thought several others will share his fate. —Heard, in the evening, of poor Downes' illness, and go to bed low on his account; though they say it is not the fever, and that when the last account came he was better.

5th.—To church with the staff at 10. My dear N. full of despatches, to go by the *Cerberus* frigate to England. Our sermon to-day was very long. The clergyman that preached was a Mr. Davies, just arrived, and he treated of botany and astronomy, as well as divinity. It appeared altogether an essay, more fit for the drawing room than the pulpit. He

* Colonel, 5th West India Regiment.

dined with us, as well as Mr. and Mrs. Woodham, and Mr. Ramsey, of the 60th regiment.

6th.—Up at day-light, and help dear N. with his despatches, by copying letters.—Major and Mrs. Pye, &c. at breakfast.—The despatches sent off at 12. A quiet dinner, and a drive in the curricle.

9th.—Till after 2 this morning, the little darling was feverish and very uneasy ; but, thank God, he appears better to-day. Drive with him to Port Henderson. Only nurse and Johnson with me. General N. holding the dear child, on a leather pillow, the greatest part of the way.— Mr. Scott, of the Council, to breakfast.—A great deal of business for dear N. in Spanish Town, and he can't return till 5. I pity him, for his heart is here, and I am sure he suffers much from anxiety.

10th.—Poor N. obliged to be in town all day, to dress there for King Mitchell's grand dinner. I dined with only Mrs. Ludford, at 3, and dressed and went into Spanish Town at 8. Found a crowd assembling, for this is what they call the King's Ball ; and every one that can afford a dress is allowed to come to it. General N. &c. came at 10, and we all marched into the ball-room, to the tune of "God save the King." I danced three dances, and then played cassino till 12, at which hour we went to supper.—Began dancing again, but heard from Mr. Sherriff that the greatest danger was when the small-pox was turning, and that then some nourishment should be given. Got the carriage as soon as possible, and returned to the Penn, to change poor nurse's diet. Found that she had had a bason of fresh milk, and that both were quietly asleep.

12th.—General N. too full of business to stir from the Penn, and we gave up church to-day, but had prayers by ourselves.—A large party at dinner. Sent the sociable and four for Miss Williams and a party of ladies. All staid for family prayers ; Mr. and Mrs. Woodham, &c.

14th.—Just as we were stepping into the carriage, at day-light, an express arrived from Fort Augusta, with a de-

N

spatch for General N., to say that a packet was in the offing, and that General Carmichael, the Captain of the packet, and Mr. Mackinnon, had landed in an open boat, in the middle of the night. Drove immediately to Port Henderson, to meet the gentlemen, and full of conjectures as to the nature of the news we were to receive—the King's death, a war, a change of ministry, or some grand affair, could be the only probable causes of such an express, and such haste. —Met the gentlemen, and brought them home to breakfast. It turned out to be only the usual communication from the British Government, and the gentlemen's haste was to get ashore. They spent the morning refreshing at the Penn. We dined at 4, and then we took them to the King's House. They were Brigadier-General Carmichael, who is appointed to the staff here, Captain Fellowes, who commands the packet, and Mr. Daniel Mackinnon, on his private affairs. Found a large party assembled, for the Colts' Ball. This is a kind of subscription fête, given by the new Members of Assembly, who are always considered colts, and the Governor too, till he has gone through the ceremony of this entertainment. General N., therefore, was a party concerned ; and it was very gay, with transparencies, &c. in the supper room, and a very fine set-out altogether. I danced, and did all that *was agreeable ;* and so did General N.—Sir J. Duckworth was in a rage with Captain Fellowes, and it was with great difficulty I effected a reconciliation, and prevented his reporting him to the Admiralty.

15*th*.—A party at breakfast ; Colonel Lethbridge, General Carmichael, Mr. Mackinnon, Captain Fellowes, &c.—Am anxious all day about poor Mrs. Ludford. Do not ask our company to stay dinner. Only four sat down. All out of spirits, poor Mrs. L. seems so ill, and can be heard in any part of this thin house.

16*th*.—We all went into Spanish Town, to breakfast with Mr. and Mrs. Murphy. I say all, but General N., nurse, baby, and myself, were the party. A large breakfast. The crowd and heat great ; but dear Georgy had a cool part of

the veranda for his tiger skin, and enjoyed himself very
much. Excused myself to Mrs. Roden, for not attending
her ball this evening, as it is impossible for me to go out
to-night, and to entertain the whole town, as I must to-
morrow.

Drs. Ludford and Adolphus backward and forward, in
attendance upon poor Mrs. L., who seems to be growing
worse rather than better.—The melancholy scenes that we
are daily witnessing, the extraordinary characters that we
meet with, and the manœuvres of party which we witness,
will, I hope, be useful lessons to us for the rest of our lives,
by shewing us the vanity of all things, and reminding us
more and more of the shortness and uncertainty of this life.

17th.—A dreadful night for us all, listening to poor Mrs.
Ludford's groans. Put off our dinner and dance for this
evening, and give all our attention to her. Our great consolation at this moment is, the health and prosperity of our
dear child.—No further news of poor Downes,* so we hope
he is doing well.—The day melancholy indeed to me, as my
dear N. was obliged to go to the King's House, upon business, and did not return till 6.—In the evening no hopes
given of our friend.

18th.—Quite wretched to-day. Poor Mrs. Ludford raving
incessantly all night, and it was impossible not to hear her.
About 5 o'clock she became quiet, and we flattered ourselves that a favourable change had taken place ; but, alas !
no, the mortification had begun, and she expired at 11
o'clock to-day ! We went immediately to the King's House,
leaving my maid in charge of the Penn, and have passed a
melancholy day indeed.

19th.—Go in my night-cap and dressing-gown, with dear
baby, to Mrs. Murphy's, at daylight, and remain till late
in the day. Poor Mrs. Ludford was buried at 9 o'clock.
The procession set out from the King's House. General N.
attended, and shewed every possible respect to her memory.
Dr. Ludford set off for St. Elizabeth's (his parish) after the

* Her brother.

funeral, and we returned to the King's House, as there was
no service in the church to-day.—At 5 o'clock, send the
carriage for the Murphy family, which, with our own, made
twenty-two at dinner. It was all gloomy enough, and both
General N. and I were so worn out, we were glad to get to
bed when 10 o'clock struck.

20th.—Feel quite ill, and can't go out. My spirits sadly
low all day, and my dear N. so full of business, that I
scarcely see him.

21st.—Low and miserable all day.—Try to rally my
spirits, for my dear N.'s sake, whose greatest comfort is to
find me cheerful when he returns to our own apartments,
after the business of the day. The evening quiet again, and
this will do us more good than any thing.

22nd.—A wretched day indeed! It seems that poor
Downes has been dead some time. How sad and wretched
for his miserable wife and child! Give way entirely, and
pass a sad evening, my imagination constantly presents
such a dark cloud before me, that I am quite overcome.
But God's will be done! He knows what is best for his
erring creatures.

23rd.—Sad dreams all night. Rise very early, and drive
out. Am determined to occupy my mind, and not to dwell
upon painful subjects. It makes poor N. so miserable, and
wears out my own health and spirits.—Write to poor
Downes' widow, and try all I can to console her.

24th.—Only Mr. Cathcart at dinner ; but my dear N. is
very unwell, and overwhelmed with business, and, at this
moment, much teased with French intrigue, about getting
money at Kingston. Try to support myself for his sake,
and not add to his cares.

25th. Christmas Day.—But very warm, and so unlike
Christmas Day in our own dear country.—A shock of an
earthquake, just as I was preparing for church. My dear N.
not well, and advised to stay at home. I trust it is only
over occupation that occasions his illness. However, in
this climate, the most trifling attack is a source of alarm.

He promised to come to the Communion, and when I missed him, I did indeed feel cruelly anxious and nervous, and this was not diminished by finding him so unwell as to be lying down, and very feverish, when I returned from church. God preserve him !—At 3, the Aide-de-camp returned from visiting the French officers, on board their frigate at Port Royal, and carriages were sent to bring them here to dinner. —The Doctor says, that General N. must not leave his room, and, politically, the General does not wish to receive them, except merely making his bow, and then I am to do the honours of the dinner table. They came at half-past four o'clock, when the Vicomte de Noailles * declared himself also too unwell to sit up ; and actually followed General N. to his room, and remained there conversing with him all the time we were at dinner.—With the assistance of the staff I got through the dinner business pretty well, but in the midst of it lost my voice entirely, and yet I have no cold. Dr. Adolphus says it is nervous, and I dare say it is, for inwardly I am very low and wretched.

The Vicomte de Noailles' conversation was chiefly on the subject of St. Domingo, but he talked also of the golden key, namely, the access he hoped to obtain to the South American treasures. He told General N. that the French plan was, to put to death every negro who had borne arms, and to hamstring the others !—General N. then asked him, what would the colony be worth in that case ; but to this he was not prepared for an answer. In short, it appears, that, though the French may have had a great deal of the monkey in their composition and character formerly, they have now more than a double proportion of the tiger. For never were

* Louis Marie, Vicomte de Noailles, second son of Maréchal de Mouchy, was born 1756. Aided the insurgents in America, and was prominent at the York Town capitulation (1781). Returning to France, he took part in the revolution. Afterwards, went on a filibustering expedition to the West Indies, and became general of brigade in St. Domingo. He died at Havana, in 1804.

there such a set of cruel heartless wretches, and I rejoiced to see them depart at eight.

26th.—I was sadly ill all night. My dear N., though, much better, thank God!—He has taken, within the last twenty-four hours, no less than forty grains of calomel, and scarcely seems to have felt it at all.—The Woodhams and Pyes to dinner. I am still *speechless*, but not otherwise ill, and continue to get through the day tolerably well.

27th.—Noise of rude music, &c. &c. all night.—My dear N. better, but particularly unwell myself all the morning. The streets crowded with singing men and women. Nothing but noise and bustle all day. At dinner, Major Maitland, Dr. Gallagher, and our own party. General N. quite himself again, and my voice is returning.

28th.—As soon as it was light, set off for the Admiral's Penn, baby, nurse, and all. General N. &c. rode. Arrive at the Admiral's about 8, and find the Vicomte de Noailles and four other Frenchmen there before us. A long discussion, upon money matters, between General N. and the Vicomte ; not at all satisfactory to the latter, I fancy, who took his leave about 12, and we rested ourselves till 4, when we joined a large dinner party. Mrs. Hibbert and Mrs. Bogle were the only ladies besides myself.

29th.—Drive to Up Park, at day-break. Sir J. Duckworth in the sociable with me and baby. General N. &c. on horseback.—The 6th battalion, 60th regiment, reviewed. —General N. then inspected the works, new barracks, hospital, &c. and we returned to the Admiral's at 8, for breakfast. Colonel Mosheim, and a few officers, with us. Mrs. Griffiths came to ask if I wished to go into Kingston. Went with her to a few shops, and returned to rest a little before dinner. A larger party than usual of ladies ; Mrs. Laws, Mrs. Griffiths, Misses Stewart, Miss Cockburn, &c. &c.

30th.—The Admiral, &c. accompanied General N. to Stony Hill, at 5. I drove out with the child and maids, and then breakfasted with the Navy men here ; Captain Dunn, and Mr. Muddle, Aide-de-camp to Sir J. Duckworth, and

Mr. Headlam, his secretary. Mr. and Mrs. Peacocke soon joined us. She, poor thing, was so unwell, that she was obliged to remain in my room all the morning. She told me her history, and I really feel for her very much. She is lady-like, and well informed, and appears to be perfectly thrown away upon an unfeeling, speculating, foolish man, to say the least of him.—A large dinner party at 4. Mrs. Hibbert, Mrs. Symes, and Miss Cockburn at dinner.—A number of ladies came in the evening, and we had quite a ball. My dearest Georgy made his appearance among the dancers, and was greatly admired. I thought he looked like a little angel. General N. was particularly merry, and danced a great deal. Thank God, he bears all his fatigues so well.

31st.—Too tired to drive out. Colonel Roberts and Captain Ross, in addition to the Admiral's usual party.—A packet arrived in the night, and we got papers as late as the 23rd of November. Peace or war doubtful.—General N.'s despatches were very comfortable to his own private feelings.—After breakfast, drive into Kingston, and make a few visits. See poor Mr. Edwards, who is still very ill. At 4, go to Mrs. Griffiths', and after a short toilette, meet a large party at dinner. The heat dreadful, and am obliged to leave the table. I don't know what is the matter with me, but I certainly don't stand the climate as well as I did last year.—Return to the Admiral's Penn, at 9.

CHAPTER III

January 1st, 1803.—As soon as we had breakfasted, took leave of the Admiral, and arrived at the King's House at 12. General N. had some business with the Secretary, &c. as usual ; and baby danced and enjoyed himself in the gallery till near 3, when we got safe to the Penn, and found all so clean and nice there, that we felt the delight of being once more at home.—Only two of the staff, and ourselves, except Mr. D. Mackinnon, who has been of all our parties.

2nd.—Dine at half-past three. The Woodhams, the Pyes, Mrs. Hodges, and two Mr. Lewises, General Carmichael, Majors Ottley and Darling, and Dr. Gallagher, in addition to our own party.

3rd.—Drive to Port Henderson at gun-fire.—My dearest baby bathed in the sea for the first time. General N. took charge of him, but my heart was in my mouth the whole time, and I could not look at the proceeding. He was bathed out of a boat, and the waves splashing so high that it was really very frightful. My spirits too, are now so easily alarmed, that the least danger for my dear, dear child makes me wretched. Lie on the bed the greatest part of the morning, and find it difficult to recover my spirits. The Admiral came at 3.—Only a small dinner party. Captain Dunn went back to his ship at 8.

4th.—The Admiral and General N. rode out at gun-fire, and I took my drive with the maids and dear Georgy. Never was there a dearer baby. He is scarcely ever heard to cry, and is always well and merry. I am, however, poorly, and begin to think that something unusual is the matter with me. If I should have a dear little girl, how delightful ! Receive a packet of books from England, for

the instruction of poor children, Sunday Schools, &c. but)
alas, they can be of little use to us here !

After breakfast, General N. drove the Admiral to Spanish
Town.   They visited Mr. Edwards, and several invalids.—
A large party at dinner to-day ; Major Maitland, Captain
Jeffries, of the 4th battalion, 60th, Mrs. Rennalls and
family, Mr. and Mrs. Roden, Mr. and Mrs. Herring, Mr.
Mitchell and Mr. Lane ; in all, about twenty-four.—Captain
Johnson just returned from his voyage to New Providence.

5th.—Rise before day, and set off for Port Henderson,
where Clifford bathed my little darling in the sea before the
sun was up.   General N., the Admiral, &c. went on to Fort
Augusta.   I was not so much alarmed to-day, because
Clifford stood only in the water, close to the shore, and not
in a boat, which made it much less dangerous and frightful
to look at.—On my return to the Penn, find Mrs. Hodges,
and two Messrs. Jarvis, to breakfast with me.   At dinner,
the Admiral, Captains Dunn and Dundas, Mr. Headlam,
Mrs. Kelsall and family, Mr. and Mrs. Dolmage, Mr. and
Mrs. Ramsay, Mr. and Mrs. Woodham ; in all twenty-six.

The Admiral was so unwell that he left the party before
we removed from table.   I then had a treat, for General
N. and myself, in seeing the dear baby prepared for the
night in the drawing-room.   Just as his fresh dress was put
on, a large centipede came creeping out from the very spot
where we were playing with him ; and judge of our alarm !
The sofa pillow was thrown to the other side of the room,
and General N. soon put the reptile to death ; but we
hunted over every part of the room, and his room too, before we could put the dear boy into his cot for the night.

6th.—Am much shocked to hear of the sudden death of
poor Mr. Woolfries.   We dined with him, at the Admiral's
Penn, last week, and he was very anxious for us to visit
him in the mountains this week.   At first we partly promised, but afterwards, on account of the journey being too
long for little George, we excused ourselves ; and most
fortunate it was, for we should just have been present at
the melancholy scene of his death.   Events like these fill

the mind with horror and awe, and make us think indeed.
—Go with General N., at gun-fire, to review the 4th battalion, 60th regiment. The Admiral not well enough to be
of the party. General N. much pleased with the corps, and
commended, in particular, the rifle companies. I returned
home with my little G. to breakfast. General N. remained
for the breakfast given by the corps.—Drs. Ogilvie and
Blair in attendance upon the Admiral, who kept his bed ;
but Dr. Blair, on whose opinion I rely, thinks it merely a
bilious attack, and that shortly he will be as well as ever.—
We had a very large dinner party, and, to our surprise, the
Admiral made his appearance. Mr. Parker, of the *Leviathan*, came with Dr. Blair. There were also Mr. Halketts,
from New Providence, Mr. Mitchell, General Carmichael,
Major Darley, Major Maitland, and officers of 4th battalion,
60th, Mr. Whitehorne, Mr. Bullock, Mr. Clements ; in short,
an immense party. The Admiral soon got tired, and was
obliged to go to bed ; so the party broke up very early, and
the house was quiet by ten.

7th.—The Admiral still unwell, and can't go with us to
the dinner, given to-day by Mr. Roden, the Custos of the
parish. Order dinner for him and his secretary here, and
go with our own party to dine in Spanish Town. Hear of
much illness, and so many deaths, that my usual uncomfortable feelings were greatly added to, and I could scarcely
sit out the dinner. So very faint and sick indeed was I,
that at 9 the carriage was ordered, and General N. and I returned home, just as the gaieties of the evening were beginning, as there was a dance.

8th.—General N. and I drove with little George to Port
Henderson, so early that the moon was shining brightly the
whole way. General N., after seeing dear baby bathe, went
on with the staff to Port Royal, in the Admiral's barge, to
review the artillery stationed there.—After breakfast, the
Admiral, &c. took their leave. He was nearly as well as
ever, but his attack has been rather a severe one, and he
looks very ill.—General N. &c. all back before three.

9th.—After the service drive about Spanish Town, and find all the invalids better, and Major Drummond and Mr. Edwards recovering fast.—Only the Woodhams at dinner.

10th.—Very unwell this morning, but drive, before sunrise, into Spanish Town ; General N. on horseback. At breakfast, Colonel Barrow, from England, to take the command, as Superintendent of Honduras. General N. engaged all the morning, in giving him instructions. He staid to dinner, with Messrs. Hanbury and Cathcart, Major and Mrs. Pye.

11th.—Am so alarmed to-day at seeing George bathed, that I am determined not to be present again on the occasion. Indeed General N. seems himself inclined to give it up ; thank God ! for I am sure it does not do him any good, and it is very dangerous.

12th.—The dear child bathed again, but I could not look at it. I hope this may be the last time.—Our own family early at breakfast.—Poor Drummond so ill, that he has been removed to the King's House, to be better taken care of. General N. himself rode into Spanish Town, to give the necessary orders respecting him, and to procure the best advice, so I trust he will do well.—A packet from England ; delightful news.—Go to dinner at 4, in a *happy fuss.* Dear Miss Acheson * tells me of her intended marriage with Lord William Bentinck. God bless and make them happy ! Go to bed most comfortable to-night, and hear that poor Drummond is much better.

13th.—Mr. Griffiths came to take leave in the evening, as he is to be off in the packet. Drummond better.

15th.—Dress by candle-light, and drive to Port Henderson, where General N. reviewed the black corps (2nd W. I. regiment). A great breakfast afterwards at the inn,† and did not get home again till 11 o'clock.

* Mary Acheson, second daughter of the first Earl of Gosford. Lord William Bentinck was afterwards Governor-General of India.

† Port Henderson Inn was an inn up till about 1880 ; and until about 1898 it was a lodging house. It is now much out of repair.

16*th*.—General Carmichael, Major Darley, Colonel Roberts, the Pyes, &c. at dinner.

17*th*.—Again make my toilet by candle-light, and arrive at the race-course before sun-rise. General N. reviewed the St. Catherine's militia. We returned to breakfast at the Penn. General Carmichael, &c. left us soon afterwards. Had a present from Colonel Ramsay, who came from Port Royal, of two beautiful tiny tortoises, in a glass case.—At dinner, Mr. Unitt, from Curaçoa, who has just arrived with the Governor, Colonel Hughes, from that island, to whom he is secretary.

18*th*.—Mr. Unitt left us very early, with General N.'s instructions for Colonel Hughes. Mr. Scott, of the Council, and Miss Williams, &c. at breakfast. Various people in the course of the morning, on business of accounts, &c.

19*th*.—Send carriages for Colonel Hughes, &c. and my baby took his walk ; for, thank God, bathing is given up. Colonel Hughes, Captain Miller, Mr. Unitt, and Mr. Du Vernet to breakfast.

20*th*.—The Admiral, &c. at breakfast, and to spend the day.—Dine at 4.—General Carmichael and his Brigade-Major, Mr. Ross, Mr. Scott, &c. in addition to Colonel Hughes, and his party.

21*st*.—Start at half-past four, with our whole party, for Bushy Park (Mr. Mitchell's) ; breakfasted there, and then proceeded on to Spring Gardens, where General N. reviewed the St. John's and St. Dorothy's militia. Returned and dined at Mr. M.'s, and then home again to sleep.

22*nd*.—After breakfast, Admiral D., Colonel Hughes, &c. all went to Port Royal.—Sir J. Duckworth returned to dinner, with Commodore Bayntun.

23*rd*.—The Admiral and Commodore went to Port Royal. Saw poor Drummond after church, and he is getting well slowly.—The Chief Justice still ill. At dinner Mr. and Mrs. Woodham, Mr. Underwood, Mr. Irving, Major Maitland, &c.

24*th*.—General N. off before day, with General Carmichael, Colonel Hughes, &c. to review the militia of St.

Thomas in the Vale. I drove out with dear little George, &c. Not at all well the whole morning, and glad to be alone. Only Mr. Unitt, and one Aide-de-camp at dinner with me. General N. &c. returned before we left the table, and all our guests took their departure soon after 8.—Poor Downes's widow and her little girl came, just as we were concluding prayers.

25th.—Go to Mrs. Skinner's room at day-light. Find her and the little girl quite well, but no one disposed for an early drive. At breakfast, an unusually large party ; sixteen persons.—My morning, after a long conversation, was spent, as usual, in writing, reading, and nursing my dear little boy. —Dine at half-past four ; Mr. Mitchell, Mr. Edwards, and some officers of the 87th regiment. Mrs. S.'s spirits better than I expected. Rather sickish myself, and glad, at 9, to go to bed.

26th.—Drive with Mrs. S. and our two children, to Port Henderson. Again bathe my little darling.—At breakfast, only Major and Mrs. Pye added to our party.

27th.—Some officers of the 87th regiment, at breakfast.— Another horrid Court of Chancery, and I did not see my dear N. till half-past four. Eighteen persons at dinner.

29th.—Only Colonel Hughes, and Mr. Unitt, at breakfast. —General N. in Spanish Town, on Chancery duty.—Messrs. Irving, Cunningham, McNeil, and Mr. Brown, 87th, at dinner. Colonel Hughes and Mr. Unitt took leave before 8, and went on board the packet, to sail for England on Monday.

February 1st.—Too sick myself to drive out. Baby better than usual, and took his airing with Mrs. S. and her little girl.—Mr. McAnuff at dinner.

2nd.—Dine later, on account of the *grand* cause between Lindo and Lake not being decided.—General N. determined to settle the business to-morrow, without hearing further pleadings.

3rd.—Am persuaded to drive in the curricle early, with General N., the baby, &c. in the sociable. Colonel Ramsay,

Major Cookson, and Mr. Du Vernet, at breakfast.—To-day my dear N. settled the cause between Lindo and Lake, to the entire satisfaction of every one ; and even the parties concerned themselves acknowledge the thorough justice of the decision.　This is delightful to me, as it makes his mind so easy and comfortable.—Major and Mrs. Pye, Dr. McNeil, and Captain D'Arcy, of the 85th, at dinner.—Settled arrangements with Dr. McNeil, about poor nurse's eldest little boy, to be sent to Stony Hill, and better taken care of.

5th.—Rise before 3.　Feel very, very sick this morning. Set off, however, as soon as dressed, with Mrs. S. in the sociable, for Kingston.　General N. on horseback, with his staff.　Arrived on the race course just as the sun was about to rise, and the scene was really sublime.　The hills, and all, tinted with the most brilliant colours.　The Kingston militia were then reviewed.　The crowd was immense.　After the review, met a large party, at the Admiral's Penn, at breakfast.　After which, Mrs. Griffiths came, and we drove into Kingston, for shopping, &c. and did not get back again to the Penn till after 2.—A party of thirty at the Admiral's dinner.　Sick all the time, and wish myself home again. Set off for our own Penn as soon as we had taken our coffee.

7th.—Mr. Blair (Lady Mary Blair's son) arrived from England, with letters from Lords Westmoreland, Hobart, &c. and dear Lady Buckingham.　Invite him and his wife here, and do all that is civil and kind by them.

9th.—A delightful shower of rain.—The people from Stony Hill, with contracts for the barrack, &c.　Only the Pyes at dinner ; and to bed at an early hour.

10th.—At day-light set off, with our whole party, for the Ferry House,* from six to eight miles on the Kingston road. —After breakfast, proceeded to review the St. Andrew's militia.　Among the spectators was one of the fattest brown ladies and her child that ever were seen, and General Car-

* The Ferry Inn is still standing.　Until the building of the railway in 1845-6, it was the regular half-way house between Spanish Town and Kingston.

michael brought them up, to be introduced to me. Got
back to the Penn before 4. Notwithstanding a delightful
shower of rain, we all suffered very much from the sun to-
day, and poor little Grace's face was almost one blister.—
Prayers, and to bed at 8.—Observed forty people of our
family at prayers, this evening.

11*th*.—Have more distressing letters, &c. than usual the
last few days, and get up early, to reply to them all as well
as I can. I know it is not in my dear Nugent's power to
listen to many of them, but I will do my best, though my
task is often painful.—Send the sociable for the Admiral,
&c. to Port Henderson, and the chariot to Spanish Town,
for Mr. and Mrs. Blair. The Admiral brought Mr. and Mrs.
Ledwich * and Captain Dunn with him. Exert myself to
make the agreeable, as my dear N. had so many letters to
write, but the day passed off extremely well. Mrs. Blair is
very pretty, but I thought her ten times more so, for the
admiration she expressed of my dear little G.

12*th*.—My little darling is four months old to-day, and
has already a tooth. The nurse got a guinea and a smart
ribbon on the occasion, and is merrier, *if possible*, than ever.
—Only Mr. Minot, one of the Members for Portland, at
breakfast. The rest of the day quiet, and enjoying the
society of the dear little ones. Mrs. Skinner's little *Bonella*
is a sweet child, but so spoiled that I am afraid she will be a
little tyrant. Mrs. S., like all Creole ladies, has a number
of servants with her, and all are obliged to attend to any
caprice of the little girl, as well as her mamma ; and I grieve
to see it.—It will, however, be a good lesson for me, and I
am determined to make my dear little boy so amiable, that
he shall be loved by all, and not feared. But, in this country, it will be difficult to prevent him from thinking himself
a little king at least, and then will come arrogance, I fear,
and all the petty vices of little tyrants.—I have taken little
Bonella in hand, and she really seems already to be much

* Rev. E. Ledwich was rector for Vere ; the Rev. S. Ledwich
for Port Royal.

better in temper, and is, indeed, a most attractive dear little thing.

13th.—General N. off early for Kingston, not to return to-night, as he is to review the Port Royal militia, at Castile Fort,* to-morrow. Feel low and depressed about him, as I cannot help fancying the ill effects of so much fatigue and exposure to the sun; but he says he feels it less than so much letter-writing, &c. after anxious business. God protect him! Read and remain quiet all day.—Poor dear Clifford to sleep in my room, as I am a sad coward when General N. is away from me.

14th.—My dear N. came at 4, not at all the worse for the sun; but he and Mr. Duckworth (Aide-de-camp) nearly lost their lives, by the overturn of the kittareen, and being dragged a considerable way. Thank God, they came off with only a few bruises and scratches; but the account of their disaster made me sadly nervous.

15th.—My mind much harassed by many painful circumstances and unpleasant subjects; but this must always be the case in public situations. Keep as much as I can to myself, and took up my dear healthy child, and make myself happy. I am so thankful, too, to see my dear N. so well.

16th.—Drive to Port Henderson, and take dear little G.—General Carmichael, Captain Maclean, and Mr. Doughty, at breakfast. After they were gone, a nice long morning with my dear N., talking over many affairs, upon some of which he has made my mind quite easy, and I shall try not to be anxious about any one or any thing, as long as I see my dear husband and baby as well and prosperous as they are at present, thank God!

17th.—General N. out with his gun at day-light. I walked in the Piazza with my dear little boy, and then amused myself with reading and writing, till breakfast.

20th.—Go to church at 10.—Rain came on towards dinner-time; so we had only a snug party, instead of the many we expected. Hear a great deal of myself from Mrs. S.

* Afterwards called Fort Nugent.

People find fault with me, for having no intimates ; but
Mrs. Pye has cured me of that, and the only way to keep
clear of nonsense and party business is, I am sure, to keep
all my confidential talk for my dear N.

21st.—Drive, at daylight, both to Dr. Lind's and Dr.
McNeil's, and General N. gave them many charges, respecting the sick of our family. All are, however, better to-day,
and will, I trust, do well.—Several ladies came to a second
breakfast, and Mrs. William Bullock brought two of her
children. How injudiciously treated the poor little things
are in this country ! They are allowed to eat every thing
improper, to the injury of their health, and are made truly
unamiable, by being most absurdly indulged. I look at all
this as a good lesson for our care of dearest little George.

23rd.—Only Mr. Sherriff, Drs. McNeil and Adolphus, at
breakfast. All our invalids are mending.—Mrs. S. in
Spanish Town, visiting all day. I took charge of little
Bonella, who was as good and amiable as possible all day.

24th.—Take little Grace to Port Henderson, to go on
board the *Ganges*, after passing a fortnight here. General
Carmichael and Major Darley at breakfast.—Mr. March,
Dr. Gallagher, &c. joined the dinner party.

25th.—General N. out with his gun at daylight. I was
not quite well, and did not drive out as usual. After breakfast, General N. went to Spanish Town, upon business, and
I remained quiet.—Only our family at dinner, and about 7
we all drove to Spanish Town, to see Mr. Cussans's exhibition. It was a performance something in the style of
Dibdin.* We could not help laughing at the nonsense ;
but, at the same time, it made me melancholy to think,
that the folly and extravagance of a person who had been
brought up as a gentleman, and who is really of a respectable
family, should compel him to expose himself in that way

* This probably refers to Thomas John Dibdin (b. 1771 ;
d. 1841), illegitimate son of Charles Dibdin, the celebrated
writer of eighteenth century nautical songs. Besides being an
actor, he wrote also a large number of songs and plays.

o

to the public. The audience were of all colours and descriptions ; blacks, browns, Jews, and whites.

26th.—Dress by candle-light, and drive to Port Henderson, the Admiral's barge taking us to Port Royal. A delightful row. The water like glass, and the scene altogether, as the sun rose, sublime. General N. reviewed the 87th, just landed from the *De Ruyter* troop-ship, after which we had a fine breakfast, on board the *Leviathan.* Mrs. Blair and Mrs. S. were the only ladies, besides myself.—The ship was in high order, and we went all over it with Sir J. T. Duckworth, who did the honours himself *beautifully ;* but, I believe, we were great bores to the officers and ship's company. The Admiral, General Carmichael, &c. came home with us, and we had a large dinner party. Among the number were Mr. Douglas, just from England, Mr. Quarle and Mr. Meyler with him, and Mr. and Mrs. Roden ; in all twenty-six.

27th.—Admiral Duckworth went at 10 to church with us. After church, made a round of visits with him.—The Chief Justice, and his brother, the Rev. Mr. Kirby, Mr. Milward, Mr. Mitchell, &c. at dinner.

28th.—General N. off at 4, for Stony Hill. I had my little George in bed with me till 6, and then got up, to drive with the Admiral to Port Henderson. The Pyes, &c. came to breakfast, and I brought back little Brooke.—Mr. Affleck, a sensible sort of man, came from Manchioneal, io invite General N. to his uncle's house, in that place. Had a long conversation with him, upon education, and get some useful hints about the university part of it, that I shall reflect upon for the sake of my dear Georgy.* Mr. A. is a good classic, and, I am told, a very well educated man. He appears so to me at least.—At 5, my dear N. returned to dinner. Halkett, the Attorney-General, and Mrs. Ross, and Major and Mrs. Pye, at dinner. All go away at 9. My dear N. sadly heated, and a little fatigued ; but quite well in health, thank God !

* Georgy went to Christchurch, Oxford, and graduated in 1823.

March 2nd.—Drove out, as usual.—General Carmichael, and Mr. and Miss Ludlow, from America, at breakfast. All went soon after.—The day quiet, and to bed at 8.—Gave little Brooke a severe lecture. He is a naughty boy, and I am in constant terror of some accident happening to him, yet I can't help laughing at his tricks.

3rd.—Delightful letters by the packet from all our friends, and General N.'s public despatches most satisfactory.

4th.—Still writing English despatches, and General N. too busy to drive out, as the letters are to be sent off by a merchant ship immediately, and not by the regular packet. —Twenty-four people at dinner.

5th.—A melancholy day for me ; my dear N. so full of business, and so surrounded with visitors, and people coming for orders, that I can scarcely speak to him, and this lasted till the moment of his departure, at 2 o'clock. Had a dull and sad day after, but tried to cheer myself with my little darling. After prayers, I spoke to all the servants, on the subject of their conduct during my dear N.'s absence, and they promised the utmost order and regularity, poor creatures ! and I rely upon them.

6th.—Went with the whole family into Spanish Town.— Made a visit to Dr. Lind after church.—At dinner, Mr. ——, of the *Leviathan*, Dr. Clare, and the Pyes, &c. A delightful letter from my dear N. in the evening.—All my guests staid for prayers at eight.

7th.—In spite of myself, my spirits will sink, and I feel a thousand apprehensions about my dear N., and forebodings that I can't describe. God preserve him, and grant us once more a happy meeting.

8th.—This is, thank God, the third day of my dear N.'s absence, and I shall count the hours till we meet again.— The Admiral has, very kindly, given Mrs. S. a little vessel, to take her to Black River, close to her own home. I feel greatly obliged to him for this considerate accommodation, as it will make her and the dear little girl truly comfortable.

9th.—All the morning assisting Mrs. S. in the prepara-

tions for her little voyage.   Dine at 3, and at 5 drive to
Port Henderson in the sociable, Mrs. Pye of the party.   See
Mrs. S. and her little girl safely embarked.   Sir J. D.'s boat,
and every sort of attention shewn her.—On our return to
the Penn, the Pyes, &c. took leave, and we had prayers, and
to bed at nine.

10th.—Mrs. Pye came to breakfast, and, as she said, out
of compassion, to pass the day with me.—Have a lecture to
give the young men ; Kemble and Brown both very silly,
but I keep all their foolish démêlés to myself, and they
have promised to think no more of the nonsensical disagree-
ment.   Played cassino, &c. with the party till nine.   Then
prayers, and to bed.—A message in the evening by Major
Darley, from General Carmichael, who will be here early
to-morrow.

11th.—General Carmichael, &c. for the day.—Mr. Morelle,
at 11 o'clock, to draw my dear baby, and I hope to surprise
General N. with a nice likeness of him, which I mean to
send to meet him, across the country.—Many sketches
made, but none of them satisfactory, and I fear, after all,
it will be a sad performance.   However, not to throw poor
Mr. Morelle into despair, sit to him myself, with dear G. on
my lap.   Am heartily tired of the business, as he kept me
till 5 o'clock.   General Carmichael, &c. all talking and commenting on the subject.   Little G. stared and wondered,
but was so good, he was the admiration of every one.   Rain
came on, just as we were going to dinner, so all the party
agreed to sleep here, excepting General C., who returned to
Fort Augusta.—A delightful letter from my dear N. before
I went to bed.—Next Monday, I shall take my departure
for the country, and then we shall meet for a few days at
least ; and while I remain here I can have no rest, as, out
of kindness, people are coming continually, and I shall not
be able to avoid a large party every day.

12th.—It is a week to-day since my dear N. left me, and
this day my darling George is five months old.—The morning as usual.—Write a long letter, and tell my dear N. all

my plans for our meeting, but don't speak of the portraits, as I hope to surprise him agreeably, for dear Georgie is better represented than I expected. I am an old sharp-nosed fright.—The day as usual ; sitting for my picture, and talking, &c. with the young Aides-de-camp.

13th.—Could not go to church, as the carriage ˙was sent early for Sir John Duckworth, and all were preparing for the journey to-morrow.—Read prayers to the maids in my own room.—The Admiral brought young Baker with him, and he is to be of our party to-morrow.—General Car-michael, Major Darley, Mr. Mitchell, Mr. Edwards, the Pyes, Woodhams, &c. at dinner. Very gay and lively.—The pic-tures not approved of, and they say that Mr. Morelle has been only a cook. The Admiral, Mr. Baker, and Mr. Kemble slept here.

14th.—Up at three, and proceed first to the King's House, to give my last directions, and to take the papers lying there for General N. Sir J. Duckworth, nurse, Johnson, and baby, with me in the sociable. Mr. Baker and the Admiral's valet-de-chambre, in a curricle ; white George (a German groom), with Mrs. Clifford, in a kittareen ; Prince and Peggy in another ; then, a white groom, and two black men on horseback before us early, to get all the wains laden with sugar casks out of the way, as they are dangerous to pass on the road, being drawn by oxen ; and, lastly, two sump-ter mules ; forming in all a great cavalcade.

Nothing could be more prosperous than the first part of our journey, till we arrived at Rio Magno. Baby well and merry, and all of us in gay spirits. Just before we came to the river, we met the Speaker, and Mr. Redwood,* and Mr Blackburn,† members of the Assembly. They advised us to lose no time in fording the river, as the water was in-creasing very much, and, indeed, pouring down from the mountains, quite like a torrent. They kindly turned back with us, as not a moment should be lost, and they directed

* In October, 1802, Philip Redwood was chosen Speaker, in place of Kean Osborn.

† J. Blackburn, member for St. Thomas-in-the-Vale.

one of the black men to go before on horseback, as soon as
possible, through the most shallow part of the river.   They
next ordered our sociable to follow, and the rest to proceed
in the same line, as quietly as possible.   The servant's horse
could not well stem the torrent, and it stopped.   Ours began
to plunge, and the traces were loosened on one side of the
wheel horses.   The roaring of the water, and the cry of the
people, " Go on, go on," made it a most terrific moment.
The carriage began to move up and down ; the maids wrung
their hands ; and poor Sir J. Duckworth really turned black.
I took the baby to myself, and sat upon the back of the
carriage, with my feet upon the seat.   All I could do was
to call out for some one to take my precious child.   Good
Mr. Blackburn (I shall never forget him) threw himself into
the water, and, by the help of the several carriage wheels,
got to the side of the sociable, and held the dear baby above
the water with one hand, and making his way with the
other, got his precious charge safe to the land.   I watched
him with my eyes till all was safe, and then I felt as if all
the danger was over, though I saw poor Clifford dragged out
of the stream half drowned.—Just as I turned to Sir John
Duckworth, to say that now we had all our senses about
us, and we could save ourselves, good Mr. Blackburn
plunged in again, and asked if I would trust myself with
him.   In an instant we were struggling with the stream,
and I must have been a sad weight ; but he kept my head
above water, and we were soon safe with the dear baby.—
Sir John Duckworth mounted one of the carriage horses,
behind my maid, and Kemble, I believe, behind the nurse ;
but the confusion was so great they themselves could hardly
tell how they got out.   It seems that poor Clifford threw
herself into the water, and was saved by one of Mr. Blackburn's servants.   The groom, &c. &c. were dragged out safe,
about a hundred yards down the stream.*

The sun was pouring on our heads, and there was no

* A few years later Whitehorne, the member for St. Ann,
was drowned at this fording while on his way to attend the
Assembly.

shelter near, except an overseer's half-finished house. A piece of cloth was hung up, as a screen for the maids and myself. Little George was not at all wet, but so full of fun, that he seemed to enjoy the scene altogether. We laid him on a mat, to kick about, while we washed ourselves with rum, to prevent cold, and the gentlemen did the same, in a sort of half-finished veranda. Our spirituous bath put us all in a glow, and we were advised, each of us, to take half a glass of the same nectar ; and after waiting for nearly two hours, it was said the water was rather low, and we all again attempted to pass the Rio Magno. I was mounted on a horse, with four negroes as guides and supports, and got safe through. Darling George was close to me, on a negro's head, and supported by several others. It was a most cruelly anxious sight altogether, and, when it was all safe over, my spirits forsook me, and I fainted. However, a shower of tears soon restored me, and we proceeded on to Berkshire Hall, where we found good Mr. and Mrs. Murphy had sent a chair, and several negroes, to Mr. Videlle's, to carry me and the child to the Hall, which is seven long miles, and chiefly on the edge of a precipice. Poor little fellow, he was so heated and fatigued, that he cried sadly, which delayed and distressed us all very much. He was so thirsty, that he wanted his nurse continually ; so I put her into the chair with him, and mounted my horse, and then, thank God ! before 7 o'clock, we were all safe and well at the Decoy.—In the evening, our treasure was so well and lively, that I lost all apprehension about him, and sent off an express to General N. to let him know how prosperous we all were, for fear of evil reports reaching him.—Thank God all well ; to bed at ten.

15th.—Could not sleep all night, for the roaring of waters in my ears ; but no one was ill, thank God ; and as for myself, my strength and spirits are the astonishment of every one.—Pass a most comfortable and quiet day, with only the party in the house.

16th.—Rain all day. Very comfortable in the house.

17th.—The Admiral off early in the morning.   Send off my despatch to General N.—The day sociable and comfortable.

19th.—This day fortnight my dear N. left me.   It appears a month, and how I long to see him again.—Receive delightful letters from him, and write him a full account of the progress and improvement of our dear baby.—Quiet, and to bed soon after nine.

20th.—As there is no church near, send little George to walk, and pass the time myself till breakfast in reading.— Prayers at 11 o'clock in the dining-room.—Have a nice letter from my dear N.   On Thursday I shall see him at the Ramble, and have the delight of shewing him how much our darling is improved.—Dine at 3.   Walk in the garden, and have a syllabub, as usual.

22nd.—Up early, and started, soon after breakfast, for the Ramble.   Baby with me in a chair ; the rest on horseback.   Stopped at Pembroke Hall a short time, and then complete our journey, about ten miles, before 3 o'clock. Found two long letters from my dear husband, and both so affectionate, and so full of anxiety about the effects of our water disaster, that I cried like a ninny, and made my eyes so red, I was half ashamed to shew myself at dinner.   Only Messrs. Henry and Whitehorne, in addition to our party. My baby well, and looking beautiful, with his fair skin and bright *purple* eyes.

23rd.—At 2 o'clock my dear N. arrived, and quite well, thank God ! but has gone through much fatigue, and run several risks, from bad roads, &c.—He was delighted with little G.'s improvement ; though, at first, the little darling cried, and would not go to him ; but he soon seemed to recollect his voice, and laughed and patted his face, as if to make up for his unkind reception ; and to shew that he did then remember him.

25th.—Spend the morning with my dear N. who has much writing, and we remained almost entirely in our own room till dinner.   Then walk afterwards, see the sugar making, and amuse ourselves till eight.

28th.—General N. off early, to review the St. Mary's militia. The day quiet. The gentlemen did not return till 7. Mr. Grant and Captain Macintosh, of the 85th, had joined the party, and dined here.

29th.—Ride to the cottage, about a mile off. Have the baby taken there, and General N. and I walked with him back, by a shorter road.—Dine at 4 ; Captain Malcolm of the 60th, two Messrs. Minot, and Mr. Fitzgerald, in addition to our party.—Messrs. Henry and Whitehorne off for St. Ann's, to prepare for General N.'s reception there ; for, alas ! he must renew his tour to-morrow.

30th.—At 12 my dear N. left us. A dreary day indeed to me.—A servant came back in the evening, with a little despatch, to say he was safe over the worst part of the road to St. Ann's Bay.

31st.—A wet morning. Had a long conversation with Mr. Murphy, upon public matters. Most of it will, I am sure, be useful to my dear N. ; so I shall keep it in store for our meeting, as I don't like to write upon such subjects.—After 10 o'clock to-day, the weather was fine, and much cooler for the rain in the morning. Rejoice on General N.'s account, as he reviews the St. Ann's militia to-day.

April 4th.—Set off to return to the Decoy at 9.—Take a second breakfast at Mr. Mason's, and get to the Decoy to dine.

6th.—Walk early ; breakfast at 7 ; dine at 3.—Take syllabub, and swing in the garden.

7th.—After dinner explore the negro houses. Most of them neat, and very comfortable, with poultry, &c. &c. about them.

8th.—Good Friday.—Prayers at 11.—This day (as many lately past) has been one of much reflection and seriousness to me, for which, I trust, I shall be all the better in future.

9th.—Walk in the garden with little G., and then breakfast at half-past six.—Prince returned from Spanish Town, and brought the portraits. Alas ! the day as usual.

10th.—A pioneer, with letters from my dear N. early this morning.

12th.—This day my baby is six months old, and there cannot be a finer creature ; so fat and fair, and so full of health and spirits. God bless him. It is also Miss Murphy's birth-day, and we shall make it a day of rejoicing.—Very merry, and to bed at eight.

13th.—Young Baker left us, to join the Admiral.

14th.—Doctor Hanson joined the party.

15th.—A great deal of talk with Mr. Murphy, about black corps, &c. Treasure it all up for my dear N., that he may know general opinions on the subject.

17th.—Mr. and Mrs. Whitehorne, with their two children, and Miss Henry, Captain Johnson, and Mr. Brown, arrived just as we were taking our second breakfast in the Piazza.—Dine at 5.—The ladies in white and silver at dinner, and the children all over beads ; the party exceedingly smart.—Made many observations on Creole education, and pity the poor things, for being so stuffed with all sorts of unwholesome food.

18th.—Did not sit down to breakfast till 9, the ladies being so long making their toilette. They seem to bestow much pains and attention to their dress, and examine me most minutely.—A dance in the evening, in which I joined *politically,* and do all that I can to be *agreeable* till 10, and then am really so much fatigued, that I am obliged to go to bed —Heard this evening of the death of poor nurse's child ; poor soul ! I am indeed distressed for her, and don't know how I shall be able to break the sad news to her.

19th.—Intended to return to Spanish Town to-day, but the rain prevented me, and I am not sorry ; for thinking of poor nurse's affairs kept me awake, and I am far from well to-day. Towards the middle of the day make up my mind to let her know the sad tidings.

20th.—Nurse came to my room early to-day, with a much more cheerful countenance than I had dared to expect, and I am really grateful to her for the effort she evidently makes, to conquer her own feelings, on account of my precious boy. —Captain Palmer joined our party to-day, and gives so favourable an account of the roads, that I hope to return home to-morrow. I danced one *political* dance to-night, and got to bed soon after.

21*st*.—A sad tropical rain, this morning, prevented my thinking of moving to-day ; for the precipice roads must be so very dangerous.—Another dance in the evening.

22*nd*.—The weather fine, and the report of the roads so favourable, that I set off for Spanish Town, soon after 8. The Misses Murphy, &c. with me. All rode down to Berkshire Hall ; little George in the chair part of the time, and behaving delightfully. Got home soon after 6, all well. Had a most comfortable dinner, and a letter from my dear husband ; ånd all went to rest, with minds at ease, excepting, I fear, poor nurse, in whose eyes I saw tears as we passed on to the Penn from Spanish Town, near to where her little boy died. I could not help remarking to-day, the number of servants attending the Misses Murphy and myself. There were no less than twenty, independently of my white maids.

23*rd*.—Rise at 6, but don't drive out. A letter from the Admiral, asking for carriages for himself, the Blairs, &c. to-morrow ; and spend the day as well as sleep.—Only Major Maitland and Dr. McNeil, in addition to our party to-day.

24*th*.—Could not go to church, on account of sending the carriages for the Admiral, &c. The Admiral, Mr. and Mrs. Blair, General Carmichael, Major Darley, Major Maitland, and Dr. Clare ; in all a large party. All in high spirits.— Prayers in the evening ; the Admiral, the Blairs, &c. remaining. The rest went away at 9.—Heard of the arrival of the packet, and my spirits were rather lowered, by the reports of the renewal of the war, &c.

25*th*.—Admiral D. &c. left us. The Blairs remained till after dinner. Then, sent them on to Spanish Town in the chariot.

26*th*.—A note from my dear N. to say that he will cer-

tainly be at home by 7 or 8 this evening. Order the servants a fête in consequence, and, with the assistance of the
Misses Murphy, make all my preparations in the best manner. Dined with the gentlemen of the family, before 3,
and immediately after take our stations in the Piazza, to
see the blackies enjoy themselves.

A long table was spread on the green, with all their most
favourite dishes, of barbecued * hog, jerked hog, pepper-
pot, yams, plantains, &c. There were tubs of punch, and
each of them had three glasses of Madeira, to drink three
toasts—" Massa Gubernor, and Missis, and little Massa "—
all of which were drank with three times three, by the men,
women and children, and their sweethearts. The little
children were all allowed a little sip, out of the grown up
people's glasses.

As soon as that ceremony was over, I began the ball with
an old Negro man. The gentlemen each selected a partner,
according to rank, by age or service, and we all danced.
However, I was not aware how much I shocked the Misses
Murphy by doing this ; for I did exactly the same as I
would have done at a servants' hall birth-day in England.
They told me, afterwards, that they were nearly fainting,
and could hardly forbear shedding a flood of tears, at such
an unusual and extraordinary sight ; for in this country,
and among slaves, it was necessary to keep up so much more
distant respect ! They may be right. I meant nothing
wrong, and all the poor creatures seemed so delighted, and
so much pleased, that I could scarcely repent it. I was,
nevertheless, very sorry to have hurt their feelings, and particularly too as they seemed to think the example dangerous ; as making the blacks of too much consequence, or
putting them at all on a footing with the whites, they said,
might make a serious change in their conduct, and even
produce a rebellion in the Island.

* Cooked by slow heat, after the manner of the old buccaneers.
The barbacue was a framework of sticks set upon posts. The
name, of native Indian origin, survives in the platform used
for drying coffee and pimento.

But to proceed with my fête.—I had people on the look-out for the arrival of my dear N., and about 8 o'clock his approach was announced. I then marched at the head of the whole party, with little George in my arms, to meet him; the music playing, " God save the King." As he got out of his carriage to join us, we saluted him, with three cheers. Dear Georgy was at first a little frightened with the noise and bustle, but he soon began to laugh, and appeared to enjoy all that was going forwards, as if he understood the whole thing. We had a little supper in the Piazza. The blackies resumed their dancing, and kept up their gaiety the greatest part of the night.

27th.—Rise early, and all well and happy, to be once more settled at home.—General Carmichael, Major Darley, and the staff, at dinner.

28th.—At dinner, Colonel Roberts, Mr. Hanbury, Major Cookson, and Major and Mrs. Ottley, with Drs. Gallagher and McNeil, Major F. and M. Grandjean, made a large party.

29th.—Little Grace came to breakfast, and to take leave for England. Mr. Ince arrived from St. Domingo. He belongs to the 55th, and has just escaped from the brigands. He gives a most dreadful account of the state of that Island.

30th.—General N. full of business in Spanish Town, almost the whole day.—Only Mr. Steele, of the 87th, at dinner.

May 1st.—To church at 10, with the Misses Murphy, &c. Young Grace went early on board the *Ganges*, to sail for England. Gave him a letter to dear Lady Temple. Wish we could all have gone with him to England.

2nd.—Sent the maids to Kingston, and drove out, with nurse and my little treasure, to Port Henderson. Began again to bathe him in the sea. They tell me it is good for him, but it is a sad ordeal.—General Carmichael, Major Darley, and Major and Mrs. Ottley, at dinner.—Young Stewart arrived, with letters from his father. A most un-promising young man in appearance, but, for Colonel Stewart's sake, General N. will do all he can to serve him.

3rd.—The Admiral and Mr. Conolly were sent for early.
—Dinner at 4.—General N. full of business, and I amusing
our guests as well as I can.

4th.—At this season of the year we are really tormented
with ants. My dressing table covered. My bason, jugs and
goblets, full of them, and nothing can be more disgusting or
distressing.—Only Mr. Parsons at breakfast and dinner.

5th.—Set off, with the Misses Murphy, at day-light, for
the Admiral's Penn. A large party assembled there, to
breakfast. The heat and dust intolerable to-day. All the
morning talking with Mrs. Blair and the ladies, but thinking
of my dear little Georgy at home.—An immense dinner
party.—Had a bath from a large glass of water spilt over
me. My ball dress all dripping. Return to the company
in my dressing-gown, not to lose time to dress after dinner.
Danced three couples only. Did not get to bed till 12.—
Long to get home again.

6th.—Set off for the Penn at daylight, by a new, short,
and most beautiful road.—My sweet babe quite well, and
seeming almost as glad to see me as I was to see him once
more. General N. loaded with business of all sorts, but
particularly about St. Domingo.—The day quiet, and happy
as it can be while we see him so harassed. This is a sad
drawback to my comfort, but, thank God, his health does
not appear to suffer.

7th.—A day of trouble.—The Spanish Town election took
place. Mr. Mitchell, Mr. Redwood, and Mr. Faulkner (*sic*),
chosen; Mr. Cuthbert thrown out.*—General N. less occupied, and more with me, the latter part of the day; so we
enjoyed talking over affairs, and playing with dear little G.
together. In the evening, the young people played Pope
Joan, and *we* walked most sociably in the Piazza.

8th.—To church at 10.—To the King's House afterwards,
where General N. settled some business. Dine at 4.—A
visit from the Duchess of Port Royal. Make her a present,

* The result of the poll was as follows :—Philip Redwood, 101 ;
William Mitchell, 93 ; William Falconer, 65 ; George Cuthbert, 55.

as usual ; and these presents are, I find, rather a heavy tax ; for all my prettiest things go that way.

9th.—Send the Misses Murphy into Spanish Town, to make visits, and pass the morning with their friends.

10th.—At breakfast, Mr. F. Smith, Mr. Lawson, and Mr. Stevenson. Only Mr. Lawson remained for dinner.—At 8, went with our young ladies to a ball, given in Spanish Town by Mrs. Ramsay.—Danced one dance. Was much amused by a great deal of nonsense, and ashamed of laughing so much.

11th.—A despatch at daylight, to tell General N. of the arrival of some French officers, with some communications from St. Domingo. Send off carriages for them immediately, but the wind coming on to blow almost a hurricane, prevented their landing, and at 5 the carriages returned empty.

12th.—Send young Stewart to Port Henderson, to go on board the *Desirée* frigate.—The Admiral came to breakfast, but left us soon after, to return to Port Royal. Then came General Carmichael, &c. for orders.—All in a fuss about the news from St. Domingo. The French officers were sent for again, and four of them made their appearance at 3 o'clock. After a little discussion with General N., dinner was ordered, and the conversation was unusually lively and gay, though how they could keep it up with such spirit I cannot imagine, after all the horrors they have been witness to in St. Domingo. But they are light-hearted Frenchmen. The gaiety on our part was assumed, and in a certain degree political, to prevent the introduction of serious subjects, as they have come, (poor souls !) to ask for assistance that cannot be granted to them ; and, in short, my poor dear N. is in a sadly embarrassing situation with them and their affairs. When little G. was brought in to them, *to be admired*, after dinner, he amused us all very much, by the profound attention he paid when the Frenchmen spoke, and then saying, *Mo, Mo*, which appeared as if he asked to hear more ; and this, in fact, was the case, as nurse has taught him this word, and he makes use of it, as a signal to repeat any thing he likes.—After dinner, we had coffee in the Piazza, and then got rid of our French friends, as soon as we could.

13*th.*—A refreshing breeze, at 5 this morning, which they say portends the continuance of the May rains, which have never fairly set in, and the last two days we have had nice showers, regularly at the same hour. General N. full of business all day.

14*th.*—An officer from Antigua, with despatches, and brought an account of the *De Ruyter* troop-ship having put in there in distress. Left the *Trent* at sea, in even a worse condition, and much fear is consequently entertained for her safety ; as she was, according to the sailor's phrase, less seaworthy, when she left Port Royal, than the *De Ruyter*, though not so old a ship.

16*th.*—Have a conversation with Dr. McNeil, on the subject of Dr. Clare, and decide upon having the attendance of the latter.—Drive to Port Henderson.

18*th.*—Rise at daylight. Bathe my boy at Port Henderson.—Mr. and Mrs. Woodham brought their little girl, four years old, to breakfast. Measured George with her, and, except in height, he is much the largest ; but she is the most puny thing I ever saw, and all from bad nursing and improper food, I am sure.—A large party of gentlemen at breakfast, and all upon business. As soon as General N. could get away, he mounted his horse, in spite of the broiling sun, and rode to Spanish Town, having appointed to meet many gentlemen of the country there, on particular business —Captain Loring, and another Captain of the Navy, Mr. and Mrs. Ross, Mr. Stevenson, &c. at dinner. Before we parted for the night, I gave Captain Johnson a good deal of advice, about precipitate marriages, but I don't think it will do any good.

19*th.*—Drive early to Mrs. Tonge's Penn, and see her little baby, but don't get home till 7, when the heat was so overcoming, that we were all subdued, and I am determined not to be out so late again. Mr. Smith. recommended by Lord Fingal, dined with us.

25th.—My dear N. still harassed with business, and in the Court of Chancery ; and I shall be on the *qui vive* till it is all over. At 5, a large dinner party.—Mr. and Miss Milward, Attorney-General, and Mrs. Ross, Doctors Clare, Broadbelt, and Adolphus, Major Maitland, General Carmichael, and Major Darley, &c.

26th.—Mrs. Roden and two Misses Rennalls at breakfast. Sent for the Admiral, Captain Dunn, &c.—General N. in Spanish Town all the morning, but joined our party at 4. Mr. Campbell and Captain and Mrs. Lomax, at dinner also.

27th.—The Admiral and Captain Dunn set off, at 5, for Port Royal. General N. went out with his gun.—Most of our family dined at the Ferry House, on the Kingston road, and our dinner party was very small.

29th.—The Misses Murphy did not go out. Mr. Woodham ill, and no church service. Assemble the family, and read prayers at 10. Duckworth and Rogers in great disgrace, and have a severe lecture from General N. They dined yesterday at Fort Augusta, and returned home in such a state that they are absolutely objects to-day ; they having their faces cut and scratched, by making their way through the fences, it is supposed, not being able to find the direct road. In fact, it is quite a mercy they were not both killed.

About 2 o'clock, there was an alarm of fire, the sun having caught the penguin fence, that separates the guinea-grass field from the lawn. All the neighbouring Penns sent assistance, the instant that one of our blacks blew the shell, and it was soon got under; though the grass and everything were so dry, that they seemed to burn like touchwood. The poor rabbits* ran out of the fence by dozens, and many of them were half roasted ; and, in short, it was a scene of great confusion. While the servants were engaged in the field, we were very near being burnt in the house ; for

* Until the advent of the mongoose, escaped tame rabbits used to live in the bush. Or Lady Nugent may have mistaken coneys for rabbits.

P

Monsieur Baptiste left his kitchen, and ran out with the rest to assist, and during his absence, a log of wood fell out of the fire, and burned several articles, and the house would certainly have been the sacrifice, if one of the maids had not fortunately smelt the fire, and had the courage to run in, and pull out all the burning linen, &c. ; which, with the aid of a few buckets of water, soon set all right again. At dinner, only General Carmichael and Major D. with our own party. The disgraced gentlemen did not make their appearance till quite late in the evening.

30th.—The day as usual.—The gentlemen of the family, excepting Duckworth and Rogers, all dined on board the *Leviathan ; they* staid at home with us quietly, to hide their *scratches.* The young ladies helped to console them, and the evening was very sociable.

31st.—Rain, with thunder and lightning, the greatest part of the night. Thank God for it ! It has cooled the air very much, and I feel particularly happy and comfortable, in consequence.—General N., for a wonder, made use of the chariot, to go into Spanish Town to-day, it rained so very heavily ; but his business pressed ; Chancery, &c., &c.

June 1st.—A Mr. Black, from Ireland, with letters.—Mr. Waterhouse, too, upon business.

2nd.—Poor Varty died this morning.—The Misses Murphy were afraid of the damp air. Mr. Clements, from America, Mrs. Dolmage, and Mrs. Ramsay, dined with us. A great deal of Creole conversation, and many prejudices that amused me, but I cannot enter into them.

3rd.—A delightful though very hot morning.—My dear N. closed the Court of Chancery for this quarter, at 4 o'clock. Only Major Otway, of the 85th, at dinner.

4th.—Rejoice that my dear N. has no Chancery business to-day. He has, however, to hold a levée at the King's House, at 1, and to give a grand dinner, in honour of his Majesty's birth-day.—General C., Major D., &c. at breakfast, and to attend General N. into Spanish Town. Salutes were fired, and all manner of respect shewn on the occasion, but I remained quietly with the Misses M. at the Penn.

5th.—No service again to-day.—Read prayers to the family, as usual. Colonel Roberts, Captain and Mrs. Emmerson, and a Miss Kempsey, came from Stony Hill to dine.—General N. closed and sent off his despatches for England.

6th.—Send the young ladies and gentlemen into Spanish Town, in the sociable, &c. ; they brought back a large party of the Murphy family to dinner ; Mr. and Mrs. M., with their daughter Eliza, having arrived there yesterday.

7th.—Mr. and Mrs. Murphy join our breakfast party, and the ladies remained with me all the morning. The rest accompanied General N. to town, as this is his first audience day.

8th.—Major and Mrs. Ottley, and Dr. McNeil, at dinner.

9th.—Mr. C. Grant and the Murphy family at dinner.—In the evening, had to settle a dispute between the young gentlemen. Made them mutually apologize, and shake hands ; but Miss Murphy is playing a foolish and girlish part, which adds much to these misunderstandings. Give her some good advice.

10th.—General N. out with his gun at day-light. I had to rest, as I have some fatigue to encounter to-day ; but the musquitoes were more intolerable than ever. They are indeed in such swarms, that it took more than an hour last night to get them out of my darling George's net, who could not sleep for their tormenting him. When, just as we thought all was safe, close to his cot crept out a large centipede, and renewed all my distress and anxiety about him. —The Admiral, and a large party, at breakfast ; and at 4, an immense dinner party. The Murphy family, Mr. Minot, Mr. Henry, Mr. Headlam, Captain Cotterell, R.N., &c.—At 7, a crowd came from Spanish Town, and we had a dance till 11, when a supper was laid in the back Piazza, and it was near 1 before they all dispersed.—The officers of the 85th, and the whole of the Murphy family, remaining here ; but all sadly crowded, I am afraid.

11th.—Colonels Lethbridge and Turner, of Vere, with the

family, made our party to-day.—The musquitoes intolerable.

12*th*.—Drive to Port Henderson, and bathe dear Georgy ;
but the sea was turbulent, and I was rather unhappy.
Breakfast before 8.—Mr. and Mrs. Murphy, with their
family, and some of ours, dine at Mr. Roden's. We had a
snug party of ten.—Only Captain Cotterell and Dr McNeil,
with ourselves, and the disengaged part of the staff, at
dinner.

13*th*.—Send carriages, soon after 5, into Spanish Town,
for the Murphy family, who slept there. Soon after breakfast, General N. set off with Mr. M. in the curricle, to visit
the estates between this and Kingston, called the Camoens.*
—After second breakfast, Mrs. and the Misses Murphy with
me in the sociable. The rest of the party in kittareens,
phaetons, and on horseback, all proceeded to the Ferry Inn,
to meet the Admiral and a large party at dinner. We had
sent on to order the dinner, a few days before, and all that
Jamaica produces was ready to be served up. The poor
Admiral, however, was so overcome, with fatigue and the
heat of the day, that he was quite ill, and obliged to leave
the table. In consequence, we all separated early. Mr.
and Mrs. M. went with the Admiral, and are to be his guests
till Wednesday. I took my seat in the curricle with General
N., and all our young people went in the sociable ; and,
really, if it had not been for Sir J. T. Duckworth's illness,
it would have been a merry party. As it was, I was much
entertained ; for the Inn is situated on the road, between
Kingston and Spanish Town, and it was very diverting to
see the odd figures, and extraordinary equipages, constantly
passing—kittareens, sulkies, mules, and donkies.—Then a
host of gentlemen, who were taking their *sangaree* in the
Piazza ; and their vulgar buckism amused me very much.
Some of them got half tipsy, and then began petitioning me
for my interest with *his Honour*—to redress the grievance
of one, to give a place to another, and so forth ; in short,

* Caymanas.

it was a picture for Hogarth.—When we got home, a packet had arrived, announcing the certainty of a war.—I had a merry hour with the young ladies and gentlemen, who are all good friends now, and in high spirits.

14th.—Receive private letters, and all delightful.—General N.'s audience day.—Mine spent with dear baby.—Captain Lawson, Mr. Vidal, and Major Codd, at dinner.

15th.—My dear N. so harassed with business, that he is very unwell, and I tremble for his health ; this keeps me in a state of the greatest anxiety, for fear it should be seriously affected.—Only General C. in addition to our party.

16th.—General N. too unwell to join the breakfast party. I drove out with the Murphy family, and then had eighteen people to breakfast with me. Amongst them was a Mr. D'Arcy, from Cork, recommended by Baron Hussey, &c. &c. General N. joined the dinner party, but felt so unwell he left the table, and I rejoined him, when they all went, and I could be with him. Dr. McNeil says, however, he has no fever, and only requires quiet. Thank God !

17th.—General N. had a much better night, but is still far from well ; and, contrary to Dr. McNeil's advice, would go into Spanish Town, as this is his audience day.—It is said that much mischief is brewing in the country, and that it is connected with the St. Domingo French, &c. ; but all this is secret information, and must be enquired into privately.—An old acquaintance of General N.'s arrived to-day —a Mr. Brent. He, with Mr. Codd, and the Doctors, and our staff, made up the dinner party to-day.—In the evening, I drove, with the Murphy family and dear Georgy, into Spanish Town. Mr. and Mrs. Murphy, with their daughter Mary, remained there, on their way to the Decoy. The other two ladies returned with me.—Prayers, and to bed at 9.—Heard from my dear N. that there was much further information respecting the plots, but still all is very obscure. He is, however, thank God ! much better, and I try to keep my mind at ease.

18th.—Think all night of the late discoveries, and fear

this wretched country is devoted to the same destruction that has overtaken St. Domingo. Should anything decidedly take place, we have agreed that my best plan would be to go on board ship, and remain there till after my confinement; but I will not think about it, in my present helpless state, but hope and trust all will yet be well.— General N. still complaining, and so full of business of all sorts, that we scarcely meet a minute in the day, except at meals.

19th.—No service in the church to-day, Mr. Woodham being absent at Port Royal, on account of health. Read prayers to the family in the back Piazza.

20th.—Drove to Major Cookson's Penn, and returned before 6. After breakfast, heard Bessy and Becky their prayers and catechism, &c.

21st.—This is General N.'s audience day, and he is very busy all the morning. Messrs. Sherriff and Perry, and Mr. and Mrs. Rennalls, from Up-Park, the Admiral, and Captain Loring, at dinner.—Many people ill in Spanish Town, about whom I am very anxious.—Mr. Campbell, Dr. McNeil, &c. Hear better accounts of them this evening ; and go to bed more comfortable.

22nd.—About 12, an express from Port Royal. The *Hunter* brig arrived with the news of war with France and Holland. This obliged the Admiral to leave us, and put us all in a fuss ; for the certainty of war with France, just now, adds much to our embarrassments here. God protect us !

23rd.—The day as usual with me, all but my being with poor N.—Only Mr. Younghusband, of the Artillery, recommended by Mr. Addington, in addition to our party.

24th.—General N.'s audience day.—At 5 o'clock a large dinner party ; among which were officers of the 85th, and 2nd West India regiments, &c. Messrs. Sheriff and Robertson, &c. Asked Mr. S. for his vote for Mr. Lyon, as Agent for the Island, and hope to get it.—Some of the 85th staid for prayers.

25th.—General N. set off early in the curricle, for King-

ston. At 1, I followed in the sociable, with the Misses
Murphy, to meet him at the Admiral's Penn, to celebrate
Mr. Duckworth's birth-day.—A large party ; very merry,
dancing, &c. The heat, however, was dreadful, and I got
to bed as soon as I could.

26th.—The Admiral had given notice to the clergyman at
Kingston, that we should attend the service ; otherwise I
would not have gone, for we were obliged to pass close by
the pole, on which was stuck the head of the black man who
was executed a few days ago. We came so late, that we
found all the congregation had been waiting a long time for
us. The church is pretty, and well fitted up, but the service
was miserably performed, by a *Scotch* reader, and a *Welsh*
preacher.* The latter is the vicar. The other, a respectable looking old man, who is curate, bears an excellent
character, and General N. says he will give him a living, as
soon as possible. I own I made interest for him. After the
service, we had to run the gauntlet quite, for a lane was
formed from our pew to the carriage door, and all were
standing still till we passed ; not a very comfortable exhibition to me at present, with my round-about figure, in a
high wind. After church, General N. went to inspect the
messing of the regiment, in the King's barrack. The Admiral
and the ladies returned with me to the Penn. At 5, a large
dinner party.—Little George made his appearance both before and after dinner, and was the admiration of every one.

27th.—General N. off with the whole staff to Stony Hill,
to inspect the 85th, who give him a grand dinner to-day.—
The Admiral and my party all dined at Mrs. Griffiths'. The
heat wonderful, and nearly intolerable, and we managed to
get away at 9.—General N. almost at the same moment, at
the Penn.—The Admiral went to-day on board the Spanish
ships of war, to invite the officers to dine with him to-
morrow, and we also have asked them for Wednesday.

28th.—Returned to the Penn.—General N. remained in
Spanish Town, this being his audience day. I should explain, that these audience days are to prevent so many

* Rev. Thomas Rees was rector of Kingston from 1784 to 1805.

people coming constantly to the Penn upon business, and it answers perfectly well.

29th.—The morning as usual till 9, when the Admiral and his party came, and soon after the Spanish Commodore and his suite ; for we had sent carriages for them all to Port Henderson.   There were six Spaniards, and we had a very pleasant and lively dinner party.   Two or three of them spoke French, and translated for the others.—General N. made them happy by speaking Spanish, which they insisted upon, and spoke rather with disgust of the frivolity of the French.   Then we discussed matrimony, which seemed most particularly to interest the Commodore, who, like all old bachelors, is fond of talking of a wife ; though they never mean to have one.   They all smoked their cigars, and, after coffee, set off again, so happy that we heard them begin to sing, as soon as the carriage drove off.   Captain Cotterell, &c. then took their leave, and we all retired to rest.   Only the Admiral slept here.

30th.—The Admiral off at daylight.   Only Mr. Woodham and Mr. Craskell to-day, in addition to our usual party.

July 1st.—Messrs. Edwards and Baillie, and Major and Mrs. Ottley, at breakfast.   The two latter remained, but Messrs. E. and B. accompanied General N. to his audience. —Young Stewart drawing bills, and proving himself worthless, to our great annoyance.—Mr. Lawrence, of the Navy, is also in disgrace.   Write to the Admiral respecting him, who will shew him all the favour his case will admit of.

2nd.—General N. very busy all day with English despatches, &c.   Have the Rev. Mr. and Mrs. Ledwich, and Messrs. Brent and Kemble, from Kingston.

3rd.—General N. received an express, from Mr. Henry of St. Mary's parish, with an account of several negroes having suddenly disappeared, from the different estates in that neighbourhood, and that from his own place fifteen had gone off at once.   This is indeed alarming, and especially when coupled with the late intelligence of a conspiracy, &c. God preserve us from the horrors of an insurrection !   To church at 10. Not well the whole time, and my mind harassed by the sad reports of the morning.—At 5, a large dinner party.—The Woodhams, Captain Craskell, Mr. Brent Mr. William Murphy, &c.—Feel sadly low, but was rather comforted after dinner, by General Carmichael's account of the state of the country, and the observations he had made on his little tour, from which he returned this morning only, and has spent all the day at the Penn. To bed in rather better spirits, about the state of opinions on the subject.

4*th.*—The Misses Murphy set off at 6 to-day for the Decoy, escorted by their brother and some of our young men.

5*th.*—General N.'s audience day. He is much occupied with the situation of this government, both externally and internally. We drove early to Major Cookson's Penn. After that, I passed the day quietly with my dear boy, till dinner time, when the staff came with my dear N. They all left us soon after dinner, and we had prayers, and were in bed before nine.

6*th.*—Get up at half-past four, after an almost sleepless night, thinking of the state of this wretched country. The heat, too, most overpowering. Drive with General N. and dear Georgy as far as Port Henderson, where we were met by General Carmichael, Major Darley, and the staff, and they all proceeded to Fort Augusta, while I returned to the Penn.—Ordered my solitary breakfast in the boudoir, which I have lately made in the Piazza. Mr. Parsons came, but I ordered his breakfast in the dining room, and did not admit Colonel Irvine,* who also came to breakfast, but sent him to join Mr. Parsons. General N., &c. returned in a most dreadful heat, their faces quite scarlet, and their hair black with perspiration.

7*th.*—From the reports to-day, the country appears in a sad state, and there is every reason to think, that the French have their emissaries among us. God protect us ! I try to support myself, but my spirits are at times deeply affected. Yet I must bear up, for the sake of my dearest N., whose cares would be greatly increased by my alarms.

* Colonel Irvine was Island Barrack-Master-General.

8th.—A night of terror and anxiety, but I must not give way, for the sake of my dear N. and all around me.—We had a nice drive round the race-course early ; and after breakfast, General N. full of business, as usual, in Spanish Town.—General Carmichael, Mr. Wm. Murphy, Kemble, &c. at dinner.

9th.—A most awful night. For several hours the sky was quite a sheet of fire, and the thunder came, peal on peal, with scarcely a second between them. The house shook so that the servants declared it was an earthquake. We intended to breakfast with the Admiral, but sent off an express, to prevent him from waiting for us, and mean to go to dinner.—Dearest little G. slept through the whole storm and is perfectly well this morning.—Soon after 10, set off for the Admiral's Penn. At dinner, the Spanish Commodore, two French naval commanders, General Morgan, and his two Aides-de-camp, with the Admiral's and our families made the party.—In the evening, played cards, and had a great deal of conversation with the French General, upon his sufferings, and the present state of St. Domingo.—To bed at 10, and certainly not in high spirits with all I have heard to-day.

10th.—Returned home.—Only private prayers to-day. —Only the Woodhams and the staff at dinner. A storm threatening, they all dispersed very early. Had prayers directly, and were in bed when the gun fired for 8 o'clock.

11th.—The heat dreadful.—General N. read prayers to me very early, and we then walked with little G. in the Piazza, till breakfast time.—At one, sent a carriage to Port Henderson, for Sir J. Duckworth, Captain Bayntun, &c. ; and at 3, the sociable for the French gentlemen. At 5, our party were all assembled ; Messrs. Scott, Mitchell and Edwards, the civilians ; General Carmichael, and Colonel Lethbridge, the military ; then the Spanish Commodore, and his officers. I was the only lady, as usual, but the dinner was exceedingly cheerful. In the evening, an express, with an account of the taking of St. Lucia and Tobago, by our troops, and decided hostilities with the French. For the first few minutes General Morgan, &c. seemed to feel a little, but, like true Frenchmen, soon recovered their spirits ; and I am sure are glad to be prisoners, and to have nothing to do with all these disasters.—At 10, we sent them all to Spanish Town, where we had provided beds for them at Charlotte Beckford's,* and the Admiral with Captain Bayntun remained here.

12th.—Send carriages into Spanish Town for the gentlemen, who all arrive to breakfast by 8. An immense crowd and three tables laid ; fruit, wines, &c. and the gentlemen all took their bottle of claret, in addition to coffee, and the usual breakfast. Much discussion between General N., the Admiral, and General Morgan, on the subject of the French officers being on their parole in Spanish Town, instead of Kingston. General N. does not quite approve of the arrangement, but so I believe it is to be. I don't like General Morgan, he appears so inimical and designing, notwithstanding all that has been done to make him comfortable ; and indeed seems to be a real enemy to every thing English, though he affects to profess the reverse.—Tuesday being General N.'s audience day, he made an early move, and the whole party accompanied him to Spanish Town.

15th.—Both of us had a restless night.—Drive to Port Henderson at daylight.—General N. reviewed the 2nd West India regiment.

16th.—Wrote letters, in favour of Mr. Lyon, and sent a present to Mrs. Sherriff, which will, I hope, secure Mr. S.'s vote.—Mrs. Skinner, with her little girl, and Miss Williams, came at 1, with a cavalcade of blackies. Her brother, Mr. W., soon after.

17th.—Go to church at 10. At dinner, the Woodhams, and Major and Mrs. Lomax, in addition to our party.—Mr. W. read the prayers this evening, and General N. has

* Afterwards Miss French's lodgings, at the north-west corner of Whitechurch and Ellis Streets.

given Mrs. Woodham's brother, Mr. Craskell, the fort at the Apostle's battery ; so all were well pleased.

18*th.*—Drive out early with Georgy and the ladies.—Sad accounts from St. Domingo.—General N. full of business all day.   General N., Major D., and the Grandjeans, at dinner.

19*th.*—A sad night.   Those poor wretches in St. Domingo prey upon my spirits.—The morning as usual.—Colonel Roberts, a Mr. Nugent * from the north of Ireland, Mr. Hanbury, and Mr. W. of the Artillery, &c. at dinner.

20*th.*—Had Major Lomax and the Grandjeans to spend the day.   Mrs. Cookson and her little girl came to see me, and the nurse brought her own little black child to shew me. It was only seven months old yesterday, and could stand by a chair, and crawl about anywhere ; and really seemed, in every respect, like a child of a year old.

21*st.*—General N. and I walked, in our dressing gowns, for an hour in the Piazza, before the sun rose, with little Georgy as our companion.   All the rest of the day preparing despatches, to go by the *Leviathan.*—At 5, a large dinner party ; Dr. and Miss Grant—like them much.

22*nd.*—General N. so full of business and letters, that he could not drive out with me.   Miss Williams went into Spanish Town in the chariot, and brought out Mr. and Mrs. Campbell, of the 60th regiment, to dinner.   Poor people, they are full of gratitude to General N., who has appointed Mr. C. Barrack-master of Spanish Town.   Sent them back happy in the evening, and went to bed satisfied.

23*rd.*—An anxious day.   Much teasing business, and much misconduct on the part of many in whom we placed confidence ; but I must try not to think of these things, for the sake of my health.   General N. much engaged all day, with arrangements for the emigrants and French prisoners, that arrived in Spanish Town to-day.

24*th.*—To church at 10.   Several of the French officers (prisoners on parole) there, so I suppose they are Protes-

* In September, 1803, a Mr. John P. Nugent was appointed Master of Wolmer's Free School, Kingston, in the place of the Rev. David Duff.

tants; but some say they only came out of curiosity, or to
pass away time. Drove to the King's House afterwards,
and had a talk with Dr. Clare, as now it is probable I shall
be confined there, instead of the Penn, and we made arrangements for the family being accommodated elsewhere.
At dinner, only the Woodhams and Kemble from Kingston,
in addition to our own party.

25*th.*—The heat dreadful, although we got in from
our drive before the sun was up half an hour. Persuaded General N. to sit to Morelle for his portrait,
though more out of charity than any thing else.—About
12 o'clock, a frightful tornado, but it lasted only a
short time.

26*th.*—Take out little G. and Bonella, with only nurse and
Johnson. Find B. very docile when she is without her
mother. Send for the Admiral, &c. in the morning.—Dine
at 5.—The two Mrs. Rennalls, Miss Rennalls, Mr. Mitchell,
&c. at dinner. Mr. M. brought me two plums of the
Orleans kind (black); the first that were ever produced in
Jamaica.

27*th.*—The Admiral, &c. left us at 5, and General N.
walked out with his gun. Mr. Whitfield came to breakfast,
and to receive orders, respecting the French emigrants. A
long discussion on the subject, with General N., who will do
all in his power to make them comfortable, consistently with
the security of the island; but they must be watched a
little, under present circumstances.

28*th.*—This day two years we landed at Port Royal, and
I was strongly reminded of it, by the salute that was fired
for Sir J. Duckworth, who went out of harbour on a cruise.
I feel truly thankful to God Almighty, who has been pleased
to spare our lives thus far, for the health we have enjoyed,
and for the addition to our happiness in the birth of our
dearest George; and now, for the near prospect of having
another darling. May we ever be grateful, and shew that
we are really so, by our obedience to the commands of the
Almighty, in all things, and by doing all the good we can
to our fellow-creatures! The day quiet and more comfort-

able than usual ; yet my plans for being confined here, or at the King's House, are not quite settled, and so I can make no decided preparations.

30th.—General N. off before daylight, to go on board the *Vanguard*, which brought into harbour, yesterday, a French 74-gun ship, *Le Duquesne.* He did not get back till 12, when the heat was dreadful.

31st.—The heat so great, that I was advised not to go to church. The rest of the family went.—Only the Woodhams and the Grandjeans, with Mr. Airy, at dinner.

August 1st.—Send off the sociable very early, to Port Henderson, to bring the French deputies, from St. Domingo, to breakfast here. Messieurs Fitzgerald and Guien, with Monsieur Hillier of the Navy, came. We breakfasted at 7, and they remained the rest of the day. Their mission seems to be of the greatest importance ; for the wish of the planters and remaining inhabitants is, to give the colony up to the English—they have been so ill treated by the French troops, and suffered so much from their rapacity and injustice, that they say it is impossible to look to them for any security. They speak indeed of their profligacy and misconduct, altogether, with the greatest disgust. It is, upon the whole, a most embarrassing situation for my dear N., and what he is to do, I can't imagine.

2nd.—General N. in Spanish Town all day.—At dinner, Major Codd, Captain Aldridge, and Mr. Chandler.

3rd.—An express, in the night, from Captain Walker of the *Vanguard*, which General N. was obliged to answer immediately, and to desire Captain Walker to breakfast here, which he did, and there was much discussion all day, on the subject of St. Domingo, &c. which, indeed, was carried on till a late hour, after the family had retired to bed.

4th.—General C. and Captain Mackintosh, of the 85th, came to spend the day. The Rev. Mr. Simcocks, from Port Royal, got a severe lecture from General N. about his marrying a young naval officer with some good-for-nothing woman there. The rest of the day occupied by St. Domingo discussion, &c.

5th.—Sent a carriage to Port Henderson for Captain Perkins, who had much business with General N. He returned to his ship soon after breakfast, and General N. was in Spanish Town the rest of the day.—Am much shocked to hear, in the evening, that young Stewart had forged a bill, and must be got out of the country as soon as possible. How unkind of Colonel Stewart to send out such a young man to us !

6th.—General N. out on horseback early. I amused myself with little G. in the Piazza. Send carriages to Port Henderson for Captains Walker and Perkins, and Dr. Blair, R.N. The latter gives a fearful account of the jail fever, brought from St. Domingo by the last prizes. At 4, send carriages for the French Commodore, &c.—A very large party at dinner, at 5. Have a great deal of conversation with the Commodore, who is the ugliest creature my eyes ever beheld, but who asserted, that at twenty he was " *beau comme l'amour*," that all the ladies were in love with him, &c.—very modest indeed, with a nose like Bardolph's, eyes that look *transversely*, and teeth of all sizes, and shapes, and colours, green and black predominating ! But it was all very amusing, and made us very merry after he was gone.

9th.—A crowd of Frenchmen at breakfast, for whom the carriage was sent early. I did not make my appearance, as we have agreed it will be good policy for me to be declared unequal to society, till after my confinement ; and so all will be settled, and I shall know by that time what ladies to receive.—The French Commodore, with his friends, and Grandjean, went on board the *Vanguard,* to dine with Captain Walker ; while General N. went with General Fressinet into Spanish Town ; he to his business, and they to their lodgings.

10th.—The day quiet, but the heat dreadful. It is now so long since we have had a shower, that every thing is burnt up, and even the well is, I fear, getting dry.—Remonstrate with some of our young men upon the improper lives they lead, and the miseries that must result from the horrid connections they have formed. Get very fair promises, but fear that is all I am to expect, from my exertions to save them from ruin. This is, indeed, a sad immoral country, but it is of no use worrying myself.

12th.—General N. went into Spanish Town as usual. Captain Dundas, R.N., General C., &c. came to visit me. Drive out, in the evening ; meet a large party of French people—Madame Fressinet, &c. Affect to lie back in the carriage, like an invalid, to keep up the character I have politically adopted.—In the evening despatches from St. Domingo, and much harassing business for my dear husband.

13th.—The heat excessive. Drive out, in the evening, and avoid Spanish Town, for fear of encountering the French again.

14th.—General N. rode out early, and went with the staff, &c. to church, at 10. I read my prayers at home.—The Grandjeans at dinner, with Monsieur Bellause, from St. Domingo. Mr. B. came to express the wishes of the inhabitants of St. Domingo, to place themselves under British protection. A difficult card for my dear N.

15th.—A cloudy day, and some tremendous thunder and lightning, with heavy rain. We all rejoice, for the moisture of the air is refreshing to the poor animals, as well as ourselves, and they seem to enjoy it as much as we do. This is the first whole day of clouds that I have ever seen in this country.* The sun has not been visible, and what a treat the comparative coolness is !

16th.—Send off carriages for the Admiral, who came to discuss St. Domingo business, &c. with General N. ; and, as soon as their talk was over, the Admiral hastened back to Port Royal, and General N. into Spanish Town. For reasons too long to explain, the French Commodore, &c. dined here, with General Carmichael, Major D., &c.

17th.—General N. off, before day, for the Admiral's Penn. While I was at breakfast, came Monsieur Bellause, with Monsieur Grandjean, upon St. Domingo business. Finding

* This is somewhat remarkable, as she had been in the island more than two years.

General N. gone, nothing would satisfy them, but laying all their papers before me, and it was with great difficulty I got rid of them, by 12 o'clock.—General N. at 4. All more satisfactory. Evening as usual.

18th.—Send a carriage early, for Monsieur Bellause, &c. and General N. arranged a great deal about St. Domingo. After they left the Penn, General N. wrote to the black chiefs, and sent also his secret instructions to Captain Walker and Mr. Cathcart,* &c. who are to proceed immediately to St. Domingo.

12th.—A present of cake and a pin-cushion, from the Duchess of Port Royal.—Was much shocked, in the evening, to hear of the sudden death of poor Mrs. Ottley, who expected to be confined in a few months.

20th.—The day as usual, but my spirits a good deal affected by the many deaths announced within the last few days, and particularly among the young, and those newly arrived in the country. Keep quiet, and have the comfort of my dear N.'s society, almost the whole day.

21st.—The Woodhams, Dr. and Mrs. Broadbelt, Mr. Husband, &c. at dinner.—Sad accounts to-day of the many deaths at Up-Park camp.—God preserve my dear husband and child !

22nd.—The carriage sent early to Port Henderson for Captain Dufour, Aide-de-camp to one of the Brigand generals. He is a much more gentleman-like sort of man than I expected ; and, although a mulatto, is not very dark, and has a pleasing countenance. The account he gave of the conduct of the French general officers, as well as those under them, was dreadful indeed, and their cruelties were not to be contemplated without horror. I was surprised at the good language he spoke. At 10, he left us, and at 4, we sent the sociable for Generals Fressinet and Merck, Commodore Querangall, Captains Courvoisier, &c. who, with General C., Major D., &c. dined with General N

* Hugh Cathcart, Clerk to the Council, to the Court of Ordinary, etc.

Q

I kept close to my apartment, till they took their leave, and then we had a snug little supper, and went to bed at ten.

25th.—The heat quite overpowering, and I feel it, now, more and more every day. All the world about me, however, seem to suffer from it, except my little darling, who is as well and merry as ever, and is scarcely ever heard to cry, or be at all fretful.

26th.—A long conversation with my dear N., about the misconduct of some of our young men, in forming improper connections, and thus involving themselves in future.—Poor foolish Captain Johnson is in great distress, about an ugly mulatto favourite, who has been accused of theft. General N. will give all the good advice he can ; but *cui bono ?*

27th.—Duckworth, &c. went early to Kingston, to bear testimony to the amiable character of the mulatto lady ; but the stolen shoes were found in her pocket ! However, they all say it was a conspiracy, and Captain Johnson's constancy is unshaken.

28th —All go to church but me.—Only the Woodhams at dinner. Am not a little disgusted with him, as they say he got tipsy, and beat his wife the other day. I can't believe it, and yet he is not at all like any idea I have formed of a clergyman.

29th.—General N. in Spanish Town all day. Much to do with the prisoners and emigrants.

30th.—Drive out, and bathe dear little Georgy. He and nurse dance and sing all day, in spite of the heat, and neither of them appear to suffer from it; but I fainted to-day, and felt very poorly in consequence. However, my dear N. stands it well, and so shall I, I trust, after a few months more.

September 1st.—General N. &c. not at home till after 10 at night. He and all the staff went, at 2 o'clock, to the ferry-house, to meet a large military party, at dinner.—My day quiet. Drive out with Mrs. Skinner, Bonella, and little G. in the evening. Prayers, and to bed at nine.

3rd.—Dr. Adolphus at dinner, and consult him about poor

dear Clifford, who seems much debilitated by the climate, and he promises to do all he can for her.

4th.—Little G. slept last night, for the first time, in his new bed, and my mind is much easier about him.—All the family went to church.—Only the Woodhams at dinner.

5th.—High wind, and a prospect of rain, thank God ! A slight shower, but scarcely enough to wet the surface of the ground, which is now as hard as marble.

6th.—General N. in Spanish Town all the morning, and I wrote all my notes and letters, as I shall soon not be able to write.—Obliged to send Mr. Heslop a negative, about Rock fort ; but don't feel much for him, he has so little delicacy in his applications, and so indeed have very many people, as well as him.

7th.—Henry Rogers taken ill at breakfast. Send for Dr. Adolphus, and have the comfort of finding it only a bilious attack. General N. as usual, very busy, and in a state of great anxiety about St. Domingo.

12th.—Here has been a great chasm in my journal. But to-day I must write a few lines.—My dear N. is gone to Kingston, and I am sitting on my sofa, a truly happy creature, and most grateful to God Almighty for the great and undeserved blessing He has bestowed upon me. I will try, in spite of the little nervous weakness which I feel at present, to give a detail of the last four days. About ten minutes before 4 o'clock, on Thursday the 8th, I was awoke with slight pains. The house was immediately in a bustle, and an express was sent for Dr. Clare, who arrived about 5, and found me in bed safe, with my dearest little fat girl by my side.* My illness was literally nothing, for I was actually speaking, and walking towards the sofa, the instant before it was all over. No words can speak my delight and grati-

* This event is thus recorded in the *Royal Gazette* for Sept. 3–10:—

" BIRTH

ON Wednesday, in Spanish Town, was safely delivered of a daughter, Mrs. Nugent, the amiable consort of His Honour the Lieutenant-Governor."

tude, or the joy of my dear N., who, as well as myself, I am
sure, expected great and protracted suffering for me. I was
immediately so well, and in such spirits, that, in the course
of the day, I saw, not only the doctor, but all the gentlemen
of the family, who came to enquire after me and the dear
baby.—Had some anxiety, on account of the misunder-
standing of my deaf maid Johnson, but am too happy to let
any thing dwell upon my mind that is at all unpleasant.
My dear little George delighted with his sister, and this is
his monthly birth-day. He is now eleven months old, and
never was there a more lovely child.—I am happy to be
allowed to nurse my little girl ; but, alas ! I fear, from
my anxiety, and the heat of the climate, I may not be able
to do her justice, and this lowers my spirits a little. My
dear N. was delighted, when he returned from Kingston
this evening, to find the baby with me, and all going on
well. He brought each of the maids a present, and I
had quite a scene with poor Johnson, after she received
hers, for she thought she had not deserved it. However, she is penitent, and I am sure I forgive her with all
my heart.

15*th*.—Quite a different creature, from having had a better night. Dr. Clare at 10. Surprised to find me up, and
walking about my room. Drank some porter at dinner, for
the sake of my little Louisa.

16*th*.—Saw Dr. Robertson* and Colonel Irvine, for a short
time this morning.—Make an excellent *day nurse*, and feel
quite happy.

17*th*.—Major Pye, Captain Johnson, and Mr. Brown, were
admitted for half an hour to-day.

18*th*.—General N. read prayers to me, and we passed a
most comfortable morning. A shower of rain, and hope for
more, as the heat is intolerable, and the *prickly heat* almost
insupportable. Had two of the family to dine with us, for
the first time.—Feel it rather a fatigue.

19*th*.—General N. in Spanish Town, engaged in the horrid
Court of Chancery.—My darling little girl quite the admira-

* He succeeded Dr. Lind as surgeon of the forces.

tion of the whole house ; just as healthy, quiet, and good, as dear Georgy.

20th.—Dear baby seems to have a cold, and is a little feverish. Am afraid the taking two milks may disagree with her. Consult with Dr. Clare, and am fearful poor dear Georgy must be weaned, and resign his room to his sweet little sister.—Rather better towards evening, and go to bed more comfortable.

22nd.—All well and happy.—A packet, and private letters most comfortable ; but I fear poor Ireland is in a sad state. My baby quite well, and dear little Georgy prosperous. Admiral Duckworth at breakfast. Mr. Murphy at dinner.

23rd.—The prickly heat most distressing.—Major Pye and Mr. Brown at breakfast.—Dr. Clare came, and ordered me saline draughts for the prickly heat ; but I don't think they do me much good.

24th.—General Carmichael and Captain Johnson at breakfast.

25th.—Colonel Irvine and Dr. Robertson with Duckworth and Kemble, to breakfast, and all go to church with General N. I read my prayers at home. Am rather low, as dear little George must be weaned, and I must give up all charge of my sweet little baby.

26th.—Mrs. S. and Bonella accompanied General N. and little George, and spent the morning at the King's House. This is our first *real* attempt to wean the dear child. My heart is heavy, but I am thankful, and will not repine. He returned in good spirits, dear boy, and we gave him to nurse again for the night, Mrs. Moore resuming her charge of baby.

29th.—I long for the Court of Chancery to be over, for it is a sad drawback to our comfort.

30th.—Assembled all the servants, and made them presents, for my dear little girl ; or rather, she did, for everything was put into her little hand, to give them. Read the family prayers, and a thanksgiving for myself, and now all will go on as usual.

October 1st.—General N. drove me out ; Mrs. S., nurse,

and the children, went in the sociable. All the family at breakfast. Doctor Clare, to announce that he had vaccinated two healthy children, from the virus sent from England, and if the infection takes, my darling little girl is to be vaccinated, the latter end of next week. This day, at 4, the Court of Chancery for this quarter was finished, and now my dear N. will be less absent from home.

2nd.—No service in the church to-day, Mr. and Mrs. Woodham being absent, on account of health. General N. read prayers at 11.—Hear of poor Captain Henry, of the Navy, being given over. These are melancholy times, and indeed these annual visitations are most trying to the spirits.

3rd.—Drove to Port Henderson, but returned quite melancholy, on hearing minute guns firing, for Captain Henry's death. General N. and I feel deeply for him.— Alone all the morning, my dear N. holding an Ecclesiastical Court, in Spanish Town.

4th.—General N. off, at 3, for Stony Hill. Returned at 4 in the afternoon, having gone forty miles to-day, besides walking a great deal, inspecting barracks, &c. ; but he does not seem at all the worse, for either the great heat or the fatigue—but many of the staff could not come to dine ; only Colonel Irvine and Dr. Robertson, and they did not go to Stony Hill. Drury is, I find, so much of an invalid, that, by the advice of the Doctor, he is to be sent to England, as soon as possible.

5th.—General N, off again, very early, for Fort Augusta, to review the troops, and to inspect the barracks, &c. there. I drove with Mrs. S. and the babies to Port Henderson. At 5, General N. brought a party to dinner.—General C., Major D., Captains Cassan and Dobbin, and Mr. Cowen ; but he had previously been at the King's House, transacting business for the prisoners, and emigrants from St. Domingo.

7th.—Drive to Port Henderson. Both little G. and Bonella bathed in the cold salt water bath there, and behaved extremely well.   General N. obliged by business to be in Spanish Town all day.

8th.—From daylight till dinner time my dear N. was shut up with papers, and did not even appear at breakfast.—My time as usual, till 12, when Dr. Clare came, with a nice little mulatto child, from whose arm my dear baby was vaccinated in both legs.   Feel much agitated, and wish this could be deferred, till after she is made a Christian ; but Mr. Woodham's absence may delay that too long, and it is best not to run the risk of small-pox.   God grant that this may succeed !   Colonel Roberts, in addition to our dinner party ; he came to take leave for England.   An express, to say that Mr. Woodham had returned, and there will be service to-morrow.

9th.—Little G. not well, and complaining with his teeth, but try to compose myself for church ; yet was so nervous, that, when the congregation crowded round me, I was near fainting.   A few remained after the service, and I returned thanks, and took the Sacrament.   After which, we drove to the King's House, where Colonel Roberts took our English despatches, and set off for the *Lord Charles Spencer* packet, in which he sails to-morrow.—Only Messrs. Woodham and Airy, in addition to our party.—Talk of fixing the day for the christening, but don't decide, for reasons too long to detail to-day.—Dear baby's legs both look rather red, so I hope the vaccine matter has taken.   Her name is to be Louisa, and I think it very pretty.

10th.—The early morning as usual, and then sit up for company ; but rain coming on, Captain Johnson and Captain Duckworth, the Aides-de-camp for the day, to hand up the ladies, actually sat down and nearly devoured all the cake and caudle themselves, to the great amusement of us all.

11th.—General N. at the King's House, and full of business all the morning.—At 12, the ladies began to come, and I had a crowd around me, till 4 o'clock.—In the evening, drove into Spanish Town to inquire how little Eve, who has got a little daughter, is to-day.

12th.—This day, my dearest, dear George is one year old complete. God bless and preserve him, and grant him many, many happy, very happy years ! Drove out, with my precious children, to Port Henderson. All prosperous. Little G. quite well ; baby the same ; and this is to be a day of joy.—At 5, the company began to assemble.—The Admiral and his party.—The Messrs. Mitchell, S. Taylor, Edwards, Cuthbert, General Carmichael, Major Darley, Mr. Cowen, the Doctors, &c. &c. After dinner, little G.'s health was given with three times three, and he was led about the table, to receive the compliments of the company. Before we took our coffee, we went to see the blackies enjoying themselves, who had also a grand entertainment. After which they drank young *Massa*, with a sort of shout, that was more like an Indian war-whoop than any thing else. Then young *Missis*, with the same vociferation. *Old Massa* and *Old Missis* came next ; and, in short, they were very merry. A ball afterwards, and all dispersed before 12. The 8th of November is fixed for my dear baby's christening. I wish it was sooner ; but, for *reasons of state*, thus it must be. It is not, however, quite comfortable to my dear N. or me.

13th.—In the morning the Admiral, &c. to make enquiries. Colonel Lethbridge and Mr. Nolan, at dinner.

14th.—Drive early to the King's House. Little Eve's child like a wrinkled old monkey. But she thinks it beautiful, no doubt.—At 12, a crowd of ladies. Every one, indeed on my list, but one family, that is out of town.

15th.—Dr. Clare early. His opinion, alas ! is, that my sweet baby has not taken the cow-pox. So that disagreeable and distressing operation must be gone over again, or perhaps, after all, we must give her the small-pox.—Drive to Port Henderson, with little G.—At breakfast, Major Nugent Smith, of the 55th regiment, Mr. and Mrs. Cunningham, of Montego Bay, Mr. Taylor, and Mrs. and Miss Corovants, from Kingston. All leave us soon after.—Poor little Drury, from Stony Hill, and appearing very ill indeed

17th.—Set off for the Admiral's Penn, to pass a few days, for change of air. Leave my little cherub with her nurse, under the care of my dear N. ; but take little G. as my companion. Mrs. S. and Bonella went to Kingston, on a visit to a cousin of hers. Get to the Admiral's to breakfast. Only Navy men at dinner ; a large mixed party, but only two ladies, Mrs. Moore and Mrs. Griffiths. Cassino in the evening, and to bed at ten.

18th.—Dream all the night (when I did sleep) of my dear N. and sweet Louisa.—The musquitoes so tormented little G., that more than half the night was spent in watching him.—Drive early to Greenwich, to the Admiral's bath. Just close to me, when I jumped in, was a large turtle. Dear little G. had only been dipped an instant before. It looked frightful, though they say there is no danger ; but I was so unwell, after I returned to the Penn, that Dr. Blair advised me not to attempt to bathe any more.—At dinner, Mrs. Ross, Mrs. Symes, and a large party of men.

19th.—Go into Kingston in the morning, and am much diverted with the easy manners and familiarity of the ladies and the shopkeepers, who all seem intimate acquaintances. At dinner, only the Misses Stewart, with Mrs. Ross, the rest all gentlemen.

20th.—Mrs. Yates and Mr. and Mrs. Cole at breakfast.— At dinner, Mrs. and Miss Grant, Mrs. Ross, and Miss Williams.

21st.—Drove into Kingston, and visited till dinner time. On my return to the Penn, receive the dreadful account of an affray in the 85th regiment, and the death of poor Captain Cassan. Am much shocked, and am sure my dear N. must feel it very much.—Mrs. and the Misses Johnstone were the ladies at dinner to-day. A number of gentlemen as usual, and Captain Scovell, who gave a most horrible description of the evacuation of Aux Cayes and Port au Prince ; barbarous and strange beyond conception indeed !

23rd.—All well, only the Woodhams, and Captain and Mrs. Craskell, in addition to our family party.

24th.—Drive to the Penn, before breakfast, with the dear

little ones.   All the morning, a bustle, and crowds of gentlemen visitors.   Mr. Dobbs, from Ireland, amongst them.
An immense dinner party of gentlemen, who sat very late.
I dined quietly in my own apartment, with Mrs. S. and her
sister, Miss Mary Williams.

28th.—A very large party at second breakfast.   Then,
at 5, a party of French people.   Received them in the ball-
room, and dined in the Egyptian hall.   Generals Fressinet,
Brunet, d'Henin le Fevre, Commodore Querangall, Captain
Fogue, &c. &c. with Madame Fressinet, Mônsieur and
Madame Grandjean, Mademoiselle Robert, Captain Murray,
&c. &c.   I really was much amused.   I sat between Generals
Fressinet and d'Henin.   The first a gentleman-like sort of
man, but, like a true Frenchman, did nothing but compliment me, and almost make love to me.   They say he was
a barber, before the Revolution, and I can easily believe it.
He did nothing but talk of himself and his wife.   He said
she was a most charming person, and so clever, that she
could talk upon any subject ; physics, metaphysics, &c. &c.
in short, all subjects of conversation were equal to her.   In
the evening, eight or ten more French gentlemen came, who
belonged to the staff of the several Generals, and we had a
dance.   I got up a French country dance for Madame
Fressinet, but the exhibition was so extraordinary, that I
almost repented my civility ; for her clothes were very thin
and she kicked about, and looked as if she had no covering
at all.   She is very pretty, though the least creature I ever
saw ; and I cannot help pitying her, for the disastrous
scenes she has gone through ; though she talks of all the
St. Domingo horrors with astonishing *sang froid.*   At 12,
all dispersed.

31st.—At second breakfast, Commodore Querangall, Monsieur Courvoisier, Mr. Fogue, &c.   My dear N. far from well,
heated, and much harassed with business.   The Commodore
&c. took leave for England.

November 1st.—Many members of the Council and Assembly called, and were very civil indeed.

2nd.—The Admiral, &c. at 5. A larger dinner party than usual to-day. The ladies were Mrs. Broadbelt, Mrs. Milward, and Mrs. and the Misses Perry. All the rest gentlemen.—Much *politics* going on, and many deep schemes laid, by some of the old members. I hope all may end well, but I fear there is a great deal of vexation likely to arise to my dear N. therefrom.

3rd.—A second breakfast, Madame la Marquise de Piquieres and her daughter. The latter was brought up in America, and speaks sad English !

4th.—A large party of gentlemen at dinner.—In the evening a crowd, amongst whom where General and Madame Fressinet, La Marquise and Mademoiselle Piquieres, &c. &c.

6th.—Several at second breakfast ; Mrs. and Miss Grant, the Rennalls, &c.

7th.—I don't know how it is of late—I have no time for keeping a journal.—It is a task to me. I see a great deal of company. I have a large and *anxious* household to attend to. I have constant applications and notes to answer ; and then, my dear little ones occupy too delightfully my leisure moments, to allow of my giving any sort of description of persons or things, or what is going on here. Besides, I regret to say, that my dear N. has many and great vexations, which, added to the heat of the climate, fill my mind, more than anything, to make me constantly tremble for his health.—Drove out this morning, as usual, but at second breakfast a chill came over me. Drs. Drumgold and Adolphus were here, and they both advised me to go to bed. I really was in a fever till near 12 o'clock at night, when my head was relieved, and I got a nice sleep.

8th.—Take bark and saline draughts, and do all I can to be well to-day, to receive my company, and have my dear baby made a Christian.—At 1, we all assembled in the chapel ; Mr. Simon Taylor, and Mr. Edwards standing proxies for Governor Nugent and Major Osborne ; Mrs. Rennalls and Mrs. Skinner for dear Lady Temple and Lady William Bentinck. Mr. Mitchell (King Mitchell) gives us a grand dinner to-day, and I am to have a ball upon this happy occasion.—But I should mention, that my dear little girl's names are Louisa Elizabeth.—After the ceremony cake, wine, &c. ; all the servants had the same ; and, in short, health and happiness was drank to the dear little Christian, with every demonstration of affection and joy. Find myself, after all this, not quite equal to the dinner party ; so send my excuse to King Mitchell, and take a quiet little repast at home.—At 8, dress for the ball. A numerous company. Don't dance, but play cards till 11, and then take leave of our guests, and go to bed.—The gaieties were kept up till one.

9th.—Much better this morning.—A packet from England, with most comfortable letters, and a parcel containing more of the vaccine virus. Send for Dr. Clare, who immediately inoculated my little Louisa with it. God grant it may succeed !—Poor little Drury does not gain ground at all, and General N. has sent him to make a cruise in the *Hercule*, in hopes of his recovering, and not being obliged to return to England.

10th.—Only Mr. Dobbs and Miss Grant at dinner, with our own family.

11th.—General and Madame Fressinet to take leave. To-morrow they go to Kingston, to prepare for their voyage.

16th.—Thirty-three people at dinner. Doing the honours and making the agreeable, was a severe task to me to-day, for my heart was in the nursery.—At dinner to-day, Mr. Redwood (the Speaker), Mr. Roden (the Custos), and his lady, Mr. and Mrs. Sherriff, Mrs. and Miss Tanner, King Mitchell, Mr. Simon Taylor, Mrs. Affleck, Mr. Minot, Mr. Christie, Mr. Lewis, Mr. Johnstone, Mr. and Mrs. Herring, Mr. and Mrs. Marshall, Mr. Stewart, Mr. Shand, and Mr. Edwards. In short, we go the round of society, I think, over and over again.

17th.—Hear from Mrs. Skinner and her sister very amusing accounts, of remarks made upon General N. and myself, and find that every word, look, and action, and article of dress, is canvassed ; but what does it signify ?

A large party at second breakfast, and all the conversation about a sad affair that has just taken place. A Mr. Irvine, in a fit of jealousy, having murdered one of his servants. It seems the favourite was a brown lady ; and, to mend the matter, Mr. Irvine is a married man, and his unfortunate wife has been long nearly broken-hearted, as his attachment to this *lady* had occasioned his treating her often with the greatest cruelty even. His own brother endeavoured to secure him after the murder, but he has made his escape. It is to be hoped that he may lead a life of penitence, if for the present he eludes justice.—We had a quiet dinner party to-day, and we rejoiced at it, for we heard, just before we sat down, of the death of poor Mr. Hillery, after a very short illness. It is indeed shocking to hear of the many deaths that occur every day, and my mind is constantly anxious for those I love. Thank God ! our family have been unusually healthy hitherto, and I pray that we may continue to be equally fortunate.—Dr. Clare, as usual, three times a day. He thinks dear little G. decidedly better ; but we are still cruelly anxious about him.

18th.—Dear Georgy rather better. Doctor Dancer,* as well as Doctor Clare, to-day. They both give a comfortable opinion of the dear child.—A large party in the evening, but I could not dance, and was glad when 11 o'clock came.

20th.—A great lecture, in the papers of yesterday, to the gigglers at church, and a fine *puff* for General N. and me, for our conduct there, &c.

21st.—Packed up the necklaces, to go by the *Cumberland*, to dear Lady Temple and Lady Mary Grenville.

22nd.—General N. made old Grandjean a present of the

---

* Dr. Thomas Dancer is well known for his " Medical Assistant, or, Jamaica Practice of Physic," which appeared in 1801. He lived in Jamaica from 1773 till his death in 1811-12. In 1779 he went as chief of the hospital staff on the Nicaragua expedition. He was physician to the bath at Bath, and also island botanist.

house and garden that he has hitherto rented of Dr. Robertson. I was much affected by the manner in which the poor old gentleman expressed his gratitude.—This is, however, only paying *one little part of our debt.* If ever this meets the eye of my dear Nugent, he will quite understand it, and know all I mean.

23rd.—All the morning obliged to listen to long histories, of the events of the evening before ; and to accommodate all differences, as well as I can. The brown ladies, as usual, concerned. Don't let General N. know of these disagreeable affairs, as it would only make him uncomfortable, and he has already enough to do, with public business.

24th.—The Admiral, Mr. Waterhouse,* &c. at breakfast.

25th.—Colonel Lethbridge, Captain Campbell, and several gentlemen from Kingston, at dinner.

26th.—A large dinner, and go, in number between thirty and forty, to see Mr. Rounie perform. We were all much amused with his ventriloquism.

29th.—King Mitchell brought his brother, Mr. Robt. Mitchell, who had just arrived in the packet, to introduce him to us. Mr. Edwards, also, at breakfast. General N. then held a Court of Appeal, in the Council Chamber, which took up his whole morning, and I received visitors for him. Amongst them was Mr. Holland, just arrived as Judge of the Admiralty. He has brought his wife with him. She was a Miss Eden, and will, I hope, be an acquisition to our society. I asked him to dinner. At 4, General N.'s Court was over, but he was so full of business, with the House of Assembly, that Captain Johnson, his military Secretary was sent with repeated messages to the House, till 6 o'clock, the private Secretary being confined to his room with a fever, though nothing dangerous. Much fuss about the troops and their pay, &c., and my poor N. had not a moment to join the company at dinner, till near 7.—We both like Mr. Holland's manner much.

30th.—A Court of Errors, or Appeal, again this morning,

* Of the firm of Willis and Waterhouse, merchants, of Kingston.

and I am sorry to say it is to continue a fortnight. I pity poor dear N. very much, for he really has not now one leisure moment; and I pity myself too, for I scarcely ever see him, but in a crowd.

December 3rd.—A large dinner party to-day for the Admiral, &c., but the only ladies were the Misses Murphy, except those in the house. Mr. Holland drank so many bumpers of claret, that he got into high spirits, and gave up, in the Court of Admiralty, every point of which he had been so tenacious in the morning.—Though this is the very beginning of December, we all agree it is like the dog-days; and, even while sitting still, the perspiration bubbles out, and drops from the forehead, nose, and chin, so that many of the company really looked like so many living drip-stones.

5th.—Hear that poor Captain Murray has the fever. Of late I have omitted to mention illness, for it only makes one melancholy and miserable; but there are, in fact, only three subjects of conversation here,—debt, disease, and death. It is, indeed, truly shocking.

6th.—General N. all the morning in the Court of Appeal.—A small dinner party; and, at 8, the company began to assemble for the King's ball.* The Admiral, with a large party, Mr. and Mrs. Holland, &c. came from Kingston; and every one seemed merry and well pleased. Supper at 12. To bed at two.

* The Ball was advertised as follows in the *Royal Gazette* :—

"KING'S HOUSE, *Oct. 27,* 1803
KING'S BALL

There will be a BALL given by His Honour the LIEUTENANT-GOVERNOR on Tuesday evening, the 6th day of December next, in honour of

HIS MAJESTY'S BIRTHDAY.

To prevent confusion, Ladies and Gentlemen are requested to order their carriages to come by the Old Court House, and go off by the Long Room.

"N.B.—No Gentlemen can possibly be admitted in boots, or otherwise improperly dressed."

7th.—Only Captain Adam, of the 55th, and Mr. Nixon, of the 85th, at dinner.

8th.—A large party of the Members, with their wives and daughters, at dinner. Mrs. Broughton is quite a character. She had been married before, and we asked her if she had had any children by Mr. Roper, her former husband, of the firm of Roper, Cocker and Co. She replied " No, nothing at all like it, no chance whatever of it ; no such thing, I can assure you." Just before the company assembled at dinner Dr. Clare came and inoculated my little darling Louisa. God preserve her to us ! After much discussion, we agreed to have the puncture made in her dear little leg ; for if the present fashion of excessive short sleeves lasts till she grows up, it will not be becoming to expose a scar on the arm, which I now see disfiguring many pretty young ladies.—A ball given to me to-night, by the Attorney-General. With our party of nearly forty persons, we proceeded thither about 9, and were received with much ceremony and kindness. Mrs. Skinner and Miss Williams were much pleased with the attention shewn them. A gay dance, and supper at twelve.

9th.—Poor Captain Murray was buried yesterday, but, as I had much to do, they did not tell me, till to-day, that he was no more. He was a fine young man ; and how I pity his poor mother, Lady George Murray, when she hears of his sad fate !—Only two new gentlemen, from England, at dinner ; the Rev. Mr. Humphreys and Mr. Skelton. The usual Friday dance. Mrs. Skinner very unwell, and poor Duckworth taken very ill in the course of the evening. If not better to-morrow, the Admiral must be sent for.

10th.—My morning spent in nursing, and anxiety, for my dear N., too, is very complaining. The Admiral came at about 3, and is in a sad state about his son, and almost despairing. General N. not able to leave his room for dinner. Mrs. S. still in bed, and all the family in distress. Doctors Blair, Clare, and Adolphus, in constant attendance. Sit down to dinner with the gentlemen, and do all I can to comfort the Admiral, and support my own spirits. In the evening, the Doctors were astonished at the quantity of calomel General N. had taken in the course of the day ; and I was indeed alarmed : but he says it is his only chance of cure. Before we went to bed, all were evidently better, and Doctor Blair speaks most favourably of poor Duckworth ; so his father went to bed, much more at ease.

11*th*.—Mr. Duckworth better. Mrs. S. out of bed, and, about 10 o'clock this morning, the Doctor pronounced my dear N. without fever ; but says, he must never take such a quantity of calomel again ; nearly, if not quite, forty-two grains ! and he must indeed have a wonderful constitution to bear it. The Admiral left us before dinner, but Dr. Blair remained in attendance upon Duckworth. Part of my dear N.'s illness, I am sure, is owing to worry, and the battles he is obliged to fight with the House of Assembly, to carry into effect the measures of Government. In private society we are all good friends, but, as Governor, they speak most harshly of his conduct, and try to bully him into giving up his intentions, &c. I wish the session was well over, and they were all once more peaceably settled at their homes, and we at the Penn again.—Did not go to church, but had the Woodhams, General Carmichael, &c. at dinner. Leave us at 8.—General N. is very much better, thank God !

12*th*.—On our return to breakfast, find Henry Rogers taken ill. Don't wait a moment, but give him a good dose of calomel, and, in two hours after, some castor oil. Duckworth better, and General N. quite himself again. Write to the Admiral, and give him an account of his son, which will, I am sure, be a great comfort to him. Keep H. Rogers upon water-gruel all day, and in the evening he was quite well. I adopted this plan from an old lady, who told me, there was nothing so safe, in this country, as scouring out the patient immediately.—At dinner, only Drs. Blair and Robertson, and Captain McDonald, in addition to the usual party and staff.

13*th*.—I spent half an hour in the chapel alone, and com-

R

fortably. Christmas Day, Easter, and Whitsuntide, are the
only days in the year for the Communion, and I am anxious
to be well prepared to take it the next time, if I live, please
God !—In the evening, many unpleasant and alarming reports, respecting the French prisoners on parole and the
negroes in this town.   One of the black men, a Dutch negro,
had absented himself from prayers, and it was observed, by
one of the staff, that he was seen making signs to one of the
sentries, from a window.   This, together with the rumours
all day, of an understanding between the French prisoners
and the free blacks, and their tampering with the negro
slaves, was indeed most frightful.   Before we went to bed,
General N. sent to the officer of the guard, and made enquiry
respecting the two sentries, placed at the front door of the
King's House, during prayers ; and found that they are
Irish convicts, of notoriously bad character, and the rest of
the guard chiefly recruits, from the French prisoners.   I
cannot describe the anxiety I suffered, nor the thousand
horrid ideas that pressed upon my mind ; and, especially,
as there has appeared of late a general apprehension
throughout the country, and various reports have been
made, within the last few weeks, of the alarming state of
the negro population, &c.   Before we went to bed, General
N. secured his own arms.   All the staff, too, were on the
alert, and, as the nursery door did not lock well, I begged
to have it nailed up for the night.

14th.—The alarm continued, though secretly, all day.
French prisoners coming in constantly, and it is suggested
that the best plan will be to disarm them.   Many Members
of Assembly closeted with General N., but he tells me that,
with the precautions taken, nothing is to be feared.—The
Murphy family at dinner.

15th.—General N. much engaged with the state of the
country.   Several messages passed between him and the
House of Assembly, on the subject of the French prisoners,
&c. &c.   A petition also from the corporation of Kingston
—they seem all sadly alarmed ; but he says, with the ar-

rangements he is making for stationing the troops, &c. that he can answer for the security of the island.   God grant that all may go well.

16th.—At breakfast, the Admiral, &c. General Carmichael, Major Cookson, and Major Darley.   An unusually large dinner party, and a crowd in the evening.   All danced and were very gay.   Many flirtations going on, but the season is now drawing so near to a close, that many looked anxious, and I fear there will be several disappointments.—To-day, the Assembly have expressed much anxiety for the arrival of the troops, and I hope, indeed, they will be here to-morrow, at the latest.

17th.—Drive out early with General N., and meet the troops marching in ; and what a relief to the minds of the Assembly, as well as mine !   A few days will end the session. —A large party of members and their ladies, at dinner.   In the evening, several took their final leave, and the civilest things were said on all sides.   Much as I wish for quiet, I have received so much kindness, from many of them, that I was quite sorry to say, adieu !

18th.—Fred. Berkeley, R.N. (a son of Earl Berkeley's) came on a visit.

19th.—Warwick Lake, R.N. (Lord Lake's youngest son) came to us.

24th.—Write letters to go by the *Revolutionnaire*.   The *Leicester* packet arrived.

25th.—*Christmas Day !*   Rise very early, and prepare for church.   The Communion well attended.—A large dinner party ; but before we joined the company, General N. had written *private* letters, to the Duke of York and Lord Hobart, which I copied for him, as he did not wish even his secretary to see their contents.   Some part of them related to a secret business with Spain.

26th.—The general negro masquerade began at daylight, and nothing could exceed the noise and bustle of the day. Little G. was delighted with *Johnny Canoe*, and with throwing money for the blackies to scramble for.—Our usual

dinner party late, in the back drawing-room ; for the hall
was public property, the whole day. Scolded General N.
for being as silly as his little boy, in throwing money for
the blackies to scramble for, and really some of them had
all their finery torn to pieces in the struggle, and very
narrowly escaped in whole skins.—In the evening, a report
from Stony Hill, that the regimental chest had been broken
open, and nearly £2000 taken out.

27th.—An express very early. One of the men has
turned King's evidence, and has impeached the others.—
The town and house still in an uproar ; but it is really
diverting, and very astonishing too, to see the mixture of
savage and civilized amusements.—The heat great, and a
large military party at dinner, in a room too small for such
a number, added to it greatly.

28th.—More intelligence from Stony Hill. Many people
implicated in the robbery ; but as yet no chance of recovering the money. The sum is now said to be £2400.—Have
not driven out these three days, but General N. has rode
and drove, and the little ones have had their exercise and
air regularly, and are, thank God ! quite well.—A military
party at dinner again. Obliged to give Drury a lecture, for
his very improper conduct.

29th.—Write early my thanks to Dr. Clare, and send him
a present of two hundred pounds from General N., for his
attention to me, &c.—Dine at 2 o'clock, and then set off for
the Apostles' battery, with General N., General Carmichael,
Major Darley, Colonel Irvine, and Captain Johnson. A
beautiful situation, but the house quite a hovel. However,
it is all to be made quite comfortable, and we have decided
to go there the 8th of next month, for the benefit of sea air,
and bathing the dear little ones. Home again by 8 o'clock.

30th.—Mrs. S. and her sister, with little Bonella, off early
for Kingston, on a visit to a relation of theirs. Little G.
will miss his companion very much, as he is very fond of
little Bon.—General N. busy, writing a paragraph for the
newspapers, in answer to a false statement, respecting some

measures of his government. He sent it off before dinner.
—Young Drury in great disgrace, and to be sent to his
regiment immediately. He is a foolish and tiresome boy,
and it is the more provoking, as he has some talent, and
many good points. Write him a long letter of advice, but
I fear it won't do much good. To-day, also, I had a long
conversation with Major Fraser, on the subject of his
officers ; and then on some of the emigrés. Send them
what relief I can. This was a day of *contretemps*, for, in
the evening, the Inspector of Hospitals was so urgent with
General N. about returning to England, and giving up his
charge here, that he got a most severe lecture, in the presence of all the staff. Poor man, he is lately married to a
young wife ! He is alarmed at the climate, too, I believe
(although he had been previously ten years at a time in the
island) ; and, in short, ever since his arrival, has never been
a day without annoying General N. with his complaints,
though in perfect health the whole time. The whole party
were aghast, and I was more distressed than I can describe.
He had come out on promotion, so that, in giving him leave,
ultimately, General N. told him that he went at his peril,
as he should report his conduct to the Duke of York.

31st.—As soon as I could, I sent Colonel Irvine to Dr.
Robertson, with a message, which will, I hope, set his mind
at ease, and make all comfortable again.—General N. feels
hurt, that he spoke so warmly to him ; but his anxiety for
the service, and more especially the medical department,
obliged him to do so, and he says that were he to give way
to all such applications, the fears of every one would soon
take them back to England, and we should have none left
to do the duty here.

CHAPTER IV

JANUARY 1, 1804—SEPTEMBER 2, 1805

January 1st.—After the service poor Dr. Robertson came by appointment. Had a long conversation, and arranged matters for him with General N. It was quite shocking to see the state he was in, crying and sobbing like a child; and with such a robust figure as his, made the scene altogether most deplorable.—Woodhams, Grandjeans, and the usual Sunday party.

2nd.—All out before day, to review the Spanish Town garrison. A grand breakfast after. The rest of the day with Johnny Canoe, &c. for the last time this year, or at least till Christmas.

3rd.—General N. ordered a Court of Enquiry, upon a Monsieur la Violette, for his cruelties to British officers, when prisoners of war, at Guadaloupe. If they are true, he must be a wretch indeed.

4th.—La Violette found guilty of the dreadful crimes laid to his charge. At least the evidence against him is as strong as possible ; but to-morrow he is to make his defence, so we must not prejudge him.

5th.—La Violette has most completely condemned himself, by contradictions and prevarications. He has been sent on board the prison-ship, in the most ignominious manner ; even his own countrymen and brother officers detest and despise him, and say that his cruelties and murders are beyond belief. In short, that he is a monster and a complete *mauvais sujet*. What a horrid world ! and to this man I had shewn kindness and the greatest civility !

6th.—More company than usual, both at breakfast and

dinner. At the latter, a large party, and all military, excepting the Rev. Mr. Donaldson.* No ladies; but before we left the table, they began to come, and we had a very gay dance, till 11 o'clock. Then, as this is to be my last party this season, another hour was asked for, and the evening ended most merrily. How glad I am!

7th.—During our drive this morning, General N. talked to me a great deal, about my taking the children to England in the spring, and not waiting for his being relieved; but we could neither of us make up our minds quite to part, and so will not think any more of it at present. The dear little ones have their health now, and the quiet life I hope to lead, with the good air of the Apostles' battery, will, I trust, soon restore my strength.—Receive a favourable answer from the Admiral, to a letter I wrote to him yesterday, about one of the French prisoners; Lieut. Babor and his son. Send off Major Fraser instantly, with the glad tidings, to the poor man.

8th.—To church, and hear a very good sermon from Mr. Campbell, jun., just arrived from England, to whom General N. has given the living of Portland.

9th.—A visit from poor Mr. Babor and his son, Thomas Jermyn, to return thanks, and they are to be off for France as soon as possible.—Dine at 2, and set off, with the darlings, to the Apostles' battery; all well, and delighted with the beautiful view.

10th.—The maids and little ones bathed in the salt-water bath, at the bottom of the rock, and all seemed to enjoy it. The cook went over to Port Royal, to market for us, and we passed the day most agreeably. Only Major Ottley and Captain Iseltevin called, but we did not ask them to stay dinner. This situation is beautiful. The house, if it may be so called, stands on a high rock, overlooking the sea; Port Royal, Port Henderson, Fort Augusta, Kingston, and the Liguanea mountains, are all in sight.—In short, it is enchanting, and really very tolerably cool in the evening.

* Rev. Colin Donaldson, rector of St. Mary.

12th.—Soon after breakfast, Mr. Dolmage * came to announce the sudden death of poor Mr. Holland, which shocked us both very much. Doctor Blair and Captain Dundas, with Major Cookson, came at three, and stayed dinner. We took a little walk in the evening, on the rock, and examined the twelve guns, which give the name to the fort.—The company all left us soon, and we went to bed at eight.

16th.—Major Codd and Major Fraser, to breakfast. We hoisted our flag for the first time, and the Admiral came over from Port Royal, to visit us ; but they all left us before dinner, excepting General Carmichael, Majors Darley, Fraser and Codd. General C. not well, and glad to get away early. His nephew very ill, at Fort Augusta.

17th.—Doctor McNeil came early to tell us that General C. was in great distress, and very ill, too, himself. His nephew, Mr. Cowen, died in the night, of convulsions, after the fever had left him, and he was supposed likely to recover. These awful circumstances, do indeed affect the spirits, but we must try not to think of them. Our boat (the *Maria*), came for the first time this evening, and we rowed to Green Bay, where we were received by an old man, of 72, a Mr. Robertson, formerly the purser of a man of war, who was expecting us, as an Aide-de-camp had gone the day before, to let him know we should probably make him a visit. It seems that he has settled the place entirely himself, and lived in it forty-two years. The purser of the *Blanche* was on a visit to him, for his health ; and he has a white housekeeper (Mrs. Washbourn), who begged that my ladyship would allow her young ladies, Clifford, Johnson, and nurse Hamilton, to pay her a tea visit, they would be such *pretty company*. As soon as the sun got behind the mountain, we explored the place, which is very wild, romantic, and pretty. A great deal of cotton growing,† and altogether

* Adam Dolmage was island storekeeper.
† Of interest in view of the present revival of the cotton industry.

very curious. But the most wonderful thing we saw, was
the tomb of a man, who was swallowed up in the great
earthquake of 1692 ; but I have sketched the tomb and inscription exactly, and that will give the history, without
my repeating it.* We returned home delighted with our
little voyage.

Here lyes the Body of
Lewis Galdy, Esq.
who departed this Life at Port Royal,
The 22ᵈ December, 1739, aged 80.

———

He was born at Montpelier in France,
but left that Country for his Religion,
and came to settle in this Island, where he
was swallowed up in the great Earthquake,
in the Year 1692,
And, by the Providence of God, was by
Another Shock
thrown into the Sea, and miraculously
saved, by swimming untill a Boat took
him up. He lived many years after in
great Reputation, beloved by all who
knew him, and much lamented at his
Death.

———

Dieu sur Tout.

18th.—Captain Dundas's barge ready for us, at gun-fire,
and with little ones and all, went on board the *Elephant*
immediately. The Admiral, Commissioner Stirling, and a
large party, to meet us, spend a very pleasant morning,
walk over the ship, and little George much amused and
astonished at all he saw ; all the sailors admiring him very
much, as well as dear little Louisa. On our return home,
at 12, salutes were fired from Fort Augusta, Fort Charles,
and all the ships of war at Port Royal. Captain Craskell
was at the Apostles' battery, and fired a salute also. Little
L. did not mind the noise, but little George started and

* Lewis Galdy was an affluent merchant and churchwarden
of Port Royal. He represented various parishes at different
times, from 1707 to 1718, in the Assembly. His tomb still
exists. Lady Nugent put a skull and crossbones, in error, for
the Galdy arms—a cock: two mullets in chief and a crescent
in base.

jumped every time that I did so, and at last was so much
frightened, that he cried sadly.   Kemble, Duckworth, and
Rogers, came over in a canoe, from Kingston, to dinner, and
returned at night ; it was rather a hazardous voyage, which
we begged them not to repeat.

20th.—Mr. Hinchliffe at breakfast, full of gratitude for
his appointment, as Judge of the Admiralty Court, and to
take the oaths, &c.   Dr. Robertson also came to breakfast,
and seems perfectly satisfied with the justice of General N.'s
conduct towards him.

22nd.—General Carmichael, Major Darley, Mr. K., &c. at
breakfast.   The question respecting the Inspector of Prize
Tonnage decided satisfactorily in the evening, before the
party broke up.   I rejoice, for, although I don't like to
have anything to say to public matters, I can't help hearing
all about them, and they are very often a great worry and
anxiety to me.

23rd.—Just as we were going to dinner, Duckworth,
Brown and Rogers, with Majors Codd and Fraser, came and
stayed till eight.

24th.—Received a present of two macaws, and a Spanish
hammock, by a Mid from the *Hunter* brig, just arrived from
Honduras.—Some of the staff at dinner.

25th.—Captain Perkins of the *Tartar*, at 7 o'clock.   He
arrived last night, from St. Domingo, and brought back
Mr. Corbet ; who was sent by General N. with proposals
for a treaty of commerce, &c. to His *Excellency* General
Dessalines, the black Emperor.   Then came the Admiral,
the Commissioner, and several Navy men, Mr. Corbet, and
Doctors Robertson and Edgar.   In short, our little front
drawing-room was so full, that many sat in the veranda.
Mr. C. has not succeeded in his negotiation.   General Dessalines wishes to make some terms on his own part, that
certainly will not be acceded to by General N.   Moreover,
General N.'s intention is, I believe, to send Mr. Corbet over
once more, and then I shall state all matters in this book ;
at present, therefore, I shall be silent.   The Admiral, &c.

took their leave before dinner, but the rest remained to dine ; and, immediately after, we began our voyage in the *Maria*, to Fort Clarence ; old Mr. Robertson, from Green Bay, having come in the morning, and offered to pilot us thither. We were much pleased with our excursion, and got home at 8. All the young men returned to Spanish Town—Only Henry Rogers slept here.

26th.—The horrid Court of Chancery begins to-day, and will interfere sadly with our comfort. General Carmichael came, most provokingly, to spend the day, and stayed till General N. returned, at 4, to dinner.

27th.—General Carmichael and Major Darley, with fifty men of the 2nd West India regiment, came to mend our roads, and they are so good natured, and so anxious for our accommodation, that I feel quite angry with myself, for not enjoying General C.'s society yesterday, and preferring my dear nursery party. As soon as General N. returned, Mr. Corbet and Mr. Whitfield came, on St. Domingo business, and we were not left to ourselves till near 8. Then, we enjoyed the sea air a little while, before we shut up for the night.

31st.—Made Duckworth read me one of Blair's Sermons,* and he really seemed as much interested in it as I was.

February 2nd.—Mr. Duckworth off, at daylight, to fish.— Brought home a shoal of fish of all sorts.

3rd.—I am afraid the climate has at last disagreed with me, for I was near fainting twice from actual weakness, while I was dressing for my platform walk, with the little ones.—Mr. D. off again to fish. I hope he will not be in the sun as late as he was yesterday, for it is a sad risk for him ; but he is so fond of the sport ! General Carmichael and Captain Ross came at 7, to spend the day. I would have excused them for omitting the kindness they intended me.

5th.—The Admiral and Captain Garth surprised us, just before we went to dinner, and six of the staff. So our little Fort room was quite crowded ; but we had a pleasant

* The Rev. Hugh Blair had died in 1800.

dinner, and all were off at 8, and we walked down the rock with them.

6th.—A white man from the Admiral, with a letter to me recommending him as a butler, but declined to take him. Then came a madman, who talked of General Brunet, and plots among the blacks, &c. but it all ended in asking charity. General N. gave him a guinea, and he was seen safely down the rock ; though I own his stories made me go to bed most uncomfortably, and revived all the alarms of plots, &c. &c.

8th.—General N. and H. Rogers (who returned to sleep in the Fort) off at daylight, to fish and shoot. Returned at 4, having been all day coasting, and a great risk I am sure they have run, by having been so long out. They brought home immense sport, having shot two pelicans, and a variety of other birds. The pelican is indeed a curious bird ; the bill is very long, and the sides of it as sharp as a razor. The chest is of an elastic texture, and stretches to an enormous size. General N. talks of getting some of his day's sport stuffed and preserved, to take home with us.

10th.—Captain Whitby, of the *Désirée*, came just as we were going to dinner.

11th.—General N. out again with his gun, till breakfast time ; and then again till 1, to see the Look-out * with General Carmichael, and some of the staff, who came to breakfast.

12th.—Walk on the platform till 7. Prayers after breakfast, and then prepare to return to the Penn.—About 12, I laid down again, with little G. by my side, and soon after was seized with a most dreadful spasm in my head, and so suddenly, that, although I knew all that was going forward around me, I could not utter a word, the pain was so violent Most fortunately, I had the presence of mind not to let go of my dear G., who was in my arms at the time ; otherwise

---

* The look-out was erected by Rodney on the top of the Healthshire Hills, in order that he might spy thence the enemy's fleet coming from the windward. Ruins of it still remain.

he might have been killed. Doctor C. was sent for ; but, before he arrived, dear good Clifford, at the risk of her life, had gone off to Spanish Town, and procured every necessary medicine for me, and when the Doctor arrived, he found nothing wanting. Several of the staff, &c. were coming to dine with us. Poor Clifford had a side saddle put on the first horse that arrived, and, at the hazard of her existence, rode off to the Penn. Never shall I forget her kindness. She came into my room, streaming with perspiration, and loaded with bottles of medicine. I saw, but could not speak to thank her, or express my fears for the risk she had run. —Till 4 in the morning my agony was great. Doctor C. remained on the sofa, and poor dear Clifford on the floor, by my bed-side, on a mattrass. Doctor Clare says, that my complaint is a *Coup-de-Soleil*, owing to the sun pouring upon the low roof of the battery room, and I suppose it is, for there is no ceiling, and the roof is as hot as a furnace. He advises my return to the Penn without delay.

13*th*.—Rejoiced to be once more at the Penn, which has been put into the nicest order, for our reception.

17*th*.—An express from General Carmichael to General N. He has discovered a spring of fresh water close to Fort Augusta, which will be a great acquisition indeed.

20*th*.—General N. held a Board of Forts, &c. which kept him all day in Spanish Town. Have several notes, about *white ladies'* disputes and little gossip. Keep clear of it all as well as I can.

22*nd*.—General N. off before day, with the doctors and several of the staff, to see and decide upon the newly discovered well, at Fort Augusta.

23*rd*.—Mr. Humphreys at breakfast.—General N. made him happy, by giving him the living of Vere, vacant by the death of poor Mr. Underwood. No events ; only they say the wild cats * have destroyed a great deal of our poultry.

25*th*.—A packet arrives ; all prosperous, both public and private, except, that from Trinidad there is an account of poor Edward Rogers's death, which we have the melancholy

* Domestic cats run wild.

task of breaking to his brother Henry. He was much affected, poor fellow, and I made him my companion the rest of the day.

26th.—In the evening unfavourable accounts from Curaçoa.

29th.—Took the Admiral to Port Henderson at daylight. He is in a sad fright about Curaçoa and not at all in spirits, as he undertook the whole affair, without saying a word to General N., and so feels that all the responsibility will rest upon himself. But General N. has met his very late communication, of the state of affairs there, in the kindest manner ; and in this, as in every other case, has set aside his own private feelings, and only considered the pubilc service. The poor Admiral seemed rather humbled, and very grateful ; and I sincerely hope their joint arrangements will not prove to be too late.

March 3rd.—Dearest little Louisa stood to-day, for the first time, all alone by a chair, and she will not be six months old till the 8th. It was a *beautiful* sight ; she is so very short, so fat, and so very pretty. At least we think she is. She is indeed like a little fat wax doll. But I have desired that she shall only be allowed to stand now and then, as a show ; but not long at a time, for fear of making her dear little legs crooked.

4th.—The heat excessive. Mr. and Mrs. Affleck, and Mrs. and Miss Rennalls, &c. at dinner. Go to bed with a thousand apprehensions, and in low spirits. People here are so very imprudent in their conversation. The splendour of the black chiefs of St. Domingo, their superior strength, their firmness of character, and their living so much longer in these climates, and enjoying so much better health, are the common topics at dinner ; and the blackies in attendance seem so much interested, that they hardly change a plate, or do any thing but listen. How very imprudent, and what *must* it all lead to !

7th.—No guests to-day, excepting Mr. White, recommended to General N. by Lord Fingal. He is very importunate to get some place or appointment.

8th.—Settle Madame Jolie's affairs, by writing to Captain Saville, &c. More information received from General Merck.

10th.—Drive to the King's House early. Call at several places, and surprise some of the staff, whose secret ménage was unknown to us before ; but this is a sad, sad country ! See the fattest black baby I ever beheld, quite a little monster, and all owing to stuffing it with food. How unwholesome it must be ! Mine, I am determined, shall at least be fed moderately, and I take care that none of the blackies shall ever give them a morsel.

11th.—Hear from Major Fraser a great many distresses of the St. Domingo emigrants, and give him all my gold pocket-pieces, for distribution, though they won't do any great good, I fear.—Begin to take jelly to-day, and think it promises to agree with me.

12th.—Colonel and Mrs. Horsford arrived from England yesterday. He breakfasted here, but she only comes to dinner.—We invited them to be with us till they can get a house, and accordingly they come to-morrow.

13th.—Colonel Ramsay, and Major Cookson, at breakfast. —The latter to take leave for England.

15th.—Mr. Edwards, of Vere, joined our party.

17th.—Spoke to Mrs. Horsford, as a friend, on the subject of her *vivacity*, occasionally, in speaking to her husband. Now that I have a daughter of my own, I feel interested in the conduct of every woman. She took it in good part, and has promised to command her temper.

18th.—Finish my letters to go by the *Duquesne*, in which poor wretched, but now happy, Doctor Robertson sails for England.

20th.—Dr. Robertson at dinner, for the last time. He was full of gratitude and happiness.—Mr. Cathcart, and Mr. Fitzgerald ; the latter just arrived from Cuba. He gives a dreadful account of the suffering of the poor people in St. Domingo, and of the treachery of the French Generals, before they left the island.

24th.—An immense yellow snake was shot close to the house.

26th.—Dress by candle-light, and drive with the whole party to Port Henderson. Find General Carmichael's boat waiting for us. Land at Fort Augusta soon after sun-rise. See the West India regiment out, and all the new recruits. They made a most savage appearance, having only just arrived from Africa ; all their names were written on cards, tied round their necks ! Saw the regimental school, after which General Carmichael gave us a grand breakfast, and we left Fort Augusta at 11.—The heat was excessive, but when we came near the newly discovered spring, I could not resist getting out of the carriage to explore it ; though the sand burnt my feet, and the sun scorched my temples and nose sadly. Mrs. Horsford was certainly more prudent, in not leaving the carriage.

31st.—Dress by candle-light, and our whole party proceeded to Port Royal, where the Admiral gave us a grand breakfast on board the *Hercule.* All the Captains of the Fleet, the Murphy family, &c. &c. Lord Wm. Fitzroy was the only new Captain, and is a very nice-looking young man. The *lion* for the morning, for the gentlemen, was a large cannon, taken from the French, but I own it did not interest me much.* Saw poor Captain Walker, just before he left the *Hercule.* Never was there a truer picture of woe, and most sincerely do I feel for him.

April 1st.—Easter Day.—Go to church at 10.—Mrs. Horsford was not well, from the fatigue of yesterday, and could not go. The church was strewed with pimento and orange blossoms, and the pews were ornamented with branches of both. The scent was most refreshing. The Communion was tolerably well attended, and Mr. Rose (who now has preached) assisted Mr. Woodham. Saw Colonel Dessource at the King's House afterwards, and asked him to dinner. We had an unusually large party, and the servants, too, had

* There are several French cannon of interest still in the island—notably two, from the *Ville de Paris,* now in front of Rodney's statue.

a feast, and were made very happy ; General N. having ordered an ox to be killed for them last night.

4th.—Drive very early to Port Henderson.—General Carmichael, Major Darley, and the Rev. Mr. Rose, at breakfast, and stayed all day. Mr. Nugent was added to our dinner party.—Hear a salute fired, while we were at dinner, and at 8, receive notes from Admiral Dacres,* announcing to General N. his arrival, to assume the naval command on the station, and to me the arrival, under his care, of two boxes ; one full of straw bonnets from dear kind Lady Buckingham, and the other, lace veils, &c. from dear, dear Lady Temple. Go to bed in high spirits, at having heard from our beloved friends ; for Admiral Dacres sent me a large packet of letters from them all.

5th.—Mr. O'Keeffe, recommended by the Duke of Clarence, came to pay his compliments, on his arrival in this country.—We had a large dinner party ; several officers of the 60th, Messrs. Fishback, Petrie, Campbell, &c. and Mr. (Chancellor) White.

6th.—Colonel Mellefont, just arrived to join the 85th, with Major Otway and Mr. Spears, at dinner.

9th.—Hear of the arrival of the *Queen Charlotte* packet. Meet our letters on our morning's drive. All delightful, and the dear old King much better than we had dared to hope from our last accounts. The Murphy family, and Mr. Minot in addition to our staff party, at dinner.

10th.—Mr. Sharpe just arrived, and Captain Hance of Rock Fort.

11th.—General N., with the staff, off at gun-fire, for Port Henderson. My morning as usual.—Poor Brown taken ill at the King's House. One of my little black boys in a

* Admiral James Richard Dacres, who was Commander-in-Chief at Jamaica from 1804 to 1808, detained in Jamaica for its protection four of the six ships (of Cochrane's squadron, which had come out in chase of Missiessy), which Nelson had hoped would reach him at Barbados, when he came out in pursuit of the French fleet under Villeneuve, immediately before Trafalgar.

S

dangerous way, and poor little Hortense *in labour.* In short, I was anxious all day, and saw only the doctors, who all staid dinner.—General N. returned about 4 o'clock, having done all he wished of business and civility to-day ; and he likes Admiral Dacres even better on this second visit, than on the first.—All the invalids better in the evening, and wretched *little* Hortense, has a great German boy.

15*th*.—Mr. Croft, with letters of introduction from England, and Major Campbell of the 60th, in addition to our usual Sunday party.

17*th*.—General N. off before day, to review the 60th on the race-course. Mr. Hall, and Mr. C. Grant, member for St. Mary's, at dinner.

18*th*.—Up at half-past two, and arrive at the Admiral's Penn soon after daylight. Admiral Dacres there, with Sir J. T. Duckworth, to receive us, with a large party of Navy men and a few civilians. Like Admiral Dacres very much ; he seems such a good natured, *domestic* man, always talking of his family. The morning spent in gossiping and talking nonsense, but we were all merry and much amused ; and I should have been very comfortable, if the dear little ones had been here.—At dinner, the party was added to, by Captains Bligh,* Croft, Vansittart, Evans and Dunn, General Carmichael, Mr. and Mrs. Symes, and Mrs. Ross.

19*th*.—General N. &c. off at daylight, to review the 6th battalion of the 60th regiment, at Up-Park camp. Large dinner party at 5 o'clock.—The ladies were Mrs. and Miss Grant, Mrs. Ross, and Mrs. Affleck.

After dinner, I begged them to excuse me, and I would lie down a short time before the ball, which I was sorry for afterwards, as I found, on my return to the drawing-room, the ladies looking very odd, and certainly cool to each other ; for poor Mrs. Horsford had injudiciously talked nonsense

* There were two Captains of this name on the station at this time, J. Bligh, and William Bligh, best known in connection with the mutiny of the *Bounty.* From 1796 to 1799 Richard Rodney Bligh ɥad been second in command at Jamaica, under Sir Hyde Parker.

about the *natives*, and offended them all very much, as I
learnt from the gentlemen, in the course of the evening.
Began the ball with Sir J. T. Duckworth, and then danced
with several other Navy men, as well as military and
civilians ; and, in short, in spite of the remains of my head-
ache, did all I could to be *agreeable*. Never since we have
been in this island have we been shewn more kindness, nor
have we ever been received with more respect and distinction ; and this proves to me, that, though they may not
like many measures that my dear N. is obliged to enforce,
yet that they cannot help liking him, as a man, and appreciating his character.

   20th.—At breakfast, Commodore Barré, and Monsieur
and Madame Vatiere, in addition to our party. Am very
much amused with the French people. When they quitted
us, we drove into Kingston, and were imprudently out till
3 o'clock, in a broiling sun. However, we were none of us
the worse for it.

   At 5, a very numerous dinner party indeed. The ladies,
Mrs. Marshall, Mrs. Griffiths, and two Misses Stewart.—In
the middle of dinner, a sad scene occurred. A scorpion
crept from under the flap of the table, up one of the Misses
Stewart's sleeve, and stung her severely. It was really
frightful to see the reptile under the thin muslin sleeve,
striking with all its force, and the poor girl in an agony ;
and it was some time before it could be got hold of. Mr.
Hinchliffe produced a little bag of indigo, which he wetted
with water, and applied to the wound, and it seemed immediately to allay the pain, and by its cooling quality certainly
prevented the part from inflaming, for the young lady did
not feel any bad effects from it afterwards. I sat opposite
to her, between the two Admirals, and could not help crying
from real fright.—To-morrow we did intend to go home, but
alas ! it will now be Sunday, before I see my dear little ones
again ; for Mr. S. Taylor expressed great anxiety to give us
a dinner to-morrow, and, from *political motives*, it was
thought we should not refuse. Indeed, in the present situation of my dear N. with the House of Assembly, we ought to

do everything possible, to conciliate the Members, and must not consider our private feelings.—Cards, and to bed at ten.

21st.—Hear that poor Miss Stewart has not suffered from the odious scorpion.—Visitors and gossip till 4 ; then proceed to Mr. Simon Taylor's Penn, where there was a grand entertainment.   Mr. S. T. was more than ever kind to me, and he spoke in the highest terms of my dear N., and ended by saying, " Ah, he is an honest man, though I don't like some of his measures."—Saw a number of black and brown ladies in the evening, to please the old housekeeper ; but I don't know whether the white ladies, whom I left in the drawing-room when I gave audience, quite approved of my conduct.   Back to the Admiral's Penn soon after 10, and to bed immediately.

22nd.—Start at daylight for home, and find my dear little ones quite well, and rejoiced to see us return.   Particularly delighted with the toys I bought for them in Kingston.*

24th.—The Navy were full of the Kingston business, and say, that the ladies have got a Directory, in which they have discovered, that Mrs. Horsford's father, Mr. Brocksopp, is a slop-seller at Wapping.   I do lament her being so silly, and bringing all this upon herself ; though probably she will never hear of the offence she has given.   I shall give her a friendly hint, to be more discreet in her conversation in future.

25th.—Brought young Berkeley home with us, as he has leave of absence, from the *Blanche,* for a few days.

26th.—Mr. Smith at breakfast, who expressed much gratitude to General N. for appointing him Island Engineer, though only *pro tempore.*

May 5th.—At 7, send the chariot for Mrs. Wright, from Carolina, and Mr. La Motte.   The lady was introduced to me by an old friend, Mrs. Middleton.

9th.—Hear of the death of Mr. O'Keeffe and poor Miss Bigsby, whose fate is indeed a lamentable one.

* Kingston on its formation, a century before, at once took the lead in commerce, in spite of the fact that the Governor lived in Spanish Town.

12th.—Mr. La Motte and Captain Dobbin at breakfast. A deputation, composed of Messrs. Kelly and Markland, from the merchants of Kingston, to General N., to detain the packet for one week. After much discussion, this was acceded to.

14th.—Mr. Harris (of the *Nonsuch*) at dinner.—General N. played Colonel Irvine rather a naughty trick, by ordering an extraordinary fricassée for dinner, of which the Colonel ate twice, and highly commended it. It passed for chicken, but was really a guana. When he hears, to-morrow, what it was, I expect to see wry faces, and a good laugh too.

15th.—At breakfast, the story of the guana * made the party very merry; and, as it had perfectly agreed with those that ate it, they joined in the joke; indeed, it is considered not only a wholesome dish, but a great delicacy, by many Creoles; but the sight of it, while living, is disgusting, as it is covered with scales, and looks frightful altogether. We had two at the King's House, but one of them fell into a covered tank there, and was lost; the other pined, and its death was decreed, to prevent it from sharing the fate of its companion.—It is, in fact, to give some idea of it, nothing in appearance but a small crocodile.—Wrote to Mr. S. Taylor to-day, about Mrs. Wright's affairs, and did a great deal of business for several people, all of which, I hope, will spare my dear N. some little trouble.

16th.—Colonel Gordon, Major Drummond, Mr. Edwards, &c. at dinner.

22nd.—Send the sociable at 2, for the Admiral and Captain King, who, with Mr. Hinchliffe, &c. made our dinner party.—Sir J. T. Duckworth and Captain Loring staid all night. The latter to take leave on going to England.—Admiral Dacres is on a cruise for the present.—I shall no longer speak of my own health; it is a stupid and monotonous subject.

25th.—Only Mons. de Mansigny at dinner, in addition to

* The iguana lizard is now only found on Goat Island, in Old Harbour Bay.

our party.—He is a sensible, gentleman-like old Frenchman, and I like him much.

26th.—General Carmichael, Major Darley, Major Ottley, Captain Kingscote, &c. at dinner, and Colonel Lethbridge to take leave for England.

27th.—Kemble came from Kingston, to announce to us his intended marriage.—Foolish man ! but I wish him well with all my heart.

29th.—The early part of the day as usual.—Colonel Mosheim, Major Campbell, and Mr. Bowles (a solicitor in the Court of Chancery), at dinner.

30th.—Captains Dundas and Lake, R.N. in addition to our dinner party.

June 4th.—Our dear old King's birth-day.—I pray that he may receive the reward of his virtues in a better world. —The Doctors advise for me an immediate change of air, and Colonel Mellefont came in the morning, to settle about my going to Stony Hill.

5th.—Hear of the serious illness of poor Captain Cathcart. He is a fine young man, and I trust may be spared.—General N. in Spanish Town all the morning, holding a Bishop's Court.—Mr. Alexander, of the 85th, was the only addition to our party at dinner.

6th.—We all went melancholy to bed, having heard not only of the death of Captain Cathcart, but also of five of his officers !

7th.—General N. rode with Mr. Smith at daylight to Fort Clarence.—General Carmichael and Mr. Hinchliffe at breakfast ; after which, General N. rode again to inspect the Apostles' battery, to see with his own eyes all that may be necessary to be done there.

9th.—Set off from the Penn at 4 o'clock ; both the dear children quite well. Arrive at Stony Hill before 8. My dearest N. my escort and comforter.—At dinner, Colonel Mellefont, Major Otway, Captain Austin, with C. Meredith. The band playing for me till 8.—Nothing can exceed the kindness of Colonel M., and indeed every officer of the regi-

ment.—Colonel M. has given up his apartments in the
barrack to me, and the other officers are so anxious to do
every thing for my accommodation, that I am only distressed for fear of putting them to great inconvenience, by
their desire to study my comfort.

10th.—And my dearest N.'s birth-day. Most fervently
do I offer up my prayers for his health and happiness.—
Before dinner, saw all the gentlemen of the regiment ; the
Lieut.-Colonel and Major taking their breakfast with us.
At 3, my dear N. left me for the Admiral's Penn, and
I dined alone ; but Colonel M., Major O., and Captain
M., spent part of the evening with me.—The band
played, and all the women and children, too, were
paraded. I went out and spoke to most of them, but
felt so exhausted at last, that Dr. Doughty (the surgeon
of the regiment) advised me to go to bed, and take a
composing draught.

11th.—Major Fraser and Mrs. Wright came to breakfast.
—Colonel Mellefont and the Doctor also joined the party.
My dear N., after reviewing the St. Catherine's regiment,
returned to Stony Hill, about 3 o'clock.—At dinner, Captains D'Arcy and Macintosh, with the Colonel and Major ;
the band playing as usual in the evening.—Sergeant Murphy,
a fine tall handsome man, was appointed my orderly, and
to be constantly in attendance.

12th.—Feel rather better this morning, and try to be well,
that I may fulfil my promise of dining with the regiment
to-day, at the mess.—Mrs. Piercy and Mrs. Nolan, with a
large party of officers, to call upon me in the morning.—At
4, went to the mess, and walked afterwards for a short time
on the parade. Have some of the party to take tea with
me, but at 8 retire to my room.—General N. has promised
that my dear little ones shall come up to me, as soon as
possible ; to-morrow or the next day, I hope.

13th.—After breakfast, Colonels Mosheim and Unwin,
Major Drummond, &c. to call upon me. General N. set off
for the Penn at 3 ; and, at 4, Colonel Mellefont, Major

Otway, Captain Wilkins, and Messrs. Longfield, Grant, and Campbell, dined with me.

14*th.*—The Rev. Mr. Campbell, the Lieut.-Colonel, the Major, Captain Etherington, Lieutenants Cully and Cruize, dined with me, with Ensign Sutherland. Feel better, and in better spirits, for I shall see all my darlings, (please God !) to-morrow.

15*th.*—Up at 4, and prepare for my dear babies, who are to come at 8. All well and happy. Spend my day with them, and my dear N., most delightfully.

16*th.*—General N. rode early to Bellevue, in hopes of engaging that place for us, but was disappointed.

17*th.*—Mrs. Burrowes and Mrs. Chapman, of the regiment, dined at the mess, and a large party came home with me to tea. Get rid of the ladies as soon as possible, and left General N. to manage the gentlemen, who stayed talking till near ten.

18*th.*—General N. went at daylight, to review the St. Andrew's regiment.—A quiet dinner in our own apartment. —In the evening we went to the parade. I preceded General N., the children being anxious to go out, and was received by the regiment like a general officer, according to Colonel Mellefont's order.

19*th.*—Mr. Plunkett came early this morning, to offer us Mount Salus.—General N. rode over to see the place, and has engaged it.—Colonel and Mrs. Horsford came to spend the day, and we had the Lieutenant-Colonel, Major, Captain Austin, and Mr. Plunkett to dinner.

21*st.*—General N. off before daylight, to review the Kingston regiment.

22*nd.*—Walk out before parade, for a short time ; Cupid carrying my chair, and the orderly sergeant Murphy following.

25*th.*—At breakfast, Mr. Watson, and several of the staff. I have now had every officer of the regiment at dinner, and must begin the list again.

26*th.*—The two Admirals at breakfast. They remained the whole day.

July 5th.—A stormy night, General N. up from 1 till 2, writing letters, to postpone the execution of the poor deserter, which was to take place at 5, this morning. Poor soul, it is only a short respite !—General N. and I writing, or arranging his tour round the island, and my moving to Mount Salus on Saturday.

We are invited to see Mr. Cully, Adjutant of the 85th, married to Mrs. Chapman, a Kingston widow. Went there, with the Colonel, Major, &c. &c. at 4 o'clock. A sad scene, the bride was shut up, and in tears, not having been able to get any white satin ribbon from Kingston, nor any onions or sage, to stuff the ducks, that were to appear at the wedding feast. Sage and onions, it was not in our power to bestow ; but, fortunately, I had a whole piece of white satin ribbon, for which I sent to my room immediately ; and, while she was decorating herself, General N. stood godfather for Mrs. Burrowes's little boy ; who was christened *Doctor* George William David, to the great astonishment of the Clergyman and us all ; but his father very sagaciously accounted for it, by saying, he intended him for his own profession, and it might save a diploma.

As soon as that ceremony was over, the bride made her appearance, all over bows of white satin, having cut up the whole piece of ribbon to ornament herself ; which was rather an annoyance to me, as I could not replace it, without sending to England. General N. stood papa, and gave the lady away, and we then sat down to a sumptuous dinner, with no less than two couple of ducks smoking on the table, but, alas ! without sage and onions. There was a large party of the regiment at dinner, and the whole business was very entertaining.—Before 8, General N., the Colonel, and I, returned to our barrack, and then our thoughts took a different turn, as my dear N. is to get up at 3 o'clock to-morrow, on a most painful service, that of shooting a wretched deserter, who has been already pardoned sixteen times.

6th.—We neither of us slept much, and General N. was up at 2 o'clock. At 3, he was off for Halfway Tree, where

the poor man was shot.   He was attended home by a large
party to breakfast ; among whom were a lady and gentleman, that he called Donellan or Donaldson ; but we found,
when they were gone, that the name was Campbell.   However, the hospitality was the same, and they seemed much
pleased.—Dine at the mess ; order the regiment grog, and
the same entertainment, as a take leave, that they had on
our arrival.   After the parade, saw the women of the regiment all assembled, and then called upon the bride and the
ladies of the garrison, and took a *tender* leave of them all.

7*th*.—A little after 4, we mounted our horses, and had a
most beautiful romantic and tremendous ride, over the
mountains, and on the edges of precipices, to Mount Salus.
Find the house and every thing very comfortable, and feel
myself much better, and less fatigued than I could have
expected.   Mount Salus appears really almost out of the
world, and, although I have a guard, I dread my dear N.'s
leaving me, though his tour this time will be short.*—The
late rains have made the insects and reptiles appear in
swarms innumerable, and their hum is quite extraordinary.
—Our gentlemen all took leave, and I hope got over the
precipice road before dark.

8*th*.—The air was so cool and pleasant, that we quite enjoyed the early morning.   Read prayers at 11, and at 1
my dear N. left me to dine at Mr. Taylor's, and to commence his tour round the island.—The afternoon was extremely rainy, with tremendous thunder and lightning.
Awful as it was to me, now alone with only the poor *blackies*
and my guard, I occupied myself with watching it over the
plains of Liguanea, from the Piazza.   At times, all was
clear above, while the storm raged below ; the thunder
roaring, and the lightning flashing on the dark curtain,
which hid all the plain from my sight.   It was indeed most
impressive, and added much to my sad and melancholy
contemplations, in being absent from my dear husband and
children.

* Mount Salus is in the Red Hills, not far from Bellevue.

9th.—Two Messrs. Pinnock, and Mr. G. Cuthbert, with four officers of the 85th, to breakfast. The latter stayed and dined at 3 o'clock, and then returned to Stony Hill.

10th.—When I was writing in the veranda this morning at half-past six, Colonel Mellefont and Mr. Austin came to breakfast with me; and, soon after, Captain Meredith escorted Mrs. Wright up the mountain, having gone to Kingston for that purpose. Hear a great deal of the sickliness of the season, and of many deaths in Kingston, &c. ; but this is always more particularly the case at this time of the year.—Three officers of the 85th at dinner.

12th.—Nurse and my darling little girl came.

16th.—Hear of the deaths of Major Otway and Mrs. Burrowes, at Stony Hill.—Go very melancholy to bed.

21st.—At dinner, Mr. Horwood, Mr. Longfield, Mr. Dugard, Mr. Grant, and Mr. Nixon, and all go away at six.

22nd.—Rise very, very early, and at sun-rise had the happiness of seeing my dear N. and little Georgy, all well, thank God ! and the dear boy most wonderfully improved in health and looks ; and the two dear little things were so happy, to see each other again, that they never left each other's side, but were hand in hand all day, and at night it was difficult to get them to go to their respective little cots. Never did I say my prayers with more fervent thankfulness than I did to-day.

23rd.—Walked in the evening to Mr. Pinnock's mountain ; almost too much in my present situation, and contrary to Dr. Clare's injunctions.

24th.—Rev. Mr. Humphreys at dinner. Much disgusted with his cant of vulgarity, and am ashamed to say, that I was barely civil to him at last, and heartily glad to get rid of him at eight.

29th.—Soon after breakfast, Captains J. and D. left Mount Salus. Mr. Nugent came, and bored us all day. Severe thunder and lightning, and much rain.

30th.—Only our own party at breakfast, with Mrs. Wright, and young Browne, who is here for his health. Soon after General Carmichael and the Rev. Mr. Campbell came to

spend the day. From Stony Hill came Mr. Grant, Mr.
Campbell, Mr. Nixon, and Captain Hance. All left us at 6.
Little G. and L. amused the party very much, and are, indeed, remarkably intelligent, lively, little things, and oh !
how I long to shew them to our English friends !

31st.—General N. off early for Kingston, and did not return till 3.—General N. found much consternation at Up-
Park barracks, to-day, on account of several soldiers having
died, in consequence of the bite of a spider. It is described
as a small, round, black spider, with a red spot at the tail,
containing a subtle poison. In fifteen minutes or less, after
the person is bitten or stung, he goes into convulsions, and
very often it proves fatal. General N. saw a man in the
hospital, a few hours after he was bitten, and says that his
agonies were dreadful, and the doctors thought he could not
possibly live. Before we went to bed, I had all the rooms
thoroughly examined, and my darling children's cots in particular. God protect them !

August 1st.—Only young Hylton at dinner, who came to
thank General N. for his King's commission, which was in
the 85th regiment. Write several letters to the young men
of our staff, and endeavour to guide them to what is for
their future welfare. I have daily fair promises from many,
but alas ! this is a sad country for the morals.

2nd.—Captain Meredith's servant, this morning, brought
in, from a little plantation close to the house, a curious nest,
of one of the little black venomous spiders, that have been
so fatal at Up-Park camp ; at least it answers the description given of it. It is a little round black thing, with a
very red spot close to the tail, or rather almost under the
stomach. We have it preserved in rum, and I look at it
with horror, thinking how fatal such a reptile may be to
those I love. Our watchfulness and care will now be
doubled, and I have desired that the children may never be
allowed to touch any thing, not even a fly, for fear of that
dreadful venomous creature.

3rd.—Amuse my dear children, by shewing them a little

Humming-bird's nest, the progress of which I have been
watching for several days past. The little mother is
scarcely larger than a bee, and her nest is like a very tiny
tea cup. It is placed under the leaf of a tree, which shel-
ters it like a roof, and keeps even the dew from her young.
The nest has a small branch running through it, as a security, and contained two little eggs, which are now hatched.
The young birds are really not larger than what we call in
England horse-flies, and are indeed the most ridiculous
things. We were much amused, in seeing the little mother
taking such care of them ; and it was with difficulty I could
get George and Louisa to allow themselves to be carried
into the house again, they were so delighted with the sight.
—Not a little melancholy, as, alas ! to-morrow, my dearest
N. begins his second tour.

4th.—A melancholy day indeed ! Dear N. off at 6.—The
little ones were asking for papa all day.—Meredith went to
Stony Hill, and brought back Drury, to spend a few days
here. Gave them both a great deal of advice.

5th.—Another letter from my dear husband. He is well
in health, thank God ! but greatly harassed with a variety
of business.—Speculations upon his resigning the Government ; politics ; shabby and ungrateful conduct of many
whom he has served, &c. &c. In short, he is very much
disgusted with many, and so am I.

6th.—Our young men all off to see a race, between the
silly boys of the 85th, who will, no doubt, suffer severely for
their folly.

11th.—An express from General N., to say, that *the King
of the Musquito Indians,** and his uncle*, wished to come to
Mount Salus, and that I must receive them in his absence.

13th.—The King, &c. did not arrive till 9, on account of
the heavy rain, which has made the mountain road very
difficult. I must now describe his little savage Majesty.—
He is about six or eight years old, a plain puny looking child,

* Till 1856 the Mosquito Shore was under the protection of
England ; the King was under the Governor of Jamaica.

but seems to have a very high and determined spirit. His features are rather better than those of negroes, and his hair is so much straighter, that he is evidently of a mixed breed ; but his uncle has the woolly hair of the negro, with flat features, and a very wide mouth.—It is said that, many years ago, a large slave ship, from Africa, was wrecked on the Musquito shore, and no doubt this may account for the hair and features of the uncle, and for the mixture of the breed.

The young King was dressed in a scarlet uniform, and wore a crown upon his head, of which he seemed very proud. The crown was of silver gilt, ornamented with mock stones, and was sent from England, some years ago, for his father. Both the little King and his uncle seemed to hold it in high estimation. When it was placed on the table, and little G. and L. wished to handle it, the uncle got up, and placed it in a little box, brought with him for that purpose, shaking his head and saying, *na, na*, all the time.—Mr. Doughty, Mr. Cully, and Mr. Grant, arrived from Stony Hill, and then General Carmichael, Major Darley, Captain Etherington, and Mr. Nixon, composed our party.

At dinner, the uncle (Count Stamford, or the Duke of York) for he announced himself to have both these titles, ate of every dish, or rather devoured every thing that came within his reach. The little King had a small table for himself, and was helped by his uncle, who seemed to attend him quite as a servant. The uncle did not drink much wine, but what he did take soon got into his head ; and as for the little King, he became quite savage in a short time. He cried, roared, and yelled horribly, and began to pull off all his clothes, in the most violent manner, and was nearly naked before we could have him carried out of the room. He was then put under the care of some of the negro women, for the night, but he shrieked and roared several hours, before he went to sleep. The uncle soon lost all his diffidence, and began to talk to us so freely, of the good and hospitable customs of his country, that I spoke to General

Carmichael, to get him also put to bed.   Poor General Carmichael had, I am sure, drank too much wine too, by his manner, and therefore the 85th gentlemen were my greatest comfort.   They got the General to bed, and also the Duke of York, placing a black man to guard the door of the latter, and then Captain Etherington, and Mr. Grant, got each a blanket, and laid themselves down at Mrs. Wright's door, and mine, and were our guards for the rest of the night.

14th.—At daylight, to my great joy, all the party set off for Stony Hill, and I hope never to see the like again.   Dear little G. and L. were quite sorry that the little King and his crown were gone, but thought him very naughty to say so much last night.   I promised myself a quiet day, but, to my great annoyance, came Mr. Campbell, and Mr. Horwood, of the 85th, to dinner, but they went away in the evening.

18th.—Receive several letters, from different members of the staff, and all full of fair promises, but I have lost my faith very much in them.

22nd.—A most kind note from Mr. Simon Taylor, with a present of grapes and other fruit.   Took the opportunity, in reply, of being equally kind and flattering ;   and so I do hope, if he is not an active friend, he will not be an im placable enemy to my dear N. the next session.

26th.—Read, &c. early, as usual on this day.—At breakfast the eternal and tiresome Mr. Nugent.—Prayers at 10. —The rest of the day quiet and comfortable.

29th.—Preparing letters for England all the morning. General N. wrote a long epistle to dear Lord Buckingham, about a residence in Bucks, and Oving in particular.   Duckworth, Brown, Kemble, and Rogers, came to spend the day, but all left us in the evening.

September 5th.—At 7, the Admiral and Mr. Hinchliffe, to spend the day.—The fact is, that this situation tempts many to come to breathe a little fresh air.—Talk till 3, when we dined, and they left us soon after 6.—Both General N. and I dreadfully fatigued, with our long talking day.

6th.—Hear from the Admiral, of Mr. and Lady Margaret

Cameron and their family. Mr. Cameron is on his way to the Bahama Islands, of which he is governor.—Despatches upon despatches, and all the early part of the day devoted to papers, by my dear Nugent.—Dine at 3 ; and, soon after 5, mounted my horse, and General N. walked by my side, to see a house from a neighbouring mountain, from which we had a most magnificent view. Returned, just as the day was closing in, much refreshed.—Settled that we would go down to Spanish Town, to receive the Camerons at the King's House. Both of us full of regret, but it can't be helped, and we must make up our minds to it.

9th.—Rise at 4, and all set off, to go down the mountain before the sun rose. All the party on horseback, excepting myself, who performed the journey in a chair, carried by four pioneers, and the little ones in men's arms. Find the carriages waiting for us, at Swallowfield estate.* Proceeded to Spanish Town, where we arrived about ten.

11th.—At 8, Mr. Cameron, Lady Margaret, and four children, arrived in the carriages we sent to the Admiral's Penn for them, last night. He was received with the ceremonies due to his rank as governor, and we had a grand dinner, and a ball in the evening. I like Lady Margaret very much, and he appears an excellent, good, and most pleasing man. The children are plain, but good-humoured and intelligent, and exactly what children at their age ought to be. They are delighted with my little loves, and particularly Louisa, who has been with them almost the whole day.

13th.—Have, at 11, a second breakfast, of fruit, wine, cake, &c., and, at 12, all set off for the Admiral's Penn ; Lady M., her young people, and myself, in the sociable, with our two black postillions, in scarlet liveries, but with black ankles peeping out of their particulars, and altogether rather a novel sort of appearance, to Europeans just arrived. General N. and Mr. Cameron in the curricle. Aides-de-camp, servants, &c. in kittareens, and on horseback ; and all arrived in grand procession, at the Admiral's, at about 3.

* Swallowfield, one of the oldest sugar estates in the island, was originally owned by Colonel Barry of the army of occupation.

Refreshments were ready, and then we all creolized till 5 o'clock. A large party, of the Navy chiefly, at dinner.

14th.—Immediately after breakfast we all went to see Kingston, and make purchases.—Left Lady M. C. a short time at a milliner's, and called upon Mr. and Mrs. Kemble to make her acquaintance, for the first time. Return to the Admiral's about 2. A second breakfast was ready, of mutton chops, &c. Then creolized till 3, when we went to dinner in our morning dresses; and, notwithstanding the late second breakfast, the whole party did ample justice to the Admiral's dinner. At 5, the carriages came to the door, and we all separated with real regret.—The Cameron children sent toys to little G. and L., and I gave them all keepsakes, at the jeweller's, in their names.—Governor Cameron and his family went to Greenwich, to embark for the Bahamas,* and we returned with our party to Spanish Town. Get home at 8, and found both our children quite well, and go to bed as soon as we could.—Lady M. Cameron and I amused ourselves to-day, on the subject of precedency. I was obliged, as Governor's lady, to take rank of her, but have promised her, her *revenge* in England, and shall be delighted to give it.

15th.—Breakfast in my dressing-room this morning. Soon after, General Carmichael, and the young Indian King, with his uncle, came to spend the day. Amuse his little Majesty in my apartment, with sugar-plumbs and the children's toys.—General C., Major D., &c. returned to Fort Augusta in the evening. The King and his uncle remained with us. The latter was taken ill, but it is thought to be merely from eating too much dinner.

17th.—Drive to the Penn at daylight. At 10, General N. began his quarterly Court of Chancery.—Obliged to send the little Musquito King *forcibly* to school; but not before, in his rage and reluctance, he had broken the poor orderly sergeant's watch to pieces, and scratched his face sadly.

* Charles Cameron was Governor of the Bahamas from 1804 to 1818.

T

The uncle was still ill, and so we had all to manage for him ourselves. George says, "naughty, naughty boy."—A staff dinner only, and to bed at nine.

23rd.—The Duke of York so well, that we sent him off, before dinner, to Fort Augusta, to embark for the Musquito Shore. He took a great many presents with him, which he considered very handsome.

25th.—Try to learn to play at *brelan.*—To bed soon after nine.

26th.—The early morning, as usual.—Went to the gallery, and heard Mr. White make his first speech in the Court of Chancery.—Mr. Campbell, Mr. Storer, Colonel Unwin, Major Drummond, &c. at dinner.

28th.—In my drive this morning, met several of the unfortunate half-black progeny of some of our staff; all in fine muslin, lace, &c. with wreaths of flowers in their hats. What ruin for these worse than thoughtless young men ! But advice is of no use, and they must stand the consequences ; yet I cannot help pitying their families, and it makes me truly melancholy to think of their future distress.

October 4th.—Mr. Gaven, recommended by the Irish Chancellor, at dinner, with our staff.

11th.—Alas ! poor Dr. Clare is no more. He breathed his last before the day dawned, and we have indeed lost a most excellent friend and agreeable companion, as well as an able physician.

12th.—My darling little George is two years old to-day, and it was to have been a day of joy and thankfulness, but the loss of poor Doctor Clare has thrown a sad cloud upon my spirits. The house full, all day.—Little G. was dressed in boy's clothes, for the first time, and little L. had a pair of shoes for the first time also. Two grand events, that occupied the whole family, as well as their dear little selves.— A grand dinner at 5, and a large party, or rather a ball. The band played all dinner time, to George's great delight, and Louisa danced round the shades on the dinner table, to the amusement and astonishment of every one. At 11, the party separated, and all the noise ceased, to my great joy ; for what with the drinking of healths, the huzzaing, the music, and the contrast of my own feelings, I really was worn out. But may God bless my dear boy, and may every future birth-day be as happy to him as this has been, for he and Louisa have been almost wild with spirits, the whole day.

15th.—Hear all the new blackies their prayers, &c. previously to their being made Christians.—The *Chesterfield* packet sailed to-day, with General N.'s despatches.

16th.—Messrs. Sedgwick, Donaldson, and Taylor, and General Carmichael, &c. at dinner.

17th.—Captain Trollope and Mr. Markland at dinner.

18th.—A large garrison dinner party to-day.—A Mrs. Campbell was the only lady, who entertained me with histories of land crabs, &c. and all the disasters of a poor military man's wife.

21st.—Mr. Woodham, &c. at dinner. At 7 o'clock, all repaired to the chapel, where all the new servants, and infants lately born, were baptized ; and I trust in God, they may turn out good Christians, and peaceable members of society at least ; for I have tried to make them understand their duty.

22nd.—All day the house was in a bustle, crowded with visitors. Eighty-five people at dinner. The band playing, the huzzaing, &c. were almost stunning, and I did not go to bed till after 11 o'clock. Poor General N. was obliged to sit up much longer.

23rd.—The gentlemen did not separate till after 1 this morning, and yet we were all up at 6, as usual.—Several people at breakfast, and at 11, General N. held a council. At 3, the House of Assembly came over in a body, when he delivered his speech.—At 6, an immense crowd ; the House of Assembly, the public officers, and the military, all at dinner, and exactly the same bustle and noise as we had yesterday. I pity poor dear N., who must go through it all, and with so much business on his hands, at the same time.—I got to bed at 10, but the party in the great hall did not break up till three.

24th.—A quiet day, thank God ! at least I hope so, as I have not heard of any company being invited.—Ten o'clock. —My dear N. writing in my room, the greatest part of the morning, and amusing himself with the children, till dinner time ; and then only the Rev. Mr. Donaldson was added to our party.

25th.—Our new medical Inspector-General (Mr. Rocket) arrived from England.

¡ *28th.*—Major Watson, just from England, the only addition.

29th.—Mrs. Wright, the young widow staying here, and who was introduced to us by Mr. and Mrs. Middleton, now Minister at the Court of Russia, has, I am afraid, taken a fancy to Mr. Rocket, and all the gentlemen of the staff are already making a joke of her *attentions* to him. I am sorry she makes herself so foolish, but it can't be helped.

30th.—A ship had arrived from England, with private despatches for General N. and Sir J. Duckworth. Strong rumours of a Spanish war, so we must be additionally alert now.

November 2nd.—Frederick Berkeley came early, and is to spend a few days with us. He is an excellent creature, and a great acquisition.—A comfortable day altogether. Some visitors, and military men in the morning, and at second breakfast.—At dinner, Messrs. Malcolm and Perry of the Assembly, with Colonels Unwin and Gordon, and in the evening a very large and very merry party. Young Berkeley enjoyed his dance beyond anything, and, as he sleeps in the house, and does not run the risk of a chill afterwards, the exercise is good for him.

3rd.—Mr. and Mrs. Kemble came on a visit.

5th.—Heard of the old President of the Council being ill. —Only our own party, and Mr. and Mrs. Cully at dinner ; but the table is now crowded every day.—Just before we went to bed, heard of the poor old President's death. Several hours previous to it, his *disconsolate* widow had sent to know how he should be buried, what the ceremony ought to be, &c. &c. ! !

6th.—Drive out early.—This is to be a day of bustle, as our very grand ball takes place to-night.—Dined at 3, and at 4, my dear N. went to attend the President's funeral, which was conducted with much pomp and state ; and I hope his widow will have all the consolation possible.

15th.—*Our wedding anniversary*, and may every future one find us as happy in each other, as we really are this day !—All the morning as quiet as possible. At 6, the Admirals, with Captains Dunn, Gardner, Hawker, Temple, &c., Messrs. Mitchell, Edwards, Hinchliffe and Scott. Got through it all very well, and very merry we were. The children came in after dinner, and behaved delightfully.

22nd.—I am wicked enough to wish a month of my life over, for I am most heartily sick of dissipation and politics, and long for a little rest of body and mind.

23rd.—The late rainy season has produced millions of horrid reptiles, and I found a large scorpion on my dressing-gown this morning.—Mr. Gaven, and Mrs. and Miss Fermor, in addition to our staff dinner.

24th.—Drive out early with the dear children. After breakfast, a scene with poor Mrs. Wright, who took her leave for Charlestown.—Mr. Rocket was particularly cold yesterday, and she shed many tears in remarking upon his conduct ; but I dare say she will soon forget all about it, as she seems rather *volage* in her feelings.

25th.—To church at 10.—Returned home much fatigued with the length of the service, as our old chaplain preached, and he is so worn out, that he can hardly utter a distinct word ; and his pauses, hesitation, and mistakes, kept me in a constant fidget.

30th.—Sent the sociable at 6, for Colonel and Mrs. Smith and family, who have lately arrived from England. She seems a pleasing woman, and her sister, Miss Wauchope, a good humoured, " bonnie lassie."

December 1st.—Dr. Clare (our poor friend's brother, but

alas ! how inferior) came to see me, and he and Mr. McAnuff were the only additions to the dinner party to-day.

2nd.—Captain D'Arcy, Mr. Piercy, and Mr. Doughty, of the 85th, at dinner.

10th.—The Colts' ball. Young Berkeley and Lake, with the Kembles, delighted with all the fuss and noise of the day. Soon after 8, all were assembled, and we proceeded in great state, up the ball room, to the tune of "God save the King." Supper at 12 ; very magnificent, with transparencies, and finery of all sorts. My chair was decorated with wreaths of flowers, and, in short, it was a gay affair altogether. Toasts, &c. were given, and all were as merry as possible ; many lamenting that this was likely to be the last of our gaieties this session, and probably our last in Jamaica.

12th.—Several people called to take leave to-day, and our chaplain, Mr. Warren, was quite pathetic in bidding adieu to the *Prince of Wales,* as he calls little George.

15th.—A quiet day.—Discuss with Mrs. Horsford the advantages of a public situation. She says, that people don't take the trouble to find out her good qualities, while all mine are exaggerated ; and that I hear nothing, from morning till night, but my own praises. I said, not *my* praises, but those of the *Governor's lady.* Her reply had some truth in it, for she said, "Aye, that may be in some respects, and yet all your good qualities are found out, by the trouble people take in enquiring into them, while I am passed over and unknown, merely because no one thinks of examining into my character."

18th.—The morning full of company, and my dear N. so much engaged in business, that I scarcely saw him. At half-past five, he prorogued the House of Assembly ; but not without having first gained his point, for the £500 due to the 4th battalion of the 60th regiment. At 6, a large dinner party of members, &c. Mrs. Levingstone the only lady, except those belonging to the family at present.

Every body in great good humour, and we did not break
up till 11 o'clock.

22nd.—Take my drive, and Mr. and Mrs. Kemble set off
for Kingston, at the same time. It is a foolish marriage,
but I hope they may prosper.—After breakfast, little G.
distributed money to the black servants for Christmas.

24th.—All the blackies half mad with their preparations
for to-morrow.

25th.—Christmas Day.—We both went to church, at 10.
A long service, and, in my present weak state, very fatiguing.

26th.—Nothing but bonjoes, drums, and tom-toms, going
all night, and dancing and singing and madness, all the
morning.—The Horsfords, the Grandjeans, &c. at second
breakfast, and to see the sports at the King's House. Some
of our blackies were most superbly dressed, and so were
several of their friends, who came to join in the masquerade ;
gold and silver fringe, spangles, beads, &c. &c. and really a
most wonderful expense altogether. General N. gave the
children money, and threw some himself among them from
the gallery, and in the scramble all the finery was nearly
torn to pieces, to my great vexation. However, they
seemed not to mind it, but began dancing with the same
spirit as if nothing had happened, putting their smart
clothes into the best order they could. We gave them a
bullock, a sheep and a lamb, with a dollar to every person
in the house, from the oldest individual to the youngest
infant ; besides a complete new dress, with two changes of
linen.—This is the case every Christmas, and at all festivals
they have a present of clothing. Perhaps, however, it is
more than is usually done ; but, for the short time we are
with them, we will make them as happy as we can.

27th.—Noise all night ; and, if possible, to-day worse than
ever.—At dinner we had only Captain Trail of the Artillery,
in addition to our little party.—At 9, all was profoundly
quiet throughout the town ; for almost every woman as
well as every man was so exceedingly tipsy, they could do

nothing but sleep; and I may say, too, so thoroughly fatigued with their dancing and masquerading, poor things! though people say, they are all really so drunk they are unable to move.

28th.—Order again restored, and all going on as usual.— Poor General N. much harassed and vexed, by the dispute between Colonels Horsford and Gordon. They are both married men, and have families, which adds much to his anxiety to reconcile them.

29th.—After breakfast General N. had the two Colonels with him in the Council Chamber, and insisted upon the quarrel being made up in an amicable manner. After a length of time, all was settled, satisfactorily, and poor Mrs. Horsford was made quite happy.

January 1st.—Go to church at 10. Much noise of tom-toms, &c. all the morning. After the service, the whole garrison came to pay me the compliments of the season. A grand collation of wines, fruit, &c. was laid out in the ball-room, where I received them, and we made ourselves mutually agreeable for an hour, when I was glad to get to my own room. Only our own party at dinner.

2nd.—My only visitor, Dr. Rennalls.—General Carmichael blistered, &c. and hopes are entertained of his recovery.—The same dinner party, and evening, as usual.

7th.—General N. received despatches from England, early this morning, by the *Princess Augusta* packet. I got delightful letters from all my family and friends, and dear Lord Buckingham has sent me a most beautiful lace cloak.

9th.—To-day we had unexpectedly a large dinner party, chiefly of French; Monsieur Mansigny was of the number. —To bed at 9.—I can't spell the Frenchmen's names, for I did not hear them distinctly pronounced.

10th.—Monsieur Mansigny, &c. again.—All day poor General N. had to discuss their affairs with them. They dined here, but, to my great joy, set off for Kingston, in the evening.

11th.—General Carmichael so well, that we sent him in

the chariot to the Rev. Mr. Campbell's, near Kingston, for
a change of air.—Surprised by the two Admirals coming to
breakfast, and to spend the day.—Sir J. T. Duckworth to
announce his approaching departure for England, and
Admiral Dacres to succeed him in the command of this
station.   They stayed till quite late in the evening, and
then slept in Spanish Town, to be off for Port Royal, at
daylight to-morrow.

22nd.—In returning home from our drive this morning,
we met a gang of Eboe negroes, just landed, and marching
up the country.—I ordered the postillions to stop, that I
might examine their countenances as they passed, and see
if they looked unhappy ; but they appeared perfectly the
reverse.   I bowed, kissed my hand, and laughed ; they did
the same.   The women, in particular, seemed pleased, and
all admired the carriage, &c. One man attempted to shew
more pleasure than the rest, by opening his mouth as wide
as possible to laugh, which was rather a horrible grin.   He
shewed such truly cannibal teeth, all filed as they have them,
that I could not help shuddering.   He was of Herculean
size, and really a tremendous looking creature.   They were
all dressed in new clothes, and the women had tied their
coloured petticoats round their waists as aprons, and the
rest had very little covering.

February 1st.—At dinner, Mr. and Mrs. Tucker (a new
lawyer and his wife) in addition to our own family.

5th.—Only Mr. Griffiths, of the Artillery, in addition to our
party to-day.   He brought letters from Sir W. W. Wynne.

7th.—At dinner, Captains Winyeates and Younghusband,
to take leave for England.

8th.—All the morning, visitors.—Mrs. J. Mitchell, &c.
from England.   Mrs. Rennalls, to introduce them.—At
dinner, Mr. Sill, Captain Campbell, Mr. Hylton and Drs.
Read and Doughty, of the 85th, and our own party.

12th.—Send carriages early for the officers of the Artillery,
just arrived from England.   Colonel Smith came, and introduced Captains Dickson and Campbell, and Lieutenants

Lindsay, Scott, Chambers and Foley, who stayed the whole day.

14th.—Mr. Storer officiating as Aide-de-camp for the first time, and seems much pleased with his appointment.

16th.—Drive out to meet my dear Nugent, on his return from Kingston. Mr. Edwards and Mr. W. J. Hall were with him, who dined with us. Saw Mr. Edwards in my own room, who shewed me the intended addresses for the Admiral,* on his leaving this station. He made a joke of most of them, the phrases were so high flown and so bombastical; and indeed I think it would be much better, if they were in a plainer and more sensible form.

18th.—Conversation with Sir J. T. Duckworth, before dinner. At 9, he took leave, and actually shed tears. I envy him his return to dear old England, and wish we could at least be of the party.

20th.—The carriages were sent, before daylight, for Commissioner Dilkes and his lady, Colonel and Mrs. Smith, and Miss Wauchope, Captain and Mrs. Dickson, Mr. Brown, &c. who all arrived at eight.

25th.—The *Pickle* sloop of war, with despatches, arrived; and, just before we went to bed, we learnt that a Spanish war was declared.

28th.—At dinner, Captain Humphries, of the 60th, and Mr. Doyle, of the 55th, in addition to our party.

March 2nd.—Only Mr. De Boss, of the 60th, in addition to our family party.

4th.—See Martin's (the Duchess of Port Royal as she is called) daughter, soon after breakfast. It is a sad thing to see even this good kind of woman in other respects, so easy on the subject of what a decent kind of woman in England would be ashamed of and shocked at. She told me of all her children by different fathers, with the greatest *sang-froid.* The mother is quite looked up to at Port Royal, and yet her life has been most profligate, as we should think, at least in England.

* Duckworth.

8th.—After a great deal of discussion, before we went to sleep last night, decide upon going at daylight to Old Harbour, to see the *Augustus Cæsar*, as we had promised the owner, Captain Bell, that we would, if possible, this morning. Every thing looked so nice and comfortable, that General N. settled with him about our accommodation, &c. and so the die is really cast !—After our return to the King's House, what with the dust, the fatigue, and the agitation of my own mind, I was quite ill, and could not leave my room.—General N. had a party at dinner ; all gentlemen, however ; but it was hard upon him, as he was almost as far from well as I was. Then, in the evening, just as he came to my room, intending to have half-an-hour's quiet, before we went to bed, an express arrived from General Myers, to say, that several French ships of war, with troops, had appeared to windward. They had attacked Dominica, but their success there, and future destination, were not known ; but this island was their object, probably.—Of course, my dear N., ill as he was, was obliged to set about immediate arrangements for our defence, as well as to prepare all the dependencies of Jamaica for theirs. This kept him up, with his Military Secretary, in my dressing-room, the greatest part of the night. We had, in consequence, scarcely a doze. However, dear little G. was so very unwell, that, if we had not had this express and alarm, we should have been kept awake by anxiety on his account.

10th.—After church, General N. full of business, and crowds of people continually coming ; all much alarmed at the idea of a French force coming to this part of the world. —As soon as we had taken a 3 o'clock dinner, General N. set off with us to Port Henderson. An express from the Admiral overtook us, giving an account of the capture of Roseau, &c. After staying a couple of hours, to see us settled in our new house, he was obliged to return to Spanish Town, and all his anxious business.

14th.—An early walk on the sea-shore with the dear children, who picked up some shells, and were delighted. Did

not see a creature the whole day ; heard from and wrote to
General N. At 4, ordered a boat, and rowed with the maids
and little ones to Fort Augusta. General Carmichael much
better. Got back soon after 6, and was in bed before eight.

15*th*.—Row again with the children, &c. to Green Bay,
and get back before seven.

17*th*.—No church to go to.—Put the children to sleep as
soon as we could after breakfast, that they might look well,
and be in spirits to receive dear papa, who came soon after 2,
and found us all improved in looks. He seems sadly worn,
and sun-burnt, though he says he is quite well ; but he has
undergone immense fatigue, walking seven miles up the bed
of a river, under a broiling sun, and over rocks, &c. where
no horse could be of use. Captain Meredith, who came
to Port Henderson with him, tells me, that all the party
were knocked up. Thank God! however, he has not
suffered in health in the least. Took a nice walk in the
evening, and the little ones delighted to shew papa the
shells, &c. &c.

18*th*.—General N. sent off the despatch to windward, to
Admiral Dacres ; and extracts from General Myers's letter,
&c. to the printer.—A few of the staff to dinner. Get rid of
them at 6, and take our nice little walk again.

21*st*.—General N. off again to inspect the black corps at
Fort Augusta, and returned at 11 o'clock. All the staff
then proceeded to Spanish Town, and we dined *tête-à-tête*
at 3. At 5, however, he was obliged to leave us. Our little
ones went part of the way with us, and when we were obliged
to take leave of dear papa it was a sad scene, and they could
scarcely be prevailed upon to return with me and the maids.
I could not help remarking the difference between the feelings of a boy and of a girl. George did not shed tears, but
kept calling for the black horse, on which his papa rode,
while Louisa covered her dear little face, and sobbed, Papa,
Papa, for a length of time, before we could pacify her.
During the evening, before she went to sleep, she called for
papa, and seemed to think of nothing else ; while George

took his little whip to bed with him, and would make me
tell him stories, about the black horse, &c.

 22nd.—Take an early walk with the children. Find the
Commissioner on my return, waiting to ask if I will go
to Port Royal to-morrow, to see the *Theseus* man of war
laid down. Appoint 12 to-morrow, when he is to come
for me.—Have little G. to dine with me, at 12 to-day,
and order a guinea-fowl, with bread-sauce, with which
he was delighted.—My new boat and boat's crew came
for orders. Fix 5 o'clock, and take a nice row. Home
again soon after 6.—A comfortable letter from dear N. ;
all well, thank God! but he is sadly harassed with
business, I fear.

23rd.—Rise early, not to disappoint the children of their
row. On our return find the old Commissioner, with the
Admiral's barge, waiting to take me to Port Royal, as the
ship was to be laid down at 8 or 9 o'clock, instead of 12,
as he said yesterday. Feel quite vexed to be so hurried,
but set off without delay, and get to Port Royal about 8.
A great many Navy officers to meet me. Mrs. Smith and
Miss Wauchope, the only ladies. Stayed till near 11, under
an awning, put up for that purpose, before the ship was
fairly on her side ; and then, indeed, it was a very fine and
a very wonderful sight. The dexterity of the sailors accomplished the whole affair in a most astonishing manner. As
the water flowed in, it was extraordinary to see the number
of reptiles that tried to escape up her sides ; scorpions,
centipedes, cock-roaches innumerable. We then returned
to the Commissioner's, where numbers of the Navy captains, &c. came to pay their compliments to me, but only
the Admiral and Captain Balderson, with a few military,
were of the dinner party at 4. At 6, my dear N. surprised
us by his appearance, just as I was stepping into the
Admiral's barge, to return to Port Henderson. Poor
fellow ! though I was rejoiced to see him, I was sorry he
had come, for he had had a most fatiguing day. A ride of
twenty-four miles in the sun, and no dinner, or any refresh-

ment.—Get home at half-past seven, when he had a comfortable dinner, and seemed quite well.

25th.—Two whales made their appearance in the harbour yesterday, and to-night were seen close in front of the house. Explained all about them to little G., who wishes to see them again.

27th.—My morning was spent in writing about Mrs. Wright's affairs. Settle them all, as well as they will admit of.

28th.—Despatches from the north side of the island. All the arrangements perfectly made, and all well.

30th.—Row to Port Royal early. At breakfast, the Admiral and Major Gould. Did not stay to dinner. Just as we sat down *tête-à-tête*, came Mr. Brown of the Artillery, with the intelligence of a French fleet being seen off St. Domingo, steering this way. The account was brought by a vessel, that left Port Royal this morning, and had seen some of them. General N. desired him to return to his duty immediately, then drank a glass of wine, and ordered his horse. I will not say what were my feelings, when he took the dear children in his arms and kissed them, for perhaps the last time. He wrote a few lines in his pocket-book, which he left with me, and which I found, after he was gone, were instructions for the safety of myself and children. I ordered the maids to put everything ready to move at a moment's notice, and then sat down almost stunned, and could not think clearly of any thing.—An express from the Admiral in the course of an hour, to tell me, that it was thought the enemy was not so near us as had been reported in the morning. In consequence, I decided upon remaining here, for fear my dear children should suffer, from being exposed to the night air, and a journey at such an unusual hour. Wrote to General Carmichael, and sent my boat's crew to Fort Augusta, to join their regiment there. Write also to Captain Dobbin, at the Apostles' battery, and arranged an express, in case of alarm, or any information coming during the night. Saw all the

doors fastened, and said all I could to quiet the alarms of
the maids, &c. At 10, prepared for bed.—I soon after received an express from my dear N., advising me to remain
at this place, till further intelligence of the enemy's movements could be obtained. I replied immediately, giving
him every comfort in my power, respecting myself and the
children.—In the course of the night, Henry Rogers came,
but only stayed a few minutes, just to see how we were.—
The rest of the time was quiet, and I rejoiced to see the
day dawn, without further alarm.

31st.—Major Fraser early, with a letter from General N.
All at the King's House were up almost the whole night,
writing circular letters, and copying General N.'s orders,
&c. for different parts of the country ; and he himself was
off before day for Kingston, where he will probably remain
till all is over. God bless and preserve him from all dangers,
and grant that all may soon end happily for us !

Eight o'clock in the evening. This day has indeed passed
most miserably. Not a creature have I seen since the
morning, but have walked in the Piazza the whole day,
with a glass in my hand, looking continually towards the
sea for the enemy. Nothing has been heard but the scaling
the guns in the different forts and ships in the harbour, and
the practice of the artillery. The ships of war have
manœuvred, and are now arranged as a sort of battery
across Port Royal harbour, and when the Admiral's ship
had her sails hoisted, and moved to her station, I could not
help smiling at George and Louisa, calling it "*Grandmamma*" ; for, being talked to of their grandmothers being
two great people, they thought such a large and splendid
object must be a grandmamma at least.

As soon as the sun would allow us to go out this evening,
I went with them to Port Henderson, where we had an
extensive view of the sea. It was a dead calm, and, as far
as the eye could reach, like a sheet of glass. Not a speck
was to be seen on the horizon, and God grant an enemy may
not cloud it ! I have just received a letter from my dear N.

He is in Kingston, and undergoing wonderful fatigue, in assembling a force for the protection of that place, and in making the best arrangements possible, for the defence of the island, by placing in the most vulnerable situations all the troops he can collect ; but, with our present force of regular troops, it is impossible to do this effectually. For, alas ! all parts are vulnerable, and our force, from sickness and various other causes, is very small and inadequate. Martial law is to be declared, and to-morrow he means to hold a Council of War, for that purpose.—I try to be as composed and as calm as possible, but I can't fix my attention to any one object for comfort, nor think distinctly on any subject.—I see the dear little ones put to bed, after saying a little prayer for dear papa ; and may their dear little innocent voices be heard !

April 1st.—We have passed a sad night of alarms. Several shots were fired from a house near, and our black servants said it was to frighten thieves, as many were seen about in the evening. General Carmichael sent back my boatmen to me this morning ; and, as they appear to be trusty people, I have desired they may sleep in the stable every night, till General N. (please God !) returns.—Dear Clifford returned here yesterday, and she is so courageous that she is a great comfort to me ; but she tells me that, before she left Spanish Town, the negroes appeared to be inclined to riot, and to make a noise in the streets, when the troops marched out, but they were soon dispersed by the militia. The black servants here seem to rejoice at the bustle, but, as they profess to hate the French; their pleasure is only that of change ; for, like children, they are fond of fuss and noise, and have no reflection.

2nd.—After another anxious and sleepless night, I rowed with the children round the ships in Port Royal harbour. Saw and spoke to several Naval friends, who were all most friendly and comfortable. About 10 o'clock, a letter from General N. He writes in tolerable spirits, and is quite well, thank God ! The Council of War was held in Kingston, and martial law declared yesterday. The day passed in my usual anxiety and watchfulness, and I have now fixed the glass in the Venetian blinds, so that I can look out constantly, without the fatigue of holding it. Every now and then I feel quite blind, but getting into a dark corner, and shutting my eyes for a few minutes, enables me to see clearly again.

The sea was rather rough this evening, and I took a walk with the little ones, instead of a row. We met a horrid looking black man, who passed us several times, without making any bow, although I recollected him as one of the boatmen of the canoe we used to go out in, before we had the *Maria*. He was then very humble, but to-night he only grinned, and gave us a sort of fierce look, that struck me with a terror I could not shake off.—This evening, nurse sung again to the children, who had their usual dance, and went to bed happy, dear little innocent souls ! Clifford tells me that all the black people know there is some alarm, but are ignorant of the cause of it, and most of them, it is to be feared, are ready for every sort of mischief. However, I feel confident in our own servants, who all seem as anxious to secure the house, and to be as much afraid of depredators, as I am.

3rd.—How little do we know what calamities may befal us in this world ! Yesterday I thought my cup of anxiety was full, but to-day I have been near losing my dear George. He was romping with his nurse and little sister, and fell from off the bed, with his head against the corner of an open drawer. He gave a shriek, and then appeared quite stunned with the violence of the blow. The wound was directly on the back of the head, and it bled frightfully. We immediately sent off for Dr. McNeil ; but, in the mean time, I took courage, and had him laid upon my lap, and held him there, while I cut away all the hair near the wound, and then applied some court plaister, upon which I kept my hand, till Dr. McNeil arrived, when he found the dear child in a nice sleep, and the blood quite staunched. He

U

said I had done all he could have done, with only this difference, that he would have sewed up the part, to which I had applied the court plaister, and this did quite as well. After a few hours, thank God ! the little darling was as well, and as playful as ever ; but it will be many days before I can cease to think of the past without trembling.

Mr. and Mrs. Edward Bullock, and their family, arrived at Port Henderson to-day, but I was too much agitated to see any one. I sent, however, to offer them all civilities, and the use of the boat, &c. &c. for taking the morning air. In the evening, I myself took to Fort Augusta my answer to my dear N.'s darling letter, and the children were of the party, that General Carmichael may be able to tell General N. how we all are, and to give a good account of them ; but don't mention the accident little George met with.—The evening cooler than usual, but the weather is now dreadfully hot, and my anxiety is great, for fear my dear N. should suffer seriously from the heat of Kingston, which is, I believe, the most broiling place in the universe.

4th.—A letter from General N. All in the same anxious state, but we are now prepared, as far as possible, for the worst.—Mrs. E. Bullock, and Mrs. Whitehorne, with their little ones, came, and spent a few hours, to the great delight of my children.—Dined with little G. at 12, and at 3, drank tea, and then ordered the boat, and took a long row, which delighted my little party.—Home, and to bed at 8.—Little G. quite well, and seems not to have suffered in the least from the fall.

5th.—At gun-fire take Mr. and Mrs. E. Bullock and their little ones a nice row round the fleet. Soon after breakfast, a Navy officer, with a despatch from the Admiral, to tell me, that, after the French Fleet had reinforced the city of Santo Domingo, they had shaped their course towards the Mona Passage, and that consequently we had much less to apprehend from their attacks ; at all events no immediate descent on this island can be in contemplation. Write to my dear N., and am all joy, to think the danger is at a distance at least.—Have Mr. and Mrs. E. B., Mrs. Whitehorne, Mr. Andrews, and the little people, all at dinner at 3 o'clock. A table laid in the Piazza, for the children, and enjoyed the scene very much myself ; dear little G. and L. doing the honours *beautifully*.—Soon after 4, rowed with the whole party to Port Royal, and, on our return, they all took leave.—A nice letter from my dear N. ; he writes in great spirits, and will be in Spanish Town to-morrow. Thank God ! thank God !

7th.—About 4, an express from Port Royal, with despatches from Barbadoes and England. A letter from Sir W. Myers, announcing the near approach of an English squadron to windward, and the prospect of our Naval force being sufficient to pursue and chase the enemy out of these seas. The Minister's letter from home, giving much the same intelligence, and expressing great anxiety for these colonies in general, &c.

13th.—Pack up, and all return in the sociable. Quite happy to be together again, and all in much better health than when we left Spanish Town.

14th.—To church at 10. A full congregation, and all the church strewed and ornamented with pimento.

15th.—Much hurry all the morning, and General N. was obliged to dictate his speech, for me to write, as he went in and out of the room, to receive different Members of the Assembly, who were continually coming. Before 2 o'clock it was ready, and he delivered it in the Council Chamber, the House having come over in state, with the Speaker at their head, as usual. At 5, an immense dinner party. Every one much pleased, and all went off extremely well. I was complimented very much, upon the improved looks of myself and children, and I only wish I could feel as much improved as they say I appear to be. At 10 o'clock all was quiet, and martial law had this one good effect, that it obliged us all to be much more sober, and to keep earlier hours, than we should otherwise have been, or felt inclined to do. Yet the great flag, flying in the middle of the square, and the number of red coats moving about in different directions continually, gave a warlike appearance, and all looked too hostile to give one very comfortable or pleasing contemplations, in considering the future.

16th.—The Assembly all in great good humour with General N., approve of all his measures, and seem really grateful for his activity and arrangements for the protection of the island.

18th.—All sorts of arrangements making for future defence. All in good humour, and every one anxious to do his duty. General N. satisfied, and more comfortable in spirits than I have seen him for a long time. The 18th regiment is very unhealthy, and I am sorry to say, are to be sent to Stony Hill, and then the poor fellows there must encounter this hot, unhealthy town.—A review this morning, at daylight, on the race-course. Took little G. in the carriage, dressed in an Aide-de-camp's uniform ; scarlet, with blue facings and gold embroidery, a staff hat and feather, and he really looked lovely ; in my eyes at least.

19th.—The 85th marched into Spanish Town, early this morning, and alas ! many of them, I fear, will suffer from the dreadful heat of this town.—A party at second breakfast, and another at dinner.—All glad to meet once more, but many are *gone* since I was at Stony Hill, and my thoughts in consequence are most melancholy.

20th.—Admiral Cochrane * and his Flag-Captain at breakfast. Make the agreeable to them till 12. My dear N. very busy as usual, but to-day he had a most flattering address, and an answer to his statement respecting American intercourse, and all of the most gratifying nature. He will now make his prorogation speech, with much more comfortable feelings.—Visitors innumerable coming in, and interrupting his business all day.—A large dinner party— King Mitchell, Colonel Edwards, Mr. Hinchliffe, Aide-de-camp (for he is now one of General N.'s militia Aides-de-camp, which gives him the rank of Colonel), Major of

* He had come out in chase of Missiessy, and was then commander-in-chief on the Leeward Islands station. He played an important part in Duckworth's victory of St. Domingo (6 Feb., 1806), for which he was made a K.C.B.

Brigade Pallmer, Aides-de-camp Ross and Bullock, General
Scott, and Major Grant, of the Artillery, with the Admiral
and his Captain, made our dinner party. Have a great deal
of talk with the Admiral, who knows all my family, and it
is wonderful, at this distance, how great an intimacy is
formed immediately with those that know them we love.

22nd.—Lament the change in the poor 85th. Within one
month three officers have died of the yellow fever, and
several once healthy looking young men are now quite
ghastly. If the climate has affected them so much in the
mountains, what may they not suffer in the lowlands !
Poor General Carmichael, too, who slept here last night, is
so ill, that General N. has given him leave of absence, and
advised his going to St. Thomas in the East,* for change of
air, which the doctors say is his only chance of living ; that
he never can recover his health here. Poor little man ! It
is a great pity he can't make up his mind to go to Europe ;
but, unfortunately, his finances are in such a state, that his
emoluments are of the utmost consequence to his family ;
and, most probably, his life will be the sacrifice.—Mr.
Vernon brought young Gordon, of the *Northumberland*,
to-day, and we are glad to shew him any kindness, on
account of his family, and he really is a fine boy.

23rd.—Arrived at the Admiral's Penn at 3. At 4, an
immense party, chiefly of the Navy, and almost all of them
the new arrivals. Most of them seemed sadly alarmed
about the climate, and afraid to eat or drink any thing, and
are making constant enquiries about the yellow fever.

24th.—Start for the King's House, the carriage loaded
with toys. The children were delighted to see us. Dine
at 5. The heat overpowering, and feel the fatigue of the
day sadly.

25th.—Beg Colonel Mellefont not to turn out the guard
to me and the children, when we take our morning's drive.
It is fatiguing the men, and makes us appear quite ridiculous, I am sure.

* Probably Bath was intended. The parish generally was
never considered healthy for Europeans.

26th.—My dear N. has had the painful task of deciding upon the fate of the 4th battalion of the 60th regiment; they are now to be drafted, a necessity that could not be avoided, owing to their continual broils, their insubordination, and constant cabals, and party business, against their commanding officer, Colonel Unwin. He is quite delighted with the idea of getting home, and leaving this horrid climate, and I only hope and pray, that the Duke of York may approve of the step General N. has found it so necessary to take.

27th.—The dinner party rather melancholy to me. Captain Bell, of the *Augustus Cæsar*, dined here, and the whole evening there was nothing but discussions about our voyage, sea stock, &c. ; and now there is no hope of my dear N. being relieved in time to go with us.—The thunder and lightning so very dreadful this evening, that none of us went to bed till 11 o'clock.

29th.—Take the children, at daylight, to the review of the Kingston regiment. A good breakfast, at Mr. S. Taylor's, afterwards.—At 5, a very large dinner party, or rather parties, for there were two rooms full. Mrs. Holgate,* Mrs. and Miss Farmer,† and the two Misses Stewart, were the only ladies.—Don't get to bed till after 11, and very much fatigued ; but particularly anxious about dear little G. and L., who, if I had not taken the greatest care, would have been stuffed with all sorts of trash, and so perhaps made quite ill, from the derangement of their dear little stomachs. I am determined never to take them out again, while they are so young.

30th.—The children had a nice night, and were quite well this morning, thank God ! After breakfast, leave Mr. Taylor's hospitable mansion, and return to the King's House, all well ; and here ends another month, and our whole party alive and prosperous, thank God !

* William Holgate was Alderman of Kingston and an assistant judge of the Supreme Court.

† Jasper Farmer, barrister-at-law, was colonel of the Kingston foot militia.

May 1st.—Write and read till breakfast time. Poor Mrs. (Lieut.) Campbell came in the morning. I kept her all day. Made her all the useful presents I could, and in short said and did all in my power towards her comfort. Lieutenant Campbell came to dinner.

2nd.—Rise very early, and settle various affairs, public and private ; and at 10 set off, with General N. and the children, to Port Henderson. At 3, General Carmichael came to dine with us, and to take leave, on going into the country for his health. He looks sadly, and, in all probability, it is the last time we shall see him in this world ; though he talks boldly of his recovery. Poor Doctor Read, who has attended him so faithfully, during his long illness, is actually dead of the fatigue, &c. and was buried yesterday. I could not help remarking the nervous effects of this climate, in a circumstance that occurred in our walk this evening. Just as we were returning home, we heard a horse coming full speed towards Port Henderson. We both stopped, with a sort of shuddering, and, when we explained our thoughts to each other, it appeared they were the same, and that General N., as well as I, imagined that it was an express to announce the death of poor General Carmichael, who had just left us. So suddenly and so frequently do these melancholy circumstances take place, that the mind is constantly prepared, and constantly anticipating them too.

3rd.—General N. and the children, with the two Misses Rennalls, were of our rowing party this morning. At 7, we breakfasted, when Mr. Longfield, of the 85th, made his appearance, and, after a most extraordinary conversation about conspiracies, &c. &c. we discovered that he was really mad. The children were playing about, and I really dreaded that he would do them some mischief ; he seized upon their toys, and eyed them in so odd a manner. General N. and I kept him engaged as well as we could, till Major Fraser arrived from Spanish Town, and we persuaded him to accompany him back ; but it was with much difficulty we got rid of him. The poor man looks the shadow of what he was when he first arrived from England, about a year ago. Then he was a fine-looking, healthy young man, and now he is a poor, emaciated, wrinkled old man.

4th.—Our usual row early. Return soon after sunrise. Captain Smith of the Engineers, Meredith, and Rogers, at breakfast. Colonel Espinasse, and Mr. Baker, of the 85th, and Mr. Brown of the Artillery, at dinner. A short walk in the evening, and to bed at 8.—Poor Longfield is in a strait waistcoat.

7th.—Colonel Mellefont at breakfast, and had a full account of poor Longfield's situation. He is really insane, but the doctors think change of climate may restore him, and he is to sail in the next packet. The Honourable Captain Gardner came from Port Royal, and sat with me some hours.* I was in a fright all the time, as the newspapers were on the table, with a full detail of his elder brother's affairs, his wife's trial, &c. General N. came at 5, and asked him to dine ; and, in the evening, we all accompanied him to Port Royal, and drank tea with the Commissioner. To our great surprise, Captain G. offered to come back with us, and, after a little supper, opened the whole history himself, and discussed all his brother's affairs fully ; so my delicacy in the morning was not at all necessary. The night was beautiful, and Captain Gardner returned to Port Royal at eleven.

8th.—Did not row out, we were so late this morning. While we were at breakfast, Captain Reeves, of the 18th, came to ask leave to return to England. Poor man ! he seemed ready to resign his commission, rather than remain here ; he is so much alarmed about the climate. General N. was obliged to leave him with me, and go into Spanish Town. As soon as he was gone, poor Captain Reeves frightened me very much, by being seized with a cold shivering fit. He told me he had felt quite ill all the morning, but did not like to complain to General N., for fear he should think it

* The son of Alan, Lord Gardner, commander-in-chief of Jamaica from 1776 to 1790, who, as captain on the station, had married, in 1769, Susanna Hyde, daughter and heiress of Francis Gale and widow of Sabine Turner.

was only owing to alarm about the yellow fever. I begged
him to take some Madeira, that was on the side table, and
advised his going back to his quarters, as soon as possible.
After taking two large bumpers of old Madeira, he returned
to his boat, and I hope to hear to-morrow that his illness
is of no material consequence.—Dr. Rennalls in the morning.—General N. brought home with him, to dinner, Colonel
Irvine, Mr. Smith, and Dr. McNeil. The doctor says, I
could not have prescribed any thing better than the
Madeira wine for Captain Reeves, so probably his complaint is chiefly on the spirits ; a disorder so frequent, and
often so fatal in this country. A dreadful thunderstorm in
the evening, and the gentlemen obliged to sleep at the inn.

9th.—A row round the ships at Port Royal again, this
morning.—Mr. Scott of the Artillery, and Mr. Dundas, at
breakfast. Poor Mr. Scott is just out of the fever, and
looks like a ghost. When these gentlemen left us, and just
as we were congratulating ourselves upon the present quiet
state of the island, and our prospect of being safe in England
by this time next year, Captain Bouverie arrived, in the
Mercury, with despatches from Sir John Orde. The Toulon
squadron passed Cadiz, on the 9th of April, and is supposed
to have steered westward ; so we are all again in bustle
and confusion ; and most likely no convoy will be able to
leave Jamaica, till the hurricane season begins, and then it
would be madness to think of going.—Colonel Drummond
came to spend the day, which was certainly not very agreeable to either General N. or me, as our minds were so occupied, with the despatches, &c. that we had much to think
of, and could not give our attention to any other subject.
—Mr. Scott and Colonel Drummond at dinner.—Hear of
poor Captain Reeves, who is desperately ill.—A thunderstorm again obliged the gentlemen to remain at Port
Henderson.—Little G. slept in his new bed in my room,
for the first time.

10th.—We attempted to row out in the evening, but I
was so nervous, and so much alarmed at every thing, that

we returned almost immediately. A quiet little talk calmed and comforted me a good deal, before we went to bed.

11th.—Captains Bouverie and Hardyman at breakfast, and to take leave. The former takes the mail to England, and, in consequence of this, the regular packet will not sail till Monday se'en-night. Mr. Smith,* the island engineer, on business, the greatest part of the morning.

15th.—General N. early in town, as he holds a Council to-day, on the subject of American intercourse, and various other matters.

17th.—One of the lieutenants of the Apostles' battery came as we were going to breakfast, to announce the death of poor wretched Captain Dobbin. He died without seeing his children, and it is said has left all he is worth to his black mistress and her child. This is, I am afraid, but too common a case in Jamaica.

19th.—To-day, three events here—Little Becky, a black child, bitten by a conger eel, a large centipede found in the nursery, and a snake close to the window. Have all the house well searched, before we went to bed, as the late storms have brought reptiles without number out of their holes.

22nd.—The heat dreadful, but the sea as smooth as glass, and the scene altogether beautiful. We were so early in our boat, that the sun did not quite get from behind the mountains till we were returning from our row, when the whole atmosphere was of a silver colour. General N. received an express from Admiral Dacres, to tell him, that, after all, it is not thought that the Toulon fleet is coming westward.

23rd.—General N. off at 3, to review the Saint Catherine's regiment, before he begins his Court of Chancery. I remained quietly by myself, writing, &c. till 12, when Mr. Brown came from Port Royal, with despatches, by the packet, and alas! some from the windward, announcing the arrival of the French combined force there.—To describe the state of my mind is quite impossible, and now

* J. H. Smith.

I tremble so much, I can hardly hold my pen, and my mind is really half distracted, with various distressing thoughts that assail me ; I have sent off an express to my dear N., and begged to join him and the little ones, in Spanish Town, immediately, and am now waiting with the greatest impatience for the result.—About 4, he came in the chariot, and after taking a hasty dinner, we set off for the King's House, where the affectionate caresses of my dear children enabled me to shed a plentiful shower of tears, which relieved my head and heart wonderfully ; and I shall now, I trust, resume all my courage and cheerfulness, and be a comfort, rather than a burthen, to my dear husband, whose mind is at present sadly harassed.

24th.—At 10, General N. held a Council of War. Martial Law was declared, and the great flag unfurled in the square, immediately after.—Got all our private letters, and (thank Heaven !) all our friends well and happy in England. General N.'s private despatch, from Lord Camden, is particularly comfortable, and I now look forward with the hope of his being able to go home with me, if I am detained here much longer by the circumstances in which we are now placed ; or of his joining me soon in England, if we are obliged to separate.—The morning full of bustle. All the colonels of militia in their uniforms, coming continually. Orders issuing in every direction, and expresses going off, to every part of the country. Every now and then my strength fails me, and I run to my own room to lament, and stretch myself out for a short time on the bed, and then I can return with fresh vigour to the business of the day.

25th.—Send the maids and children out in the sociable. Remain with my dear N., who has passed a day of continual business, writing and giving audience, etc. Don't dine till near six.

26th.—To church at 10 ; an immense congregation, and all in scarlet. The heat extreme. The poor Jews looked uncomfortable the whole service, but they would have lost

their pay, of five shillings a day, if they had not attended.
A large party at second breakfast, and the Attorney-General
was of the number ; he is wishing for leave to go home, if
possible, on account of ill-health, and indeed, he does look
sadly.—All the day full of bustle ; militia generals and
colonels coming continually. George and Louisa were
much amused, with seeing all the red coats parading the
square, and I could not help smiling, to see a militia soldier,
with a black boy carrying his firelock behind him, and the
serjeants, with each an attendant carrying his halbert, &c.
Major Gould arrived, before dinner, with various reports,
respecting the enemy, as well as *domestic* affairs.—The
clergy as usual at dinner.—Much anxious discussion, before
we go to bed at ten.

27*th*.—Go out early with the children.—Poor General N.
shut up from daylight, and not a moment to breathe
scarcely, he has so much writing and business of all sorts.
Breakfast at 7 o'clock.   Till 3, incessant business and visiting.   Then an express, with a confirmation of the enemy
being in these seas.   If they really do come, we have the
comfort at least to know, that we are as well prepared as
we possibly can be from the nature of our situation, re-
sources, &c. &c. ; and that we have nothing to accuse ourselves of, in point of negligence, or being off our guard.   In
fact, the security of this island depends mainly upon our
superiority at sea, and the vigilance of our squadrons.

Poor General N. has been particularly harassed to-day,
with business, and teased and vexed at the same time, by
the new militia General officers.—They are all so tenacious
of attention, command, &c. !   King (now General) Mitchell,
is quite *sulky*, and out of humour, because he is not given
enough to do, and that General N. has given more orders
to General Farmer than to him, the last day or two.—We
had a large dinner party, and many people also in the evening, and all paying me the greatest attention, King Mitchell
in particular ; and this has always been the case, whenever
he is displeased with General N. for any of his measures.

Then, I am sure of being overpowered with flattery and fine speeches.

28th.—General N. again too much engaged to go out with us before breakfast ; and, as soon as that was over, was at his desk again before 8.—General Carmichael surprised us with his appearance to take the command of the troops, and General N. has appointed him a Lieutenant-General,— good, little, zealous, but *broken down* man ! Colonels Melle- font, Horsford, Irvine, Rainy, &c. are all Major-Generals. —A crowd of military at dinner, and in the evening ; my- self the only woman.

29th.—General N. off, before day, to Kingston, and I drove out with the children. Breakfast at 7, with the gentlemen of the family that remained. Mr. Knox, lately from England, came, and I asked him to dine, as he is in- troduced by Mr. Staples and my brother Cortland.— General N. returned at 5, and the reports of the enemy are less favourable. My spirits are not a little depressed, as he hinted the necessity of perhaps sending me and the dear children into the interior of the island, where Mr. Mitchell has kindly offered us an asylum ; but I am sure that the blacks are to be as much dreaded as the French.—Messrs. O'Hara and Knox at dinner, and a large party in the even- ing ; Mrs. Rennalls was of the number, to hear the news.

31st.—A stormy night, and the thunder dreadful.—Busi- ness, visitors, and anxiety all day. When will our suspense be over ? I really rejoice at every hour that passes, in hopes that the next may bring some tidings to put an end to it.—An unfortunate man of colour was brought into Spanish Town, to-day, to be tried for mutiny. He is a serjeant in the militia, and his abuse of his colonel, and white people in general, has had, they say, already a most serious effect ; among the men of his company in particular. —At dinner, only the staff, but so many gentlemen in the evening, and about a dozen ladies, that I thought it was best to set them all dancing, and this kept up their spirits till 11 o'clock. To-morrow several of them go into the

country, where most of the women and children are gone
already ; as the interior of the island is now considered the
safest place.   So it certainly is, from the French, but how
will they guard against the insurrection of the negroes ?—
Poor Captain Campbell, of the Artillery, is dead, after a
very few hours' illness ; I am afraid that fatigue and exposure to the sun, for some days past, have been the cause.

June 1*st.*—The day as usual, full of business and anxiety,
from reports of all sorts, and of a contradictory nature.
General N. half angry with some of the staff, for telling me
all the rumours.—In the evening, a crowd of people, as
usual, for nearly three hours.

2nd.—*Whitsunday.*   Dreadful thunder and lightning all
night.   The rain and the storm altogether continued, and
it was so very damp, there was no service in the church.—
The maids, &c. all in a bustle, preparing for the marriage
of Mrs. Cummins (a nursery maid) with Ensign Brockmüller,
which is to take place before dinner.   The rain, &c. they
say is a bad omen, and occasions, I observe, many anxious
looks and mysterious remarks.   The storm kept the party
from assembling, till it was so late, that we went to dinner.
At 7, Ensign Brockmüller made his appearance, and soon
after was united to nurse Cummins, who is now an officer's
lady, and has, in consequence, thrown off her cap, and been
dressed in her own hair.   Yet the Ensign offered to let her
remain, and do her *work* here, as long as I remained in the
country ; but I declined so great an honour, and she returned with him, in the evening, to his quarters.

3rd.—The wretched serjeant of militia's Court Martial
began at 12, and I am sadly afraid he will be condemned ;
for an execution at this moment would be such an addition
to our horrors !   The 55th regiment, commanded by Major
Chalmers, marched in to-day, and have had a dreadful and
dangerous march across the island, on account of the torrents of rain that have fallen during the last few days.

I received a distressing letter, from one of our staff, whose
history is a most unfortunate one.   He has a young woman

living with him, that he seduced in England, and brought over here. His remorse is great, and as she has behaved well, and he is still attached to her, I have advised his marrying her, without loss of time, and particularly for the sake of his two nice children ; and also because the mother has been no further culpable than he has made her. Every thing is now arranged privately, through his friend, Colonel Irvine. General N. has promised a licence, and so a few days, will, I trust, put an end to his misery and remorse, and make all parties respectable as well as happy in future.

All the family dined at the mess to-day. General N. and I *tête-à-tête*, with the dear babes, as our greatest treat.— In the evening, before we went to bed, a despatch arrived from Antigua.—The French are still in the same position, as far as any intelligence can be obtained. Soon, however, our suspense must be at an end.

4th.—At 12, the several forts and ships, in Port Royal harbour, fired a salute, in honour of the day.* Soon after, the garrison were drawn up in the square, in front of the King's House, and fired a *feu-de-joie*, and then passed General N. in the usual manner, as he and all the staff, with the new general officers, &c. stood in the portico. Then, General N. held a levee, which was very fully attended.— At 6, nearly two hundred people sat down to dinner, and at 12, all was over, to my great joy ; for the dear children were so delighted with the noise and the music, that they would not be persuaded to go to bed, till all was quiet.

5th.—The poor sergeant is condemned, and the wife came this morning, to petition me to save his life. She has six children, poor wretched creature. Write to Mr. Mitchell for his advice, and whether I should ask the favour, or not, from the Jamaica Government. He thinks the example would be so bad, that he must be left to his fate, and especially with St. Domingo before our eyes. I still do, however, hope, that some punishment, short of death, may be substituted for it.—Major Chalmers, and the officers of

* The King's birthday.

the 55th regiment, at dinner.—The poor man's sentence is solitary confinement for two years, and a fine of £4,000. As he is rich, the money is not of much consequence ; but at sixty, in this climate, the confinement is almost as bad as death. However, it is a reprieve, and I trust, if he lives, he will come out of prison a better man.

6th.—Awoke before daylight by an express from England and the Windward Islands. The French force is detained in the harbour of Martinique, by a malignant and contagious fever, and the Minister informs General N. that he may soon expect a strong reinforcement in this part of the world. Our minds are more at ease, and I hope all may soon be well with us, and our suspense at an end.

7th.—All the family writing ; for we have English letters, as well as circulars, &c. to get ready. Much happier than usual towards evening, having obtained the pardon of twenty men, of the 85th, who were to have been punished to-morrow.—The staff dinner only ; but a large evening party, and a dance, as it is Friday.

8th.—Meredith very ill to-day, and all owing to his own imprudence. It is melancholy to think, how young men throw away their health in this country ! The doctor says, however, that he will soon be well, with a little care and discipline.—A number of young officers at dinner, and in the evening more of them.—Don't feel comfortable myself, and fancy that I smell a fever. Dr. Rocket made me gargle my mouth with Madeira wine, and go to bed at 9 o'clock. He says that fancies of that sort often lead to much evil.

13th.—I was much amused this morning, with the account of poor Mrs. Brockmüller, who is not even allowed to sit down to table with her lord and master, the Ensign, but is obliged to wait behind his chair ; and he has in fact married her to have a good servant, poor thing !—News of the French towards the middle of the day. Part of their force has proceeded south, and it is thought with the intention of attacking Trinidad. Soon, I trust, our fleet will arrive, to put an end to their depredations and our alarms.

15th.—At 5, a dinner party, but I remained in my own room. Soon after, an express arrived from Lord Seaforth, &c. announcing to General N. that an additional French force had made its appearance, from Ferrol, and part of the squadron also from Brest had joined them, making in the whole about thirty sail of the line, and that a great number of troops was supposed to be on board. Lord Nelson arrived at Barbadoes, but was sent by a false report to Trinidad. However, an express has followed him, and shortly, it is to be hoped, we shall have some certain account of their destination and proceedings. In the mean time, all our suspense must continue, and our anxiety is cruelly renewed. For my own part, I feel really almost worn out, with watching and expectation, and my poor dear N. is so harassed with business, that I dread the effect upon his health.

All the house engaged to-day ; and after all, the despatches could not be sent off till 12 at night.—In the evening, I received my company as usual, and the party was numerous, all wishing to hear, or to tell what they had heard ; and, among other things, I have been told, by the few ladies who remain in Spanish Town, such horrid things of the savage ideas, &c. of the slaves, on the estates in the interior, that I am determined, if my dear N. is obliged to leave me to meet the enemy, that I will take my dear children on board a ship, or any where near the coast, from whence we may make our escape, rather than accept of the asylum offered me by Mr. Mitchell, &c. &c.

16th.—The church shut up, on account of the heavy rains. —General N. engaged with despatches all day, to go by the *Staunch* brig, which sails for England to-morrow.—Just as we were going to dinner, heard of the arrival of a packet. All anxiety to hear the news, and General N. and I, in particular, to learn our fate. At half-past seven, came the public despatches. They are all that is comfortable. Sir Eyre Coote is to come out with a dormant commission, and to place himself under General N.'s command, till the alarms

x

here are over, and the latter wishes to resign.*　This has raised our spirits very much, and if Lord Nelson can but send us a good account of the French fleet, we shall be happy indeed.

17th.—A great deal of business still for my dear N., and the arrangements for Honduras, &c. are very troublesome.

18th.—Another day of uncertainty and anxiety.　An express from the Admiral, to say, that Lord Nelson, not having found the French fleet at Trinidad, had come on to Martinique as quick as possible ; but we are still uncertain, whether the enemy remains there, or has come this way, as there are two accounts in a letter from St. Vincent's.　The one states that the French had left Martinique, and, by the course they steered, it was supposed would have returned to Europe.　The other, that the whole fleet was seen proceeding towards St. Domingo.　Whichever may be the true report, our suspense must soon be at an end ; but it is a painful state for us all, and a horseman does not come up quick to the door, day or night, but I tremble all over, and almost lose my breath from anxiety.

20th.—Both my dear N. and I are out of spirits.—He says, that he cannot leave Jamaica till matters are a little more settled, and that he must wait Sir Eyre Coote's arrival. Yet, if the French leave these seas, he is anxious that I should go with the children to England, as soon as possible; but it will be a miserable separation to us both, and it will

* Sir Eyre Coote succeeded as Lieutenant-Governor when Nugent left on 20 February, 1806.　Ill health and the effect of the climate on a weakened constitution compelled Coote to retire.　He brought the news that the Imperial Parliament had passed a law with drastic restriction on trade between Jamaica and other West Indian islands and the United States ; and also that the African slave trade was abolished.　He was succeeded on 12 March by the Duke of Manchester as Governor, and on 13 April, 1808, by General Villette as Commander of the Forces.

be a severe trial.—Only Berkeley and Lake in addition to
our staff party to-day.

21st.—General N. reviewed the 55th and 85th regiments,
and the St. Catherine's militia, on the race-course, at daylight. I could not summon strength or spirits to go. How
different I feel from what I did on my first arrival, and
indeed for a long time after ; then I had strength, spirits,
and activity, for any thing. Now, all is an exertion beyond
my strength, and probably my not sparing myself the first
year or two, as well as the constant anxiety of late, have
done as much as the climate, in wearing me out.

At 7, I met all the party from the review, at breakfast.
Mr. Simon Taylor came soon after, to take leave of me ; as
he says he is now sure that all our alarms will be soon over,
and that I must lose no time in going to England, for the
sake of my health and that of the little ones. General N.,
he says, is a *rock*, and will stand any climate. In the course
of his visit his expressions were so kind, and he seemed to
feel so much, that I was as much surprised as affected by
his manner, for he has the character of loving nothing but
his money ; and yet I have experienced such continued
kindness from him, that he has shewn me almost the affection of a father. Indeed, I feel that I know him much
better than the world does, and shall always feel gratefully
affectionate towards him.—A Council of War held at 12
o'clock, and it was unanimously agreed that martial law
should cease at 12 o'clock to-morrow night in case no further intelligence arrived to prevent it.—A meeting also of
the Assembly to be called for the 2nd of July.—A large
second breakfast, of the 55th and 85th officers.

At dinner, Colonel Pollock (St. Mary's), and Mr. Vaughan
(Trelawny). Had a long conversation with the latter, on
the subject of making Christians of the negroes, and of his
experience of the advantages of teaching them their con-
sequent duties, &c.—On his estate (Plumstead), he has
christened all his negroes, and has induced many of them
to marry, and lead regular lives. He says, they have in

consequence improved in all respects ; are sober, quiet, and well behaved ; and the last year twelve children were born of parents regularly married. The new negroes are attended to, the instant they arrive on the estate, and are taught their prayers most zealously, by the oldest black Christians, and those best instructed and most capable. How delightful this is ! I wish to God it could be made general, and I am sure the benefits arising from it, in every point of view, would be incalculable. I gave Mr. Vaughan several of my catechisms, made for our black servants, and several good little books for their instruction, with which he seemed much pleased.

In the evening a very numerous party. I can't flatter myself that my departure is so much regretted, as they tell me, but still it is comfortable to feel that no one wishes me ill ; and many indeed not only made strong professions of regard, but actually shed tears ; but what was most gratifying to my feelings, were the very kind and handsome things said of my dear Nugent. They all agreed, that he was one of the most moral and able governors they ever had, and wished us, a thousand times over, a happy meeting in our native land. All this I really felt very much, although I am not so vain as to take all the flattering things they said of myself, otherwise than as proceeding from their kindness, infinitely more than from any merits of my own.—We sat up longer than usual ; for, after the 11 o'clock dancing, there was much to be said, in shaking hands, and bidding good night.

24th.—At second breakfast, Mr. and Mrs. Woodham and their little girl. Immediately after, we all went to the chapel, where Harry and Eve's child was made a Christian, and now I shall not leave one, belonging to this house, unbaptized.—Continual visitors till 4 o'clock. Then, a deputation from all the *brown* people in the town, wishing to take leave of me. Received them immediately, and then shut myself up in my own room, to rest, and try to be equal to the further exertions of the evening.—At 6, a large party

—King Mitchell, and Mr. and Mrs. James Mitchell, Messrs.
Hinchliffe, Edwards, Bullock and Ricketts (Lord St. Vincent's heir*), the commanding officers and our own staff ; in
all thirty persons.

25th.—A long conversation in the evening with Colonel
Drummond, about his affairs, &c.—Give him the best advice
I can. General N. and I agreed to send off an express to
the Admiral, with our excuses, as I am really unfit to undergo the fatigue of such a visit, nor has my dear N. spirits for
it either.

26th.—A long letter from the Admiral, who thinks we
are quite right, not to encounter the fetes which were intended to be given at Kingston, had we visited his Penn.

27th.—Rise early.—All day the house is in more than
usual bustle, and I am glad of it, for I can't sit down, or
think comfortably of any thing, or write or read, or even
interest myself much in my dear children, God bless them !
—General Carmichael and several others at dinner. I left
them early, and assembled all the servants in the chapel,
and, after prayers, spoke to them on the subject of their
future conduct every Christmas. I gave them each a catechism, with a certificate of their baptism ; and deposited
with old Phœbe a sum of money, to be divided among them.
But to Cupid I gave a written character, and something to
buy a keepsake.—Poor creatures, they were all in tears, and
expressed the most affectionate regret, at the prospect of
my departure. Before I went to bed, I received a message
from the garrison, wishing to attend me on horseback, to
the port where we embark. As it is twelve miles, I begged
they would accept of my best thanks, for their kind intention, but not to risk so long a ride in this dreadfully hot
weather. No news of the French, or of Lord Nelson, and
to-morrow is fixed for the Fleet to sail !

28th.—We never slept, and were in bed scarcely three
hours. Poor dear N. and I were both up and dressed,
before 4 o'clock, though we had sat up so late writing and

* And as such afterwards proprietor of estates in Westmoreland.

talking. Found all the servants assembled, and a large party of gentlemen on horseback at the door, who all insisted upon accompanying me, a few miles at least.—The parting with the poor blacks and them, with other friends on the road, was painful indeed. At 7, arrived at Old Harbour. A breakfast for all the staff, on board the *Augustus Cæsar*. Only my dearest N. remained afterwards. Sit on deck and can't talk of to-morrow ; yet we can think of nothing else ; and the thoughtless, playful innocence of the dear children, while we pretended to be amused with it, brought tears to our eyes, and it was difficult to restrain a burst of grief.

29*th*.—Neither of us could rest, and we did nothing but complain of the smell of the sugar, and the dreadful heat of the cabin, all night, or rather for the few hours we were in the cabin, for at 2 o'clock we were both up, and remained conversing, and trying to make up our minds till 8, when, as we were nearly down the Harbour, and the sea breeze was very strong, it was thought best that General N. should proceed no farther. God bless, and grant us a happy meeting once more.

The morning wretched. All sick, even the dear children. I believe that I was for a short time out of my senses, for I lay upon the cabin floor for several hours, in a most deplorable way. About 2 o'clock I went to bed, and before evening was tolerably composed, and the dear little ones were as merry as possible, only calling for papa, and it was difficult to pacify them, before they went to sleep.

30*th*.—In the morning we were off Negril Harbour, the port of rendezvous for the Fleet.

July 1*st*.—At 9, the *Theseus*, and the rest of our convoy, appeared in sight, and Captain Bell came to tell me it would be necessary for him to go on board the Commodore, for instructions, but that he would not be absent more than an hour.—The weather was beautiful when the boat was lowered down, and we watched him till he was safe on board the Commodore's deck. Soon after, a most sudden and

dreadful squall came on. We were lying in the midst of
the fleet, when our cable broke, and we were in the greatest
danger of driving against a man-of-war, that threatened
to fire into us. Fortunately, however, the mate was a good
seaman, and he steered us safely through the ships, and
quite out to sea, but we were, for some time, in a state of
the greatest danger and alarm. They told me, afterwards,
that I went to the helm, to give my assistance. I dare say,
in my distraction, I might have done so ; but I only recollect kneeling down, with my two children in my arms,
and resting my head on the cabin floor, while they lay in
dismay by me. As we stood out to sea, another danger
presented itself, from the Spanish pirates, &c. One vessel,
at no great distance from ours, was boarded. The crew
escaped in their boats, but first set fire to her. Our mate,
however, manœuvred us so well, that, towards evening, we
had nearly got back to our former station, when the captain
came on board, and declared he would never leave the ship
again, till he saw me and the children safely landed in
England.

2nd.—About 10 o'clock, Captain Bell was so fortunate as
to anchor the ship nearly in the very spot from which we
had been driven yesterday, and to-day they hope to get up
our lost anchor.—The dear little ones passed a quiet night,
in spite of the great heat ; and the maids, &c. seem well
this morning.— I ought to mention my two fellow passengers, and who compose my family, Colonel Irvine and Dr.
McNeil, with my three maids, and two dear little children.

All day watching the labour of the several vessels, in re-
pairing the damage done by the storm. One ship is on
shore near us, but they hope to get her off, and that she has
not suffered much injury.—I had many visitors in the
course of the day. Mr. Griffith, of St. Elizabeth's, came,
and took charge of a letter for my dear N. Mr. Hylton
arrived soon after, with one from him, and told me that a
report had come on to Spanish Town, of our ship having
gone on shore, and that we were in great distress. I there-

fore sent off another letter immediately, to set his mind at ease on our account. Captains Ross and Boger came to offer their services, and, at Captain Bell's request, I asked for two good helmsmen. Then came Captain Drury, to apologize for having scolded us so much, and threatened to fire into our ship, during the squall ; but he said it was tor our sake, more than his own ; as, had we come in confact, his ship was so much stronger than ours we must have gone to the bottom.—The rest of the day passed quietly. The weather quite calm, and all well.

3rd.—No alarm or incident during the night. At 6, this morning, a letter from my dear N., and I wrote to him in return, before I left my cabin.—The heat dreadful, and the smell of the sugar almost suffocating ; so that we must live on deck very much.—About 10 o'clock, Captains Temple, Drury, Crofts, Tucker, and Douglas, Messrs. Edwards and Griffith, Captain and Mrs. Dickson, (Artillery), and young Berkeley, all came to see me, and staid nearly two hours on board.—Little G. and L. much admired for their intelligence and great spirits, as well as pretty looks and engaging manners.

About 1, the signal was given, and we all weighed anchor for sea. This seemed to me like a second parting from my dear husband. Soon after we set sail, a heavy squall, with tremendous thunder and lightning, did not at all contribute to raising my spirits ; but, before I went to my cabin for the night, the Commodore sent me a nice long letter, from General N., who is well, thank God ! and promises to keep up his spirits, and take the greatest care of his health, with the hope of our meeting in happiness once more.—About 12 o'clock at night, we were fairly out to sea, and the ship tossing about very much, from the agitation occasioned by the late squalls. I could not rest, but sat looking at the fleet, and watching, for the greatest part of the night, the winds and the waves.

4th.—The weather fine this morning, but the sea rough. However, all around me are well, and the little ones run about the cabin as if they were on shore ; for, having no shoes on, they don't slip about much. Only we are in constant fear of a sudden roll of the vessel doing them some mischief. The confinement alone seems irksome, and they are continually asking, when we shall go to the Penn, &c. —Dined at 4 in the round-house, with the two gentlemen and Captain Bell, and at 8, retired for the night.

5th.—Heard this morning, by chance—for they did not intend I should know it—that the carpenter was found dead in the very act of putting up his tools, last night ; and that some of the seamen are ill also, on account of getting wet, and striking in the prickly heat, during the heavy rain, the first night or two after we sailed. Tell Captain Bell to use all my stores, in any way that may be of service to the invalids.—See the Grand Caymanas, just before we went to dinner. It is inhabited by people who subsist by catching turtles, and procuring articles from vessels, that are unfortunately wrecked there.—A little rain in the evening, but the night calm and quiet ; though the heat was so great, that the children could not rest, but were crying all night for water, which was so warm when they got it, that it would not allay their thirst, and only distressed them the more. Dear little L., in her impatience to drink, actually bit a piece of the glass fairly out, and it has cut her little lip and cheek a good deal.

6th.—A calm this morning, and the ship rolling about with the swell of the sea, and very uncomfortable. The Grand Caymanas near us. It appears a very low miserable island. It is a dependency on Jamaica, and that gives it an interest with us, as being under the command of my dear Nugent. I look at it with a sort of melancholy pleasure, as something belonging to him, but as if we were again leaving him behind us. Soon after breakfast, Lake and Berkeley came, and brought the man Captain Temple had promised me, so now we are very tolerably off for steersmen. —A dead calm the whole day.—Little L. with a violent heat all over her, in addition to the prickly heat. The doctor says, their best diet for the present will be rice and arrow-root, and for George a little port wine.

16th.—There has been a sad chasm in my journal ; but, in spite of my present state of nervousness and weakness, I will try to fill it up.—In the night of the 8th, we were spoken to by the *Magicienne* frigate, to tell us, that the Havannah was clear, and no enemy in that quarter, or in the Gulf of Florida, so that we might steer our course, without any further fear. The Captain was anxious to know how we were, that he might tell General N. all about us, on his return to Port Royal. I was so anxious, for fear that Captain Bell would mention the illness on board, that I jumped out of bed, and ran to the cabin-window, to say, all is well, and to beg Captain B. would tell the Captain of the *Magicienne* so. In an instant, I was struck, as with a great blow, or, rather, as if I had received a shot ; and, from being in a profuse perspiration, and in a violent heat, I became instantly almost stiff with the cold.—Poor Clifford, who, in spite of her own illness, got up to see what was going on, got a blanket, and covered me up, but all would not do. I went up to breakfast, but was in such an odd way, that Dr. McNeil, who came to see how I was, ordered me to bed immediately. Vomitings then came on, and I was tortured with pains in every part of my body, as long as any recollection remained ; but for twenty-four hours my head was in a sad state, and I knew nothing that had passed. Since that, my weakness has been dreadful, and the fever coming and going, so that I could scarcely move from my bed, even to have it put in order.—On Saturday, I was brought upon deck, and soon I hope to recover my strength.—On Wednesday, my sweet Louisa was seized with almost the same sort of fever, and for three days the darling little thing was in a sad stupid state, neither sleeping nor waking, nor taking notice of any thing. My own maid was also, on Wednesday, taken so ill with a fever, that she was put into bed and covered with blisters ; and, to crown all, the doctor again took to his bed, on Thursday, with a fever.—Miss several

poor sailors from the deck, since I was taken ill, but ask no
questions, for I am afraid to hear sad tidings of them.

17th.—Clifford is rather better to-day, but my dear little
boy is feverish, and very complaining with his bowels.—He
and Louisa are both ordered to have port wine and biscuit,
at 11 o'clock, every day, and they take their little glass
with great pleasure. Two of our best seamen were taken ill
to-day, and their lives are despaired of. For my own part,
I am so miserably low and weak, that I can scarcely support myself at all. However, I have made an effort to
continue my journal for my dear N., in the usual cheerful
strain, for his mind would be distracted, did he know our
real situation.—We were obliged to lay to all night. To-
morrow, however, I hope we shall get rid of this horrid Gulf
of Florida, and be in a more open sea.

18th.—My only attendant, since my illness, has been a
tall old man, the steward of the ship, and he has thought
of a plan for restoring my strength, which I have promised
to adopt to-night. It is to take a piece of toasted bread,
dipped in porter, and then sprinkled with sugar, just before
I lie down to sleep.—Write my journal for General N., as
now I must soon send it off ; a midshipman was sent to-day
by the Commodore to apprize me of this.—Still in the Gulf
of Florida, and the ship obliged to lay to all night. The old
steward will not resign his office, but still attends me, and
to-night I shall take his prescription of toast and porter.
His name is San Fiorenza, for he was born in a church of
that name, during the great earthquake at Lisbon, and was
immediately baptized by an officer, that happened to have
taken refuge there with his mother, &c. He comes to my
bedside every morning, and kneels down to take my orders,
and the same at night, and never offers me any thing, when
I am ill and in the cabin, without going down on one
knee. His language is very curious ; a mixture of English,
French, Italian, and Portuguese. Altogether, he is quite
a character.

20th.—Rise very early, and have the comfort of finding

we are getting clear of the Gulf of Florida.—I must not omit to mention, that while I was ill one of my finest macaws flew overboard, and the same day my most intelligent parrot died. I wish we had no greater losses to lament; but, alas! many of the crew are missing, and have, I fear, also found a watery grave.—Lat. 29, at 10 o'clock this morning.—Very light winds, but fair.—At 12 o'clock, sent my journal, for General N., on board the schooner.

26th.—I forgot to mention, yesterday, the immense dolphin, that had been for several hours about our ship, was taken. Many of the sailors said, they had never seen so large a one. There were many smaller swimming about, and the men were much amused, with trying to harpoon them. The large one was brought upon the deck, and when it was dying, it looked beautifully; being green, blue, purple, yellow, with stripes and spots of mother of pearl, or silver; and the dear children were much astonished at the sight.

31st.—I do indeed dread a long passage, for the smell of the sugar is so bad, it destroys every thing. All the cabin is covered with a sort of leaden surface, which comes off upon one's clothes, and even our skins seem to be dyed with it. I am shocked at the dingy, dirty appearance we make, but this is not the worst part of the business, for I constantly feel my throat and lungs affected by it. Every thing *tastes* of the *smell* of the sugar, and I am in continual apprehension, lest my dear babes should suffer in their health by it.

Here ends the month of July.—This evening, Captain Temple was so good as to take our madman (Gardiner) on board the *Theseus*, as he became mischievous, threw one of the turtles overboard, and threatened, every night, to get into the cabin, and to murder all the women and children, which, as we had no means of confining him, made our situation by no means pleasant. Many a sleepless hour has it cost me, since I have been on board.

August 1st.—Young Berkeley came on board to dinner.

He says that there are several of the ships missing. Some went on shore in the Gulf of Florida, and were lost ; others are supposed to be taken ; and some to have parted company in the heavy squalls we have had of late.

3rd.—All our party are quite well, and the children are mending very fast ; but the smell, and the dirt, occasioned by the sugar, seems to have increased with the damp weather. Every thing feels clammy, and if you touch the wainscot, it comes off like the marks of a black lead pencil, and no water can get the stain out. My nose seems always dirty.

7th.—I really believe that the putrid steam of the sugar disorders my stomach ; for it turns every thing of a dingy lead colour, and the maids complain of the continual nausea it occasions them.

8th.—In the afternoon the tiller was put in order, and as it was necessary, for that purpose, to open the trap-doors in our cabin, the heat and intolerable stench from the sugar were indescribable. The vapour that arose from it blackened every thing, and was as hot as if it came from a boiling cauldron. The men, who went down, returned as if from a warm bath, and their faces all discoloured.

17th.—We are now about two or three hundred miles from the banks of Newfoundland, and may look forward to seeing dear England in about three weeks, or perhaps sooner. Our voyage has been sadly tedious, with calms, squalls, and contrary winds ; but now, I trust, we may look forward to more settled weather, and in three weeks, or a little more, we may leave this uncertain and tremendous element.—Spoke a ship from New Providence ; Governor Cameron and his family quite well.

21st.—Still a fair wind, and the fleet pretty well up, as the *Theseus* took a vessel in tow yesterday, and made several of the fast sailing merchant ships do the same.—I don't think I have ever mentioned how I pass the day on board ship. I will now detail the dull routine. As soon as I awake in the morning, the old steward comes into my

cabin, with either a dish of ginger tea, or coffee, or sometimes a piece of a shaddock. I then have the children
brought to me. They kiss papa's picture, and pray God
to bless him. After playing with them a little time, I say
my prayers, and then dress for breakfast; before which,
I generally walk a short time with the gentlemen on deck.
As soon as breakfast is over, I go down into the cabin, and
see that the maids wash and dress my little ones, who come
on deck with me ; and the morning is spent, between reading, walking, and playing with the children. At 12, I always open my map, and mark on it the progress of my
voyage. At 11, the children have each a biscuit, and some
port wine and water. Louisa then goes to sleep, and George
eats some chicken, or some thing or other, when we take
our luncheon at 12. At 2, they have strong soup, either of
mutton or chicken. At 3, I go to my cabin, read, and then
dress for dinner. Soon after 4, we dine ; and at half-past
seven, I leave the gentlemen to smoke their cigars, and to
drink their brandy and water. Soon after 8, I am always
in bed, and the babes sound asleep. The old steward then
comes to my bedside, with a large tumbler of porter and a
toast in it. I eat the toast, drink the porter, and generally
(when the sea and wind will permit) rest now tolerably well.

   To-day we lay to, about half-past one o'clock, for the dull
sailers, when Captain Bell went on board the *Theseus*, and
I took the opportunity of sending some sweetmeats, half-a-
dozen of Malmsey, and a nice little roasting pig, of the
Chinese breed, to Mrs. Dickson. Captain Bell heard, from
Mr. Lake, that they were all sadly off in the wardroom, for
fresh meat and porter ; so we made them a present of three
or four pigs, a sheep, some poultry, and some porter, &c.

   26*th*.—Not much wind, and that little is against us ; and,
as it is at east, we feel it very cold ; but I enjoy it, and the
children don't seem to suffer the smallest inconvenience
from it.—Lay to, the greatest part of the day, for the dull
sailers, forty or fifty of our fleet being out of sight behind us.

   27*th*.—Rise early.—Not much wind, but it is fair, what

there is of it ; however, we are obliged to go back again, to collect some of our fleet, which have appeared in sight this morning, though at a great distance off. A captain of one of the merchant ships came on board, and brought two London newspapers ; one as late as the 26th of July. I am quite out of spirits ; Sir Eyre Coote had not left Cork on the 12th of July ! * Alas ! I had flattered myself that my dear Nugent was already relieved, and on his way home. God bless and preserve him !—About 2 o'clock, a strange frigate, which proved to be *La Loire*, Captain Maitland, joined us from Cork ; only six days out. This makes us feel ourselves near home. Soon after, the *Cerf*, Captain Chamberlain, spoke us, and gave us an account of the naval engagement between Sir R. Calder, and the combined fleet from the West Indies, &c., with the promise of bringing us the papers as soon as possible ; one as late as the 10th of August.

29th.—Spoke the *Cerf* again, soon after 12, and sent on board for the newspapers. Sir R. Calder in disgrace, for not following up his advantage with the enemy. Sir John Orde superseded, for not following the Toulon squadron to the West Indies, and Lord Nelson is at Gibraltar.—Not a word in the papers about Sir Eyre Coote ; so I hope and trust he sailed for Jamaica on the 13th of July, as the papers we had yesterday seemed to think the troops would leave Cork about that time.—Captain Chamberlain came at 4 o'clock, and dined with us, and never in my life did I hear more scandal than he told us of the whole fleet.—Such quarrels, such discontents, and party business ! I do indeed rejoice that I did not accept of the accommodation on board the *Theseus ;* for Captain and Mrs. Dickson are perfectly detested and looked upon as the greatest incumbrances. What should I have been, with children and maid-servants, all

* On the 25th of August at Abbey Church, near Clonmel, Ireland, Sir Eyre Coote, K.B. and M.P. for Queen's County, was married to Miss Bagwell, daughter of Colonel Bagwell, of Marlfield, M.P. for the County of Tipperary.

sick, and of course unavoidably troublesome.—I sat up till near 9, and the gentlemen did not quit their cigars, &c. till near twelve.

30*th*.—Captain C. has promised to get me some newspapers from the *Loire*, by which I hope to find out the exact time when Sir Eyre Coote sailed, that I may judge of the probable chance of my dear N.'s leaving Jamaica, before the season for another meeting of the Legislature there.

September 1*st*.—The *Loire*, with the ships for Bristol and Liverpool, left us early in the night, and were out of sight this morning. Alas ! one of my most beautiful Curaçoa birds died in the night, from the inclemency of the weather. He was very large, with a dark variegated plumage, and a purple tuft upon his head, or rather a lilac one ; for it was too light a colour to be called purple. I examined it after death, and it appeared to be a hard sort of crumbling substance, like the inside of a bone. I am much afraid that I shall lose more of my birds, for, unfortunately, they are all moulting at present.

2*nd*.—Towards the evening, very cold to *us Creoles*. Louisa did not seem to feel so much as George, who looked very grave at first, and then said his fingers were sore, which was a very natural idea for a child, who had never before known what cold was.

CHAPTER V

SEPTEMBER 3, 1805—JUNE 18, 1815

September 3rd.—Six o'clock in the morning.—The land just announced from the mast head, thank God ! thank God ! a thousand, and a thousand times !

4th.—The morning beautiful, and the wind directly fair, to take us into Weymouth. The fear of quarantine, and apprehension of falling in with some of the enemy's cruisers, and our convoy being very much scattered, decided us upon going on shore, and at 10 o'clock, we took our leave of the *Augustus Cæsar*, and good Captain Bell, and crowded all the sail our little vessel could carry. We had a sad, tedious time, till after 6 o'clock, when we came into Weymouth Harbour. There we were obliged to remain, for the health officer to examine us.

Before I describe our landing, I must mention our appearance. Colonel Irvine and Dr. McNeil were in old brown or pepper and salt clothes, that they had worn some years before in England. My three maids were in their best bonnets, &c. but the shape sadly old fashioned, as we soon found, and all their gowns and trimmings much tarnished, by the climate of the West Indies, and by the sun, air, &c. The children we put a second frock on, so as to supply the place of warm clothing ; but their ankles, arms, and necks, were covered with beads ; and for myself, in my hurry, and anxiety to get on shore, I forgot the dress prepared for me, and put on a full Lieutenant-General's uniform, that I had used as my dress of ceremony on the voyage. It was a scarlet habit, with embroidered fronts, and two large gold epaulettes on my shoulders.—In short, we made a most extraordinary appearance altogether.

Y

Captain Bell was rather reluctant to our leaving the ship, at such a distance from the land, but provided us with sea stock, for a day or two, for fear of accidents ; among which were, a large ham, and a large roasted turkey, which we immediately exchanged, with my Captain of the fishing vessel, for some brown bread, butter, and fresh cheese, upon which we all feasted.

At 8, the health officer made his appearance. He told us that the Duke of Gloucester had just been buried, and the king and royal family, then at Weymouth, were all shut up ; but he had been invited, by some of the attendants, to dinner, and this kept him so late. In fact, he appeared to be almost tipsy, but this was fortunate for us, as he was in high good humour, in consequence of the good cheer. My gentlemen, who, as well as myself, had been reading the rules respecting quarantine, on board the fishing vessel, began with assurances of our health, although they confessed we had been ill. This put me in a fright, and I ran to the side of the vessel, with the two children in my arms, making a most pathetic speech, about the hardship of our having got through all the dangers of foreign climates, and then to be left to die of the night air in sight of our native shore. This won the little man's heart ; and, in his anxiety to be kind, and to tell us all about the quarantine regulations, &c. he jumped on board our little vessel ; where, in a moment recollecting himself, he said, " Well, Madam, now it is all over, as, if you are to perform quarantine, I must perform it with you : so all we have to do is to remain quiet for a little while, and then keep our own secret after we land."

As it was getting darker every minute, we were soon in his boat, with our trunks, &c. ; but I could not help laughing at his evident fear of the plague, notwithstanding all our assurances of all the party being in perfectly good health. The little light that remained, when he came on board, shewed him our sallow sickly faces, and I don't at all wonder at the poor man's alarm. During our short row to the shore, however, he resumed his spirits sufficiently to

give us his whole history. First, he shed tears about his
poor partner, whom he had laid under the sod, three years
ago ; but he smiled again, when he spoke of the daughter
she had left him, now sixteen, apprenticed to a milliner,
who was patronized by the princesses ; all this would have
made us laugh too, if we had not been expecting to land
on our native shore every moment.

How shall I describe the instant when we left the little
vessel ! It was then so dark, that no one could see me, and
my first movement was, like Columbus, to kneel down and
kiss the earth, and return fervent thanks to Almighty God,
for his mercy and goodness, in bringing us safe through all
our perils and dangers. Then I embraced my dear children,
and vented my feelings in tears and congratulations to all
my fellow passengers. Our kind friend, the health officer,
hurried us up some back lanes to our inn, where we were
placed in confidence, under the care of his friend the landlord ; and he also got some other friends, in the custom-
house, to pass our baggage. All was done for a fee of five
guineas, which I was directed to entrust him with, to pay
all expenses, and keep all secret. My agreement with the
captain of the sailing boat was twenty guineas, so I begin
to think, that I shall not have money enough to take me
to London. However, it was too late for the bank last
night, and, though we can't leave Weymouth, on account
of the review this morning, which will engage all the horses
till 3, it is thought most advisable not to make ourselves
known, till we have left the coast a little way. Nothing
could exceed the attention of the people at the inn, except
the delight of little George and Louisa, at the novelty of all
around them. George seized upon the tongs with astonishment ; and, before I could prevent her, Louisa had possession of the bell rope, and rung such a peal, that she brought
up the waiters, &c. in a great hurry. In short, they were
like little mad things, and it was late before they could be
composed to sleep ; and, even then, nothing but real fatigue
induced them to close their dear little eyes. My gentlemen

and I had a nice supper of partridges, and all went to bed happy and thankful.

6th.—We left Weymouth before 4 o'clock, and, on our arrival at Dorchester, heard there were some officers in the house, that Sir Eyre Coote had not yet sailed, and that the time of his departure for Jamaica was quite uncertain. Then, upon examining the state of my purse, found that my Weymouth bill had sadly diminished its contents. I applied to the landlord, therefore, for money for a draft. He referred me to his wife, who was even more hard-hearted than himself, and dropped some hints, about *odd people* travelling about the country, &c. This set me on my mettle, and I collected all my gold pieces, and found I had sufficient to pay for a good dinner, apartments, &c. ; and so I went to bed last night in good spirits ; for I make no doubt the next stage I shall meet with kinder people. I must, however, say that there is some reason for the fear these poor people seem to have, about our being respectable, as I sent the landlady to a Colonel *somebody* in the house, last night, to ascertain the truth of General Nugent's being in Jamaica, &c., all of which was vouched for, but he had never heard that *General Nugent was married ;* so no wonder the woman would not trust me—but I must dress, and be off with my dear little ones for Blandford.

7th.—A nice breakfast at Blandford, yesterday morning, and the landlord in an instant ran over to the bank, to get me a hundred pounds for a draft upon Messrs. Drummond ; and, on opening my desk, I found a letter of credit upon them, from General N., for any amount ; and this, owing to my stupidity, I had never thought of since I landed.— Gave the children some dinner at Andover, and slept at this place, Hartford Bridge.—Now we are off for London, where we expect to be in time for the dear children's dinner to-day.—Drove to Berkeley Square, and found that the Russian Ambassador had taken possession of all the apartments at Thomas's Hotel. Then to Grosvenor Street, and find the house empty. My sister Fraser and all out of town.

At Reddish's Hotel in St. James's Street, we got excellent apartments.

8th.—Before 10, my dear sister Fraser from the country, &c. We went to St. George's church together. Delighted at being once more allowed to return thanks to God, for all his goodness and mercy. I wrote from Weymouth, to tell our dear friends at Stowe of our landing, and Dempsey was sent up to town to-day, to take charge of us down to Stowe. He brought a most kind and affectionate letter, from dear Lord Buckingham himself ; offering even to come to town, if I could not immediately go to the country, and insisting upon my making Pall Mall my home, &c. and not going to an hotel.—Lord and Lady Westmeath, and their nice family and, in short, abundance of friends, coming in every minute. Doctor Fraser spent an hour with me this evening, and thinks I had better remain a little while near him, as both the children and myself require a little care yet.

9th.—Lord Westmeath came, to accompany me to Downing Street, where I had made an appointment with Mr. Cooke yesterday. He assured me that General N. would certainly be at home by Christmas, or very little after, and that Sir Eyre Coote would sail as soon as General N. would have time to take his passage, on board the November fleet, unless (alas !) some circumstances should arise, to prevent his giving up the command in Jamaica. He spoke to me about the anxious wish of General N.'s friends in the government, that he should accept of a baronetage *now*, as giving him claims for the *ribbon*, which General N. prefers. —He stated that there are objections to his being made a Knight of the Bath at present, which makes all that espouse his interest, and the Duke of York in particular, anxious that he should accept of the favours now offered him. I will tell him all they say, and his judgment and feelings must decide the point. Our long conference ended with many praises bestowed upon my dear husband ; and he does indeed deserve them, and I rejoice his conduct is so well understood and appreciated

On my return to the hotel, Drs. Blair and McNeil. The former is going back to Jamaica. Mrs. Pye, also, was one of my visitors to-day, and made me almost fancy myself at the King's House again, she was so full of all the gossip of Spanish Town. Her brother is going to be married to a lady, with neither youth, beauty nor fortune, but she is well connected, sensible, and amiable ; and so I trust he will be happy. Met Colonel Robinson in the street, who did not know me at all, at first ; but says now, it is because *I am looking so well !*—Dined with Lord and Lady Westmeath to-day.

10th.—Find Lord Temple (alas !) a little changed too, for he has become a man of the world, and is now paying great attention to Lady Castlereagh. It may be a joke, but it is not right. Lady Lucan has forsaken her husband and family, and become quite abandoned.—How wretched ! Poor Lady Frances Vandeleur is in a melancholy way, and so nervous as to alarm and distress all her friends very much. Sir Eyre Coote is married, I find, to one of the Misses Bagwell, who is to accompany him to Jamaica, and this accounts for his delays. D. Mackinnon is married to a Miss Rose Elliot, or going to be. She is a cousin of Lady Le Despencer and Lady Cosby. General Wellesley has arrived from India. I wonder if he will now renew his flirtation with Kitty Pakenham !* All these little affairs I shall make news of, for the amusement of my dear N., whose mind I will try to distract from business, and divert as well as I can.

12th.—A conversation to-day with Lord Westmeath, &c., and was advised to apply for the command in Ireland for my dear Nugent.

13th.—Awoke early, and composed my letter to Mr. Cooke—*Private and confidential.*—I left my *grand* letter in Downing Street, or rather saw the servant deliver it, as we sat in the carriage.

14th.—Drove out with Lord and Lady Westmeath, inspect my new carriage, and see several houses, that I may

* He married her on the 10th of April following.

report to my dear N. the one most likely to suit us, when he comes home. Settled my dear little party in Sloane Street.

19th.—Dined in Grosvenor Street, and had a delightful nice sociable evening.

20th.—An agreeable surprise prepared for me, by dear sister Fraser. It was indeed joy to me, to find my dear sister Robinson and her good husband there.

27th.—Decided upon going to Stowe to-morrow. Send my man Richard to arrange accordingly, as soon as we had dined. To bed at nine.

28th.—Take leave of Madame Du Pont, soon after 8, and proceed as fast as possible to Lillies, where we arrived before 4, having given the little ones their dinners on the road. Dinner at 6, and as they had prepared for me, and insisted upon my remaining for the night, make up my mind, and put the children to bed at 8. There are now five generations in this house. Colonel Nugent, his mother, and grandmother, his daughter, and her daughter, all eating, drinking, and talking, and the old folks enjoying themselves, quite as much as the young ones.

29th.—Arrived at Stowe soon after 2 o'clock, and found all the dear party assembled. I found all looking well, but the growth of Lord George was beyond every thing. Lady Mary is now quite a woman, in size and appearance, and with a lovely face. Dearest little Lady Temple is wonderfully improved. Dear, dear Lord and Lady Buckingham are the same as when we went away, only a little older ; and Lord Temple is as good humoured, kind, and handsome as ever, and the dear little man is grown tall and beautiful.

At dinner, we were surprised by the sudden and unexpected appearance of General (now Sir Arthur) Wellesley.* He was greeted with the greatest friendship and delight, and placed on the other side of dear Lord Buckingham, who was anxious to learn all about his Indian campaigns, &c. as soon as possible ; but he seemed more inclined to talk over

* He had been aide-de-camp to the Marquis of Buckingham when he was Lord-Lieutenant of Ireland.

his Aide-de-camp days, and to tell me all the tricks played
by him, General N., &c.—In short, the two people, from the
east and west, both arriving the same day, afforded much
mirth and amusement to the whole party, and it was 11
o'clock before we sat down to supper, and past 12 before we
could think of going to bed. Only Major Moore here, in
addition to the family party.

30*th.*—My darlings much better, and amuse all the family
very much, by their little funny talk, and Creole ideas and
ways.—Obliged to write many letters, having myriads, from
all parts of the country, to answer.—A talk with Sir Arthur
Wellesley about Ireland, and Irish friends, and I think he
still retains his old feelings.—Dine at 5. A most delightful
evening. Music, and much agreeable conversation.

October 3*rd.*—In the evening, had a long and very interesting conversation with Lord Buckingham, on the subject of General Nugent's affairs, and shall write, (please
God) to-morrow, and detail all he says, as I am sure he is
a real friend, and deeply interested for us all.

4*th.*—Judge of my surprise, upon entering my own room,
when she * drew aside a curtain, and shewed me the bust
of my dear Nugent, placed on a little cabinet, close behind
the bed. It is an excellent likeness, and invaluable to me,
and I kissed her most heartily for her kindness, and all the
party seemed to share in my pleasure and satisfaction.—
The rest of the evening as usual, but many jokes, by Lord
Temple, on their giving me a husband of marble, &c.

5*th.*—Got a most delightful, long, and comfortable letter,
from my dear, dear Nugent.

12*th.*—Lady B. projected a trick for the Duc de Serant,
which succeeded famously ; but he played us one in return,
and sent us all pell-mell down stairs ; but these events took
up so much time, and made us all so merry, that we did
not get to bed till after 1 o'clock.

13*th.*—Write, &c. early. Evening church. Mr. and Mrs.
W. Fremantle, and the Misses Harvey, just before dinner.

* Lady Buckingham.

Little L. made acquaintance with them immediately, and could scarcely be got away to bed —The evening as usual.

14th.—Drove with Miss E. Harvey, in the little pony phaeton. She is a worse whip than myself, if possible.

17th.—Arrive in town soon after 4 ; found a letter from my dear N. waiting for me in Pall Mall. Sent to my sisters Fraser and Robinson, and they both came, and dined quietly with me.

18th.—Read over General N.'s letter again, and then decide upon writing and consulting Lord B. upon the subject of the letters he has enclosed to me; one to Lord Camden, refusing the baronetage offered him, and the other to the Duke of York, respecting the red ribbon.—Still my mind too anxious, and too much occupied with my dear N.'s vexation about the baronetage, and his affairs, to think much of enjoying anything else.

19th.—When I came home to dress, Mr. Birchall came to consult me, about Sir Eyre Coote's carriages. He appeared to be one of the stupidest men I ever met with, and will, I am sure, mismanage the whole thing.—I have promised, if possible, to find out some eligible party for Miss Coote to accompany to Jamaica. Some good gentleman-like steady family, if such there can be found leaving England in these times.

20th.—Dine with the Robinsons, and have a quiet evening.

21st.—Dine again with the Robinsons, in Dover Street.

22nd.—Lord B.'s letter all kindness. He has written to the Duke of York himself, and dictated a letter for me, to Lord Camden and the Duke.

30th.—Dine with the dear Robinsons, to celebrate their wedding-day.

November 3rd.—Go to church with dear Lady Temple. Lady Mary Grenville has a cold, and can't be of the party. —The rest of the ladies all Catholics.

4th.—In the evening, Lady Buckingham invented a game, called " kiss the doctor," which sent us all to bed very merry. The old Bishop of St. Pol de Leon seemed to enjoy the fun as much as any of us.

7th.—Great news! The combined fleet defeated off Cadíz, but Lord Nelson no more ! I could not help being greatly affected by the whole account, and retired to my own room, to vent my feelings. I don't know why, but all these sort of things seem to have such a connection with my dear N. and his situation, that they appear as our own immediate concerns.—The whole day talking of the great event announced this morning. Various conjectures and ideas on the subject, but I hope it may bring about a peace.

8th. After a fidgety sort of night, have the comfort this morning of hearing that Sir Eyre Coote must certainly now be soon in Jamaica, as he left Cork on the 28th of October ; and a packet is announced, so I shall soon have letters from my dear N.

18th.—For some days I have been making up my mind to pass a few weeks at Bath, and this morning, at 7, I set off for Oxford. Found Lord G. Grenville expecting me there, and prepared to do the honours of *great Tom*, &c. to the children.—Lord G. took tea with me ; after which he went to his rooms to dress, and returned to take me to the concert, given for the benefit of the widows and orphans of Trafalgar. Lord G. supped with me at the inn, and we talked till a late hour.

19th.—Get to York House, in Bath, at 8 o'clock.

21st.—Just as I was going to dinner, the Misses Kemble came, and I invited them to partake sans façon ; so we had a nice sociable evening, working, and playing with the children, &c.

25th.—After we had taken our glass of water, went with the little ones to Rosenberg's, and had them weighed. George was two stone and nine pounds, and Louisa two stone two pounds. I was six stone eight pounds. I spent the evening at Mrs. Dacres', to talk about the Admiral and Jamaica.

29th.—The dear little things more than usually lively and

merry, this morning. The old gentleman, whose name I
find is Morshead, who was so civil to our party last night,
I met again, at the Pump-room to-day, and agreed to go
to see the hospital with him, to which I have also sub-
scribed. It is for indigent people, who come here for the
benefit of the waters.—Dined alone, and then went, in the
evening, to meet Mrs. Johnson, the Bayards, &c. at Mrs.
Hering's. In the course of conversation, I happened to
mention Mr. Morshead, and heard he was a dreadful character, and had been turned out of several lodging-houses,
and indeed excluded society, for his conduct to women. So
here the Misses Kemble and myself are in a fine scrape, and
we must get rid of our acquaintance as well as we can !
How lucky it is that my appointment with him was for a
distant day ; so I cut him the more easily.

December 2nd.—Mr. W. Pitt at the Pump-room, and the
little ones called out Billy Pitt so loud, that I was fearful
he would hear them. He is very ill, only Lord Mulgrave
with him ; but all the company made a lane for him to go
up to the Pump, and shewed him as much respect as if he
were one of the Royal Family—to the great astonishment
of some French generals, that are prisoners here, and were
present.—In the evening was chaperon to the Misses Dacres
and Kemble, to the rooms. A good ball, and pleasant
evening altogether.

5th.—Lady Milnes one of the party.* Her husband was
Lieut.-Governor of Quebec, and she came home without him,
as I have without mine, and we became quite intimate, in
comparing feelings. I like her much.

6th.—Crowds of visitors. Sir Charles Knowles (for more
than two hours), Lady Call, her daughters, and the Mac-
kinnons, Lady Jane Aston, &c. all rather tiresome.

7th.—The early part of the day as usual. Made a few
visits. In the evening, with the Dacres, and heard again
the praises of my dear N. ; for old Mr. Deane knew his
father and grandfather, and remembers him one of the
finest looking and best bred men he ever saw.

* At Mrs. Dacres.

15*th.*—To church at the Abbey. Drink tea with Lady Belmore ; Miss Kitty Fisher, the young Roscia, was there. I took her home in my chair, and was much amused with her conversation, and the secrets of the theatre which she divulged. She is certainly astonishing for her age, but I much doubt her turning out any thing very superior, by and by, as she speaks so much of the labour of learning her part, &c.

18*th.*—Arrive at Stowe about 7 o'clock.

24*th.*—Write a long, and as consolatory letter as I can, to my poor sister R. whose husband is, alas ! certainly going to Jamaica, and she is quite miserable about it.

1806. *January 2nd.*—Took the children down for a short time before dinner, to be shewn to Monsieur ; both very much admired. Monsieur amused us much, by teasing me on the subject of their being so fair, &c. as he thought, being born among the blackies, they must have had a darker tinge.

The Duc de Berri said, that it was always their fate, just as they became well acquainted, and found friends, they were obliged to be off ; and in the present instance he felt it particularly. I thought he was really going to be very sentimental, and throw himself at Lady Mary Grenville's feet at once.

4*th.*—Am amused to find that my old maid, Johnson, passed herself on the French valets de chambre for having been a maid of honour, in foreign parts, where, she assured them, I had been a queen ! This accounts for poor nurse's anxiety, to be dressed smarter than usual every evening ; for I suppose she passed for a maid of honour also.

13*th.*—In the evening took profiles. General N.'s bust brought down from my room, and had a very good likeness taken from it.

14*th.*—Awake early, in hopes of letters. Only one from Grandjean. General N.'s detained at the Horse Guards. Read old Grandjean's epistle half a dozen times, as he scarcely speaks of any thing but my dear N. and his kindness to him.

15th.—Dined at Missenden, and got to Grosvenor Street in time to give my little ones their supper, and see them safe in bed and asleep.

16th.—A Dr. Gordon of the party.—Supper at 10. Prayers, and home immediately after.

17th.—Announce myself to Admiral Nugent, and let Lady Gosford, &c. know I am in town.

21st.—Dine again in Pall Mall. A sociable and agreeable, though a rather melancholy party, poor Mr. Pitt being at the point of death, and almost the sole subject of conversation. Came home, reflecting much upon the lives of politicians, and how absorbing politics are of every other feeling.

23rd.—At Mrs. D.'s met Mrs. Charles Fox, who admired my children so much, that I could not help feeling very grateful, though I declined a regular introduction to her.

30th.—Sir T. Strange introduced to me. He is just from India, and going back again, and gave me a long account of dear Lady W. Bentinck. A frigate has arrived, and brought an account of poor Lord Cornwallis's death !

February 6th.—Mrs. Card sent home my dress before 1, and all the feathers, &c. were also ready ; so I dressed, and joined the party in Pall Mall before 2, as Lady B. sent her chair for me. The dear little ones were with me while I dressed, and delighted with mamma's big petticoat. My dress was a blue satin robe, with white swan's down, white crape petticoat, on white satin, blue drapery with swan's down, to match the robe. Head dress, diamonds, pearls, and white feathers. In short, all very smart.—The drawing room was crowded. Mr. Fox and all the new ministers there. The poor King and Queen tried to look pleased, but did not seem very comfortable. I could not but remark Mr. Fox's slovenly appearance ; his stockings were loose about his legs, he had no bag on ; and the joke in the newspapers the next day was, that he was not a *Bag Fox*. Got home soon after 5. Take off my hoop, rest a little, and then meet a party at dinner, at Lord and Lady Carleton's. All in our Court plumes, and very gay, but feel very much fatigued indeed, before I get home at twelve.

10th.—Dine with Mrs. Fraser, and then dress and go to the Duchess of Gordon's assembly, or rather concert; for the Misses Anguish, and Mr. T. Moore, sang the greatest part of the evening; there were also several professors there. Did not get home till near 3 o'clock, as I stayed to see the little dance after the concert.

12th.—Remain at home all day, and only admitted Lady Gosford and Mrs. Kemble, the latter of whom has just arrived from Jamaica. Mrs. K. left my dear N. quite well, thank God! and preparing to embark.

13th.—Have a great deal of talk with Lady B., on the subject of the *Peerage*. Lord B. thinks it is not the moment, but that it may be soon; and may then be pushed for. I don't care much about it, only as far as it will satisfy the world that my dear N.'s services have been properly appreciated.

14th.—Dined at *King Mitchell's*. The dinner was given to me, and all Jamaica was there. Upwards of twenty at dinner, and an immense crowd in the evening. I was so toadied and complimented, that I fancied myself again in the King's House, but looked for my dear N. in vain. In spite of what I have said, I was greatly pleased with my party, and stayed so late, that I could not join Lady Dungannon's *Beauty* party at supper, as I had promised; and perhaps it was good policy, as I should have entirely lost, by comparison, my little reputation of the sort, which they have given me.

19th.—*Ash Wednesday*. To church with Mrs. Fraser. Then visit many Jamaica people, to have the happiness of hearing and answering enquiries about my dear N.

20th.—Sup in Pall Mall. The party there, Sir Joseph, Lady, and Miss Banks, Lady Stanhope, and Lord Mahon, Dean Warburton, &c. Lady Temple and I were much amused, and behaved very ill, by laughing at Sir J. B. and his stick, Lady Stanhope's history, &c., but Lady Bucking-

F̴ͅ.

ham's affected gravity was the cause of all; and even
Lord B. could not help laughing.

F̴ͅ . *25th.*—Arrive, at 2 o'clock, at Melchet Park.

March 2nd.—After church, walk and see Mr. Osborne's
Hindoo temple, in honour of Mr. Hastings.

8th.—Get to town about four.

10th.—General Merck came, and I really felt half afraid
of him; he seemed so odd, and looked so like an assassin.
Hear all he had to say, and promised I would detail it all
to General N., &c. and then rejoice to see him depart.

5th.—As I did not get my letters yesterday, I made up
my mind in the night, that General N. would arrive to-day,
and so rose very early, and got all the house up, the children
dressed nicely, and every thing ready to receive their dear
papa. Till 3 o'clock, in the greatest fuss and agitation,
when General Grenville came, and told me, that he had seen
a public letter from General N., and that now he would certainly not be here till towards May, as he is to sail in the
next convoy ; that is, this month or April. Receive my
letters from the Secretary of State's office, and am much
consoled by their contents. He is well, and writes in spirits,
and I see he is right, in not coming away immediately ; Sir
Eyre Coote's appointment, to succeed him in the government, being merely provisional (that is to say, the commission runs, in case of his death, or absence from the
Island, *only*); so, of course, while there is any alarm, or
prospect of an enemy, he would not leave his post ; but
thank God ! all prospect of the French being in force in
that part of the world has so far subsided, that there is
scarcely a chance of his being detained beyond the April
convoy. Dine quietly in Pall Mall, and go home immediately after supper.

21st.—Lady Temple and I went to Mrs. Fremantle, in
Stanhope Street. A large party and music. The Duke of
Cambridge sang. Mrs. Billington, Madame Bianca, &c.

April 9th.—Set off for Gosfield. Arrived there at 7.
Lord George, and Lady Mary with Miss Hernon, to meet

me at the gate. A great deal of fun all the evening, and
then some serious conversation with dear Lady B. before
we went to bed.

I shall not keep a journal of days, or rather a diary, but
speak of facts as they arise, during my stay in the country.

Went with dear Lady B. to visit the poor nuns ; and,
afterwards, to make the acquaintance of my dear Nugent's
old friends in the village, who asked a great many questions,
about *Master George*, and were much pleased to see his
children.

21*st.*—Took little G. to church for the first time in his
life, and could not help reflecting very much upon the
circumstance, of his being for the first time in the House of
God, and seated directly over the remains of his grandfather, and great grandfather, whose monuments are in the
pew, over the vault that contains their coffins. Lady B.
talked to me most feelingly on the subject, when we went
back to the house.*

* On the north side of Gosfield Church, near Halstead, Essex,
is a large pew, or rather a room with a ceiling moulded in plaster,
of George II time ; and on the north wall of the same is a fine
monument of that period, with figures of Mr. and Mrs. Knight,
the former in Roman costume, the latter in widow's weeds ;
and on an urn at their feet is the following inscription :—

" Joanni Knight
de Gosfield in Com. Essex Armig.
Qui obiit Oct. 2 1773 Æt. 50,
Anna Craggs,
Jacobi Craggs, Regi Georgio I a secretis soror
Memoriæ & Amori Sacrum
Conjugi Suo Charissimo H.S.P."

On the base of the monument are other inscriptions. In the
middle, on an oval white marble panel :—

" Anne Craggs
married
1st to James Newsham, Esq :
2ndly to John Knight, Esq :
3rdly to Robert Nugent, Esq :
Created Earl Nugent in 1755
She died the 22nd of November 1756
aged 59."

Continued on next page

On the evening of the 3rd of May, I received an express, just after dinner, to tell me that my dear N. had arrived at Plymouth. Set off early on the 4th, for town, and met my dearest N. on the road, near Chelmsford. I cannot describe the delight of our meeting, and the dear children partook of our joy, and seemed perfectly to recollect dear papa again ; for they knew him the instant he appeared at the side of our carriage. We were both going as fast as four horses could take us, and were some distance past each other, before the horses could be stopped. General N. then jumped out of his carriage, and ran back to ours, and the little ones cried and laughed with joy, to see their dear father, so often prayed for, and about whom so much and such constant anxiety had been expressed. It was happiness indeed ; and we all returned to town with hearts full of joy and thankfulness.

Lord and Lady B., and many friends, were soon assembled there, and we passed a delightful time till the 17th of June,

On the west side of this, on a similar slab of marble :—

" Edmund Nugent
Son of Robert Viscount Clare
& Lady Amelia Plunkett
his first wife
died the 26th of April 1771
Aged 39 years."

On a corresponding stone on the east side :—

" Robert Nugent
Created Viscount Clare
and Baron Nugent
of the Kingdom of Ireland.
Married
1st to Lady Amelia Plunkett
2nd to Anne widow of John Knight, Esqr.
3rd to Elizh widow of the Earl of Berkeley
Died the 13th of October 1788,
Aged 79 years."

And on an urn, over the last recorded inscription :—

" Margaret Nugent
Sister to Robert, Earl Nugent
Died November 18th 1794
Aged 70 years."

Continued on next page
Z

when we left town for Cheltenham. But I ought first to mention, that General N. was pressed very much to go as Commander-in-Chief to India, to relieve Lord Lake ; and I passed some days in anxiety and agitation, for fear he should be prevailed upon to accept the situation. However, he declined it, to my great joy, distinguished as the appointment was.

I must also mention, that we went to the King's birthday, at St. James's, which was particularly brilliant. Lady Temple and I had dresses just alike ; lavender-colour satin robes, embroidered most richly in silver vine leaves, and bunches of grapes. Our petticoats white satin, with lavender crape and satin, rich embroidery, and the draperies looped up with a silver arrow. Head-dress, diamonds and feathers, mixed ; the feathers, lavender and white. The Queen remarked our dresses, as we went up together, and said they were the prettiest she had seen.

My dear N. had business in town, so I went to Cheltenham, with my little ones only. On the 27th,* my dearest

A coffin, in the vault under the pew, bears a plate with the following :—

" Here are deposited the remains of
Edmund Robert Nugent
the son of Lieut General
Sir George Nugent
and Maria his wife.
He was born Decr 5 1807
and Died Decr 26 of the same year.
To the Great Grief of his
disconsolate Parents "

The following entries are in the Burial Register :—

" My Lady Anne Nugent the wife of the Honble Robert Nugent, Esqr, was Buried November ye 28th (1756) and Rec^d. the affidavit that she was Buried in Lining."

" The Honourable Edmund Nugent was buried May 4th 1771 aged 39 "

" Robert Craggs Nugent, Earl Nugent, died in Ireland October 13th (1788) and was buried in the Family Vault in this Parish the 26th of October aged 78 years   duty rec^d."

* June.

N. joined our party, and was much pleased with Rutland Lodge, and all my arrangements.

On the 28th of July, our little party broke up ; Mrs. Robinson and her children returned to Thornbury, and we took ours to Bath for a fortnight, when we were suddenly hurried off to town, as my dear Nugent was appointed to the command of the Western District, to succeed to General Simcoe,* who has accepted the command in India, which General N. a short time ago declined.

On Sunday evening took possession of our house at Ex-mouth, called Ormond Lodge, engaged for us by dear Lady Temple.

Took possession of our house in the Barnfields, Exeter, on the 9th of October, and on the 12th (Sunday) celebrated our dear little George's fourth birthday.   General Phipps, and a large military party, met Lord and Lady Temple, &c. at dinner.

On the 20th,† General N. off for Aylesbury, to canvass the Borough.   He and Lord George Cavendish's son, the two Government members, and scarcely a doubt of their success.

November 2nd.   Much discussion on the subject of the baronetage, which I think he will now accept.

9th.—Expecting my dear N. every moment.   He came at 3.   He has succeeded in his election, or rather canvass, perfectly.

16th.—We have given two grand dinners, to the Palks, Graves, Courtenays, and Rolles, &c. and divided the military and church militant among them, and so have made large and agreeable parties, for both days.

December 14th.—The only event this week is our sitting to Mr. Downman‡ for a family piece ; which, if the like-

* John Graves Simcoe, the first Governor of Upper Canada. He was taken ill on his way to India, returned, and died at Exeter 26th October, 1806.

† October.

‡ John Downman, A.R.A., a Devonian by birth and a pupil of West.   In 1806-8 he was practising in Devonshire.   His portraits are chiefly met with in private collections in that county.   He died in 1824.

nesses are good, will be most interesting, to us at least.
General N., the children, the nurse, and myself, are to be
the group, and we shall see.

' My ball on the 29th was particularly gay and brilliant,
and Lady E. Palk was in all her diamonds, and Mr. and
Mrs. Brummell came with the Graves' family. They were
the only new people.

1807. *January 21st.*—Left Exeter, and arrived at York
House, Bath, between 4 and 5 o'clock on Thursday.

29th.—Arrived in town, and found all the *world* (of *our*
acquaintance) there before us.

On Tuesday, March 31st, General N. visited the 2nd
battalion of his regiment (the 6th), at Ospringe barracks,
Kent; and the 1st battalion the day following, at Deal,
and returned to London, April the 3rd. On Tuesday, the
26th, General N. set off for Aylesbury, to begin his canvass.
—On the following morning, I started for Stowe, with the
little ones. We travelled with our own horses, and slept
at Missenden, and did not reach Stowe till the 30th, in the
evening. All Aylesbury in a bustle, as we passed through,
and General N. had a hard battle to fight; but he was
elected on the 9th of May, and Lord Temple for the county
on Monday, the 11th. On Tuesday evening, the 12th, they
returned triumphant to Stowe. All the house in green
ribbons, but my poor deaf maid had a sad trick played upon
her, and wore, as General N.'s colour, a *red bow ;* and a sad
quarrel was the consequence, with the ladies and gentlemen
of the steward's room.—On Wednesday, the 13th, Mr. T.
Grenville and Mr. R. Neville were elected for Buckingham,
and we all attended them in the town to witness the
ceremony.

On the 19th, Mr. Robinson arrived from Jamaica, to our
great joy, and I rejoiced with my dear sister, on his safe
return, and without his health having suffered at all, apparently.—Captain Cadogan, R.N. and Mrs. and Miss Gould,
were his *compagnons de voyage*, and we went to the inn
immediately, to shew them every civility, but they were off
for London, without loss of time.

We spent a few days again at Ugbrook, and, on the
1st of September, we slept at Tiverton, on our way to
Castle Hill, to visit Lord and Lady Fortescue, where we
spent a week, with a large and agreeable party, Lord and
Lady Temple, Lord and Lady Graves, Lord G. Grenville,
&c. &c.

At Mamhead, &c. till the 20th, when my dear N., accompanied by his staff, set off for a military tour through his
district.

November 2nd.—We had a large dinner party ; Lord
and Lady Fortescue, and Lady Anne, Lord and Lady
Graves, Lord and Lady Rolle, Lord and Miss Courtenay,
our new Bishop of Exeter and Mrs. Betham, &c.

December 3rd.—Sit to Downman for my picture a second
time, the first being no likeness at all ; now it is thought
it will be much better.

19th.—I left off writing this day fortnight, and now
resume my pen, with joy and thankfulness. A few
minutes after 5 o'clock on that day, I felt slight pains, but
I knew them to be decisive ; I therefore quietly gave
orders, for all things to be got ready, and tried to make up
my mind to what was to follow. I had, however, but a
short time to think of it ; for the doctor and nurse could
scarcely be with me, before my darling little fat Edmund
made his *entrée* into the world of woe, as it is called by
some, but may it be a world of happiness to him.

27th.—With what different feelings, with what agony,
do I resume my pen ! God has taken my darling child
from me ! He is now no more.

1808. *January 21st.*—Arrived this evening at Parrot's
hotel, in Brook Street.—On Tuesday, we took possession
of Lady Gosford's house, in Upper Harley Street.—On
Friday, Mr. and Mrs. Robinson came to us, and spent
a week, when they took apartments at an hotel, for the
season.—General N., thank God, is looking better ; but he
has great fatigue, and has caught a severe cold in sitting
on General Whitelocke's court martial. I went with
Ladies Buckingham and Temple, &c. to Chelsea, the last

two days of the trial, and could not help pitying the wretched man, though he certainly fully deserves the sentence passed upon him.

We arrived at Tunbridge Wells, on the evening of the 18th of April, and settled ourselves, on the 21st, at Cumberland House, on Sion Hill.

May 22nd.—Mr. Cumberland,* the author, was there† with his daughter.—Send the children to take their usual drive, and were at home by 8.—The carriage came afterwards, and we had the pleasure of bringing Mr. Cumberland, &c. home with us, and found him particularly agreeable and entertaining.   He lodges at Sion Hill, close to us, and we have promised to be good neighbours.   His daughter is married to a Mr. Jansen, of the German Legion, and himself a German.   Mr. Cumberland seems very fond of her ;‡ but, I am told, he highly disapproved of the marriage.   His other daughter is married to Lord Edward Bentinck, and he takes great pleasure in speaking of that connection.

July 8th.—We are now going to begin a tour, as they say that nothing is so good as continual change of air to remove every vestige of the hooping cough,§ before winter.   Arrange all our affairs in town accordingly, and General N. has obtained leave from the Duke of York, to be absent from his district till September.

11*th.*—All set out for Stowe.   Our party consisted of General N., myself, and the two children, Miss Vyse, my own maid (Johnson), nurse Hamilton, Monsieur Gênet, and Joshua our footman.   The heat was great, and when we arrived at Stowe, poor General Grenville, &c. all panting and dying of it ; the great amusement was, watching the state of the thermometer, which rose at one time as high as ninety-six.

Little Miss O'Donnel and her maid were added to our

* Richard Cumberland was then seventy-six years old.   He died three years later.
† Mrs. Sheridan's.
‡ He left her all his property.
§ The children had had it in April and May.

party. I ought to observe, that the heat was so great, as
we travelled, that many poor labourers dropped down dead,
as they were working at the harvest.

On our return to the hotel, we found little O'Donnel in
great distress. An express had arrived, from Stowe, telling
her, that Gage Rookwood had arrived there, and proposed
to her guardian for her. However, upon talking over the
matter coolly, we all agreed with her, that it would be more
delicate, and more decorous, for her to pursue her journey
to Ireland, with us, and let the gentleman either follow, or
wait her own good time for returning. Indeed, her presence was necessary in Ireland, for the purpose of arranging
some money matters ; so we continued our journey through
Wales, which we all enjoyed exceedingly, in spite of the
unusual heat of the weather.

We only spent two days in Dublin, to see Miss O'Donnel
safe to her friends, and to see how the Dublin world were
going on. The town was empty, however, and we only
heard of all the Castle proceedings of the last season ;
among which, the disagreements between Sir A. and Lady
Wellesley made the most prominent feature. We were only
two days on our road to Belvoir, where we found all well,
and my poor mother much better than we could possibly
expect, after the sad accounts we had lately heard of the
state of her health.

We remained ten days at Belvoir, the children being quite
well of their cough, and quite happy with their cousins, and
much liked and admired by all their relations and friends.
Took rather a melancholy leave of the dear party, and
crossed over to Port Patrick, from Donaghadee. Then
through Ayr to Glasgow, where we were met by good old
Colonel Murray. Stayed two days, to see the manufac-
tories, &c. ; all of which I explained to the dear children,
as well as I could, and their early age would admit of. We
then proceeded to Sir John Murray's (Lanerick Castle),
where we were most hospitably entertained, and all their
few neighbours invited, to do us honour. These were
limited to a few of the Macgregor Clan, and Lord and Lady

Doune.   We were much amused with the clannish histories, &c. ; and with hearing all the Jacobite feelings and prejudices descanted upon, just as if it was in the years 15 and 45.   In the drawing room, and in Lady Murray's dressing room, there were portraits of Prince Charles ; and General N., I am sure, shocked the whole party very much, by calling him the Pretender ; for he was immediately corrected by the Lady of the house, who said, " Prince Charles, if you please."   I saw, too, a portrait of my dear father, among many others of the Macgregor Clan, and, although a wooden sort of painting, it is something of a likeness.   We then set out again on our tour, accompanied by our kind and good friends, the Murrays, for Trinity Lodge, near Edinburgh, the seat of Colonel Murray.—Saw the Castle, Holyrood House, &c ; in short, all the lions of that beautiful city ; and were fêted by all the Macgregors and their friends, for a week.—I must not omit to mention, that I saw my pedigree, both at Holyrood House, and at the Lord Advocate's library, and was desired to be proud of my descent.

We took leave of Edinburgh, and our hospitable friends, with the greatest regret ; but had a delightful journey to London ; seeing all that was worth seeing on the way.   We were obliged to hurry away from Scotland, sooner than we wished, as my dear N. must be again in the west of England, early in September.   The poor dear little things felt this leave taking almost as much as I did, and the next day, by way of getting rid of the painful impression, of dear papa's being gone for a long time, though not to the West Indies again, as dear little G. thought at first, I took them to see sights ; and Mrs. Salmon's wax-work, in particular, was such an amusement, that it absorbed every other idea.

Soon after I came back to town, Mr. Scrope Bernard shewed me an advertisement of a place in Buckinghamshire, thirty miles from town, that seemed exactly to answer our purpose, as a *home*.   Write to my dear N., who approved of the description, and wished me to go to see it.   Mr. Scrope Bernard went to the lawyer, for all particulars, and I find

it is for such immediate sale, and so many people about it,
that I must make up my mind on the subject in twenty-four
hours. So, not to be known, order a hack carriage, and
with nurse and Georgy, go down to Marlow ; where I
arrived at about 8 o'clock in the evening. Mr. Scrope
Bernard was there before me, and Mr. Hicks appointed to
meet us, at 10 the next morning, at the house ; to give me
his opinion of the timber, and the value of the place altogether. Spend some hours with him (Mr. S. Bernard) at
Westhorpe House, and then, by their advice, offer sixteen
thousand pounds for the whole purchase, instead of acceding
to the demand of twenty thousand pounds.—Am very nervous about it, but no time is to be lost, on account of the
many people who wish to become the purchasers. Return
to town that evening, see Mr. Robson, and deposit four
thousand pounds. Then write to General N., full of anxiety
about what I had done. Receive a most kind, affectionate,
and comfortable answer, by return of post. He is quite sure
he shall like it and be satisfied ; at all events, that I have
acted for the best, let it turn out what it may. On the
second of November, I went down and took possession.
    Fortunately, General N. was ordered to town, as one of
the members of the Court of Inquiry, on the Cintra Conven-
tion, which is to sit on the 14th of this month. He arrived
on the evening of the 13th, and, as the Court was adjourned
for three days, we made a visit to Westhorpe House ;
arriving there at 11 o'clock at night, on the 14th of November. We found great difficulty in making any body hear,
to let us in, which kept us a considerable time at the gate,
before we could gain admittance. We immediately went
over the rooms, &c. ; and early the next day inspected
every thing else, and my mind was relieved from a load of
anxiety, by his approving of every thing, and seeming perfectly satisfied with the purchase.
    We brought little Miss O'Donnel to Westhorpe with us,
and, the week after our return, Mr. Frogatt came, and all
the settlements, &c. were arranged, preparatory to the
marriage. The lover also (Mr. Gage Rookwood) came,

and spent a fortnight. Poor thing, I trust she will be happy, for she is truly good and amiable, and deserves to be so ; but alas ! I fear his attachment is to *les beaux yeux de sa Cassette*, and not to herself. I must say, from what I see of him, he appears to be incapable of appreciating her worth and good qualities. But she likes him, and the marriage is to take place, as soon as possible after Lent.

My dear N. was constantly living on the road, all this time, and going up for any question of importance in the House of Commons.

1809. Lay plans for a school, and mean to curtail my soup list; after this winter, to have only the sick and old people upon it. I intend that Saturday, May the 6th, shall be the last day for their receiving soup this year, or at least till next October or November.

May 1st.—From this date, till June the 3rd, our time passed in receiving and making visits in the neighbourhood, and in regulations for our parish, and the poor, &c. &c. and in plans for the improvement of Westhorpe. Consult Mr. Bent, our builder, employed at the house in Brook Street, about stuccoing the house, as it is now a frightful, ugly, blue and red brick building, and all the window and door frames must be renewed, they are so ugly and worn out.

June 25th.—A letter came from the Commander-in-Chief, signifying his wish, that General N. should proceed, as soon as possible to Kent, and assume the command of that district, to replace Sir John Hope, and to regulate the embarkation of the troops, for the expedition to Walcheren.

July 10th.—Off for Dover. All the hotels and inns were crowded, and our accommodation was very so so.

11th.—Get a lodging house, but not very good.

18th.—Set off for Deal, on our way to Ramsgate.—The embarkation, for the expedition, a most interesting and affecting sight.—Found Mr. and Mrs. Robinson at Ramsgate, and dined with them that day. He is Commissary-General, to the great armament, and she, poor soul ! must be left behind.

21st.—Went to Broadstairs, Kingsgate, &c. and then set
off, in the evening, for Deal. Met Lady Wellesley, &c.
there, and had a nice walk on the beach. The Downs full
of ships, and the sight altogether magnificent. The poor
fellows cheering as they embarked, and I don't know why,
but I could scarcely refrain from shedding tears at their
joy ; it seemed, indeed, so thoughtless, when they were so
soon to meet an enemy, &c. But soldiers, I believe, never
think, and perhaps it is fortunate for them that they do not.

September 15th.—Saturday, the Admiral's dinner, at Deal.
—Sir Charles Paget, a judge of lace.—Am much amused
with the gentlemen's bargains, made at Walcheren, for
their wives, &c.

20th.—My dear N. much harassed by the accounts
from Walcheren. There is a dreadful fever among
the troops, and the sufferers are beginning to come over,
for a change of climate and medical care, &c.—All the
morning, he has been on horseback along the coast, and
giving orders, for every possible accommodation, &c. for
the sick.—Unfortunately, we had another large party at
dinner ; Lord and Lady Temple, Lady —, &c. who all went
with us to the ball. It was a later night than usual, and
to mend the matter, there was an alarm of privateers near
the shore, the night being very dark. One of them fired
into the town, and Lord Temple's battalion guns turned
out, to return the fire. We were in a great fuss for some
hours.

21st.—The accounts from Walcheren very bad, and
General N. was off early for Deal, &c. We followed,
a large party, in the middle of the day, and all dined at
Ramsgate, with Sir Henry Dashwood, Lady Camden, the
Ladies Pratt, &c. Mr. Mercer and music in the evening.
A late supper. My dear N.'s mind more at ease, having
to-day completed many arrangements, and given out his
orders, for the accommodation and comfort of the poor
invalids as they arrive, and the Archbishop of Canterbury
is coming to consecrate a burying-ground, to receive those,

who, alas ! have no chance of recovery, the fever being of
so malignant a nature.

22nd.—The morning very busy, and we all dined again
at Sir Henry Dashwood's.—The Duchess of Manchester, &c.
Very amusing circumstances attending the arrangement of
carriages, for the party to go to the ball, at Broadstairs.
At last the Duchess and General N. went in a hack chaise,
with the singing Mr. Mercer, as bodkin. The events of the
ball equally amusing. Old Lady Nelson shocked at Lady
John Campbell and the Duchess of Manchester, asking their
own partners, &c. She assured me, that Lady J. Campbell
must be mad, or worse ; for she wore half boots, and had a
dog called Devil. In short, we had a great deal of fun, and
came back to Ramsgate very merry, in spite of all the
anxieties of the morning, respecting the poor sick soldiers, &c.

23rd.—General N., &c. on horseback early, along the
coast. Lady T., Miss D., &c. walked on the pier, and
how different the appearance of every thing, from what
it was a short time ago, when Lord Chatham, and the Lords
Manners (his Aides-de-camp), and so many gay and fine
people, were parading about and troops embarking, and all
in high spirits ; and now we hear of nothing but sickness
and disaster.

October 1st.—My dear N.'s mind is most cruelly harassed,
by the idea of the numberless sick, coming almost
every moment from Walcheren, and almost the impossi-
bility of making them at all comfortable.

3rd.—A quiet day, and entirely given up to business by
my dear N., who is heartily disgusted with all the reports
from Walcheren.

6th.—General N. determined to resign his command, and
has written to be relieved.

9th.—Before 5, we started for Canterbury, where we
dined.

11th.—Did not arrive in town till Wednesday afternoon.
We put up at the hotel in Brook Street.

18th.—Left town in time to give dearest George and Louisa their dinner at Westhorpe.

21st.—Some of the cadets, from the Marlow military college, to take sketches in the grounds ; invite a party for dinner to-morrow.

November 1st.—A letter from Mr. Robinson. He is well, and hopes to be in England, almost immediately. She, poor thing ! was almost as much overcome with her joy, and thankfulness, too, that he had escaped that dreadful Walcheren fever, which has proved so fatal to so many on that luckless expedition, as I was by my fright yesterday.

15th.—My dear N. vexed, that he must attend a ball at Aylesbury to-morrow. The French Princes, and all the world, are to be there, as it is given to celebrate the fiftieth anniversary of our good old King's reign, as a jubilee.—He presides at it, as senior member for the Borough, and Mr. Hussey assists, as the other member for Aylesbury. But it can't be helped, and we only think that he may be back in time, to find me still out of bed, though I should rejoice if it were otherwise, and he should only have the joy of seeing the dear baby, without the anxiety of expecting it.

There is a chasm indeed in my journal, but I will try to recollect all the past, and fill it up as well as I can.

December 16th.—Towards evening, my dearest N. returned. He was met by the shepherd, nearly a mile off, to tell him it was a *dawtre*, and to get the promised reward of a guinea.

27th.—My time has been passed in taking care of my dear baby, and I have been a little nervous about her, as she certainly does not appear to have quite so strong a constitution as George and Louisa had at the same age ; but Mr. Hickman still persists in his opinion, and so I shall try to be satisfied. Yesterday, the dear little soul was made a Christian, by the names of Maria Emilia.

1810. January 2nd.—Left my darling children this morning, all well, thank God ! and dearest baby quite prosperous, though still looking rather pale, and yellower than usual, and than I like.—Arrive at Stowe in time for dinner.— Seventy-five people staying in the house, exclusive of servants, many of the French emigrants, &c.

The accounts from Westhorpe were very comfortable, and all went on quietly and prosperously with me till the 11th, when I heard of the death of my poor mother, which took place on the 4th of this month ; though the bad weather which prevented the packet from coming over, and the letters also going round by Westhorpe, delayed our receiving the intelligence, till so many days after the melancholy event.

Some future day, my dear children will have to experience the loss of their mother, and may their regrets be softened by the reflection of the comfort and happiness they afforded her through life ! And may God Almighty grant me his grace, to fulfil the duties of the situation in which he has been pleased to place me, and enable me to form the lasting happiness of those committed to my charge, by cultivating their minds and hearts, and sowing the *good seed ;* and grant that we may all, through the mercy and goodness of God, be enabled to set our fellow creatures a good example in this world, by living in a constant state of preparation for the next.

On the 29th we left Stowe.

On Saturday, February the third, my dear, my darling George left us for Iver school.

We all started for Gosfield, and spent three happy weeks there, with our dear Lord and Lady Buckingham, &c.

Passed a most agreeable time in town, till the 8th of June.

In the month of September, a sudden idea of our going to India occurred. It is a source of great anxiety to me— for my dear husband's sake, and for the future benefit of our dear children, I ought to wish it ; as he thinks it is right not to remain without employment, and that he should now exert himself for them. On the 18th of this month, my sister and Mr. Robinson sailed for Canada, where he is appointed Commissary-General.

Of late I have had many anxieties, on various subjects ; but the idea of going to India is uppermost.

In October, our good old King was seized with his former malady, and still continues in a sad state. Of course, a regency is in agitation. This has put all the political world in a bustle.

1811. *February* 18*th*.—Since I closed my journal, in December, our good old King has been so much better, that it is thought he may yet be restored. But the Prince Regent appears to be going on quietly, and doing so well that it is a pity the reins should be taken out of his hands, till his good old father is able to resume them, with comfort to himself, and advantage to the country. He has, in fact, acted with the greatest prudence and consideration towards his parent ; for, except giving to General Keppel the vacant regiment of General Craig, he does not mean to give anything away, but to leave all patronage for our good old King to decide upon, when he may recover.

Lord Wm. Bentinck, who has been for some time appointed Minister and Commander-in-Chief in Sicily, goes there soon, and she writes me, that she hopes to accompany him. Wherever they go, may they be happy and prosperous !—From some reports of late, I am in great hopes that General Brownrigg will be sent to India, instead of my dear Sir George.

My dear N. has had an audience of the Prince Regent, at Carlton House ; he was most graciously received in his private apartment ; but nothing new or satisfactory, about the Indian plan, was the result ; so I am left to my hopes and fears still.

In March, the East India plan was decided upon, and my dear husband was unanimously and with acclamation appointed by the Court of Directors. All parties seem highly to approve of the appointment, and Lord Temple told me, to-day, that instead of feeling any regret I ought to be proud of such a testimony to his character, as it is that entirely that has gained him the appointment, not one of his friends being in power.   But, alas ! I cannot help thinking of my children ; and, while I am going through all the bustle of dinners, to meet East Indians, &c. and while I am fatigued both in body and mind, with writing and various preparations, my whole heart is at Iver and at Westhorpe ; for ten days ago, my dear little girls returned there, under the care of dear good Miss Dewey.   I am impatient to get out of town to them, but can't get rid of our engagements, till towards the last of the month.

On Wednesday, the 3rd, my dear N. was sworn in at the India House, and dined with the Court of Directors, and a large party, afterwards, at the London Tavern.   Every thing went off most prosperously, and he has since settled a great deal of business.   To-day, he saw Mr. Perceval, Mr. Yorke, &c.   To-morrow night, after dining with the Nulli-secundus club, to meet the Duke of York, &c., he means to set off, and hopes to be at home by 2 or 3 o'clock on Monday evening.

This book I shall seal up, and send to Westhorpe to be put into the desk, that is in the little breakfast room, where my dear children may find it, one of these days, should I not return ; and along with it various little articles, as keep-sakes, which they will value, I am sure, as relics of a father and mother, devoted to their interest and welfare. Now, may God Almighty bless, protect, and watch over, my beloved, my darling children, and may He, in his great mercy, permit us once more, in this world, the great and unspeakable happiness of seeing them again !   My heart sinks within me, but I will not allow myself to think that there is anything of evil presentiment in the misery I feel ; for I trust, oh my God ! in thy mercy and goodness, for ordering whatever is best for us, here and hereafter.

June 1st.—After passing the whole of the month of May in London, fatigued with preparations for, and agitated by the thoughts of, my voyage to India, I arrived at the George Inn, Portsmouth, on my way to the Isle of Wight, expecting in a few days to be confined there ; Miss Macnamara, now

Countess M. T. Macnamara, kindly accompanied me.—Before dinner I saw Captain Templar, of the *Baring* East Indiaman, and made many arrangements for our voyage, &c. &c.

7th.—My mind was relieved by more comfortable letters, my dear Nugent has had an explanation with the Duke of York, and all is amicably settled about the wicked business in the House of Commons.

8th.—A happy day.—My dear brothers J. and C.* surprised me with a visit, before I was up ; I dressed while they took their breakfast ; the day spent in conversation.

15th.—About 10 minutes before 8 o'clock my precious little boy was born.

July 6th.—Our dear little boy was baptised by the names of Charles Edmund—Sir John and Lady M. Murray, Lord Cobham, and Lady Fortescue, being sponsors.

On Saturday the 20th we embarked on board the *Baring* East Indiaman—but I wish to forget all I felt on that day. . . . Passed a wretched night, and on Sunday, the 21st, the wind came round to its old point, and we returned once more to our dear ones.

27th.—Embarked once more ! a dreadful night indeed, but I will determine to conquer myself, and be a comfort to my dear husband, if possible.—All day at anchor in the Falmouth Roads.

> The hour is past—Oh hour of woe !
> Children beloved, a long adieu !
> But, though to distant climes I go,
> A mother's heart remains with you.
>
> Nor shall that heart know rest or peace,
> Nor shall that heart forget its care,
> Nor shall, while absent, ever cease
> Thy tender mother's fervent prayer.
>
> And may that God who sits on high,
> Who every thought and wish can see,
> The secret sob, the smothered sigh,
> The bitter tears oft shed for thee ;

* John and Courtlandt.

2 A

In mercy may He grant me this,
    The only blessing I implore,
The dear delight, the heartfelt bliss,
    To see my darling babes once more ;

Once more in Westhorpe's shades to roam,
    The dear ones sporting by my side,
And never more I'll quit my home,
    For India's glory, India's pride.

And oh ! may he, whose manly care
    Chases my grief in accents sweet,
My happiness be doomed to share,
    And make that happiness complete !

August 14*th*.—Saw Porto Santo, at daylight this morning, and Madeira soon after, with the two great rocks called the Desertas, lying to the south of that beautiful island. Landed about 1 o'clock at Funchal, and were received by a large party of gentlemen.

16*th*.—This afternoon, we, all embarked again from the beach, and were carried to our boats, in the same manner that we had been brought on shore, upon men's shoulders, for the surf is so high it is impossible for the boats to approach near.

19*th*.—Looking out for enemies' vessels all day—our greatest danger seems to be off the Cape de Verd Islands. —In a few days, we hope to get clear of all these apprehensions, and then, I am sorry to say, our Commodore will leave us.

September 16*th*.—The ceremonies customary on passing the line took place about 9 o'clock this morning, and lasted till 10, and that I am sure was long enough ; as in many respects it is a cruel sort of business. To keep clear of scrapes, it was first agreed, that the soldiers and cadets should be exempt from the ordeal, on paying a dollar each to the crew.—At 9 A.M. every thing being ready, the ship was hailed from the forecastle (as if from the sea) by Neptune, and answered by Captain Templar. Neptune asked what ship it was, and said he wished to come on board.—

Orders were accordingly given to hoist in his car and attendants, and they all immediately came on deck, Neptune
and Amphitrite, with their son, in a car drawn by six sea
horses, and driven by a sea god.—Several sea gods were in
attendance, as well as the barber and his mate, with a long
pole, and instruments for shaving ; there were two large
tubs near the gangway, filled with salt water, to which
Neptune and his people proceeded.   Some of the attendants
were then ordered to bring every seaman in his turn, who
had not crossed the equinoxial line before—they were taken
to the tub blindfolded, and seated there, when the barber
and his mate rubbed their faces with tar, asking them at the
same time some questions—the instant they opened their
mouths to answer, the mate stuffed a large lump of tar into
it, and the barber began shaving them, with something that
looked like a small saw ; then, while the poor man was
attentive to these proceedings, he was suddenly ducked,
over head and ears, in the tub, and escaping from that, and
running towards the forecastle, he was half drowned by
buckets of water, thrown by those of the crew who had
passed the line before, and were stationed for that purpose
to waylay him.   All the poor midshipmen underwent this
watery trial and it was astonishing to see how much the
soldiers, sailors, &c. seemed to enjoy the fun ; but I could
not help thinking of the frogs in the fable. Captain Templar, however, very properly forbid any cruelty or severe
ill treatment, as is sometimes the case if the men are not
restricted ; for the sailors have been known to revenge
themselves upon the officers, &c., that they disliked, by
shaving the skin off their faces, &c.   No accident, however,
happened on board the *Baring*, and the day ended in perfect
good humour on all sides.

October 22nd.—Stood off from the land till 2 o'clock this
morning, and then stood in again—there was a fog till about
11 o'clock ; then we distinctly saw the Table Mountain rear
its gigantic head, but it was soon lost sight of again, by the
fog returning as thick as ever.

23rd.—At day break we found ourselves very near Robbin Island, at the entrance of Table Bay, and about nine miles from Cape Town. About 12, we cast anchor, and prepared to go on shore.] An aide-de-camp, with letters from Sir John and Lady Theodosia Cradock, came to welcome us. We landed under a salute, and found a large party on the shore to receive us.—The first day, it was only a family party at the government house ; their staff, and our staff, and Johnny Cradock, their only son and heir, about twelve years old, and Captain Tilden, on his way from Batavia, with despatches from Sir S. Auchmuty, telling of the capture of that settlement.

Soon after breakfast, Sir John C. on horseback, with all his staff, and Lady T. C. in a landau, came to our door. —Sir George and his staff were also well mounted, and we all started, for the famous vineyard of Constantia.

Sir George was very busy all day with military enquiries, and told me, in the evening, that the military force at the Cape was nearly 5000, besides the Hottentot corps, the artillery, artificers, &c.

The latter end of October is the beginning of the Cape summer, so all the fruits were not yet ripe ; we had, however, oranges, strawberries, bananas, green peas, artichokes, and salads, in abundance ; and all this was a great treat, after our voyage.

25th.—Sir George and Sir John C. off early, to explore military passes, &c.

The tenure, by which lands are held in the colony, is by lease from the government, for a certain number of years, at a very small rent ; some do not pay regularly, and cannot prove their titles ; others have left the colony, with the Dutch governors, and have not yet returned to it, according to the British Proclamation.—There are consequently two parties, one British, or Stadtholderian, and the other French.—The Governor has the power to make grants of land, but, in the present uncertain state of the settlements, is very cautious of using it. The climate is mild, and

healthy, which may be judged of by the troops ; for, upon
Sir George's enquiry, he found there were not twenty sick,
in a corps of a thousand men.

26th.—There is no good timber near the Cape, but about
two or three hundred miles off it is said to be very fine ; but
how to get it down is the question.

28th.—At 8 o'clock this morning, we left Table Bay.

30th.—Some new arrangements at the dinner table, made
on my account—the medical man at the Cape saying it was
injurious to my eyes to sit opposite to the glare of the sun
on the sails.—A Captain Midwinter, of the Company's service, insisted upon keeping his seat, which would place him
and his wife next to me and Sir George ; and as this was
Captain Templar's place, and Colonel and Lady Charlotte
Murray next, Captain T. would not submit to it. There
was, in consequence, much confusion, and it ended in
Captain Midwinter retiring to his cabin, and ordering his
and his wife's dinner to be sent to them there. This was
all very uncomfortable to us, but we were not to blame, nor
had we it in our power to make either of the gentlemen
reasonable. I would have given much to be allowed to dine
in my cabin, or to have resumed my former situation, but
this was not permitted. Captain M. sent me an apology,
but abused Captain T., when, in fact, he behaved with the
most violence of the two. It seems Captain M. is a West
Indian, and suspected of being party-coloured, and these
people are always very furious, in all their passions.

November 1st.—Had an explanation with Captain T. on
the subject of yesterday, and insisted on being allowed to
dine in my own cabin. Lady C. Murray begged to be with
me, and so it was all settled, excepting that Captain M. was
not permitted to resume his seat at the table, but was desired by Captain Templar to dine below, and this he did.

December 20th.—A wretched day ; for a most painful and
distressing occurrence took place. One of the usual violent
and distressing outrages was committed by Captain Templar, in knocking down one of the soldiers. Captain Fraser

picked the man up, and remonstrated with Captain Templar, mentioning that the order given by Sir George was, that no soldier should be punished, without the complaint being made in a regular manner, and the punishment awarded by a court martial.—On this Captain Templar insulted poor Fraser, who took it most coolly ; at the same time telling him, that such gross conduct should not remain unnoticed at a proper season.—Fraser's conduct met the approbation of every one on board, and all the gentlemen came forward, declaring they would no longer dine at the captain's table.   He was so ashamed of his language and conduct himself, that he offered to dine in his own cabin the rest of the voyage ; but, after much discussion, it was agreed, that Colonel and Lady C. Murray, Fortescue, Fraser, Sir George and myself, should have a separate table, and then the rest of the passengers, at last, consented to dine in the great cabin.   Poor Fraser is so young, and just entering military life, that even Sir George thinks him right, in demanding satisfaction, but my misery is great at the idea.—I know what his poor mother will suffer, and if anything should happen to him, or if he should be the destroyer of another, I should indeed be truly wretched.— I did all I could to pacify and settle matters, without coming to such horrid extremities.   Captain Templar was ready to make any apology, but not publicly on the deck, where the offence had been given ; in short all was unhappiness, and I have never left my cabin since.

This is now the 10th of January, 1812, and this morning we anchored opposite to Saugur Island.   Immediately I heard boats lowered down, and I shuddered, guessing what was going forward.—I covered up my head, and would not leave my cot, till Fraser was conducted to my bedside, safe and well, and then my prayers for his safety were changed to thanksgivings, that all had ended so happily.   It seems they both fired together, and then Captain Templar immediately begged Mr. Fraser's pardon, and made the humblest apology for the outrage he had been guilty of.—This has been a most distressing business altogether, and the finale, although so repugnant to every feeling of religion and morality, I cannot now regret ; as even Sir George assures me, any other termination might have been a lasting injury, and a most serious disadvantage, to poor Fraser, during the whole of his life as a military man ; and so young as he now is, it would have been the ruin of his prospects.

January 11th.—While we were eating our biscuits a large centipede made its appearance over our heads, but was soon demolished by the young Aides-de-camp ; this gave me the idea of playing them a trick, and I made a pair of artificial centipedes out of a piece of rope, and put one in each of their beds, which afforded us some amusement before we went to sleep.

14th.—At day break Sir George was up, but did not land till 7 o'clock, as the fog was so thick we could not see many yards before us. The salute, however, at his landing, contributed to clear the air, by dispersing the fog a little, and we then were delighted with the scene—Fort William, the buildings of Calcutta, the banks of the river, and the odd shaped boats, formed a very striking and really beautiful scene.

When Sir George landed, he found the way up to the government house lined with military, and all the staff of the army there ready to receive him ; he was met by Lord Minto on the steps of the government house, sat down to breakfast, with all the principal civil and military personages of Calcutta, was afterwards sworn in as a member of council, when a salute was fired, and then he returned to us.

17th.—I ordered tea at 8 ; the scene was a curious one, though it did not divert me at the time, my spirits being particularly affected—I sat leaning on the table, expecting a cup of tea and a biscuit on a waiter, when the folding doors were thrown open, and the huge butler, or khanasounah, looking like the great Mogul himself, marched up towards me, followed by eight men, one with a cup of tea,

another with milk, a third with sugar, and so on—one man
with a chowrie, or silver stick, with a white cow's tail, to
keep off the flies, &c.   I begged to be left alone, and at last,
by signs, made them understand me ; however, the Mogul
would not leave me, he placed the others outside the door,
and then stood behind my chair.

February 22nd.—I doubted in my own mind, while he *
was talking, whether I ought not to try and confirm him
in being a Christian, but such an attempt would be mischievous, I am told, and would lead to unpleasant consequences, so I ought not to think of it.

28th.—I have hitherto not mentioned the hookahs, which
are indeed an extraordinary sort of things ; they are not
admitted at the government house now, but, as the late
Commander-in-chief and his wife admitted them, and
neither Sir George nor myself find the smell very disagreeable, or insupportable, and as it would be depriving half of
the community of one of their greatest comforts to object
to them, we have agreed to receive them, and a most ridiculous sight it is.—Imagine half of the men of a large company,
puffing and blowing, and the hookahs making a most extraordinary noise—some a deep base, others a bubbling treble
—the variety of cadence depends, I believe, on the length
of the snake, and the quantity of rose-water poured into
the receptacle for it.—I have generally one on each side of
me, as my place is always between two of the oldest gentlemen in society.   I have, however, set my face against young
men smoking, as it is in reality an odious custom.—Fortescue
and I have had quite a little battle about it, for he had sent
off to Benares to have one made ; however, at my request,
he has given it up with a very good grace.

March 7th.—In the evening drove to the China bazaar.
Visited the Black-hole ; the greatest part of the old fort,
where it was, is nearly in ruins, and the Black-hole itself
almost demolished.   There was a sepoy sentry near the
famous window, and the whole scene came to my mind with
such force that I felt quite sick.   A wretched looking black

* A Surkar.

man, with no covering but a piece of cotton cloth, pointed out to us the place—He, and every thing about it, bore such an aspect of misery I was glad when we left the spot. There is a monument to the memory of the unfortunate sufferers, but the inscription is entirely effaced, if ever there was one.

8th.—Went to church at 10—spent the rest of the morning in my own room.—Colonel and Lady C. Murray tiffed * with us.

27th.—Good Friday.—Mr. Shakespear introduced Mr. Chinnery† (the miniature painter), to me.—Saw Chinnery's paintings—the likenesses excellent—prevailed on Sir George to sit for me.—I begin to be very anxious about my brother Philip, whom we have been long expecting from Madras.

April 5th.—My brother arrived—it was a joyful meeting —he is much altered, and I should scarcely have known him, but he is in excellent health and spirits.

16th.—I have always forgotten to mention the birds' nest soup, that we have had at several places where we have dined ; but to-day Sir George was reading some papers upon the subject of the revenue of Java, and birds' nests are mentioned as one of the principal sources of revenue there. The Chinese consider them a great luxury, and procure them from Java in great abundance.—From what I have tasted here I should not be of their opinion ; for, independent of the natural repugnance to, and prejudice one must have against, such luxuries, the soup appeared to me a most disagreeable vapid sort of thing.

June 1st.—Sir George sat for his picture at 7 this morning, for the first time.

July 1st.—From the time I awoke, crowded with business of all sorts—Visitors, chits, &c. ; had a large party at tiffin ; and at 5 we all set off in different vehicles to our boats. About 7 we found ourselves comfortably settled, and all matters tolerably arranged about us.   Our sleeping boat has

* The word to tiff now only survives in the Anglo-Indian noun, tiffin.
† George Chinnery painted much in the East. He died at Macao about 1850.

three rooms, and is really very pretty. I did not get much sleep this night, for the noise of the dandies, or boatmen.

2nd.—At 5 o'clock we reached Barrackpore, but as the rain, which had fallen at intervals all day, was then pouring down in torrents, it was near 6 before we could land—Lord Minto and all his family were waiting for us, and the dinner was ready. The house is not large, being merely a temporary residence, built by Lord Wellesley, while a palace he had projected was building. The foundation of the latter only remains, Lord Wellesley having been prevented by the Directors from proceeding with the building ; and, indeed, from what appears of the extent of the plan, the expense would have been too great ; yet the Governor of India should have a handsome country residence.

7th.—Dinner was ordered in my brother (General Skinner's) pinnace, for the kitchen boat (or babbychee khaunnah,) was fortunately as good a sailer as we were.

8th.—At Barrackpore, I was told by Mr. J. Elliott, that he saw a poor man brought down, by his relations, to die on the banks of the river, near Santipore.—They stuffed his mouth full of mud, and left him with a person to watch him, who very composedly began to smoke his hookah, as his charge appeared likely to last some time. Close by the side of the dying man, lay a dead neighbour, who had been placed in the same situation as himself, a few hours before, and a Pariah dog was devouring it, in the sight of the wretched sick person, who seemed to regard it with particular attention, but without any of that appearance of horror we should suppose a human being would feel, in that situation.

12th.—We found the old Begum * seated on an ottoman of cloth of gold ; she was helped up by two of the women, and embraced us, after which she placed herself in a chair of silver, the ornaments of which were embossed tigers' heads—the bottom was ivory work, instead of cane. She desired me to sit down by her, in an ebony chair inlaid with

* Munny Begum.

gold. Mrs. Fagan, and Johnson, sitting opposite to us. Her appearance was indeed singular—she is very little, very old, and very ugly—her age is said to be ninety-six or ninety-seven—her dress was a pair of orange silk pantaloons —her head was covered with a muslin veil, embroidered in silver, and edged with orange coloured silk—she wore magnificent diamond bracelets on her arms—and in her ears, were large emeralds and pearls—her fingers were covered with rings—her feet were bare, but there was a pair of finely embroidered slippers, on a morah near her. The instant she seated herself on her chair, she drew up her feet under her, so that her knees served almost for a resting place for her chin. Sitting in this attitude, and with a shaking head and hands, she looked an exact personification of old age and infirmity. The conversation appeared very lively, and, from what I could learn from our interpreters (Mr. Brook and Mr. Addison), there is a good deal of that shrewdness remaining, for which she was formerly so remarkable. Many of her attendants were nearly as old as herself ; some, however, were young, but none appeared at all pretty. The men were great, fat, disgusting looking creatures, and seemed to have the whole government of the Zenana in their own power—they wore large turbans, and swords, and did all the honours to us. There was a pond near the door, in which were some wax or composition ducks, finely gilded and painted ; and making them swim about is one of the greatest amusements of the Zenana.

After we had conversed about half an hour, I expressed a wish to retire, for fear of incommoding the old Begum, who had sent me word in the morning, that she had been ill for three years past, with such profuse perspirations, that it was sometimes distressing to keep any clothes on. She immediately called for some little gold baskets, which were placed on the floor, in the middle of the room—out of these she took half a dozen different necklaces, of silver, fruit, and flowers—she took great pains to select those she thought the best, to bestow upon me, and at length ornamented me with no less than seven, sticking bunches of the same kind in my ears, &c. till I was all covered with finery ; she then gave Mrs. Fagan and Johnson, each one, with bunches for their ears.   After this, she put otto on our fingers, embraced us, and allowed us to retire.

The Munny Begum's fame has been long known in England, from the trial of Mr. Hastings, and the rhetoric of Mr. Burke ; but there are no remains of the beauty and elegance, once said to be her's ; her voice could never have been pleasing, as it is loud, coarse, and masculine ; yet, although her manners are a good deal those of second child-hood, now and then she seems to rally, and a glimmering of her former energies appears.   It is now, I believe, fifty years since the death of her husband (Meer Jaffier), and during this period she has confined herself to her palace, and the gardens which surround it, which are not more than an acre or two in extent.   Her chief amusements are smoking her hookah, conversing with her attendants, who are very numerous, and in witnessing their childish recrea-tion, of swimming little painted ducks.   The history of her life would include almost every event of importance, in the east, connected with British dominion, for nearly a century past.   She has seen her husband raised to the throne, by the aid of England, and dethroned by the same power ;—again has she witnessed his restoration, and since his death, she has lived to see her son's abdication, or rather to see him, like herself, a pensioner on the British Government. Report says she is very rich, but cannot be prevailed on to make a will, for fear of the consequences, and is always angry if a hint is given on the subject, considering the person her enemy.—Hers is indeed a melancholy situation, and I consider her a monument of the vanity of human greatness —however, to all appearance, the scene will soon close, and the famous Munny Begum will be as if she had never been.

25th.—At 6, Mr. and Mrs. Nugent called in their barouche, and we went to visit the environs of Monghier.—All the party dined with Captain and Mrs. Nugent.

I should have mentioned before, that our fleet consists of a hundred vessels, and upwards of 3,000 souls. It is wonderful, in this country, to see the number of attendants, to even the smallest family, for it appears to me, that every servant has a servant. My maid Johnson's kitmatgar, or footman, has an old man to attend upon him, who dresses his dinner, &c. and so on.—To-day we saw eight or ten sepoy soldiers, travelling on leave of absence. Each soldier had a man to hold a chitta over his head, and many had a second, to attend and carry their bundle.

Every morning, before we get under way, the maunghie goes to the head of the pinnace, fills his brass cap with the water of the Ganges, and throws it over the bow of the vessel ; he then makes three salaams, saying a short prayer, —and this is to save us from disasters during the day.—Is not there something like real piety in this ? Almost every vessel in our fleet has a garland at the head of it, which, being consecrated, is also a protection against evil accidents. There is something very striking, and even affecting, in the piety (superstition if so you please to call it) of these poor Hindoos, and, whenever I see them in the water, with their eyes lifted up to heaven, and their hands clasped, I cannot avoid giving them credit for real feelings of religion ; and I am certain, that, whatever their mistakes or superstitions may be, such prayers, offered in purity of heart, are acceptable to the Almighty.

August 1st.—In the evening, Sir George reviewed the troops at their station, after which we all visited the famous Gola, built, by the order of Mr. Hastings, by the present Major General Garstin, some years ago, as a granary for the East India Company, in case of a recurrence of the scarcity, which gave rise to the idea of having such a structure. There are various opinions as to its utility. It is ninety feet in height, and the walls are twenty feet thick. Outside of the building, there are two spiral flights of steps to the top, and Mr. F. Fitzroy (brother of the late Lord Southampton) rode a horse up them, to the great astonishment of the world here ; and it was indeed a most extraordinary and mad undertaking. There is a large hole at the top, into which it is intended to pour the grain, and four doors below, to take it out, as it may be wanted. The expense of this building is said to have been 120,000 rupees, and the intention is, a resource against famine. It is a very ugly structure, and resembles an enormously large dirty beehive. The echo in the inside is extraordinary ; the fall of a pin may be heard from one side to the other, or the lowest whisper—in this respect, it exceeds even the whispering gallery at St. Paul's. There is a large tablet over one of the doors with this inscription—

> In part of a general plan
> Ordered by the Governor General in Council,
> the 20th of January, 1784,
> For the perpetual precaution against Famine
> In the Provinces
> This Granary
> Was erected by Captain John Garstin,
> Engineer ;
> Completed on the 23d of July,
> 1786.

11*th.*—Set out at daybreak for Ghazipore.

13*th.*—In the room where we dined, at Mr. Sweetland's, poor Lord Cornwallis breathed his last. A coffin could scarcely be procured for him, and he was attended to the grave by a few invalid soldiers. We are to visit his tomb* this evening. We visited the monument, erected to the memory of Lord Cornwallis. It is not finished, but it promises to be a handsome structure.—After seeing all that was to be seen, we returned to our boats.

This place is famous for the manufacture of rose-water and attar of roses.—I have bespoken a considerable quantity, to be prepared for me against my return here. It seems it takes 130,000 roses, to make one small bottle of the attar, and this bottle costs a hundred rupees, or twelve guineas.

24*th.*—Dressed before daylight, and went out in my

---

* Still kept in repair by the Indian Government.

toujou to the Fort.—Saw the manner of defence, by rolling
immense stones over the ramparts—the situation and view
beautiful—this place is considered strong, and is kept in
repair, as a refuge for the European population, in any case
of emergency.—I went into the gallery, and placed myself
in the exact spot occupied by Mr. Hastings, during the
great battle, fought on the 22nd of October, 1764, which
decided the fate of this part of India.

September 2nd.—We have passed a most miserable week.
On the evening of the 26th, while we were at dinner, at
Mr. R.'s, English letters arrived. I would look at them,
and learned the dreadful intelligence of the death of dear
Lady Buckingham, and I left the table most miserable. A
day or two after, Sir G. made known to me, the great and
irreparable loss of my dear and excellent sister, Mrs. Fraser.

9th.—The only consolation one has, in contemplating a
conquered country like this, is the feeling, that most of the
inhabitants (the lower classes in particular) are much
happier under the present than under the former government—their property is secure, and their industry is sure
of its reward. The upper ranks, however, have much
splendour, consequence, &c., and, in short, every thing they
most value, to regret ; I should regret it also for them, did
I not know how they abused their power, and how cruelly
they oppressed the poorer classes.

Allahabad stands on a point of land, just where the rivers
Ganges and Jumna meet. The fortress gives it a most im-
posing appearance—the ancient palace, &c., looking like
one of the old castles we read of, and sometimes see the
remains of, in the days of baronial song in England. This
fort was built by Acbar, and most of the palace is still
entire—it is, in fact, partly converted into quarters for the
officers commanding in this station.—The architecture in
general is Grecian, and one of the gates, which is still entire,
is beautiful.—It is, however, considered very unhealthy,
and, although the commanding officer's quarters (where we
dined with Colonel Fergusson) are very handsome, they are

only occasionally inhabited—the heat being excessive, from
the white walls, and the style of building altogether ; the
materials of which retain the damp to that degree, that, as
soon as the sun makes his appearance after a shower, it
has the effect of a vapour bath.

I must remark here, that I now see many things almost
with indifference, which I should formerly have mentioned
in great detail.

13th.—The bank at which we came-to was covered with
a plant called the javassan.* This plant grows only in a
sandy soil, where nothing else can be cultivated. Just
before the hot winds set in, it springs from the ground,
starts up very rapidly, and sends forth a narrow bright
green leaf ; soon after the rains set in the plant droops, and
the leaves wither, and it becomes extinct. What makes it
most remarkable, is, that the plant comes to perfection
when the tatties are required, and is the best material for
making them, and the instant the rains set in, the tatties
are no longer required, and the plant dies away. I learnt
this history from Dr. Phillips, our medical men.

October 18th.—Soon after 4, set off for a seat in the neighbourhood, called Constantia, built by the late General Claude
Martine, who amassed an immense fortune in the Nawaub's
service. The house is intended to be in the style of an old
French chateau, but it is a singular mixture of all sorts of
styles ; yet it is beautiful and interesting, as well as extraordinary. It is adorned with statues innumerable—hea-
then gods, Chinese mandarins, shaking their huge heads,
milk-maids, shepherdesses, nuns, &c. all jumbled together !
—In the front of the house, a column is erected, in the style
of the Monument at London, to commemorate the life and
death of this singular man. His tomb was built by himself,
under the house, and by his desire, is, in compliance with
his will, kept constantly lit up.—It is a plain marble monument, with this inscription—

" Here lies the body of CLAUDE MARTINE, who came to India a
Common Soldier ; and died a Major-General. Pray for his Soul ! "

* Javásá, called the camel thorn, or the Persian manna plant.

At each corner of his tomb is a grenadier, as large as life,
resting his head on his arms reversed, and so well represented, in painted stone, that I was at first deceived, and
took them for real sepoys. There was something very
affecting in this sight, and I was glad to leave the place.
We then went into a Chinese garden, exactly like those one
sees on china cups and saucers.—General Martine was a
Frenchman. He left the greater part of his fortune to the
poor of Lucnow, Calcutta, &c. Constantia overlooks the
Goomty river, and a vast extent of ground is seen from the
turrets. Over the principal door is written,

Labore et Constantia.

It seems well applied to the history and character of the
founder.

22nd.—I have amused myself with writing some complimentary verses to the Vizier's dervise, which may, perhaps,
amuse my children, should they ever read them—

FROM DERVISE COLMAN, TO DERVISE NAWAUB, *with Two Half
Guineas, and a Seal, with his Arms engraven upon it.*

> In this small gift, respected sage, you view
> Emblem of friendship, lasting as 'tis true ;
> The pure gold ore bespeaks the steady friend,
> The shape denotes the friendship without end ;
> Their well match'd size, forming a kindred soul
> United, represents a perfect whole.—
> The seal, already with my arms impress'd,
> Firmly cements and ratifies the rest,
> And though we're severed, or by time or space,
> For ever shews the brotherly embrace :—
> And brothers may we be till life is o'er,
> Then meet in happiness to part no more.

LINES, SUGGESTED BY A VISIT TO THE COURT OF
LUCNOW, IN 1812—

> In northern lands, where the sun's beam
> Seems faintly through the clouds to gleam,
> Where hoary Winter's aspect wan
> Chills even the intellect of Man,

2 B

Genius in vain attempts to rise,
And infant Fancy breathes and dies :
But in this happier clime we view
Genius sublime and Fancy new,
The Sciences and Arts refin'd,
Ennobling while they grace mankind :
Yet, ah ! in vain Sol's brightest rays
Might through the azure curtain blaze,
In vain might Genius rear her head.
Or Fancy weave her varied web ;
In vain might Science or might Art
Their beneficial Views impart,
Did not a Sovereign's fostering hand
Cherish and renovate the land ;
Did not his smile benignant cheer,
And bless the product of the year ;
'Till Science, Genius, Fancy pure,
Flourish, expanded and mature.—
Thus Lucnow's Prince his influence sheds,
And happiness around him spreads,
And, by his gracious manner, shews
The heart from whence his bounty flows.

24th.—We then explored Sujah-ul-Dowlah's palace, in-habited also by Assuff-ul-Dowlah, and the present Nawaub vizier (Saadut Ally Khan), in the early period of his reign, before he purchased from General Martine the ground near the residency, and built his palace, in which he now resides. The building is quite Hindoostannee, but does not give much idea of either comfort or magnificence. Among the few pictures, is the original of one, from the pencil of Zoffany, an engraving from which I have often seen in England ; it represents Assuff-ul-Dowlah and Captain Mordaunt at a cock fight. The Nawaub keeps much of his treasure in this palace.

November 19th.—In the evening, I amused myself with writing some verses on the Taaje.

LINES WRITTEN ON SEEING THE TAAJE, AT AGRA.

Here all conspires to charm the ravish'd sight,
  And fill with wonder the admiring eye,
Here splendid gems and marble spotless white,
  That with the sunbeam and the snow might vie,
Their various beauties so commix and blend,
As nature did to art her best assistance lend.

The stately rising dome, the burnish'd spire,
  The casements, that their soften'd light impart
Each in its turn, and all alike, conspire
  To strike the wondering eye, and touch the heart ;
And while, wrapt in delight, I silent gaze,
My heart to wedded love its well earn'd tribute pays.

For not alone this pile presents to me
  Proportions fair of architectural pride,
In every polished stone and gem I see
  All that's to love or sentiment allied ;
And to the mental vision here appear,
All the affections that the feeling mind holds dear.

The basis, formed of marble white and pure,
  Pourtrays the groundwork of a well-placed love,
Which firm through life unshaken shall endure,
  Nor shall the hand of death that love remove—
For true affection, in the tender heart,
Stands unsubdued by time, or death's unerring dart.

The pale ferosah, modest azure blue,
  Emblem of truth and love the most sincere,
The brilliant sapphire's deeper regal hue,
  Tells how above all other love doth peer ;
The love which, under Hymen's blest control,
Exalts the human mind, and dignifies the soul.

The yellow topaz speaks the anxious cares,
  That ever on affection's steps attend,
And the rich diamond, as it brightly glares,
  Shews the high value of a real friend :
But far beyond the brightest gems are found
Friendship and faithful love, in one soft union bound.

These pearls, the tears that fond affection shed
    O'er the pale corse of her he loved alone,
These rubies, precious drops that heart has bled
    For her alas ! for ever, ever gone !—
And pity's eye the tribute pearl bestows,
While faintly through the heart the ruby current flows.—

But see, the emerald glads the tearful eye,
    And offers balsam to the troubled breast,
Pointing to regions far beyond the sky,
    Regions of peace, the mansions of the blest—
For Hope is e'er arrayed in brightest green,
All nature too in Hope's attire is seen !—

Sweet smiling Hope, thou soother of our cares,
    Thou first, best boon, to hapless mortals given—
Thou, who, when miserable man despairs,
    Bid'st him to look for happiness in heaven—
Whate'er of wretchedness be still my lot,
Oh ! let thy cheering ray, thy smile forsake me not !

And ye, blest pair ! so fond, so true of heart,
    Who underneath this marble mouldering lie,
Ye who have known the agony to part,
    Are now rewarded with eternal joy ;
So may fond love and truth for ever rest,
And like Jehan and Taaje eternally be blest.

22nd.—Went early, and past several hours at the Taaje.
—Wrote my name at the top of one of the minarets.—More
delighted and charmed than ever, with this beautiful unique
building, and left it with real regret, for this is, I fear, the
last time we shall be able to visit it.   I was the only lady
of the party, and we took three hours to examine it in the
minutest manner.   I could look at it for as many months,
without being tired—it is really like the most beautiful
Sèvres china, and deserves to have a glass case made for it.
—What a pity it should be exposed to decay !

December 24*th.*—I shall now say a few words, of Messrs.
Gardner and Fraser, who are still of our party ; they both
wear immense whiskers, and neither will eat beef or pork,
being as much Hindoos as Christians, if not more ; they are

both of them clever and intelligent, but eccentric ; and, having come to this country early, they have formed opinions and prejudices, that make them almost natives. In our conversations together, I endeavour to insinuate every thing that I think will have any weight with them. I talk of the religion they were brought up in, and of their friends, who would be astonished and shocked at their whiskers, beards, &c. &c. All this is generally debated between us, in a good natured manner, and I still hope they will think of it.

1813. *January 2nd.*—At 3, Sir G. reviewed Skinner's horse, as it is called. I saw the whole from my elephant, which, although it was surrounded with firing, and all sorts of noises, never stirred, or seemed the least alarmed. I saw several others, however, that turned round continually, and appeared as if they wished to make their escape.—The troops were all dressed in yellow and scarlet, the officers distinguished from the men, by having more gold upon their turbans, which being beautifully mixed with the scarlet cloth gave them a magnificent appearance ; the first movements were in the European style, marching about, saluting, &c. After that, they skirmished in the native style, firing their matchlocks, in the most curious and dexterous manner ; when pursued, they fired backwards, forwards, sideways, &c., at full gallop, the reins lying on their horses' necks, sometimes standing in their stirrups, to take better aim, at others, leaping to the ground, firing almost under their horses' bodies, and recovering their seats so quickly, it was actually like magic. They then attacked each other with swords and spears, and their figures were exactly what I have often seen, in pictures of Saracens ; the glittering turbans, flying draperies, &c., having a very novel and interesting appearance. A bottle was then placed on the ground, and they fired their matchlocks at it, going full speed ; many bottles were broken. A tent pin was then driven into the ground, and, as they passed full gallop, they dislodged it with their spears. The last manœuvre was most extraordinary. A party of men, selected by Captain Skinner (who distinguished himself particularly in all these wonderful exploits), were mounted, with each a brace of pistols, which they fired, going full speed, over their horses' backs, and under their bodies, leaping on and off, with the greatest ease. As they fired several times, they must have loaded also, but how that was done it is quite impossible to say, for their horses were the whole time *ventre à terre*.

At sunset, we left the ground, the whole regiment being previously drawn up in line, and saluting. I was then particularly struck with their appearance—the yellow flag to each squadron, ornamented with scarlet and gold, the small gold and silver flags, at the top of every spear (for every squadron had a certain number of spearmen, mixed with those who carried matchlocks), the glittering appearance of their turbans, the rays of the sun playing on them, as it set behind the fort on the right of their line, in short the whole scene, had a most lively and picturesque effect. Sir G. complimented Captain S., and we all returned from the field, much gratified.—Captain S. has the pension of a lieutenant-colonel, or rather pay I should say, he having held that rank in Scindia's service ; he and his brother were educated in Calcutta—their father being an officer in the East India Company's service.

3rd.—I believe Mr. Colman is the first clergyman who has been seen on the Delhi frontier, as the whole of this line of our new conquests is called.

15th.—We made a short excursion into the Nepaul country. The opposite shore is very mountainous and woody, and is called Holiland. The Ganges at this place is narrow, and flows quietly over its stony bed. Many people have attempted to trace its source, which is supposed to be at no great distance. We all sat down to rest ourselves, on the top of the mountain, and to contemplate the view, with which I was much delighted.—I wrote the following lines on it.—

WRITTEN AT HURDWAR

Ah ! who can wonder that the holy Seer
Should fix the dwelling of the Godhead here,
Where, from the stately mountain's snowy side,
The Ganges rolls his clear majestic tide,
And through far distant regions takes his course,
With god-like bounty and with giant force ;
Whilst all around us, in the varied scene,
The glorious attributes of God are seen ?
The mountain, fertile vales, the stream, the grove,
Speak his High Majesty, paternal care, and love.

February 15*th.*—At 7, dined with the civil station.—The dinner was given at Mrs. Donnithorn's ; three rooms were opened for dining.—A ball in the evening.—Sir E. Cole-brooke very entertaining and clever, but very eccentric.—Mr. Deane really a sensible man, without pretension.—Mr. and Mrs. Donnithorn rather pleasing, but exhibiting too much.—Mr. and Mrs. Barnes unaffected and agreeable—but I have forbidden myself ever to speak of people or characters—in the slight view I take, it is impossible for me to form any correct opinion.

March 26*th.*—Yesterday, the whirlwind blew down the tent, where the Adjutant General's office is kept, and carried up into the air some very material papers, which were all, however, recovered ; and we were particularly anxious about them, as one of the shopkeepers, in the bazaar, is known to be a spy from Rewah, and would gladly have availed himself of this opportunity, of procuring some in-telligence.

July 2*nd.*—My brother General S. taken ill, with a fever, during the night.

3*rd.*—My brother much better ; his fever quite gone, but his strength much reduced.

10*th.*—Mrs. Gordon sat with me, till 9, having also dined alone.—The moon was particularly bright ; the numerous little parties along the bank, preparing their food, and the busy scene around us, compared with the calm face of the water, formed a most interesting picture ; at a distance was heard the music and dancing of wedding parties in the village, with the paddling of boats going to and fro. I was obliged to make out conversation, when I should have preferred perfect silence, and half the enjoyment of the evening was lost.—Mrs. G. is, however, a good young woman, and worthy, in all respects, of a better fate than she has met with ; but it must be with some dear and intimate friend, or quite alone, that the beauty of a fine moonlight night can be enjoyed.

August 4th.—I feel quite ungrateful, in not having mentioned the death of the old Munny Begum. She was 97 years old, and 97 guns were fired from Fort William on the occasion.

When the Wallady Begum's Vakeel was here, just now, I made my Ayah ask him all the particulars of the old Begum's death. He said she did not appear to suffer at all, and, on the day of her death, there was no appearance of illness. A few days before, she ordered her shroud to be brought ; she desired it might first be washed in rose-water, and then steeped in attar of roses, after which it was folded up, and put in a place she directed. On the morning of her death, she was much longer at her prayers than usual ; and of late, indeed, she had passed the greatest part of the night in prayer. After going through some of her morning arrangements, she called some of her principal women, desiring them to place her on the musnud, and no sooner was this accomplished, than she leaned back, and breathed her last.

9th.—Arrived in Calcutta, between 4 and 5.

September 9th.—Up very early and write letters.—One of Lord Moira's Aides-de-camp at breakfast, Major Foster. Have a long discussion afterwards with him, in my own apartment, and hear all about the family, and am determined to like them all. A nice drive in the evening, and only a small party at dinner.

10th.—The heat oppressive. The deaths of two young

officers, who were recommended to Sir G., were announced to us, and a third at the last gasp. Fortunately, we did not know them ; but these melancholy occurrences strongly remind me of the sad scenes we witnessed in the West Indies, and which are so frequent here too, at this season of the year.

October 3rd.—The morning as usual ; but I am sorry to say, we had a large dinner party, contrary to our rule. The staff of Lord Moira were our principal guests. They are very numerous, and all, as is manifest from their conversation, expect to be soon provided for ; but I imagine Lord M. will find it an embarrassing task ! Sir G.'s patronage, I suppose, will be confined to this presidency, and he can now be of little use to his friends, or to any one ; but kindness and civility will always be in his power, and these we can both shew, in our different situations, to all.—He rests a great deal upon Lord Moira's character for generosity, and high-mindedness, and yet we cannot but both feel that his returning a verbal answer, by Sir William Keir, to the very generous letter Sir G. wrote, does not savour much of either of these qualities. However, Lord M. is now so near, that to-morrow, or next day, must bring him to Calcutta, and then we shall see what line of conduct he means to adopt.

4th.—Before we went to bed last night, it was announced, that Lord Moira had arrived nearly to Garden Reach, and would land early this morning—Sir G., in consequence, gave every necessary order, and at daylight, was ready at the ghaut, to receive him.—The troops paraded, and every thing was done which is usual on such grand occasions.

On Sir G.'s return, I heard all the proceedings, and cannot say, after the specimen that had been given, by the cool verbal reply to Sir G.'s excellent and manly letter, that I was much surprised to hear, that Lord M. avoided all direct communication with Sir G. ; referring him, in the most extraordinary, and I must say unmilitary and ungentleman-like way, to the staff for information, instead of addressing his conversation to their chief.—By the manner in which Sir G. feels it all, at present, I am sure it must end, ere long, in his resigning the command of the Bengal forces, and returning to Europe. It seems, however, that his appointment, as Commander in chief of all India, is not cancelled, but left in abeyance, to be resumed, in case of any thing happening to Lord Moira, or ill health obliging him to return home.*

6th.—I like Lady Loudon exceedingly, and heard from her a most delightful account of my dear, dear children. I admire Lady Loudon's children exceedingly, and, indeed, they are charming little people.—In short, I was charmed with my visit.—Not so my dear Sir G., who had an interview with Lord Moira, while I was with the ladies, the result of which is, his determination to resign immediately, and go home as soon as he is relieved ; indeed, he would go sooner, but various reasons oblige him to remain here till next year. I deeply regret it, but I know he must do his duty, and I ought to be resigned.—After we left the Government House, we paid a visit to Lord Minto ; and, in the evening, we had a mixed dinner party of civil and military.

7th.—Constant arrangements for the new *regime* going on, though all the communications are made through the staff, and every thing is done to show Sir G. it is meant he should be a cypher.

8th.—Sir G. in council all day.—I wrote, read, and laid plans for the future.—Civilities passed between Lady Loudon and me. Enquiries after health, &c. She wishes to come and see me, but her carriages, &c. are not ready yet.—Visit Mrs. George Elliott, &c.—In the evening take a short drive, and have a quiet party.—Heard many ridiculous and idle reports, to-day, of the intended etiquettes of Government House. I am sure they will never be carried into effect, if Lady Loudon allows herself time to learn anything of the society here, or Lord Moira forms the least

* Lord Minto was somewhat suddenly superseded in order to make way for Lord Moira (better known as the first Marquis of Hastings), a personal friend of the Regent.

acquaintance with his subjects, before the next intended drawing room.

12th.—At daylight, received a letter from Lady Loudon, pressing me to come to the Government House, to see Sir G. invested, by Lord Moira, with the Order of the Bath. The heat was great, and Dr. Leny thought I had better not risk the fatigue ; however, I decided upon going, at 12 o'clock, Lady Charlotte Murray and Mrs. Nicolls being my companions.—It was altogether a curious scene, both behind the curtain, and in the public hall, and I rejoiced, for my dear N.'s sake, when all was over. Lord Moira's speech, on the occasion, was thought most extraordinary, and several people expressed indignation, at the want of delicacy of one part of it, when he took occasion to say, that Sir G. was shorn of his honours, meaning his patronage, which was certainly an odd way of expressing it. I don't think, however, he meant any real offence, but merely to display his own grandeur and eloquence, &c. I have his speech in print, and mean to keep it, as a curious specimen of his mistaken view of things.

15th.—After the drawing room, there were two commerce* tables. I played at Lord Moira's, and Sir George at Lady Loudon's, table. A guinea each was put in the pool, and a hint given, that the winner would of course bestow it on the pages ; but old General MacDonald, when he was successful, pocketed the whole, with great glee, and did not seem at all to comprehend the hint. This was at Lady Loudon's table. I was *dead*, and so tired, I was glad to take my leave, before the General, &c. finished ; so I don't know how the matter was arranged at Lord M.'s table ; but the whole seemed to be much quizzed by the company.

17th.—We passed as quiet a day as the state of my poor N.'s mind will admit of ; but he has, hourly, vexations and worries from Government House, and it is now evident, that nothing will satisfy Lord Moira, but the certainty of his resigning his appointment, and returning to Europe.

* A game of cards in vogue at the period.

24th.—Several events have taken place, since I left off writing my Journal regularly. My poor dear brother sailed in the *Salsette* frigate, for Bombay, being appointed to the staff there, and will act as commander in chief, till the new commander in chief comes out.

December 30th.—Lord M. pursues the system he began with ; but now that Sir G. has told him he will resign, &c. all goes on more smoothly. Still it requires some *patience*, as there is such a mixture of vanity and folly altogether, that it makes one sick.

1814. *January 15th.*—My Journal is very dull, but I live in such a bustle, and such continual fatigue, that I have no time, or thoughts, for enquiry or remarks. My most agreeable occupation is, when I can steal a moment to myself to shut my eyes, and build castles, on the subject of England and my dear children.

16th.—Sir G. dined with the 24th regiment, to meet General Gillespie.

17th.—The play in the evening was very tolerably performed, and all went off extremely well. Lord M. bowed to the audience afterwards, and I am sure felt himself quite a king ; and indeed, we were all in great state, and very great people.

28th.—A grand review ; after which, Sir G. ordered a *feu-de-joie*, in honour of Lord Wellington's victory, in the neighbourhood of the Pyrenees. It is glorious, but alas ! how many aching hearts are made by such glorious events !

April 11th.—We have been to the Poojah, and a most disgusting sight it is ; and melancholy indeed to think, that human beings should so torment and degrade themselves, from a false idea of religion. But I will try to describe the extraordinary scene. First, as in all holiday meetings, there were groups of dancing people, that is, parties of men, with very little clothing on, squatting on the ground, with each his hookah, and looking at the evolutions of Nautch women, which is one of their greatest amusements. These

women were ornamented with beads and tinsel, and looked
very gay.—Then there were jugglers, all, I am told, very
expert ; but we did not stay to look at their tricks. Groups
of opium eaters, sitting in a circle, and looking like drunken
skeletons—such miserable wretches I never saw before, and
it is impossible to describe !   Then, there were poor sinners,
doing penance in various ways.   But the most shocking
sight is the swinging ; this is done by the unfortunate creature having iron hooks passed through the sinews of his
back, and by these he is suspended to a high pole.   The
wretched man, whom we saw begin this penance, appeared
at first to be in torture, for he drew up his legs, as if in
great pain, catching at the rope by which he was suspended,
as if to relieve himself ; but, soon after, he was apparently
at ease, and went round and round, as fast as possible,
distributing flowers, &c. to the mob, who all scrambled for
them, as sacred relics.   It seems these swinging people, like
many others who do penance, are hired by the priests, who
make vows, and have the option of performing by proxy.
One swinging man let fly a white pigeon, and he is most
fortunate indeed that catches it ; crowds were running in
every direction, for the prize.

As I turned, with horror and disgust, from the wretch
who was swinging, to Sir E. East's and Sir G.'s great
amusement, a man thrust his head in my face, with his
tongue out, and a great iron rod passed through it.   I
started back, and he made signs for a rupee, which was
given him.

At a little distance from the carriage, were men doing
penance, by being driven in strings, like horses, going to a
fair in England, but the reins were passed through holes
made in the flesh, on each side of them, and the pain must
have been dreadful.   But I will not enumerate all the many
horrors, that superstition and ignorance lead these poor infatuated creatures to commit, or submit to.

The Rah-Poojah, or sacrifice by carriages, is another and
still more horrid festival than either the Doorga-Poojah, or

the Churruk-Poojah. Men are often crushed under these
shocking machines, as sacrifices to their gods. *Now*, it is
not done openly, but as if by accident ; they are, however,
prepared, by dress, &c. and then the crowd presses upon
them, as if their fall was unintentional. The Ayah told me,
she saw a beautiful boy, all dressed in gold and flowers, and
in a few minutes he was under the wheels, and his parents
rejoiced, because he went to Brama. But I will not distress myself with these horrid descriptions, for I have
drawings of all the ceremonies, and they are hardly credible.
Sir G. could hardly be persuaded that all the apparent tor-
ments were not juggling tricks ; but what we saw, this
evening, were too evident to be doubted.

23rd.—Colonel Loveday was of our breakfast party, who,
upon talking of the hail storm yesterday, told me, that
formerly such an event was the signal for a jolly party, the
hail being generally sufficient to ice the wine, which was a
great treat in those days, as they had not the means of procuring the luxury of ice, which we enjoy at present.

30th.—A large party, given by the Easts to Lord Moira
and Lady Loudon. Lord M. most particularly civil and
attentive to me, and so he has been ever since he knew
Sir G. had resigned, and more *polite* to him also.—What a
world !

May 26th.—The bamboo is now in blossom, which is
quite an event, and they tell me, it has not been seen, in
the state it is at present, for fifty years, and I never saw
it before, I must confess.

June 1st.—Gilbert * with me, the greatest part of the
morning. At 7 o'clock, started for the church. By some
unfortunate contre-temps, we were half an hour beyond the
appointed time ; the bride, &c. all waiting for us. Lady
Loudon was extremely angry, and could scarcely recover
her temper during the whole evening. I was vexed about
it, and particularly on account of the poor bride. Sir G.
attempted to apologize, laying the blame upon the horses,
&c.; but the fact was, he was in the midst of papers, the

* Captain Gilbert.

chain of his watch was broken, and he did not know how time went; and, in addition to this, the horses took it into their heads to kick, and we were obliged to stop, have them taken off, and proceed with a pair only.

There were about sixty people present in the church; and, immediately after the ceremony, the bride and bridegroom repaired to their boat, which was waiting for them, just below the Bazaar. Unfortunately, a north wester must have overtaken them, and must have been (we are afraid) very detrimental to the white satin dress, &c. We were almost blown over from the church to the Government House, when we all mounted our favours, and looked like so many Medusas, for our hair was all blown into snakes, and strips, by the gale. Lady Loudon made a toilette; but we had not the same advantage, of a dressing room, so we kept each other in countenance, by smoothing our locks, as well as we could, with our fingers.—An immense dinner party, and almost all Calcutta assembled, in the evening.

24th.—Up soon after 4. All Calcutta in a bustle, for Lord M. &c. embark at Champaul Ghaut, before sunrise. The troops were out, and all due honours paid. At 10 o'clock, Sir G. took his seat as Vice-President, under a salute, and usual ceremonies.

28th.—A dispatch to-day from Nepaul, enclosing Sir G. some of the poison with which the Nepaulese rub their arrows, and are now trying to poison the tanks, &c. which is one of their modes of warfare. The poison sent to Sir G. was taken out of a tank or pool, and must have lost some of its noxious qualities, notwithstanding which, when the experiment was tried upon a poor little kid, it expired in two hours, apparently in great agony, and a fowl, that was scratched with it, shared the same fate, in two hours and a half. Sir G. was handling it and examining it, when he happened to look at the letter, which stated, that it should not be touched, without the greatest care, as its venom was such, that the prick of a pin in the finger might convey it to the whole frame.

The Nepaulese are a savage race, even in the present day. We have had communication with them lately, and have endeavoured, through the medium of a resident, to form a *peaceable* alliance with them, but were obliged to enforce our terms with military aid.—To show how unenlightened, and in what a state of ignorance, this people must be, it is said that, only some few years ago, the Rajah of Nepaul sent ambassadors to the Calcutta Government on the subject of a negociation, relative to the trading between the Nepaulese and the Company. The Rajah's orders were, to have men to write him anything new and extraordinary, that they saw. Among other things, they reported, that the River Hooghly ran part of the day one way, and part of the day another. Having no idea of tide, and knowing nothing beyond the Ganges, and the streams that issue from the mountains, and make their way into the sea, he recalled the ambassadors, as people not to be trusted, having set out with telling him such falsehoods and impositions.

September 14th.—Lady Hood soon after 8, to pass the day with me.—Sir G. not well ; so he left us to receive visitors, &c.—She smoked her hookah almost the whole morning, to my great astonishment.

November 14th.—Sir G. gave a public breakfast.—An express, to announce the failure of our troops in the Valley of Door, and the death of poor Gillespie. Alas ! I am afraid he sought his own destruction ; for, latterly, his mind was certainly sadly disturbed, and, in my long and many conversations with him, I could not but see that natural impetuosity, and his extraordinary vanity, and love of fame, had led him into false ideas, and errors, that would embitter his future life. So, perhaps, he has been taken from this world in mercy, and yet with all his failings, I fear, unrepented of. All our party were sadly out of spirits, and we separated, soon after dinner.

At Buxar, the last effort was made by Sujah-ul-Dowlah, and Meer Cassim, against the British power. Their force was immense, 50,000 against 7000, of whom only 1200 were

SKETCH MAP
of
THE ISLAND OF JAMAICA
To illustrate "Lady Nugent's Journal"
.1801 - 1805.
Compiled by
J. MELVILLE
.1905

English ; but the skill of the latter prevailed, and, after a conflict of two hours only, all were put to the rout, and most of them perished in the Ganges. I do not understand the justice of these wars, and therefore forbear remark.— The temple here, held in such high veneration by the Hindoos, is dedicated to their God Rama, the Hindoo Mars.

I was talking, the other day, to Mr. Monckton, upon the subject of some of the native prejudices, and how much some of ours must astonish them, particularly the freedom with which women mix in society, &c. He said that a Miss Clark, who is now going to be married to the younger Mr. Metcalfe at Delhi, surprised a rajah very much, by her robust appearance, and running about the house, &c. ; for she had then just arrived from England, and was what would be called, even there, a coarse romping girl, a character totally unknown among the natives. By way of a joke, Mr. M. told the rajah, it was not impossible but that she would take a fancy to kiss him some day, and enquired what he would do in such a case. His answer was, " Oh no, —hope not—if she do, I go immediately and wash body." This is not very gallant, but he would really have thought it necessary to bathe and purify himself, if this had happened ; for he seemed to consider a woman of her appearance, and manners, rather as an object of disgust than anything else. Their own women are generally very delicate in their appearance, and very timid in their manners. Indeed, they are more like silly children than grown-up females ; they are fond of toys, have no education, and spend a life of uselessness and folly, that may well make the Mahometan men believe they have no souls.

THE END.

INDEX

386

402 **INDEX**

PLYMOUTH : W. BRENDON AND SON, LTD., PRINTERS

7

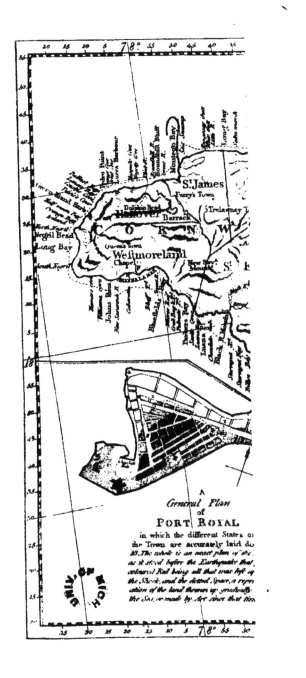

A
General Plan
of
PORT ROYAL
in which the different States or
the Town are accurately laid do
B. The whole is an exact plan of the
as it stood before the Earthquake that
coloured Red being all that was left of
the Shock, and the dotted Space, a repre
sation of the land thrown up gradual
the Sea, or made by Art since that tim